*strange!
Love,
Chris*

# CALLING

Chris Maunder

Copyright © 2010 by Chris Maunder

All rights reserved. No part of this book may be reproduced, stored, or transmitted by any means—whether auditory, graphic, mechanical, or electronic—without written permission of both publisher and author, except in the case of brief excerpts used in critical articles and reviews. Unauthorized reproduction of any part of this work is illegal and is punishable by law.

This is a work of fiction and, as such, it is a product of the author's creative imagination. All names of characters appearing in these pages are fictitious except for those of public figures. Any similarities of characters to real persons, whether living or dead, excepting public figures, is coincidental. Any resemblance of incidents portrayed in this book to actual events, other than public events, is likewise coincidental.

ISBN 978-1-4457-1341-0

*For the Theology & Religious Studies students of York St John, past and present*

# Preface

*C**alling* is a story about alternative spirituality in the twenty-first century. What shape might traditional religious experiences take in modern-day 'secular' urban Britain? Can someone who is not a member of the world's religious institutions undergo the spiritual journey; the mystic search for union with the deity; visions; the sense of a divine guiding hand?

The main character, Frances Dryburgh, a Leeds woman of twenty-nine in a routine office job, has profound spiritual encounters which lead her to life changes. Entranced by the arrival of a very desirable man in her neighbourhood, she enters into a world of religious experimentation in modern Goddess worship, with its associations with Paganism and Witchcraft. Her story reflects important themes in contemporary spirituality: personal freedom, empowerment, self-worth and the value of the natural environment.

Frances' visionary experiences take place 150 years after the famous apparitions to Bernadette Soubirous in Lourdes, France, which resulted in the establishment of a world-famous healing shrine. How do Lourdes, 1858, and Leeds, 2008, compare? Despite the differences in space and time, spirituality – both old and new – has common threads, although Frances discovers that the alternative spiritualities which enthral her are not without their challenges and contradictions.

*Calling*'s characters exist and act in plausible situations. However, the fantasy world of *The Wizard of Oz* has also made a contribution to the storyline!

The book is unusual in that its story was shaped at critical points by my consulting a randomly generated pattern of Tarot cards and, on one occasion, the *I Ching*. At these moments in the writing of the book, consultation of these methods of divination helped to determine the direction of the narrative. This seemed to me to be true to the spirit of the traditions that were being explored in the story.

None of the characters in *Calling* is based on an actual person, alive or dead. With a few exceptions – some of the dreams and one childhood memory – the story does not reconstruct any event, or any person's role, in my life. Most of the venues where the action occurs, such as houses, places of work, hotels, restaurants and pubs are fictitious, even if some of the description is drawn from visits to places that actually exist. Real places also feature in the narrative: Leeds Town Hall; Elland Road football stadium; the *Trip to Jerusalem*, a famous pub in Nottingham; the village of Avebury; chapels, churches and cathedrals in the Auvergne. The activities that take place in these venues have been created for the story. Nevertheless, they are all based on likely scenarios (Avebury does see rituals at the full moons and equinoxes; the Kaiser Chiefs did play at Elland Road in 2008; there are classical concerts at Leeds Town Hall).

I would like to acknowledge the following people who have made a specific contribution to the writing of *Calling* as I have struggled with it in all the spare moments I could find outside my professional life over four years. First and foremost, to Debjani Chatterjee MBE, poet and author, Trish and Andy Maunder, Jacqui Larsen and Sue Yore, all of whom read the script in its entirety and gave me great support and encouragement, as well as many useful suggestions. Secondly, there are many other people who have played an important part in the process of writing, either reading parts and suggesting improvements, or helping with detail, or giving information on areas of their own expertise. My thanks therefore also go to Ebony Fletcher; Jenny Vale; Becca Wilkins; Leila Roberts; Joanne Peaker; Beth Lintin-French; Trisha Brown; Kirsty Gibson. Thirdly, many thanks to Kris Waldherr for her kind permission to quote from *The Goddess Tarot* (U.S. Games Systems Inc., 1999), and to refer to her ideas and titles for the Tarot cards. The *I Ching* text referred to derives from Richard Wilhelm's 1923 version (Routledge & Kegan Paul, 3$^{rd}$ edition 1968, translated into English by Cary F Baynes). Other books mentioned in the story and the astrologer's interpretation in chapter 44 are fictitious!

## Note on the Yorkshire accent:

Where characters with strong Yorkshire accents are featured (for example Frances, Debs and Irene), this is indicated by signals in the speech (and, in Frances' case, thoughts). These signals are not intended to represent an exact rendering, something which would make the text difficult to read. They are simply devices to remind the reader that the speaker has a Yorkshire accent. These include: "wi'" rather than "with"; "were" in the place of "was"; the omission of the definite article "the"; "o'" replacing "of"; "'em" instead of "them"; the familiar "summat", "owt" and "nowt" for "something", "anything" and "nothing"; occasionally, "us" rather than "our"; "while" as an alternative for "until". However, some of these may be misleading. The abbreviation "wi'" is not universal in Yorkshire and is probably found more often in South Yorkshire and the Pennines rather than in the cosmopolitan city of Leeds, where the accent has been diluted. "Were" is often pronounced "wa'". "The" is not actually omitted in the Yorkshire accent but abbreviated to a soft "t'". Although "t'" is often used in literature to denote this aspect of the Yorkshire accent, it may give the impression that the "t" sound is actually stronger than it usually is, particularly amongst young Yorkshire people. To the outsider, it often sounds rather as if the word "the" has been omitted. On the other hand, "o'" and "'em" are among a number of dropped consonants that are common in the English language in general and not peculiar to Yorkshire. In conclusion, one can repeat that there are signals to indicate that the Yorkshire accent is being used, but there is no attempt to represent a precise rendering.

Chris Maunder, 20th May 2010

# 1

# On a Promise

A February night. Cold air streamed through a city suburb, sweeping along tarmac streets lined with rows of houses in terraced blocks. Nearby stood parkland, its trees and shrubs shrouded in black shadows. In a small unostentatious first-floor flat, a young woman slept. As the west wind passed by, a renegade eddy became detached and seemed to curl back on itself for just an instant, in order to play upon the old-fashioned sash window of her bedroom. Mischief danced in the breeze; it was attending to the business of making nightmares. And so the woman, Frances, began to waken; as she journeyed from mental rest, deepest nothingness took on forms and the forms attracted to themselves emotional charge. They required her to dally for a short while before she re-entered the world of time and consciousness…

She was peering up fearfully at the bedroom wall. High amongst the shadows there, a spectral scene was taking shape. A shimmering tableau emerged: a woman holding a baby, wrapped up so warmly and carefully that it could not be seen. The figures took on life and movement – with gentleness, the woman placed the infant in a ghostly cot and stood smiling at it, a benign and caring mother comforting her child. Then she turned and, in a deliberate movement, looked down at Frances below in her bed; her smile changed and became a menacing grin, the angelic being transformed into a terrifying witch demon. In the next moment, she began to advance down the wall aggressively and floated towards the trembling girl, growing larger as she approached, the malevolent grin more and more terrible. No hooked nose or prominent chin or warts, her features neat and regular, but her evil purpose clear. She disappeared out of sight behind the open door just by the bed-head. Terrified, Frances turned round to look at the narrow slit between the door and its frame, so near to her unprotected head. The witch was there; her eyes sparkled and she laughed with pleasure as she began to poke her fingers through the crack. She taunted her victim, relishing the terrible things that she was about to do to her...

Frances awoke with a start and looked about nervously. The small bedroom that met her anxious stare was not the one she had slept in as a little girl; it was far cosier and more comfortable, a place of adult security. The darkness was no longer hiding evil spirits. Nevertheless, she switched on her bedside lamp. She felt perplexed. She gazed up into the far corner where the wall met the ceiling and mentally asked a question of the shadows: *Why that dream again after all these years?* It was a repeat of a compelling childhood nightmare, her earliest memory. She often wondered why the first thing in life she remembered was a terrifying dream. Not like her friends' first memories – a kitten as a gift; a collection of dolls; a day out at the seaside. So was she just weird, a potential head case? Fortunately, the fears of the four year old had long since receded; witches were just figures of fantasy, entertainments to be laughed at and enjoyed, stereotyped pantomime dames. The world was a place she could handle now she was twenty-nine. Its horrors were identifiable and easily avoided, if you were careful and stuck with your friends. Children were frightened because they were little; they saw stairs as mountains leading up to dark sleeping places, full of giant furniture that towered over small people. Hardly surprising that they anticipated a host of supernatural creatures which crept in even when the locks were strong and the windows secure. Frances had long since given up believing in such things. *So why now, why has the witch dream come back?*

Maybe it was caused by depression, she reflected. The truth was that Frances didn't like herself much at the moment. She was obsessed by her failure to establish a satisfying one-to-one relationship leading to marriage and parenthood. Her twenties had seen her battle through a gauntlet of doomed love affairs, indeed to call them *love* affairs was something of an overstatement. She climbed out of bed to refill a glass with water and looked at herself in the mirror. She wasn't unattractive, was she? She was 'like a Titian painting,' someone had once said, a comment she rather clung on to when love's experiences suggested a more modest self-appraisal. OK, her face was pale and a little on the gaunt side... but she had fine high cheek bones. Sandy brown hair of unremarkable hue that she could rarely be bothered to colour... but soft and in sweeping curls. Eyes that were neither bush baby large nor adorned with long lashes... but enlivened by an unusual palette of colour: grey-green irises, with golden brown flecks that radiated out from the pupils. Teeth a little uneven, overlapping at the front... but compensated by an impish and captivating smile. A little over medium height, could be said to be on the skinny side, with small breasts... but, if the camera caught her right, a body slim and reasonably toned. She certainly received attention from men but why *those* men, she wondered? It got her down in quiet moments.

However, when out with the girls, she was good at poking fun at herself and playing the clown, hopeless and unlucky in love. A few drinks and she had the ability to dominate the conversation with her anecdotes, while friends listened on in amusement. She recalled her tipsy antics of a recent evening out, when she had held court in the recounting of heroic failures.

'Well, hunkiest guy I ever pulled were Jason; how could I seriously fall for someone wi' a name like that?... ha ha... Yep, tall, dark and handsome, sort o' bloke foretold by gypsy, *however*... (sip of vodka and tonic for effect)... blessed wi' fully matured superiority complex, really expert put-down merchant. I suffered *three years* o' humiliation and being regularly dumped for weeks on end before he came back for a bit o' comfort so eventually *I* ended it! Yay!... (gulp, more vodka)... Yet Jason *once again* held trump card, oh yes, as soon as I blurted out my big decision, which had taken me weeks agonising, he gave out a long, loud sigh o' relief, put his arm round my shoulders, laughed and, *totally calm*, said in his plummy accent, "Thank goodness for that. I wondered how long it would take you to realise that we were never going to finish up together"... what a bastard!'

'(Next vodka) Rob were really much nicer person than rat Jason, not so hunky though but OK, if you know what I mean... (nods exchanged)... but *not* a man who found decision-making easy. Oh no! "Whatever" were his favourite word. Do you want to go to Ibiza on holiday, Rob? Whatever! Do you want pizza or Chinese take-away? Whatever! Do you want a million pounds? Whatever!... ha ha... A life with Rob, well, it revolved around TV, pub, fish and chip shop... (serious look, combined with long slug from the rapidly emptying glass)... Mind you, we were OK for a few month but when my *ex*-friend Becki saw how weak he were and started flirting, quite successfully I would add, I saw that as a signal to move right on!'

'Move on straight to Dave, that is – chances are that you will go out with a 'Dave' at some point... (giggle)... *This* particular specimen o' 'Davehood' were great to be with on your *own* – talkative, funny and really quite good in bed, but he had nasty habit o' losing it with your best mates and sometimes your family too, for *no* obvious reason... (toss of head for disapproval)... So, I said to myself, choose between them good moments alone together and just about everyone I knew. No contest, Dave! You were weakest link... goodbye!'

*Well, it made the girls laugh,* Frances reflected with a smile. Some women are born romantic heroines, others comics. Rarely both. Yet there was method in her madness. When she told stories about her men in conversation with girlfriends, Frances always listed Jason, Rob and Dave first, because they represented the only proper relationships that she could claim to have finished. Also in the affairs file were the half dozen or more who had done the indecent thing to her first. Men attracted by more captivating rivals; men who had a mission to travel the world alone; men who found a new job in another city; men who whined: 'I've changed, it's nothing to do with you'. One even became a Catholic priest (good for the ego to be the woman who finally helped you discover the celibate life). These men ceased to have claims to names in her accounts of the past; she denied them the power to continue hurting her by deleting their identity. 'Don't remember him *at all*,' she insisted when someone mentioned a man quite prominent in her thoughts and feelings some years before.

But why would she be suffering from loneliness and depression this week of all weeks? There was no need. Maybe, just maybe, things were looking up. In the cold dull weeks of February, a potential Mr Right had wandered into her life. The day before, she had told Sal about it, her workmate at G.R.C. Engineering, Finance Department...

'On Monday, I just needed cheering up, so I went to this local pub wi' Cyn and Jo. Well, we were just thinking, this place is a bit dead, let's get out o' here, when *he* walked in. So we thought, well probably we need to stay for a bit, as us legs have suddenly gone numb! He were pretty gorgeous, I can tell you. Tall bloke, blond hair, tanned skin, great looking, late twenties, good clothes, seemed nice. On his own. I thought, I'm out o' this, Cyn is younger and sexier than me, while Jo can charm rattlesnake at fifty yards. They'll ditch their men for this one! But then Jonathan called Cyn on mobile and she would have felt too guilty after that to do any serious flirting. Jo seemed a bit down that evening, what with all that nasty business here at work, whether she should claim harassment, etc. Anyway, she finally seems to be making a go of a relationship. So I were only one up for it and he were *pretty interested* in me, I'm sure of it. He kept looking over, then he came to our table and chatted for a while. Said he had just moved into area and needed to check out his new local. If it hadn't been for you lot, he said, I might have walked straight out again!'

'His name were Nathan. We talked to him about local nightlife, giving him some of our thoughts on the bright spots o' Leeds. He's come up from London to new job at University. Summat to do wi' Library. He didn't stay long, more unpacking to do and work tomorrow, he said. I might have been put off by that, but then he added – talking to us all but looking straight at me in a meaningful sort o' way – maybe we can meet up next weekend and you can show me where it's at in Leeds. OK, I said, meet us at Hyde Park Corner on Friday at half seven and we'll take bus in. I can't, said Cyn (a bit mournful, like), Jonathan's back at weekend and he'll want some quality time. Count me out too, said Jo, I'm going back to Mum and Dad's to get some advice on things at work. Just me then, I said, looking a little nervously at our new friend, in case he backtracked on rendezvous now that it were one-to-one. No problem, he replied, wi' *really genuine smile*. I really do think I'm on a promise there, can't believe it. Oh God, Sal, this time, surely!'

So there was no need to feel down now, was there? Frances stood the glass on her bedside cabinet and slipped back beneath the warm covers. *Good things eventually happen to nice people. Eventually. Don't get into the habit of expecting failure, you'll bring it on.* Back to sleep...

The nightmare melted back into the archives of memory during the following day. Frances tried to stay upbeat. With only twenty-four hours to go before the big Friday, ensconced in her one-bedroomed flat for a quiet evening, she played lots of female singers on the CD player, to give her a kind of 'girl power' confidence. K.T. Tunstall, Sandi Thom, Amy Winehouse. She looked up in the middle of jigging to the music; the pictures on the living room wall seemed to reflect back her excitement. She had an idiosyncratic penchant for images of the Madonna and Child, something lost on her friends and not easy to explain to herself (*maybe it's a way of reminding myself that I once studied art history at college – OK, I were a crap student and I did it because I couldn't think of owt else to do*). For whatever reason, they had become an indispensable part of the background in her gloomy, cramped little first-floor domicile. On three separate walls were hung: an imposing icon all in metallic silver, known as the 'Virgin of Iviron'; Raphael's *Sistine Madonna*, a beautiful film star in a flowing gown; Giotto's *Majesty*, a regal lady in black gown set against a golden background, surrounded by saints and angels. In addition to these were several smaller icons as vignettes on the mantelpiece and sideboard. Apart from exuding a feeling of maternal warmth, the images were part of Frances' attempt to brighten up the dingy flat as well as she could. It represented the best single-occupant rented dwelling she could find in her attempt to strike out alone and escape quarrelsome or chain-smoking housemates. But tonight, for once, it felt like a palace.

As the meeting with Nathan approached, it was as if the normally stern Madonnas smiled like the *Mona Lisa* and the precociously serious Infant Jesuses gurgled happily and spun their orbs round like tops. Soft lighting from bulbs in wall brackets covered in old-fashioned conical shades, with splits in the fabric here and there, radiated happiness. The TV was off; 'nowt good on Thursday night,' she said to her beloved companion, a young black female cat named Cassius ('I thought it were a boy when I named it'). The quiet TV screen enjoyed its rest, with the little statuette of naked Venus on its top dancing contentedly; the fireplace had the gas fire on in addition to the ineffective central heating; the scattered candles above it on the mantelpiece were not burning tonight ('I'm scared to light 'em since number 209 went up in smoke'); a clock made in China ticked round at a good rhythm. Behind her, the second-hand oak bureau and bookcase stayed serene, the contents not minding Frances' neglect of them on this one evening.

Friday came. Yes! Frances went for the make-up, not too much, not too little, not too tarty, not too dowdy; sandy brown shoulder-length hair drawn back over the ears, with a little ponytail, nice look, highlighting the cheek bones. *Makes me look younger,* she thought, *top and skirt tonight, put them jeans away, girl, your legs aren't bad, heels but not too high, tights, yes, you might feel warmth o' love but it's also February, the air is cold and your skin is white. Couldn't eat, maybe we'll catch summat later, very nervous, at my age why do I still feel like this, it's even worse than when I were sixteen.* Plans: 'Stay in main part o' town,' Sal had advised, 'You don't want to be in rough end after 10.30, or someone'll deck him and spoil evening'. Food for thought: *avoid Red Lion, that bitch Becki goes in there and I'm not losing this guy to her; in fact stay away from regular haunts to avoid trouble, although hopefully a few girls from work might see me on my way through town and be jealous, good for some crowing to cheer up dreary Monday morning.*

A little pang of guilt... she hadn't really considered 'people in need' this week: her mum, with all those panic attacks and fainting fits; Jo, who really was going through hell at work, same company as Frances but different department; that lonely elderly neighbour who always seemed to be available for a chat whenever she put her head out of the flat door ('he must wait out there for me'). It was at times like these when she wanted to feel right with her conscience, wanted Fate to be on her side. *I'll give them all some time next week,* she thought, as if speaking silently to the invisible spirits of love and luck, so that they might let her off the sins of omission. *Maybe Nathan will help me out as I go round for my acts o' kindness!*

On my way out, no – back in, feed cat... Out again, no – back in, did you turn taps off?... Third time out, no, third time in again, *good idea to take switch card, bit rude to have no money on first date. He won't mind stopping at cash point; maybe with him protecting me from muggers, I can get fifty quid out all at once, instead o' going back and forth for twenties... Last look in mirror, OK, maybe chew some gum to make sure breath is fresh, add a little extra perfume. Cass! Don't walk in front o' my feet, not right now!... Dark outside, but not far to bus stop and lots o' people around. Really chilly, might be going to snow or summat. Stay on side o' road away from dark trees on Woodhouse Moor and always try to keep respectable-looking people in sight. Walking alone as a woman in this part o' Leeds takes special street skills. Cyn gave me good advice: 'If a weirdo comes near, call someone – anyone – on your mobile phone and he'll not touch you while you're talking to someone, will he?'*

Standing at bus stop, a bit early, looking at shapes as they go by. *Is it him, no, too short, too fat, too jerky, too drunk!* Planning conversation pieces – *he seems educated, maybe talk about music or my one-time interest in art and tell him things to do in Leeds, or summat. No, don't want to be responsible for conversation, let him take lead! I'm only part-time feminist – when I want cooking and cleaning done by men! But what if he turns up with his real girlfriend! Or maybe wife? He would have mentioned it, surely? Not another evening o' disappointment? Just him on his own, please. Is that him?! Is there somebody with him? It's not going to be one o' those situations, is it? No, please!*

But the spirits of love were capricious tonight, because Nathan, coming closer and beaming at her as he emerged from the shadows into the street lighting, was certainly not alone.

# 2

# Something Special

Nathan approached cheerily and touched her on the shoulder.

'Hello, nice to see you again.'

She might have been thrilled to hear the South of England tones emanating from such handsome lips, but the pleasure was diminished by the presence of the strange-looking person standing nearby to his left side. Her reply was uncertain.

'Yes... and you.'

'Can I introduce Debs?'

'Oh, yeah, nice to meet you, Debs.'

'Hi.'

Frances went through the motions, her mind racing. *He's bringing a woman along on first date? Can't be right. I should walk away, right here and now.* But something stopped her. She had always been accused of being an impulsive person and, as she got older, she was trying to fight it and be more 'rational'. 'You always react too quick,' her dad often said. 'Just hear people out, give 'em a chance.' *OK, Dad. There might be a good reason – perhaps this woman friend bumped into him on road; perhaps she rang up suicidal, just before he were going out and he couldn't say no; perhaps she's just coming to city centre and meeting up wi' boyfriend. We'll see what happens when we get to town.*

They waited for a couple of minutes at the stop, the conversation initially staying at the level of bus routes and timetables, then Frances said how she had often stood at this same stop as a little girl. Debs had not spoken since saying hi. Frances tried to glance at her sideways in the evening gloom. This wasn't too difficult, as Debs was looking anywhere but at her; on the contrary, seeming rather uninterested, she peered at the shop windows near at hand, still wearing her iPod headphones. She was a black woman, about the same height as Frances and roughly the same age. Frances couldn't see her face well in the light, but there was no obvious sign of great beauty. Her dark hair was just longer than shoulder length, stuck out in an unstylish mass; in the curls she had several apparently randomly placed small ribbons. A quick survey suggested someone rather dowdy (which was a relief!), wearing a metallic grey puffa jacket horribly faded and outdated; it made her look overweight and somewhat masculine. Her choice of clothing seemed generally cheap, more than a little battle-scarred, blue jeans above scuffed black shoes. She wore no obvious make-up. *'Don't go on first impressions, they'll mislead you!' Get out o' my head, Dad, I'm twenty-nine now.*

The light inside the bus confirmed it. Debs *was* plain, with a long face and large, rather mournful eyes, which seemed to stare into an unknown dimension. Starting to sense that the woman was not a rival, Frances bit the bullet.

'So are you meeting someone in town, Debs, love?'

'We're all meeting up with Jose,' Nathan replied instead. 'When we get there, I'll call to tell him where we are. I hope that's OK with you.'

Not really... but oh all right, anything to stay in with Nathan.

'Yeah, fine by me; your boyfriend is he, Debs?'

Finally, a word from Debs, although without direct eye contact.

'No, just a friend that Nathan and I have known for some time.'

Those few words suggested to her that Debs was a local girl like herself. This supposition was soon confirmed.

'Debs and Jose both live here in Leeds and I've moved here so that we can all see each other more regularly,' said Nathan, spotting the discomfort in Frances and coming to the rescue.

*Impulse to go home, number two! What's this hunk Nathan doing wi' strange girl like Debs? Why do they all want to spend time together and include her? Fight it, girl, there's an explanation somewhere! I were never into weird goings-on, but give them an hour or so to convince me it's all OK! Make sure phone is switched on!*

Despite her misgivings about the way the evening was turning out, Frances could not help but enjoy Nathan's company. He seemed so attentive to her – in a non-sleazy kind of way – that she began to be reassured that this really was a date after all. As they talked, she looked expectantly into those confident blue eyes with the long blond lashes and saw that smiling, pleasant mouth with straight white teeth, framed by nicely shaped nose and strong, but not over-prominent, chin. The golden hair fell almost onto the shoulders, fashionably unkempt but settling in pleasing swirls, suggesting that he was not someone for whom 'bad hair day' was in the dictionary. He was casually dressed for a pub night out; yet a Levi jacket and woolly scarf looked catalogue standard on him. His tan wasn't fake but light and natural, at this time of the year weathered more by wind than by sun. He reminded her of someone a bit like, maybe, that Paul Hunter, the snooker player, a local Leeds lad who had won national trophies, whom she had fancied like mad and for whom she made an exception to her rule: 'I'm not into sport, ridiculous watching men muck about wi' their balls... ha ha.' She had cried bitterly when she heard he had terminal cancer, 'I can't believe it, he's so *fit* and so young.' Maybe Nathan looked a bit like him in his prime, but the likeness was not that striking. Then there were dishy actors – a blond Jude Law with longer hair? Yes and then no. *A rock singer, maybe? Can't think. Oh well, he's just like himself and no one else.* Good-looking people had an uncanny ability to remind her of someone, but she could never quite put her finger on it.

Like many only moderately attractive people, Frances dreamed of the day that she would hit the jackpot with a partner who was drop dead gorgeous and, like the more hopelessly romantic ones among them, she believed it *would* happen. *God, let me have just a little bit o' luck!* This led her into many blind alleys and disappointed moments. She knew it was mostly foolishness although, to raise her hopes, she had seen quite a few instances of the 'can't believe *he*'s wi' *that*' category.

The bus dropped them at the bottom of Vicar Lane.
'Should we call you Fran?' Nathan was a little late in asking.
'No.' Frances made a face. She was unashamedly old-fashioned about her name. 'Just Frances. I knew a Fran once and there's a Frankie at work, wouldn't want to be like either o' them. What about you, Nath?'
The attraction took its first steps into an attempt at a tease.
'Good one! No, I'm happier with the long version too.'
Frances felt slightly embarrassed that Debs had been excluded so far from the chit-chat. Then she remembered that she wasn't supposed to like her, an interloper on her jackpot moment. 'Bleeding hearts just make a mess on the carpet,' Jason had said. Maybe he was right on that one; she couldn't go through life worrying about every small discomfort that near strangers suffered. It was her character, however, to care for everyone she met – an irrepressible impulse.
Nathan hadn't finished with the questions.
'And what's your surname?'
Frances didn't like this question but she answered nonetheless: 'Dryburgh.'
Nathan nodded in acknowledgement. What was he thinking? Dryburgh. Not a good name when you're a school kid. Dry

equals frigid, dull, humourless, barren. 'Hey up, here's Miss Dryfanny.' She took great trouble to appear warm and light-hearted in order to refute the name. She couldn't wait to get married to a man to get a name that was more exotic, more appealing.

'And yours?' she retorted, in great hope of hearing the surname that would frame her future.

'Oh, yes, just good old commonplace Smith, I'm afraid.'

Oh well, Smith was bearable, if you were walking up the aisle with Nathan Smith.

'Debs, what about you?'

Frances couldn't help but try to bring her in. But Debs was somewhere else and didn't hear the question, so it was left to Nathan to smile with a shrug and answer for her: 'Lewis'.

Frances suggested *The Black Bull*, but Debs, the headphones finally removed, said that she preferred *The Airedale*. She knew the Leeds scene too. Frances asked her which part of the city she came from. 'Chapeltown' was the terse reply. So they were both from working class areas of the northern suburbs: Debs from Leeds 7, Chapeltown and Frances from Leeds 6, Hyde Park.

Before entering the pub, Nathan phoned interloper number two, Jose. Frances thought there might be some compensation if he were a handsome Spaniard. *How about that, out wi' dark and blond citizens o' hunk city all in one evening and only Dowdy Debs as competition.* They went in. As they waited at the bar, Frances looked around. Not her normal scene at all, the pub was long and narrow and felt rather cramped and dark, thanks to the low ceiling and mahogany panels all round the walls. Away from the bar stools, the customers were seated on cushioned mock leather. Lots of real ale options. Mirrors with brewery adverts inscribed. A middle-aged pub, not the bright wine bars of Greek Street or the Cornmarket in which she usually hung out. Oh well, she wouldn't be bothered by party crashers and those slags that she knew from school days. Nathan interrupted her thoughts by passing her a glass of red wine and asking if her friends of the other night were OK.

'Well, if you ask me, Cyn is struggling wi' that Jonathan; he's right boring, never goes out.' *Shouldn't have said that, don't want to tell him Cyn might be up for it.* 'Jo, she's not a happy bunny right now, problems at work wi' bosses getting on top of her; oops, didn't mean it like that... ha ha... No, it's serious, shouldn't laugh. They're pushing her around, making her feel bad, destroying her confidence.'

The small talk was amiable, but still Debs did not say anything, staring round at the crowds with the pub getting busier as Friday evening progressed. Frances didn't care, nor did she mind how scintillating the conversation was, as long as she was sharing it with Nathan.

After twenty minutes or so, Nathan gave a wave to someone behind her and she turned to see the newcomer. There were no sexy Spaniards in sight, no brooding tennis players or bullfighters. The only person heading in their direction was a small Asian man, dressed neatly in a shiny brown jacket with an open-necked yellow shirt underneath, smiling pleasantly but not someone who would set a girl's heart on fire. He limped awkwardly.

'Hi, guys,' he called, 'How's things? I got a bit delayed.'

He had a definite South Asian accent with a slight Leeds twang to it, but he was also what her mum would call 'quite well spoken'. He held out his hand to her before sitting down.

'Jose's the name.'

'Oh yes, hello, pleased to meet you, too.'

For the second time in the evening, Frances struggled to sound genuinely pleased, because she wasn't. She was disappointed and not a little bemused. Who were all these people? Then the direct side got the better of her, as it often did.

'I were expecting Spanish man, given your name.'

'That's what everyone says.'

Jose laughed. He was clearly a more sociable personality than Debs, as well as being a smarter dresser.

'I'm from Goa, an Indian province which was Portuguese until some forty-five or so years ago. My family is Catholic and many of us have Portuguese names. Mind you, I've been here in Yorkshire for nearly twenty years now.'

At first, Frances had mixed feelings about the arrival of Jose. On the one hand, he was a lively character, a little on the camp side, and his presence brought the conversation to life; he certainly entertained Nathan and even Debs managed a smile or two. On the other hand, her little tête-à-tête with Nathan was most definitely compromised. Nathan and Jose drank Old Peculier, a strong Yorkshire brew, and indulged in some good-natured banter about whether nobby Nathan was a fish out of water up here in the north. Then Jose taunted him about his job in the library.

'Going on a staff training course, are you, Nathan? This week, we are going to study how to put books in alphabetical order. A goes before B and then comes C... OK, that's enough for today, work on that overnight and we'll do D tomorrow.'

Nathan responded in kind.

'Well, the great man speaks. He who organises should we say, *dis*organises – bus timetables. Mr da Silva, how do you respond to the relatives of those thousands of people who have died waiting at bus stops?'

'It's a lovely way to go, Mr Smith. Better than expiring of boredom in the University Library. Ssh! Please drop dead quietly, people are trying to read!'

The best part of an hour went by. Nathan and Jose dominated the talk for a while, then tried to get Frances involved by talking about the city in which she had lived all her life. It was difficult for her to feel comfortable; she began to feel awkward, like a stranger at a party. She didn't really know any of these people and she hadn't yet had any confirmation of a love interest from Nathan. There was no one else in the pub she knew that she could turn to – no interruptions meant no rescuing, either. Her more pessimistic side started to take an upper hand. Although enthusiasm often welled up in her, passionate soul that she was, taking her along exciting new paths, quick disappointment and easy discouragement were powerful forces too and they wouldn't let her free from that sinking feeling.

'I must go soon; I can't stay out too late.'

'Ah, perhaps then it is time for us to get to the point,' said Nathan, giving her a tender smile. Frances looked back, puzzled. If he were about to say something romantic, this seemed an odd time to be doing it, in front of his two friends. 'There's something special about you,' continued Nathan, suddenly looking serious, his blue eyes more intense than ever. 'I noticed it last Monday in the pub. I wanted my friends to meet you to see what I saw.'

'Special? Don't know what you mean,' replied Frances, looking anxious. She was now too far down the road to self-doubt. *This is some kind o' scam,* she thought frantically. *I want nowt to do with it!* 'No, sorry, I really must go,' she insisted. 'I'm worried about my mum. I said I'd pop in.'

The lie dispatched, she got up quickly, grabbed her bag and shot out of the bar, just in time so that they couldn't see the tears starting to gather in her eyes. *I must look right mug, me! Special, eh? A special kind o' mug who parts with her hard-earned cash, I suppose.*

Only a few yards from the pub, Frances heard swift footsteps behind. She supposed hopefully that Nathan was striding after her to try to talk her into staying. She turned as the pursuer touched her arm. Big surprise – it was not Nathan, but Debs. For the first time since they met at Hyde Park Corner, the big dark eyes looked straight into hers and the person who had seemed something of a nonentity until then took on a new dimension. Frances, despite trying to suppress the feeling, could not escape the fact that she experienced an unexpected feeling of rapport with this stranger, although she could not think why. Perhaps it was because they were both working class lasses from Leeds.

'Please don't be upset, Frances. We're not trying anything on or owt. There in't any catch. Nathan's very sincere when he says he were drawn to you. Come back and let him explain.'

Frances tried to make the best of it and keep her panic under control.

'I'm sorry, but I can't. I've lost it now. Maybe another time. I need reassuring that there's no funny business going on. Tell Nathan to call me, I gave him my mobile number.'

Then she walked off in the direction of the bus stop. Jose couldn't be a bad bus schedule organiser, after all, as there was one waiting for her there, affording a quick getaway.

Frances spent the next day doing very little, cursing Nathan, Debs and Jose for spoiling her Friday evening, a sacred event in her weekly calendar. Lots of wine. Stayed in, rare for a Saturday.

On Sunday, she found herself with an agonising internal battle – she was still embarrassed and upset but, on the other hand, she wanted Nathan to call. But he didn't. *Bad thing, drinking alone. Even cat seems to be avoiding me. I'm coming on too, that don't help.*

Back at work on Monday, trying to avoid Sal and others asking awkward questions. Held out until lunchtime.

'Yeah, very nice evening, Sal, don't know where it's leading but here's hoping.'

'You don't sound very positive, Frances, love.'

'Just don't ask me yet, Sal. Give it time.'

Depression kicking in during a lonely evening at home. *Special? What did that mean? No wine in house, too drained to get some.*

Tuesday – things got worse. As she had tried to keep out of the other girls' way on the Monday, the news came as a surprise. Jo hadn't come back in on Monday and she had sent word saying that she was leaving the firm. Evening – couldn't get through to Jo, just left a message. Nothing from big N. He had mentioned the number of his place in nearby Springfield Terrace. But what was it? She might go round and give him a piece of her mind. Bought more booze on the way home.

Wednesday – the pits. Called in by the Administration Manager, a woman of forty-something with very short hair and speaking very carefully, as though from a script; 'professionalism' seemed to pervade her very being, like the name 'Blackpool' through the length of a stick of rock.

'Frances, we think it's time you had a change, as we like our staff to face new challenges and not get stale. As you may have heard, Joanne has given us notice and she's now on sick leave until she goes. We need someone quite urgently in the Ordering Department. We have decided to transfer you to take her place.'

Frances, open-mouthed, let this sink in. The 'department of hell' Jo had called it: 'Managed by brute who's in with senior executives, you can't touch him. Runs place as if you were soldiers fighting in Afghanistan. Control freak.' Frances winced but words of resistance wouldn't come out. She knew it was *fait accompli*.

'OK,' she said.

She thought, *I can't do it, well maybe just for a bit while I look for another job.*

'When do I start?' she asked.

An inner voice pleaded, *please not yet!*

'Monday,' she heard.

*Better get Yorkshire Post and see what's in,* she decided to herself. Evening – *very down. Need company. Cat in tonight – come here, I need to cuddle you. Lots more wine. Alcoholism? – yes, definitely. Who cares? Actually, I think it were number 11.*

Thursday – feverish conversations with Sal. No solutions. Very bad day. Confidence just about shot. Evening – text from Jo, inviting her to call, but then couldn't get her. Desperate – *nowt to lose, might as well go and see him. Deep breaths. Yes, make-up and a change of clothes, a girl can't sink that low…* Number 11, Springfield Terrace. *One of those three-storied terraced houses and not divided into flats. Is he rich then? Is this his place? Yes, it must be. It's him who's answering door.*

# 3

# Spiritual Adventurers

Nervousness, pent-up frustration, anxiety, uncertainty – all of these served to make Frances very defensive when she saw Nathan smiling a friendly welcome at her. She couldn't help feeling short-tempered and irritable. *Why am I doing this to myself? I hardly know him; he looks good but might just be a bit of a weirdo.* But she hadn't been able to stay away and that annoyed her even more.

'Well, thanks *very* much for calling me.' Frances pushed past him into the house; Nathan began to look sheepish as Frances went off on one. 'Thanks for calls night and day, asking how I were and whether I were upset last Friday. My phone was so blocked wi' messages from you, no one else could get through!'

Nathan started to slide from embarrassment to amusement. He was discovering that Frances could be funny, especially when she was in angry sarcastic mode. But he tried to stick with the apologetic look, on the surface anyway.

'I didn't want to call you and put you under pressure,' he argued. 'I wanted you to make your own decision whether to see me or not. I couldn't have you thinking we were trying something on.'

'Well maybe staying quiet's just a clever tactic,' came the reply. 'Whatever... I just wanted to come round and see why you thought I were so *special*.'

And she all but spat out the last word, to try and play down the genuine curiosity that was proving stronger than the bad temper.

Nathan showed her through a narrow hall into a living room. The size of the house suggested wealth; the interior contradicted that supposition. It had that bachelor look, neat but uninspiring. The room was large and well-lit with a high ceiling and decorated plain white all round, which made it look bare. The feeling of emptiness persisted, despite the prints hanging: two impressionist paintings and a poster of *Rebel Without A Cause*. A couple of sprawling spider plants stood by the long windows, mothers with several offspring growing on the stalks. The mantelpiece was bare except for a nondescript cheap clock and a rather full wallet to one side, with a few coins splattered around. There was an oak veneer bookcase, probably IKEA, with plenty of books inside, on top and all around it on the floor. A tall lamp stood in the corner with a shade part-covered in dust. The suite was two-piece in beige, a single armchair and a long cheap-looking sofa sporting a couple of white square cushions. They had carefully been arranged in diamond shapes, as if Nathan was one of those men who went around straightening things but without noticing any other detail about them. Newspapers and magazines covered the little coffee table.

After asking for Frances' drink preference, Nathan poured her a lager, which she sometimes fancied when not wanting to ask a host to crack into a bottle of wine. He then sat down next to her on the sofa and took a deep breath.

'I *do* want to get to know you better, Frances. I really do think you have special qualities and maybe you don't know it yourself.' Was that patronising? Nathan seemed to sense that a correction was needed. 'Or maybe you do, of course – I don't know you well enough to know one way or another but I want to.'

When she was upset, Frances tended to become extra-impulsive, like someone drowning who grabbed onto every piece of passing driftwood. She suddenly decided that all this talk was a shy man's way of trying to get off with her. She shuffled closer to Nathan and made a move as if to kiss him. But he drew back, trying to compensate by putting an arm around her shoulder.

He said, very softly, 'Steady on. I wasn't meaning that.'

Frances could easily have made hasty exit number two within a week. But she didn't really have the energy for any more indignant actions. She leaned into his arm and started to sob. *Good one! Now I'm Ms Dryburgh-Desperate.* He held her compassionately, keeping the composure of a man who had done this kind of thing before.

'Please let's be friends, Frances. I'm really not that good with romantic relationships.'

A few more soothing words later and Frances graduated from deep sobs to tissues and sniffles. Then she pulled herself together with a big sigh and sat upright, pulling away from him.

'OK. Friends it is then. I need one right now.' Resignation in the voice, trying to make the best of a bad job, then Frances qualified the agreement. 'But I need to know what you're up to. Why do you hang around wi' such strange people as Debs and Jose?'

Nathan smiled as if recalling them fondly.

'The three of us have come together, firstly because we get on well and, secondly, because we're...' He paused for thought as if he wanted to ensure that he used the right wording. 'We're *spiritual adventurers*, Frances.'

She gave him the look of a working class girl who didn't bear pretension too gladly.

'Go on, what does that mean? You've come to wrong person, I've not been to church for owt except baptisms, weddings and funerals since my mum sent me to Sunday School up to age ten because she thought she ought to.'

Nathan gave a brief laugh.

'No, I didn't mean that we're churchgoers. Far from it. We're *adventurers*. That means we want to explore the world of the supernatural outside the straightjacket of organised religion.'

Nathan went to get more drinks. Frances reflected for a few seconds. The thinking didn't come easy, with all the background brain noise of trouble at work, disappointment in love and a general feeling of unease. She looked down at the magazines and saw a *Pagan Dawn* amongst the copies of *The Independent* and *TV Quick*. *Pagan, what exactly does that mean, a tree-hugger? Where do I fit into all that? OK, I've made trips to clairvoyant in town, none of her predictions ever came true, but Cyn and me kept going back because we liked talking about ourselves to someone. She couldn't prophesy owt to save her life! I should be married and rich and living in Seychelles by now! Then I suppose there's them pictures o' the Virgin Mary in my flat, they make me feel somehow secure in all the mess of life, when things go wrong. Do Madonna pictures make me spiritual? Actually, I just want to find a man! I'm an 'adventurer' who's on hunt for men! Here's another one escaping the net!* Frances laughed bitterly and only just managed to stop herself sliding back into tears through wretched self-pity.

'It's like this.' Nathan had come back into the room with two more bottled lagers as he spoke, the sentence beginning somewhere down the hall. 'I spent years looking for something to feed my soul, tried various churches, religions and all that. Nothing really made sense. Then I decided to widen my interests and met Debs and Jose at a Druid camp in Somerset. It was about three years ago. I suddenly realised, as we were talking there one night, that it was not some *thing* I was looking for but some *people*! Not a club of believers all with the same belief, but some people with whom I could go on a kind of journey that would take in any kind of faith and spiritual idea that attracted us, as long as they're healthy.'

Frances felt out of her depth with this talk of spiritual journeys and switched the conversation to more familiar territory.

'Did you ever find a *woman*, Nathan? Wouldn't that have satisfied you?'

Nathan began to look less comfortable, which seemed odd for someone usually so attractive and self-assured.

'No, Frances.'

A chance maybe for him now to reassure her that there was nothing wrong with *her*.

'I just don't feel right when I get into a relationship. It lasts for a few weeks, maybe months sometimes, but then I usually end it, unless the woman's got frustrated and dumped me first. I'm not gay or anything... (aside) Jose wishes I was!... but I just wasn't made for one-to-one relationships. I feel better in a crowd.'

Frances wasn't impressed; she'd heard this patter before: 'It's not you'; 'I need to find myself'. Her arms flopped into her lap in resignation.

'Maybe you should become a monk,' she said, remembering the guy who went off to be a priest.

Nathan ignored the remark.

'Let's start again, Frances. Why don't you come out with Debs, Jose and me tomorrow night? This time we can really talk. You can find out what we're about and we can learn something about you. The other two agree with me, you *are* special. There's just something about you, you have a kind of charisma. I'm sure that you're a very spiritual person.'

Frances was in sceptical mode now. *Men are double-talkers. They might call you special, but they don't act on it. They flatter whenever it suits 'em and turn away when you get a bit demanding. This guy seems a bit different, true, he's not after casual sex. But he's all promise and no delivery, like rest of 'em.* So, once again, she tried to change the subject.

'Actually, I don't feel that special right now. My work's going down toilet. I'm just nobody there, pushed round wherever they want me. Just dogsbody who they give fancy title to, to get me working harder for virtually nowt. Senior Administrator. Yeah, yeah. On Monday, I'll be working for Adolf Hitler's twin brother and he'll walk all over me and I'll have to get out and go somewhere else, that's if I can wi' bad references he'll write me.'

Frances began to recount the whole story about Jo and the situation in Ordering. As she did so, a ring on the doorbell announced a second visitor. It was that familiar situation – just as she got going, pouring her heart out, the phone rang or the doorbell went and her listener found a way out.

It was Debs, in what looked like the same clothes that she had been wearing the previous Friday.

'Oh, hi,' she said, in her non-committal way.

Nathan seemed not to want Frances to be distracted, however.

'Debs, Frances has just been telling me about her work. Perhaps you could fill Debs in with the story, Frances, I'm sure she would want to hear it.'

Oh, genuine interest! Well, we'll give him credit for that. As Frances re-started the story, within a couple of minutes she could not help noticing how much it felt better to talk with Debs there. Nathan had been sympathetic, but a girl somehow tuned in better when other girls needed to talk. As soon as she realised she needed to be in listening mode, Debs seemed to switch like a light from indifference to absolute focus. It was like the moment when Frances left the pub the other night; as soon as there was trouble, Debs had the gift of plugging in and turning on. Frances once again felt that pull between the inner voice prompting her to dislike the apparently unfriendly woman and some other strange instinct telling her that she might actually have a good deal in common with her.

Frances described what it was like in the office, how she had managed a measure of independence and job satisfaction in her present position in Finance and enjoyed working with Sal and some of the others; how the Ordering Department where she was now going had a terrible reputation for being a happy stamping ground for sadists and a graveyard for more sensitive folk; how her friend Jo had been hounded until life was unbearable so that she was on anti-depressants and visiting a counsellor at thirty quid an hour; how Frances always knew that she would be broken if she were ever to be in that situation, despite all her bravado; how she didn't want to move jobs because it was reasonably paid and, anyway, she wasn't someone who found it easy to make changes; how she really didn't know what she wanted to do with her career; how she had thought she might do better with her degree, even if it was only art history at a small college, which she had started on impulse because she used to like painting and had the desire simply to be the first one in the family to do a degree course; how she was nearing thirty and seemed to be going nowhere; how, how, how…

When Frances finished, she just looked at her two new friends and shrugged as if to say: but there's nothing you nor I can do about all this, is there? Debs looked straight back at her with intensity.

'Frances, give me while tomorrow to consider what you've said today. If you want me to advise you, I'll speak to you in pub. Think about it, I don't want to rush you. But you *will* be there, won't you?'

And then, giving Frances a friendly squeeze on her arm, she wandered back out into the street in deep thought.

'Didn't you want that coffee?' Nathan called after her.

Yet Debs, true to form, ignored the light things of life as she dwelt on the serious matter in hand and said nothing as she left. She had not even taken the puffa jacket off.

'Tell me about her, who is she?' Frances asked, looking straight at Nathan.

Something very odd had happened in the last few minutes. The handsome blond man had lost his position at the centre of her attention; now the dour black woman was more compelling somehow, as if she might hold the answer to Frances' life, stuck as it was in a deep rut.

'Well, she's had a bit of a tough time, you know.' Nathan had a serious, reflective look as he described Debs' life. 'Her mother was a prostitute and she never knew who her father was. She was brought up in a house full of instability, abuse, violence and hard drugs. In her teens, she too turned to prostitution and drug taking, spent time in prison for pushing, then a period in the mental hospital. I don't think she started living like a normal human being until she was well into her twenties. Then something happened to her to change everything. She doesn't say much about it, except that she 'took control' with the help of a group of women whom she met while in a refuge hiding from a psychopathic pimp. But it hasn't been easy; she is still technically an addict and that is why she is so quiet normally – she has to concentrate minute by minute to keep her mind together. She gave up with psychiatrists, that's just another kind of drug abuse, she says. Her spiritual search began as a necessity, unlike myself and Jose for whom it started as a diversion, a hobby. She tried so hard to change her life, she impressed Social Services who gave her a chance, a job as a care worker specialising in domestic violence. It's something she knows about.'

Nathan paused and took a moment to hold Frances' hand gently, in a way that avoided any hint of sexual interest. She had begun to look pale, as if the last hour or so on top of a depressing week had drained the blood out of her. But she didn't want him to stop telling the story. There was something that drew her into the dark secrets of Debs' past; it was like going down a whirlpool that, for some reason, she didn't want to escape.

'Tell me about her "spiritual search",' she urged. 'What does she do?'

Nathan looked uncertain and tongue-tied all of a sudden.

'Well... It's to do with changing of her consciousness. She tries to see the positive things in her life and taps her inner potential so that she can control her destiny instead of being the victim all the time.'

Frances wasn't sure that she understood this claptrap, but on the other hand she was quite cheered to think that Debs might have some experience that would be of use in helping her in her present work situation. OK, work problems weren't as terrible as drugs, violence and back street prostitution, but they could be just as damaging to her; she didn't have much steel in her below the bubbly personality and flashing eyes.

She sensed the apprehension in Nathan as he struggled to explain Debs' spiritual journey and in what sense she was an 'adventurer'.

'Go on, tell me more,' she said, with a firm gentleness that she had not managed since she walked through his front door an hour or more earlier.

'Well…' Nathan started to say something. He knew he had to respond to her; after all, it was he who had brought the subject to this point. But he was clearly uncomfortable, not with whatever it was that Debs was involved in but with the impact that it might have on Frances. He took a deep breath. 'Debs got involved with a group that taught her a lot about spiritual things and the way to handle difficult situations positively. They practiced a very ancient belief system that is ever more popular now and of course no longer has the negative stigma attached to it that it once had; indeed, many teenagers are quite interested in it…'

'You *are* prattling on,' interrupted Frances, now feeling on top of things enough to tease him a little. 'Just say it.'

'Witchcraft,' said Nathan, cursorily.

Frances took in a breath, as she recalled the fears of her childhood. Why had she re-experienced the witch nightmare recently; was there a meaning? Was it a warning to stay away from Debs? But she was desperate, there were no other options. She would have to suppress her misgivings for now.

'Thank you,' she replied. 'I guessed it five minutes ago. Now why did you imagine that would upset me?'

# 4

# Working through the Heart

The next day, Frances couldn't decide whether she had done the right thing the evening before or not.

'I'm not right good wi' couple of bottles o' lager – they go straight to my head and then I agree to anything!'

But in saying this to Sal during the morning tea break, she exaggerated. In reality, although drink was quick to slur her tongue and blur her vision, she usually retained a good measure of control over her words and actions. Can someone be impulsive and self-controlled at the same time? If so, one such person was Frances. Impulsive, when her instincts told her that she was safe and when her heart took her in a certain direction. Self-controlled, even when drunk (actually, especially when drunk), in circumstances that could lead to embarrassment, unwanted obligations and possible danger. At Nathan's flat, she had opened her heart about her worries; well, she needed to offload some of the pressure and that was fine. Uncertainty came with the possibility that she was now going to have to enter into some kind of group activity over which she had no say. When Frances had pooh-poohed the idea that witchcraft held any terrors for her, she was really meaning that trivial kind of witchcraft you try when it doesn't really matter: teen spells, playing at being Harry Potter. But Debs was a serious person and her approach to spell-making promised – or threatened – to be something far more intense. On the other hand, the situation at work was so dire that, whatever Debs came up with, it could not make it worse.

'You'll clear out your desk and move your things on Monday morning. Before you start in Ordering, I will give you a briefing and then Mr Ballard will speak to you about what is expected of you in your new role.'

Great, the Administration Manager was doing her professional thing, saying terrible things in a matter of fact, everything's under control kind of way.

'She's just bloody Nazi robot,' exclaimed Frances, when out of earshot.

To make it more difficult, this was the day that old friends, feeling neglected recently, began to call or text for a Friday evening date. 'Jon out, wd lv 2 mt u 2 nite – Cyn.' Jo got through on the office phone and suggested a night out during which she could add yet another 'briefing about Ordering', this time from the bottom up perspective. Mum, too, got through.

'What's up wi' you, love? Me and your dad haven't seen you in weeks and we're only a bus ride away.'

All were put off: Jo and Cyn until Saturday, both complaining that this wasn't so convenient. Mum was postponed to Monday. Somehow, Frances had to stick to her guns and keep her meeting with Debs et al. She was desperate to find out what strange witchy strategy was going to be suggested, so that perhaps if it was nonsense, she could dismiss it and get on with worrying in her own way; however, if it was helpful, then she'd have a plan to help her through the weekend. She also felt just a little nervous that a cry-off to follow the walk-out last Friday would put Nathan off completely. How could you resist pursuing a good looking heterosexual man who didn't have a girlfriend? His going incommunicado for six days had sown enough doubt for her not to want to risk it.

This Friday, Nathan would call at her flat and walk with her to the corner to catch the bus. They would meet Debs and Jose in the *Airedale* as before. Different kind of urgency, similar feeling of collywobbles. More workmanlike approach to dress and make-up: jeans and trainers, albeit with a pretty top with flared sleeves and low-ish neck. Variety is always right in the hair style department: loose and well-brushed, not the drawn-back look of the last two meetings. Frances was a bit of a rebel against the straight hair look so fashionable at the moment, she felt that her curls had a timeless charm and so she resisted the 'you need to do something wi' that hair' brigade. 'It's just way I like to look, it suits me'. 'Do you want to get bloke, or not?' 'Not sort o' bloke who goes for fake tan and false straight blonde hair Barbies!'

On arrival, Nathan was complimentary and she couldn't resist the 'well, why don't you do something about it' look. *Nice to walk down Hyde Park Road with him, even if we're not holding hands. Girls will still be green with envy!* Soon they stood at Hyde Park Corner; Jose was spot on with his timetables again – the bus was there as expected. Frances took the chance to find out more about Nathan, as he was hardly the type to talk about himself. *Bit of a closed book,* she decided, *so let's get some facts.*

'Well, if you really want to know, Frances, but it's not that exciting.'

Born in South London, father a GP, mother looked after the home and the three of them, an older brother and sister and himself. They moved to Hemel Hempstead when he was six. During his mid-teens, his father left them and went to practice in his beloved United States. Mother married again, a financial advisor. Nathan went to Southampton University and studied Chemistry but didn't really get into it, scraping a $3^{rd}$ class.

'Oh, only a $3^{rd}$. You're not in *my* class then, I got a 2.2 in art history.'

'Well, I had no idea that I was speaking to someone so intellectual. Please sign my copy of your book when you've written it.'

'But would a thicko like you be able to read it?'
'Art history? Most probably not!'
Frances smiled.
'To be honest, I don't think I could get through a book on art history myself now and I didn't really understand them then!'

Nathan continued with his life story. He drove a cake delivery van for a couple of years, then did a postgrad in librarianship. Worked in Brunel University for a time, while living in rented accommodation in Hayes, and took a year out to travel. It was while in India that he got the spirituality bug, until then only a nominal Church of England type, i.e. rites of passage only.

'Except I did read the gospels at the age of twenty. Thought I might like to be a minister for a while, but then someone mentioned that you normally needed to go to church regularly before they let you become one.'

'You'd make a good vicar. All smile and bullshit.'

And so on to Druid camps, Buddhist meditation courses, meeting Debs and Jose. He had talked about moving to live nearer them for some time and became so sick of the perpetual clog of the London suburbs, with the anonymity of life there, that he was delighted to get the job in Leeds.

'So this is where you came in, Frances.'

No, Nathan, *you're* the one who came in.'

The repartee was good and once again Frances could not help loving his company despite her resentment at the lack of sexual advances from him. There was energy around when they were together. She forgot about her anxiety for just a little while and was glad of the traffic jam that prolonged the short journey into town.

'Perpetual clog o' London suburbs, Nathan? Look out o' window! Is Leeds any better?'

'Yes, much better, Frances, you've no idea what London is like. This is countryside compared to it!'

And then, the *Airedale*. Jose and Debs had arrived ahead of them; Jose was charming and friendly just as he had been the week before. *I don't get that Debs! She were nice as pie last night and now she's looking into space while I say hello.*

'Oh, drinks – red wine again tonight.'

Nathan and Jose ordered real ale, Debs stayed with orange juice and lemonade. Small talk then, prompted by the others, Frances' life took centre stage.

She retold the work story for Jose's sake. For some reason, she played down the problem, perhaps feeling that she was overstating it. *When you're outside a situation,* she reflected, *it can seem more trivial than when you're there in the thick of it.*

'Maybe Jo exaggerated and it were partly her fault. I could reason wi' Ballard, show him I'm keen, so it might be OK.'

'What do other people say about him?' asked Jose.

He looked as intense and engaged with the matter as Debs had been the previous evening.

'Well... that he's a bastard, I suppose. And that he is such a control freak, that you can't please him, however hard you try.'

Jose was quick to respond to the contradictions, although he was gentle in pointing them out.

'Ah, so how are you going to reason with him? You don't want to sell your soul to the company by slogging every hour of the day, do you? How will you enjoy your work and keep him happy at the same time?'

'I don't know... shit, it's such a mess. Surely he can't be that bad?'

Hearing this, Jose switched into lecture mode and there was nothing soothing about his words.

'In the seventeenth century, the Spanish and Portuguese worked South American Indians to death in mines and executed them on whim. In the eighteenth century, slave ships were crossing the Atlantic; half of the African human cargo perished en route, the rest toiling without end on plantations from which Europeans became rich. In the nineteenth century, Irishmen were starving to death in their tens of thousands as the British aristocracy looked on, only interested in how it was affecting their own incomes. In the twentieth century, as we know, the world saw many great wars, with the wilful slaughter of innocent millions. So why, so soon afterwards, do we think that, in a company department in Leeds in the twenty-first century, the boss will be 'reasonable'? There is no reason to believe it. In his little world, he is a human being enjoying power and he has inherited the ruthless gene of his forefathers. He will only be as reasonable as the law, his employees and his own interests *force* him to be.'

This was quite depressing for Frances, who was about to sink into a deep hopelessness, but then Debs came in.

'And so you have to do some work on him, Frances.'

Frances looked sceptical.

'How?'

Debs was unperturbed.

'Tell us more about department where you're going to work. Who works there?'

Frances took a deep breath before replying.

'Well, in Ordering, maybe eight people altogether. There's Mr Ballard; he's got an assistant manager and then there's several administrators and…'

Debs butted in.

'Yeah, but what *kind* o' people are they?'

Frances shrugged.

'I don't know 'em. I've heard some are nice, but they have to keep their heads down. Bosses on other hand are right Nazis. They don't give anybody room to breathe. There's lots to do; any mistakes and you're staying late to put it right. Staff come and go, but they always get new people because pay's OK. It won't be like where I am now, where we can have a laugh, though we still get job done.'

Debs looked suddenly confident, as if she had solved the dilemma on the slenderest of information.

'You'll have to take a more proactive role in your department,' she said, as if it were the most obvious thing in the world and then lowered her voice like a conspirator. 'We call it working through the *heart*.'

'Whose heart?' queried Frances, looking round quizzically at Jose and Nathan.

They grimaced with slight nodding motions, as if to say: we don't know what she means exactly, but keep listening to her.

'The heart o' the department,' replied Debs with conviction. 'Every group o' people is like a body; the group has a head and a heart. The head? That's your bosses, they're the ones doing thinking and making plans for everyone. Often the head goes forward without considering rest o' body. But the heart? That's made up o' those ordinary folk who have to get on wi' job. The heart is vital to whole body; if it stops beating, then body dies. If the heart starts to cause trouble, the head begins to worry, because it depends on it, you see.'

Frances looked a bit disappointed at this; it didn't seem that Debs understood the extent of the problem. Fostering unrest would make no difference.

'But the bosses can ignore the workers as much as they like,' she said, despairingly. 'If there's trouble, they can sack the workers, because there's many more people out there willing to take job.'

'No, you misunderstand,' said Debs, not put off by this. 'The heart does not cause pain to the head by petitions and sit-ins, or whatever, although sometimes you can use those means as well. No, it sends out its message through *magic*. It's impossible for bosses to do battle with that. And it's up to person who knows about it to do magic on behalf of group. That person is working through the heart.'

Frances was still fairly confused but, such was the certainty with which these words were spoken, and such was the clear backing of the two men for Debs and her strange project, that she wanted to know more.

'How do I work through the heart?'

Debs continued, obviously relieved that she had her pupil still on board.

'Well, there's two parts to it,' she replied, her voice almost in a hushed whisper now. 'Firstly, get to know ordinary folk. Put up with things for a bit while you get to understand them and what their problems are. How would they like department to be run, that kind o' thing.' She looked up at Jose, who had stood up and was waving his hands about trying to get everyone to agree to another round without disturbing the conversation. 'Same again, ta.'

'Yeah, me too, thanks, red wine.'

Frances smiled at Nathan as he got up to help Jose at the bar and she then settled back to listen to the plan.

'Secondly, practice magic in your own home, in private. There's no rules on how you do it. Use something important to you, maybe with some spirit connection. Use that as the focus for ritual o' some kind. Make up your own. Do it regular. Candles are good. Summon spirits to help you. Then keep workmates in your mind as you do ritual actions. I can give you some ideas on what to do, but it must be *you* who does it, as it's your workplace we're talking about.'

*Magic? Oh God, is this really happening?*

The men were taking a little while, as the Friday night crush was beginning to slow down service at the bar.

'Where did you get all this?' asked Frances. 'Is it in a book of spells, or summat? I did spells once, for love, but they didn't work out too well!'

'Noooo…'

Debs was dismissive of the idea. Teen Wicca books were clearly not what she had in mind.

'I learnt it from women in refuge where I stayed a few year ago,' she replied, looking away from Frances. 'Women whose hearts had been broken. Women who were used to being victims o' men who controlled their lives. Men who insisted on being the *head* and forcing their will one way or t' other. So these women had to work through the *heart,* you see, to stop it being broken forever. And they found that, when their hearts worked together as one heart through magic, they could be strong, so that the men had to listen, sometimes without realising what was happening. Things started to turn out better.'

Jose and Nathan finally returned. They were still in respectful mode, allowing the women the space to talk, and passed the drinks around without speaking. Debs tried to push Frances into taking the thing further.

'So what will help you make connections wi' spirit? Is there summat in your home, a little statue of a Goddess or Buddha, maybe?'

Frances thought of the little naked Venus on top of the TV, brought back by some admirer from a holiday in Cyprus, but that didn't seem appropriate. *But of course!* She smiled.

'My Madonnas. I can use my Madonnas.'

The icons and paintings seemed to have been waiting for this moment; the idea of involving the Madonnas made it all seem a little less spooky. Debs frowned, however.

'It's up to you, of course, but Virgin Mary has not been that helpful to women, you know. She's held up by Catholic priests as a model of humility and virginity, to keep women subordinate and to suppress their sexuality.'

But, hearing this, Jose wanted to come into the discussion.

'Speaking as a Catholic,' he said, with a broad smile and mock self-importance, 'I can tell you that the Virgin Mary is not quite what the Vatican would want her to be. She is a powerful wonder-worker and can be a figure of subversion against the world of male domination. She has much in common with the mother goddesses that preceded her in Pagan Europe. She can certainly be asked to help Frances with her problem. Anyway, all this talk about heads and hearts – it's straight out of St Paul's letters. Christianity can be radical too, you know.'

Nathan saw his chance for some banter; the evening was too serious.

'You had better not tell your priest, Mr da Silva, that you are dragging the Virgin Mary into a world of witchcraft. You will finally – and not before time – get excommunicated! Off to the Vatican with you; you will have to hand in your rosary beads.'

Jose laughed.

'I wonder what kind of ceremony it would be, when you got *un*confirmed. Perhaps you would have to stand there in St Peter's in the nude, wearing nothing but a condom.'

As the jokes continued down the road of the silliness that comes easily with the downing of drink, the evening switched from serious business to just letting off steam. Even the teetotaller Debs seemed relaxed and, although still the quietest of the four, was clearly enjoying the company. There was plenty of zany laughter, something at which Frances was quite a natural, so she gave as good as she got with Jose and Nathan. But Frances was also enjoying private thoughts. One was her excitement that, finally, she had found a purpose behind her little collection of Virgin Mary images. There was a new found hope there. *I don't know what I believe in but I really think she can help me.* The other was acknowledgement of the fact that she was enjoying the company of three companions whom her other friends would regard as strange. *They seem to be taking me on their journey, to I don't know where.* This caused her a moment of apprehension.

'About this *adventuring*? It's not, like, a bit kinky or owt, is it? Do you sit and chant for hours in a field? Or hug trees? And what about witchcraft? Debs, are you in a coven and do you use daggers and robes and all that?'

Debs shook her head, thoughtfully.

'No, the group did consider working with an athamé, what you call a dagger, and black cloaks, but we decided that it were just like playing at being Christian priests. High ritual and all that. Covens – it's all so 1960s! People can do that kind o' thing if they want but not us. We decided that our female bodies were themselves sacred objects in our rite. They have power to create life, you know! But being a strictly women-only group in those days, women who had been hurt in connection with sex, we certainly didn't do nakedness or owt. It's true that sometimes we used certain objects to enhance rites, like a broomstick, mirror or cup. But they are ordinary household objects. We kept it low-key.'

Frances nodded in some relief, but then Nathan turned and looked round long and hard at her. She suppressed a gasp; he was coming across as pretty creepy all of a sudden. Perhaps she had put her finger on it – they were a bunch of weirdos, after all.

'We can't reassure you, Frances,' he said, with slow deliberation. 'You just have to trust. We're not in charge of what happens. Being an adventurer is like waiting for a wind to blow the ship and then seeing where it leads. We don't believe in certainties. There is a something else – or maybe a *somebody* else – who decides.'

Frances looked away and explored as deeply within herself as she could. Her life was hollow right now and held no other promising possibilities. There was something about handsome Nathan, witchy Debs and limping Jose that she couldn't resist. And that *somebody* else, well, she just had to find out who that was. There was no alternative. She would have to forget her nightmares. Acceptance came and, with it, relaxation. She smiled, first to herself privately, then across at the others. *Yeah, why not, I'll go along with the three adventurers; I've a feeling that it'll be good for me.*

# 5

# Somewhere over the Rainbow

Saturday – not good. A hangover raged for the best part of the daylight hours. 'Working through the heart' seemed a bit loony in the sober light of day. Then, later, an evening out with Cyn and Jo that had nothing of the jollity of the night before. Cyn was struggling with the relationship with her partner.

'He's just holding me back; he doesn't want to do owt, or let me do owt, either! You've no idea how much I had to argue to come out tonight.'

Jo was so pessimistic about the department in which Frances was about to replace her that the fighting talk in the pub took on an unrealistic feel, a piece of bravado in a losing situation.

'You best just look for new job, Frances, as quick as you can. I've not found owt yet, I admit. I think we're going to have to take big pay cut looking at what's available.'

Frances' friend and one-time colleague, usually so attractive, looked ill – pallid skin, eyes slow and pained. Cyn wasn't helpful in the situation, either; she was so obsessed with her own troubles that, at one point, Frances snapped at her for not listening when Jo was speaking.

'OK, Cyn, we *know* that Jonathan's a pain. But don't you think that Jo needs bit of air time tonight?'

Sunday – with one day to go, the time had come to put the magic into action. Debs had phoned her the day before with some practical ideas. She needed to start the rituals: at first, fairly basic, light candles, call nature spirits and ask them to help in her struggle with the Ordering Department bosses. Maybe she could get something from the office that one of them had handled to use it as a focus for spell-making. Frances oscillated between laughing at herself for making such a big deal out of a small problem and sinking further into anxious despair because of it. But neither of these moods helped in the creating of magic. Probably she wouldn't have done anything at all but for a surprise visit from Jose early in the afternoon.

Jose had come to offer support while passing, having spent the morning playing for a chess team in a club nearby. On the Friday evening, Frances had noticed how garrulous he was; so now it was no surprise that he talked at her nineteen to the dozen. He was not as guarded as Nathan about his personal history and Frances had no need to prompt.

'My parents – surprise, surprise, after all, they're Asians! – run a small newsagent's in Hunslet... I'm thirty, but I still live with them... we need the wages from my nine to five bus timetabling job and so I can't really afford to rent or buy elsewhere... my gammy legs from childhood polio cause my family to be over-protective and do you know what? I've never really had the courage to set up my own home... I haven't got a partner.... indeed,' he added in a matter-of fact way, 'I haven't really experienced anything other than brief flings.'

It took Frances a couple of minutes to realise that Jose was talking about relationships with men. He chatted on about his life quite openly, with plenty of humour at his own expense, for which Frances, also something of an adept in this area, could not help liking him. Then there was childhood in Goa; Roman Catholicism, which he both loved and hated; chess; classical music; books. *You're proper geeky, aren't you,* thought Frances, while smiling benignly.

As Jose maundered on, Frances studied him. Short, trendily spiky dark hair framed a small face with large black eyes, which might have made him attractive were it not for a long nose, protruding teeth and dimpled chin. His skin was drained of its brown colour in the depths of the English winter, his face slightly scarred by one-time acne. Nevertheless, his charm, expressed through a broad smile and those entrancing eyes, compensated to some extent. His voice was smooth, reassuring and not loud, despite the constant chatter. He wore a beige woollen polo neck jumper – slender, bony hands emerged from the sleeves, which gesticulated constantly as he spoke – with combat trousers and hiking boots, which looked strange on a man so obviously unfit for any kind of physical exertion. He wouldn't accept an alcoholic drink during the afternoon but preferred Earl Grey tea, sugared and without milk.

Eventually, Jose got round to the point of his visit: Frances' spiritual battle against the powers of darkness in Ordering. Frances, finally managing to complete a sentence, told him about the little ritual that she had agreed with Debs.

'So *that's* witchcraft,' smiled Jose. He was looking at an icon on the wall in the central place above the mantelpiece, 'the Virgin of Iviron', the dark Russian Madonna in a silvery cloak, the Child on her left knee. 'A quiet space, spiritual contemplation, some candles and a holy picture. Sounds like prayer to me. You're sure you're not a Catholic?'

Frances didn't know enough to contradict him; all she could do was to slowly shake her head.

'No... I don't know...'

Jose helped her out.

'Well, maybe it's *not* Catholic because I don't think Catholics call up the elements of earth, air, fire and water, do they?'

'Maybe not,' replied Frances. 'I don't really know what I'm doing, to tell truth. I haven't started. I don't know how to.'

Jose smiled sympathetically.

'What grabs you?' he asked, 'Amongst all these things: candles, pictures, calling on spirits? What moves you?'

Frances looked round, first at the Virgin of Iviron, then at Jose, then down at her hands and then she sighed.

'Well, I suppose it's... I'm not sure.'

'Go on!' urged Jose, although gently; he wasn't going to let it drop.

'It's like wanting a mother,' Frances responded; she was getting near to tears now. 'I think I've got those Madonna pictures up there because I need a mother sometimes. My own mother, you see, she's not very well, gets depression and everything. I don't blame her, she'll always be my mother, but I need a strong mother as well.'

'OK,' said Jose. 'Well, use all the little rituals as a way of speaking to your strong mother. Don't worry about the meaning of it all. She can be the Virgin Mary, the Goddess, the Good Witch of the North, the Lady of the Lake. It doesn't matter; I don't believe it does, anyway. It's what you *do* as a consequence. Does it work for good or for ill?'

'Right now,' said Frances, 'I'm just trying to cope wi' tomorrow.'

Jose sensed that the time to leave had come and limped out, first grasping her arm in solidarity and then giving a cheery wave at the door. As he went, he wrapped a heavy scarf around his neck before putting on his brown mock leather jacket. A slight and vulnerable figure, he disappeared lopsidedly into the February wind, the sky already dark in late afternoon. Frances felt a little pull of tenderness which counteracted the irritation she had experienced at his dominating the conversation and apparent air of superiority. Then she did her little ritual following Debs' instructions: lighting the candles, creating an imaginary circle, raising the energy of the earth (*How does it get here, in first floor flat? – Maybe through flap, wi' cat!*), calling up the spirits of the elements, asking for protection from the evils of the world, including those at work. Following Jose's suggestions, she also invoked the Goddess and spent a time of quiet concentrating on the image of the Virgin of Iviron, her own representation of the Goddess. Then she undid it all: releasing the spirits, earthing the energies, opening the circle, extinguishing the candles. Yet, rather than responding to the dramatic effect of it all, she felt nothing except the anxiety of what tomorrow would bring.

Monday – very apprehensive. Condemned woman should have eaten hearty breakfast but no, she can't even manage a half bowl of muesli. Feels sick on way to work. Company building looks like Dracula's Castle (*do come in, Ms Harker; I'll leave you now, it's getting light*). Nazi Robot Woman, the Administration Manager, introduces the new role but not much to do on first day. Read manuals, get a feel of it. Watch others. One or two of the girls say hi, but they don't linger on weekend tittle-tattle as they would do on a Monday in the Finance Department. No sign of the Führer. Out somewhere in Bradford, she hears. Stay of execution. Meets Sal at lunchtime: sympathetic looks, 'how's it going, love?', squeezing of hand. 'Nowt to worry about, so far!' Nervous laugh. Dracula jokes. Hitler jokes. Antichrist jokes. 'Count Ballard, 666 Demon Lane.' 'Dr Jekyll and Mr Ballard.' Laughter – the best medicine. *Ha ha – bleah.*

Evening – lots of texts, lots of messages. Jo, Cyn, Nathan, Debs, Jose, etc., etc. *Everyone who knows me would like to say hi.* Cass the cat even looked sympathetic in an off-hand way. *Will you be texting me too, Cass? Hope u r OK cos I need 2 h fed.* Visit to Mum and Dad. Cue lots o' fussing. *Don't tell 'em about work. Just listen. I love you really, but you're couple o' funny buggers.* 'Must go, can you give me a lift, Dad? Only 9.30, I know. Work tomorrow.'

Tuesday – enter the arch-demon Ballard himself. The 'briefing' at 10. *Managed breakfast this morning but feel right sick now!... Surprise – the Devil seems quite nice. Gentle, encouraging, can't understand it. Even a bit flirtatious. Haven't heard that it were that kind o' harassment. Not bad looking for fifty-something, tall, slim, light brown skin, grey hair swept back, balding in a not unattractive way. What am I thinking?! Smile back but BE CAREFUL!...* Started work in earnest today, arranging meetings, phoning suppliers, typing letters, usual stuff. No problem. Wednesday – no problem. Thursday – no problem.

'Hello, Debs, thanks for calling. You know, I think this witchcraft thing's working well. Yes, every night, without fail. I'll keep doing it.'

'Hi, Jo, OK so far. No, I'm not implying that you made it all up. Must admit that people aren't so chatty in Ordering. So not all good.'

Thinks: *but it might be good for me, thanks to my protecting spirits*!

Friday – OK up to 11, then called over by John Taylor, Ballard's right-hand man. In the open plan office, John's desk was just visible from Frances' through a gap in the screens around each little private space. Then... disaster. John seemed to speak, not using his thin, pale and serious-looking lips, but through his thick glasses, the eyes alarmingly large in the lenses.

'One or two concerns... must get into good habits... we don't do things like that here... letterheads... phone manner too familiar... too long for lunch... need to look smarter in case suppliers call into the office.'

Frances tried her familiar routine: a little flash of temper and abrupt, formal language.

'No-one trained me that way... You need to communicate in a more constructive way... People in business prefer friendliness; I have experience in these matters.'

This kind of thing had worked with previous bosses – she had seen them turn their eyes away nervously, clear their throat and look as if they were suppressing slight trembling, then say well, you might have a point, let's see how things go, we both need to make adjustments. No such soft underbelly with John Taylor. He looked straight ahead into her eyes and reiterated his position. He saw no need to show warmth, nor temper his criticisms, nor offer some encouragement. Neither did he raise his voice; the words and the quiet manner in which they were spoken were more menacing than any shouting. After twenty minutes of battling against a brick wall and being reminded about the possibility of disciplinary action, Frances was fighting the tears and asked to go to the toilet. She was summarily dismissed.

'Yes, fine, that's all anyway.'

After five minutes composing herself, she decided to seek out the apparently gentler Ballard. *Maybe the real Master of Darkness is Taylor.*

'Hello, Frances. I am afraid I can't speak to you now. Mr Taylor will deal with it... Ah, you *have* spoken to him... Well, I am sure that he knows what is best. He is a man of considerable experience. Please follow his instructions to the letter and then everything will go well... Goodbye, Frances (wave of dismissal), I'm very busy.'

Frances spent the rest of the day in internal conflict. She avoided Sal at lunchtime, as she wanted to sort it out in her own mind first. Option one: *Taylor has got a point, I've possibly become a bit sloppy in Finance – it's easier to go along with him, it wouldn't take too much adjustment.* Option two: *he's wrong but I can compromise – I'll do some things his way, some things my way. He'll see that give and take's best way forward.* Option three: *things really are grim – this is just beginning o' harassment that Jo's described: things were never right, work had to be done and re-done under constant stress; it were an impossible place to work.* Of these, option three was the most difficult to take – how dare they treat her like this? There was also the terrible realisation that there would not be another job this well paid out there, if any at all. But option three was also the most plausible, as it was what she had expected on Monday; the four days of relative quiet had lulled her into a false sense of security, making it all seem worse when the bad moment finally arrived.

In all the turmoil, the little rituals in front of the Madonna suddenly seemed rather futile. She knew that her emotional make-up would not let her rest either day or night under this kind of pressure. She would not shrug it off, concentrate on evenings and weekends, put it out of her mind, get a sense of proportion, get her priorities right, treasure the good things – none of the clichés about the importance of putting work troubles in perspective would wash with someone like her. What hope did the lighting of candles have in the face of the terrible power of inner anxiety? It was that self-mutilating interior churning that was the real enemy when she could not take the injustices that people were inflicting on her. Their harsh words were as nothing compared to her own anger at being impotent. How could the circle protect her from the enemy within?

And so, the day over, Frances decided not to keep her weekly rendezvous with Nathan, Debs and Jose. She would spend the weekend alone, just her and Cass, TV, music and wine, maybe some vodka too. At least having the lousy job meant that she could afford it. Calls, texts, ringing of the doorbell – all were ignored. *Coronation Street* was turned off when there was trouble at the fictitious underwear factory – too close to home. Try again later – oh no, a repeat of *A Touch of Frost* included something about a woman being harassed. In the first commercial break, she was about to switch that off too, when some music in an advert suddenly caught her ear. 'Somewhere over the rainbow...' Somewhere over her rainbow, something clicked. Images came into her head: Nathan's come-to-bed eyes and easy laugh; Debs' fierce but seemingly loyal intensity; Jose's over-talkative vulnerability. Whatever it was that was over the rainbow, she needed to find out. So she rushed down and out and into Hyde Park Road, arriving at the Corner bus stop short of breath. Yet not before having to go back after fifty yards and put cat food in Cass' bowl. And check that the gas was turned off. And make sure that she had shut the front door properly.

# 6

# New Birth

At seven-thirty, Frances didn't want to see Nathan, Debs and Jose ever again, nor anyone else for that matter. At nine-thirty, she burst into the pub, full of passion to see them and talk their strange talk. Something moved her to fight back against new enemies by throwing herself fully into the world of new friends, abandoning the reservations that she had felt towards them until now. Her eyes searched for them in the cosy ambience of the softly lit *Airedale*. They had regained the table of the previous week.

'How's it going at work, Frances?'

'Let's talk about summat else! Spiritual adventuring, man in moon, bird man of Alcatraz, anything a' all but not work!'

Knowing looks. OK, we'll go along with you. Don't mention the war. She looked battle-scarred. Wild eyes with hints of redness, make-up not quite right, hair not so carefully in place as usual, old jumper, shoes not good colour match with pink jeans.

'We're just really pleased to see you, Frances.'

They hadn't given up on her.

Jose had been sharing his view of the universe. So he resumed where he had left off.

'All life on earth is destined to die,' he said, cheerfully.

Frances looked at him with a somewhat manic stare and a fixed smile. As he paused, glancing at her with a little apprehension, she nodded her head and widened the smile sarcastically. *Go on. Great so far. Very comforting.* Jose looked away and continued.

'And yes, of course, death is something terrible and to be feared. But imagine what it would be like to be an embryo in your mother's womb that could reflect on its situation; you would fear *birth*. That will be the moment when everything supporting you breaks down; you will be ejected from the womb, your home, your umbilical cord – through which you are fed – cut forever and the placenta, in which you float blissfully, separated from you. For you, birth is death. You do not know what lies beyond or how you could survive without these essential things... (pauses for sip of ale and – possibly – for effect)... Death is like that too, we dread the day when all the things that support us, our bodies, hearts, brains, breathing cease to function; we could not imagine how we could continue. But what do we know? After the trauma of our dying, perhaps we will look out at a new world like the just-born infant.'

'So are you saying we are all living in a womb?' asked Nathan.

'In a symbolic sense,' replied Jose. 'A womb-world in which life is moving towards birth. We are given the clue in the way that life both begins and ends in pain and suffering. Birth is a trial and so is death. Death is the second birth; this is what all the great religions teach. However... (moves close and speaks quieter, to signal a great secret to be shared.)... what many religions lack, although many of the ancients knew of it, is the image of the Great Mother. She is the most appropriate symbol for the Divine Being that sustains us. We are all in her womb, you see. We've concentrated too much on the heavenly Father and forgotten the Great Mother.'

'Life after death,' added Frances.

She was still looking a bit vacant, but she was happy to go along with this diversion from the travails of Ordering.

'Well, in a way,' Jose responded, trying to encourage her to join in. 'But not necessarily *after* in a time sense. Life *beyond* death. It's in a new dimension, you see. It doesn't just go *on*, but it goes somewhere else, which used to be symbolised as *up*. *Up* is a good metaphor, as it's not before or after, it's a place from where you can see over the whole of your life and everybody else's.'

'Somewhere over the rainbow!' exclaimed Frances.

'Er... yes,' replied Jose.

She was beginning to worry him now. Debs tried to pick up the conversation again.

'I'm not sure about living in womb, Jose. Seems a bit claustrophobic to me. Shouldn't life be free and open, not closed in?'

*She does remind me o' Scary Spice,* thought Frances, *crazy frizzy black hair, from Leeds, although minus Spice Girl smile and really scary at times.* If Debs had a point to make, she always made it with conviction. Jose pondered for a second (which always involved a slightly nervous glug of whatever he was drinking) and then answered, hesitantly at first.

'Maybe you're right, but it's only a metaphor. On the other hand, life does have its limits, you must admit. We *are* closed in. Our bodies constrain us... (looks down at gammy leg)... and also our circumstances.'

Frances came to life. There had been another sudden click within her.

'If death is birth and we are like babies again in a new dimension,' she said, brightly, 'Then Madonna and Child could be meant to remind us of our new birth which will come at the end of our lives. Maybe this is why these images are so important, even to people like me who aren't really Christians.'

'That is brilliant!' exclaimed Jose. 'If we think of the holy image of Madonna and Child as referring only to two holy people, then we are left out, unworthy creatures. If, on the other hand, it signifies *all* of us, reborn on the lap of the Great Mother, then it becomes *our* story, the future for each and every one of us. I think that's what true Christianity is all about, it's the story of everybody, because that's how God actually wants it. It's the purpose of creation. We are all destined to be baby Jesus on the lap of Mary, if only we knew it.' He clapped his hands in triumph. 'Good one, Frances!'

Nathan looked to heaven in mock disgust, but his manner was friendly, showing that, while left out of the discussion so far, he was pleased to see everyone so animated. He winked at Frances. How easy it was to get her heart fluttering again! *The flirt!*

'I'll get some more drinks in.'

While he was away, the others remained quiet, lost in thought for a while. For Frances, the idea that the Madonna and Child pictures, hanging in benign splendour on her walls, could symbolise a future freedom away from the drudgery and anxiety of her life sparked a new sense of hope in her. She didn't like talking about death – the very thought terrified her – unless there was a very strong emphasis on the after-life. *Madonna and Child, my new birth, my new freedom. Somewhere over the rainbow.* She had made a connection – between Jose's religious talk and the mysteries of her own emotional attachments to the figure of the Virgin Mary. Maybe that was what being thirty would be like; she would finally get to make connections. From zero to eighteen, she hadn't known there were any connections to be made, then from eighteen, she knew there were such things as connections, because everyone kept telling her, but she didn't know how to make them. 'Critical analysis is about making links... and asking searching questions,' her college tutor had said. She didn't have a clue what he was on about. Fortunately, he gave sufficient clues as to how to scrape a pass in an Art History degree without making any links... or asking any searching questions. But now, *eureka,* she was doing it at last!

Nathan came back with the round; now it was his turn to contribute something. He felt he needed to bring in up-to-date science from time to time, to keep them earthed.

'Scientists are telling us that we will someday banish death forever,' he said, provocatively. 'With medical technology, we may be able to stop or even reverse the process by which we age. Ageing is only wear and tear, after all. Death is just the final breakdown, but it could be avoidable, if we fully understand the human body.'

Jose looked startled, even angry, at such a suggestion.

'How will the human psyche cope with that? All our ancestors for centuries before us faced and accepted death, handing down the belief that it is a gateway to a new existence. It is deep in our collective unconscious as the door into a higher world. Without it, we will be closed in forever. The womb will be closed. All we will have to look forward to is more and more frustration by the limits of our existence. If we ever manage to prevent death, it will be a disaster for the human race. We'll die of boredom! Hmm, let's see, what shall I do for the next ten million years?'

Debs agreed: 'Yes, death is that great mystery by which we return to the earth, to make way for new generations. It is the one thing that we all share, which makes us equal. We shouldn't want to live forever, it's egoistic.'

Nathan frowned. To Frances, he was so attractive, he made her think that, in each gesture, he took the opportunity to demonstrate his good looks to everyone who might be looking on (and often Frances did see other women – sometimes men – glancing over at him in admiration). Even a frown was a modelling pose. But he wanted to make a point too.

'How do we know?' he complained. 'How can we say that just because death has been seen as a gateway or new birth for generations past, that it will be that way for the human race in the future? We can't anticipate what life will be like in tomorrow's world, with or without death.'

'Maybe,' replied Jose. 'But from where we are standing now, the end of death would be a psychological disaster and scientists need to understand that. It's not just a technological thing.'

The conversation was interrupted by a sudden: 'Hello, Frances.' The four of them turned to see where the helloing was coming from. Pushing through the crowd, by now dense as the late evening wore on, was a jolly-looking young man smiling broadly. His boyish demeanour, small features, comparatively large ears and spiky hair made him seem like a playful leprechaun. His clothes matched his sanguine expression: a brightly coloured short-sleeved shirt, yellow wrist-band from some charity or other and white trousers. Frances clearly did not know the newcomer well, as it took her a second or two to remember his name.

'Oh, hi... Gary, in't it? Friend o' Jo's?'

'That's it,' replied Gary. 'We met at her party a few month back. You were with, erm... what's his name?'

'Can't remember,' said Frances firmly but cheerfully.

What's-his-name had been one of those unmentionables, a couple o' dates and he was looking elsewhere. *Good thing too,* remembered Frances, *right boring he were, took me to Leeds Royal Armouries. Just my scene – not!*

Clearly Gary wanted to join them. Frances introduced everyone.

'Now then!' exclaimed Gary, grinning amiably, obviously someone who enjoyed meeting new people.

Nathan and Jose looked comfortable; it was a no lose situation. If he was a 'spiritual adventurer' like them, he was worth talking to; if not, he might provide them with a few stupid comments to feed their mirthful sarcasm after he had gone. He was also pleasant-enough-looking for Jose to enjoy his company, although first impressions suggested that he wasn't at all gay. Debs looked the least happy and gave Gary her usual 'keep away' treatment: a short, unsmiling stare, followed by no eye contact at all. She distrusted men and was happy to confine herself to those she knew offered no threat, the not very macho

Nathan and the slightly camp Jose. Frances did not appear thrilled at the prospect of an addition to the number, either. She was loath to have anyone disrupt her new-found circle of comrades, among whom she felt she was finding a hitherto unknown part of her personality, a 'spiritual adventurer' aspect. Anyway, how could she fancy any bloke after finding Nathan?

The women's reticence meant that the men were soon deep in all kinds of nonsense talk of their own, although Gary, while happy to engage with Nathan and Jose, clearly had an eye for Frances. *Who's he staring at? I hardly know him! Where does he fit in wi' Jo's crowd? Actually, he's not bad-looking, although it's not a good time for me now. And what about Nathan? If I start seeing Gary, I'll lose my chance, won't I? On other hand, maybe Nathan'll get jealous! Oh, I don't know!* The trouble was that the arrival of Gary had taken the wind out of Frances' sails. She had thrown herself into the evening to escape her worries and now they returned, despite the glasses of wine and easy atmosphere. She began to look sombre and contributed less and less to the conversation.

Debs had seen this Frances before, on the first evening they had met. She was not good at socialising, but the one thing she could offer was advice and solace to a woman feeling down. She related to women under pressure and had done so ever since the refuge had saved her from her pitiable life that would not have lasted very long given the course on which it was headed. She turned to Frances; once again the dour, defensive woman employed that powerful empathy Frances had encountered before.

'How's it going Frances? Tell me, I want to help.'

While the men were distracted, having moved on to the ethics of sport, Frances, in a low voice, described the morning meeting with John Taylor.

'But I feel a bit better tonight, Debs. I've suddenly realised what my icons o' Madonna mean to me. They mean freedom, new birth into future new world where I will escape one day from bad jobs, bad boyfriends, my over-anxiety about things, like my family and friends and all that.'

Debs shook her head.

'No, Frances, not escape,' she replied. 'Remember what I said about working through the heart? You can't look to escape, because that would mean you'd have lost and taken flight. Working through the heart is about facing it all and still coming out on top. You must keep working on that; it's the only way. New birth comes through pain, remember?'

Frances part understood but had no words to offer by way of reply. She was touched by the way in which this one-time drug addict cared for her after such a short acquaintance. All she could do was to lay her hand gently on Debs' shoulder by way of thanks; she nodded, as if to agree to Debs' encouragement to keep trying with the witchcraft, with the 'working through the heart'.

At this point, Gary noticed the moment of quiet in the women's interchange and saw an opportunity to turn up the heat in his pursuit of Frances. Having established quite skilfully while talking to the men that she wasn't 'with' either of them, he now turned his attention to the sandy-haired woman opposite. The fact that she didn't look at her best might have attracted him more, she mused afterwards, as she would have looked vulnerable and in need of male support.

'Now, Frances, did you hear that Kaiser Chiefs are playing at Elland Road next weekend? Do you like Kaiser Chiefs? Best thing to come out o' Leeds in quite a few year, if you ask me. Maybe you'd like to come; I know someone who can get me a couple o' tickets.'

Gary was fearless; it was not a problem for him to ask a woman out in front of her friends, people he hardly knew. Frances looked at Nathan, to see if he could offer her any hope that he was considering making a move on her himself, but all he did was to give a little smile, which seemed to be encouraging her to go with Gary.

'All right then, Gary. Wouldn't mind. When is it?'

'Sat'day.'

*Ah well, I can have my cake and eat it. Friday spiritual adventuring and Sat'day doing what girls and boys do.*

# 7

# Whose Sins?

That night, Frances had a nightmare. She was in an unfamiliar place somewhere in the countryside. There had been a murder and two detectives, men that she did not know, were on the case. It was night. They led Frances by torchlight into a deserted farmhouse; after clambering through broken doors and across fallen bricks and rubble, they came to a damp and eerie room with a large empty fireplace in one wall. 'Here she is,' exclaimed one of the men, pointing into a corner. There was a corpse lying there, recognisably that of a woman but decay had set in. One of the detectives explained to Frances that the house was built on ground that had special properties. If there were to be a thunderstorm overhead, the corpse would be revived momentarily, just long enough for her to reveal one word only, the name of her killer. The sound of pouring rain could be heard now. Suddenly, a flash of lightening brightened the open glassless window just above the body. Frances felt fearful of what was to come. Then the corpse's came to life and she turned her head towards Frances with staring eyes; it was all she could move, the rest of her body lying slumped in the corner as before. Her look was one of horror as if she were realising her situation, that she had only a moment to live. Then struggling for speech, she gave a deep croak and something came out: 'Sins'. Then she fell back into death, the body stiff and lifeless once more. Frances woke up with a start. It was 3.45 a.m. For some time, she lay there, shaken, trying to reason with herself that it was only the events of the day before that had caused her to be anxious and suffer such bad dreams. When she finally had the energy to venture out of bed to get a fruit juice, she was relieved to see that Cass was in for the night, so she took her back to bed for company. Five o'clock came and went before she fell asleep again. *Sins? Whose sins were those? Who or what had killed the woman?* Just a dream maybe, but Frances instinctively felt it was important. Somewhere she had one of those 'Dreams Explained' books. She got out of bed once more – the cat fleeing into the shadows at this second interruption of its comfort – and looked up 'sins' but the word was not in the index. *Dead bodies? No. Corpse? Yes!* 'Corpse: A situation that has become difficult and which causes the dreamer to feel trapped'. *Good one. That explains that then. But what were the 'sins'? Who's done what? The sins of my bosses at work?* She was still thinking about it as she got up the following morning but an easy answer eluded her.

Saturday was a do-nothing day as it so often was when there wasn't enough money left in the kitty for some serious shopping. Frances lost the high spirits of the previous evening's sortie and re-experienced the gloomy mood. She could not really remember for sure what had caused her to feel some hope in the pub; she preferred to wallow in her self-pity, so she refused to try to recall whatever it was that had uplifted her. In the late afternoon, a long phone conversation with brother Colin, now living in Bristol and working as a chef, mostly about their parents. Then an evening drink with a friend from schooldays who came over from Garforth every now and then, leaving her husband to babysit. They talked about Gary.

'I'm not rushing into owt. Anyway, there's this other guy I really like and I'm going to take it steady to see what happens.'

'Oo, what're you like, Frances? Reminds me o' myself before I were wed!'

During sleep, another compelling dream but with a lighter atmosphere than the one of the night before. Frances was with an unknown woman walking along the towpath of a canal. The woman was saying, 'This is my parents' place.' Then all of a sudden they had to cross a major dual carriageway, taking care of the traffic. Frances saw Jason, her flame of a few years back, about to get into a limousine stopped on the hard shoulder. Then he called after her and asked if he could join them walking. Apparently, he had been travelling away to become a film star, but the chauffeur had said that he was too slow and couldn't wait for him. The three of them walked down to what looked like a large lake or inlet and, at the side of the water, Frances was asked some difficult questions about art history by her two companions. Occasionally, she made mistakes but, when she did, the others helped her; finally it was agreed that she had passed the test. At this moment, the woman began dancing. It was difficult to decide what she looked like, although it was clear that she was wearing a white dress. Frances had the impression that flames were flowing out of her feet as she twisted and turned on the lakeside. Then the woman seemed to disappear and it was Frances who was dancing. The movement was exhilarating; it impressed Jason, who was clearly in awe of her. When she stopped, he kissed her. Then the two of them returned to the canal, which Frances now had to swim across. As she found herself doing so, she looked back to see Jason standing on the bank; he could not follow for some reason but it did not seem to concern her. As she swam, she found herself clutching a letter in an envelope with a large stamp on it. Reaching the other side, she walked towards what she knew was the woman's parents' place. She was in an exultant mood and, on a large banner overhead, she saw the words CELEBRATE OFTEN. This was the end of the dream, Frances woke up in a much better state than the previous night. It was already morning.

The dream galvanised Frances into trying to remember what had made her happier in the pub on the Friday night. Maybe the woman in white in the dream was a kind of Madonna figure. She decided that this was a symbol of hope as the Madonna's lap held the Christ Child, the symbol of her new life. Not a new life through escape, according to Debs, but by facing the situation as it was and overcoming it. And the 'working through the heart', she would give that another go. She knew that it wouldn't be easy and that it was partly an act of desperation rather than confidence. The knot in her stomach just would not go away; she would have to work on her rituals with it gnawing at her rather than waiting for it to recede.

Calls: 1) Gary again on the mobile, didn't answer this time. He then sent a text, but Frances didn't respond.

2) Mum on the landline, some worry about changing gas supplier.

'Don't bother with it, Mum. It may save money in short term but at end of the day they'll get their pennyworth. And it's so much *hassle*.'

3) Cyn phoned from somewhere in town. She sounded triumphant.

'I've finished wi' Jonathan. Too heavy going. He tried to plead wi' me but I just walked off. Can't think why I didn't do it some while ago. I feel sense o' relief, to tell truth.'

4) Next, Nathan (*yes!*).

'Frances, it's about time we did some spiritual adventuring. There's a gathering to celebrate the equinox, which coincides with the Easter weekend. That's three weeks' time. It's at Avebury, the stone circle in Wiltshire. There'll be a load of characters there, Druids, Pagans, Heathens, Shamans, lots of music, wonderful indigenous instruments they play, loads of drumming and maybe a few pints too... Indigenous? Oh, the traditions of native peoples, from America and Australia mainly. And we can do some meditating and walking around the area. Lots of sacred sites. We'll go down in Jose's car. You can help pedal it. Ha ha!... Steady! No need to be rude!... All right, we'll put you down for the weekend, then... B&B? No, dear Frances, that's not very Pagan. Camping. Four in a tent, or maybe five, if that Gary wants to come... OK, OK, he's not a spiritual type. How do you know?... Right, you just know. It's what girls do, just know.'

5) Gary – I'm still not answering.
6) Cold sales.
'Miss Dryburgh? No, she's not in. I think she's emigrated.'

Afternoon – some quiet moments alone with the candles and Madonnas. The focus this time was a print of Raphael's *Sistine Madonna*, a little softer than the Virgin of Iviron, more appropriate for the sensitivity she was feeling. *Come on, concentrate. Working through the heart, the heart, the heart. New birth and hope. New birth. Hope.* The dancing dream woman came back into her mind's eye, she was celebrating Frances' getting the answers right. *Must get the answers right. Fight this feeling of sick anxiety and despair.* Suddenly, in her imagination, Frances saw the woman dancing in the Ordering department, right in front of John Taylor. He looked bewildered and angry but was unable to stop it happening. The woman had taken control of the office; she was its mistress. The heart had to be obeyed. Then the imaginary world darkened and there was the corpse. 'Sins'. Who would save the dead woman from the sins of which she spoke? Maybe the woman in white. *Hold on to hope. Concentrate. Believe.*

The silence became a struggle, so call no. 7) from Jose came as a relief.

'Hi, Frances. Would you like to go to a concert on Wednesday?'

Another concert. Could it beat the Kaiser Chiefs? Where? Who?

'The Town Hall. Poulenc!'

Jose almost shouted this word.

'Plonk who?'

'Francis Poulenc – the French composer. My favourite. Wonderful music, just wonderful! A selection of his music, instrumental and choral.'

*Wonderful indigenous instruments. Wonderful Kaiser Chiefs. The wonderful music of Mr Plonker. Exciting times!*

'Go on then, Jose, put me down for it. I'll need some cheering up by Wednesday.'

'Brilliant. I'll collect you and we can walk down. Don't worry about a thing, the concert's on me. And we'll have a drink afterwards in that bar underneath the art gallery.'

*The art gallery?* That caused a pang of guilt; Frances had intended to keep up with the art thing but hadn't been there for some years now.

Call 8) Gary. Better answer finally.

'No, Gary, can't go out during week. Got a new job, you see. Let's leave it while Sat'day… Looking forward to it. Never seen 'em live before. OK, Gary, stop phoning me. I'll see you. Don't worry.'

Reluctantly, Frances felt herself admiring Gary's cocky cheerfulness, which continued unabated despite her reserve. No hint of irritation, of impatience.

'I'll not worry, lass. The waiting'll make it even better seeing you Sat'day.'

He was a warm soul and she liked that. She was warm too but was so easily put off by the wrong word or a funny mood. Gary seemed more robust.

Finally, call 9) Debs. Had Frances heard from Nathan about the trip? 'Yep.' Was she coming? 'Yeah, sure, sounds good.'

'It'll be fantastic, Frances. So many interesting people including some members o' women's group that I were in when I lived in Nottingham. We can do some Goddess rituals.'

'OK, sounds great.'

'Yeah, it'll give me a chance to teach you about Drawing Down Moon ritual.'

'I can do drawing, Debs, did art you know.'

'Not that kind of drawing!'

'I know, just teasing you!'

'Don't tease me, Frances, I'm not right good wi' being laughed at.'

'It's just banter, Debs! I don't laugh at people I like, just with 'em. And if I like 'em a lot, I laugh with 'em a lot.'

Debs changed the subject without answering. Frances sighed inwardly; she was beginning to get used to the fact that Debs simply could not operate in the light world of gentle ragging that Frances delighted and excelled in. Some people were heavy that way. But Frances had an instinct that Debs had other qualities that were worth staying friends for. So they talked for a while about an article that Debs had read over the weekend.

'There's a strong movement all over world to force drastic action about the environment. People have finally realised that it's no good waiting while it's too late. Present targets are insufficient. There's going to be a big international initiative this year and greater pressure on major carbon-emitting nations to take immediate action.'

'Oh, wow,' replied Frances.

However, she felt a little hypocritical as she made appreciative noises. She had not been the most politically aware person in her life so far.

Evening. The sick feeling in her stomach grew stronger. Sunday was usually a stay-in night; it hadn't been before she was twenty-five, but the habit seemed to kick in after then. Too many bad Monday mornings and empty purses for the middle of the week. She found herself again in reflective mode and went back in her thoughts to the evening that she met Nathan. Not long ago, just three weeks, but it seemed like a long time, things had happened since then: new friends, new job, new hopes and, most definitely, new fears. And it was that fear that dominated the latter part of Sunday. *More rituals? No, could overdo it. TV? No, can't settle. Reading and background music? Yes, good idea... Let's have another look at that dream book. Women in White? Oh, wow, it's there.* 'The dreamer may be hoping for a wedding or, if they are already married, may need to inject new life into their married relationship.' *Bit clichéd, that: women in white equal weddings. Dancing?* 'The dreamer needs to express their creativity more – the unconscious is urging them to tap into inner energies.' *Maybe.* 'Canals: see under Rivers, Waterways.' 'Rivers, Waterways: This suggests a new departure, but the dreamer may feel inhibited from making a fresh start. If in the dream, the river forms a barrier, the dreamer will need persuading to make changes and should seek advice in the matter. If the dreamer crosses the river, fording or swimming, or sails up or down it, then the dreamer should take the step without fearing it.' *Yes, OK, could have worked that out for myself.* 'Letters: The dreamer is waiting or hoping for news. A message in the near future may have profound consequences.' *What if the letter has a stamp? No mention of stamps!*

'What about stamps?!' shouted Frances to no one as she sat alone in her flat, competing with the Scissor Sisters on the CD player. Cass looked up and yawned. She added, looking straight at the cat, 'This book doesn't include everything that it should!'

As soon as the words escaped from Frances, she suddenly felt depressed. As a cocky eighteen or twenty year old, she would never have imagined that now, at twenty-nine, she would have been sitting alone with a cat, talking to herself like a mad old woman. No, by now she should have a very fine hubby and two kids, or maybe just one kid and a bun in the oven, not working (because hubby earns big bucks), quite a sorted mature lady. But at times like these, she just felt like a lonely little girl. As this thought came to her, she imagined herself an overgrown Alice in Wonderland stuck in a doll-size house, with everything getting curiouser. The Knave of Hearts deserved to have his head cut off; he just kept running past without stopping for long enough.

'Off with his head!' she shouted, but still Cass was not concerned enough to make any response.

She then gulped, half laughing and half crying, tears beginning to trickle down at the same time as a smile came unexpectedly across her face. Now she really was Alice; the flat would be drowned in her tears and Cass would catch the infectious smile and become the Cheshire Cat. Then she thought of the morning, Messrs Ballard and Taylor and the Nazi Robot Woman.

'You're nothing but a pack o' cards!' she yelled again, imagining herself towering above them in the Ordering Department.

This time she dissolved into hysterical giggles. This helped a lot. Frances had a good sense of humour, even when she was on her own. Or maybe it was just the wine. Finally, before falling asleep in the armchair, she thought of herself as an eccentric ageing witch, living alone with her cat but giving wise advice to all and sundry, helping them overcome adversity. Then she woke at 2.30 a.m. with the lights still on, in a tangle of brown-coloured throw that wasn't really big enough for the armchair and creased up very easily; Cass was lying on her stomach, tapping into her body warmth. Then she went to bed, slept soundly, her dreams quite mundane this time. Not a white rabbit in sight.

# 8

# Plonker Music

'Job's really terrible,' Frances moaned to Jose, as they walked down together to the Leeds Town Hall, the venue for the concert. 'One week and three days and I feel like I've been harassed for months. Nowt's good enough for 'em, you have to do it all twice, nobody laughs and you can't be one minute late. I *am* trying the rituals, every night but... I don't know – I feel like I'm up against huge brick wall.'

Jose did his best to be sympathetic, but he wanted to talk about the concert. He was clearly excited; he loved Poulenc's music and he complained about how it was not often played live or on the radio.

'You won't hear Poulenc on Radio 3,' he complained. 'To get on there, his music would have to be several hundred years old, for antiquarian interest, or contemporary, avant-garde stuff.' He sighed. 'And you won't hear him on Classic FM, either. He's not mainstream enough for them.'

Frances had to try hard to suppress the feelings of exasperation. *What about my trouble at work!!! Mr Plonker, so what?* But she was keen not to turn into another Jo, obsessed and tedious in her angst and so keen to share it. So she just smiled and feigned interest.

'When did he live?'

Jose was delighted to be asked.

'He was born in 1899, a Frenchman,' he replied. 'Gay of course, a real rebellious and colourful character who enjoyed Paris in the swinging twenties! His music took a more serious and religious turn when a friend was tragically killed in the mid-1930s. He managed to combine old and new, traditional and more modern styles of music. A bit like my spiritual interests!' Frances failed to see what he meant by that, so he went on with the facts. 'Poulenc lived until 1963. In the same year, Poulenc died and the Beatles became famous. But one day he'll be better known than them, as eventually humanity *has* to acknowledge him as the greatest of the composers.'

And so: arrival at the Town Hall. Frances was not comfortable. Everybody looked elderly, or geeky, or both. The chairs were packed too closely together, despite the fact that there was a large space between the audience and musicians. Frances felt hot; she had dressed too warmly for the walk down. The first half of the programme covered instrumental music, several pieces featuring piano and woodwind instruments. It was not without a certain charm; a little wistful, it reminded Frances of the background music to one of those poignant TV dramas, with people from yesteryear wandering through cornfields in the grip of lost and hopeless loves. But she was not in the mood and, with her usual quick judgement, decided: *boring!* It went on and on, one piece to the next and there seemed to be no memorable melodies in the music. She entertained the idea that no one else really liked it either; they were all sitting there pretending to be enraptured as part of a plot to irritate her. Jose most of all. Who was he anyway? Not much like her normal friends. What would they say if they saw her now? *Hey up, it's Frances at a gig! Really getting it on down, aren't you, love? She's raving so much she must be on 'e'! Or maybe that's 'e flat' – a little musical joke there, Frances! Ha, ha. She's wi' real hunk too. Finally made it among jet set, haven't you, babe?*

As the interval approached, Frances decided to leave. She would go to the toilet whilst Jose was buying drinks and come back and say, I'm not very well, Jose, love. Must be anxiety about work. You enjoy rest o' concert, I'll get on home. So, when the time came, she spent several minutes in the loo to make it seem authentic. On the way out, she took a deep breath ready to make her excuses, but then suddenly she caught sight of Jose holding the drinks in the corridor because the bar was too full. He was not aware that anyone was watching him. His eyes were cast down towards his shoes; his body language suggested discomfort at standing amongst the towering, chatting crowd. There was an air of vulnerability about him as he stood there, no longer the ebullient, talkative character who dominated pub conversations. His loneliness came through to Frances in that moment as she glimpsed him, a little boy lost pretending to be a man of thirty. A boy who wanted men, yet whose uneven looks and idiosyncratic interests made him rather less than attractive to the gay community of Leeds. A man whose passions were, in part, a cover for someone frightened of the world and fully aware how it could damage him so easily. All this Frances saw and her intuition surprised her. She then realised that she could not leave him prematurely that night; she would have to stay until the end of the concert. She slipped through the throng of people to stand beside him, took her glass of wine and gave him a broad smile which lied and said, telepathically, I'm really enjoying myself. Thanks for bringing me. Brilliant, that Poulenc. Jose brightened immediately and smiled back. She put her hand onto the inside of his left elbow, safe in the knowledge that his sexual preference ensured he would not misinterpret her signal. In making that gesture, she thought to herself that she understood for the first time what true friendship was really about and what it demanded of her.

Part 2: choral music. Frances tried to listen, to get into it. Some classical stuff she did like, after all. OK, she was mostly into pop and party music, like everyone else she normally hung around with. However, she could feel a certain warmth hearing the *Hallelujah Chorus* or the last movement of Beethoven's *Choral Symphony*. So surely Poulenc was not beyond her. It did sound a bit offbeat, an 'acquired taste' she imagined herself saying to Sal the next day at lunch. But she made an effort to like it. And then, without warning, the choral harmonies took her somewhere else, without her even getting to like them in the normal sense. The room started to go misty. She felt as if she was being transported to another place, another dimension, a private island of her own somewhere in the sea and sky. The audience, choir and orchestra had disappeared; all that remained of them was the music. She was not asleep. It was as if she was back in the dream and saw the dancing woman, whom the choir accompanied as she slowly but gracefully gyrated around. The woman's face had not been clear in the dream, and even now Frances could only vaguely see it. There was definitely strength there, a calm resilience, ageless, the kind of face that looked back at you and gently questioned what you wanted from her. Yet the features would not remain stable. The face was dark brown, almost black, but then it turned more of an olive brown and then became pale. It wasn't clear whether the woman was thin or stout; she was first one thing, then the other. Her dress was white at first, but then it was green, becoming a blue gown with a red dress beneath. Then it turned a golden colour and, finally, it was multicoloured. Frances, entranced at this unfolding of her inmost imagination expressed in such a lovely apparition, began to feel quite ecstatic, a thrill passing up through her spine until her whole head was alive with a strange but wonderful energy. She lost track of time; she was not on planet Earth.

The piece ended; Frances came back to the room with a bump. She looked around to see if Jose or any other member of the audience had seen her strange 'turn', but they were applauding the musicians briefly before the next piece began. She tried to recreate her visionary experience as the music continued; it was not possible, although she could easily recall what the ecstasy had been like and savoured the memory. Frances looked down at the programme. What was the music that had had such an effect? *Salve Regina.*

'What does that mean?' she whispered to Jose.

'"Hail Queen",' he replied. 'It was a medieval anthem to the Virgin Mary which Poulenc set to music.'

She wondered about that. Was the dream woman the Virgin Mary? She did not look like any Madonna she had ever seen and not like any of the icons that Frances had collected, although some of the faces had the dark brownness of the first phase of the vision. She might have been the Virgin and, then again, it felt as if she might not. She was strange and alien, yet there was also something about her that made Frances feel that she had encountered her before somewhere. Whoever she was, she gave Frances very positive feelings of optimism and self-worth.

The rest of the music was not too bad; much of it had the poignant, haunting atmosphere of the *Salve Regina.* Towards the end the theme moved from religious hymns to a collection of French songs and Frances began to get a little restless. Yet she was still captivated by her earlier experience and wanted to relive it at some time in the future. When the concert ended, she noticed some CDs on sale at the back of the hall. Jose was beaming all over his face when Frances went up to buy one. The only CD with the *Salve Regina* on was part of a five CD set. Frances grimaced as she forked out £16.99.

'Not bad for five CDs,' remarked Jose.

*I never thought I would pay a hard earned £16.99 for Plonker music,* she thought, beneath her smile of agreement.

'You'll have to lend me money for my round now,' she said.

Jose laughed.

'I'll gladly buy your round without any thought of you paying me back; it's worth it to see you initiated into the fabulous world of Poulenc.'

She then had to endure an hour and a half of listening to him talk, mostly about his love of Poulenc, in exchange for three glasses of red wine and a packet of cashew nuts. Nevertheless, her good mood remained. *Maybe I were rewarded wi' that vision and nice feeling because I were kind to Jose by staying,* she thought. *Probably nowt to do wi' Plonker a' all.*

'Plonker', and Frances' 'conversion' to the brilliance of his composition, was inevitably the hot topic of the pub conversation on the Friday. Frances was secretly glad not to be questioned too closely about the week in Ordering as she did not want to betray her despair about it with the whole group gathered. She was not in the mood to hear people urge her to keep up the rituals; if she mentioned the vision, she knew that Debs would tell her not to try and escape from the grimness of the job but to take control by working through it. In her own mind, the vision *had* provided a diversion from the drudgery of 8.30 to 5 and she had dwelt on it whenever she had the chance during the working day. But, now, when questioned by the group, she felt impelled to say *something* about the turmoil of her inner thoughts and fancies, so she told them about the two dreams.

'Very interesting, that.' Debs was, unsurprisingly, the first to respond when the conversation got heavy. 'The Great Goddess is calling you,' she said firmly, with no room for disagreement. 'It's often that way wi' Goddess. She's appeared to you and she's calling you to be her priestess. You need advice. I can give you a web address for a group called "Priestesses of Delphi". You should join. Obviously, you have special powers of clairvoyance. Now, the corpse dream, that's your old life speaking to you. It will soon be gone forever. The sins mentioned were sins of your past, in which you have not expressed your powers and have given in to male stereotypes of what a woman should be, helpless, afraid, inactive, etc. In future, starting now, you can be bold and claim what is rightfully yours. You can be a living incarnation of Isis.'

*Incarnation of Isis? Sounds cool.* Frances privately committed herself to checking out the Priestesses of Delphi.

At the end of the evening, a longing glance at Nathan (the expression 'drop-dead gorgeous' always came to her mind when she looked in his direction). Would he say something and intercept the impending date with Gary the next day? He was always so sweet with her, so attentive, listening to her speak with great care and sensitivity, making sure she had a drink. She felt valued when she was with him, so why didn't he go that one step further? Despite the longing looks of women in the pub each time they went there, he seemed oblivious to them and there was still no talk of a girlfriend. Maybe gay like Jose? No, Frances didn't think so. One day she would get to the bottom of it. But tonight, no last minute gesture? *Don't see Gary tomorrow night, Frances, I've got plans for us. Oh, Nathan, I've been wanting to hear you say that since the first time we met. I've been wanting to say it too, Frances, I just needed time.* Ah, those little speeches in the head! That small stage in the theatre of the imagination, with its eager lights shining down on the actors undertaking the words and gestures that should have been. The script that was written by Fate, a playwright whom no one takes seriously these days. *Now, Nathan, we can be what we were always meant to be – spiritual adventurers together as life partners!* They kiss. Exeunt.

Saturday – Frances felt nervous. Well, she reflected, things are usually better when you finally get there and meet your date. They were. It was a great night. Frances felt exhilarated that a Leeds band could be so good, thrilled in the old way, a young person just having a fun night out, not a strange woman experiencing visions at concerts. Gary was great too. Just as attentive as Nathan, except that he was interested in making something more of it. They held hands. They snogged. They laughed. They shared jokes about people in the audience, people on the street, people in the chippie.

'Look at *them*, it's Goofy out wi' Minnie Mouse!'

'And over *there* – read all about it, Gulliver dates Lilliput citizen! Have you seen my partner, pal? Yeah, mate, you just trod on her!'

'Oh, no, I don't believe it! I've just seen Osama bin Laden in drag!'

'You're right, bloody clever disguise. The Yanks'll never find him, or is it *her*, here at Elland Road! Enjoy concert, Osama?'

But they didn't sleep together. For some reason, when it came to it, Frances just couldn't go that extra step. Gary escorted her home in the taxi, looking and sounding cool as usual, maybe thinking it was good that his new girlfriend was not a slapper. But Frances was a bit fazed by her own reticence; she didn't feel comfortable about it at all. *What's Sat'day night for, anyway? Maybe I'm just getting old. Or maybe it's not what incarnations of Isis do, have shag on first date.*

# 9

# A Little Revolution

Frances had forgotten one half of the Debs 'working through the heart' scheme until now and, in the days that followed, she tried to make up for it. As well as doing the little rituals, she should have put into practice the plan of getting to know other people in the department, to understand the 'heart' of the office. So, whenever she got the opportunity, she tried to engage the office women in conversation about how they felt, what life was like. One or two were reticent, the types who kept their head down. However, one teenage office junior, Becca, seemed to be glad of someone taking an interest in her; Frances after all, had some years experience at G.R.C. and could be of help to her. The trouble was that it was Becca's first full-time job since leaving school. She had the air of someone who would have believed Frances whether she claimed that the office was Paradise or if she had suggested it was Gulag 699. She didn't know any different.

'Do I think I'm being tret unfair, Frances? Is that what you're asking? Well, I suppose I am. We should have one o' them water machines, that's what I think! You're right, no one appreciates me or gives me encouragement. No thanks even when I do massive pile o' photocopying!'

Frances achieved a little more when sounding out Loli, a Spanish woman of some forty years who had married an Englishman at sixteen and was already a grandmother four times over. Loli was a genial person who always seemed to have a smile on her face, although rather often with the vacant look of someone thinking about gifts for very young grandchildren. She had plenty of part-time experience in offices. What was particularly promising about Loli was that her motherly kindness extended to her colleagues and so she genuinely cared about those who would not speak for themselves. Frances managed to get her to agree to meet at lunchtime and they talked in earnest. Loli didn't seem so concerned about herself, as she worked only eighteen hours a week; the job wasn't that central to her life, but she was anxious about some of the other staff whom she had known for a couple of years.

'Do you see Katie there, Frances? She was the blue-eyed girl when she first came and Ballard encouraged her to think of herself as a management candidate. Then he and Taylor got more and more critical of the work she was doing; she could not live up to their expectations. No promotion came. She began to get disheartened and depressed. However, she won't give up on her dream and so she continues to be a servant to them. Don't tell her anything you don't want fed back to them... (Frances began to regret the fact that Katie was one of the first people she had approached, unsuccessfully, to test the general mood)... Then there's Tricia. A lovely girl, a heart of gold! She reminds me of my Jacinta, so warm and friendly, always helping. But now she won't speak to me or anyone else. There is too much pressure on her, she just gets her work done and then goes home, tired out.'

Po-faced, ginger-haired Tricia looked so opposite to any notion Frances had of a generous-hearted half-Spanish woman, she wondered whether Loli was looking through rosy glasses or whether the office really did transform people into shadows of their former selves. The latter alternative was certainly a very worrying prospect. She imagined herself in five years' time as a sullen workaholic, a testimony to the 'dry' part of her name at last.

Frances remembered Katie, Tricia, Becca and Loli in her little rituals that week. She decided to move the pictures about and placed in the centre of the wall above the mantelpiece the framed print of Giotto's *Majesty*. She liked that one because the Virgin and Child were flanked by feminine looking angels – she imagined them to be all the downtrodden women in the office, with the Goddess in their midst, the child signifying the hope of the future.

'I ask the Goddess to bless Katie and keep her safe against those who would put her down... (lights candle)... I ask the Goddess to bless Tricia and bring back her warmth and friendliness... (lights candle)... I ask the Goddess to bless Becca and not let her teenage years be spoilt by worry... (lights candle)... I thank the Goddess for Loli, please bless her and keep her strong... (lights candle)... Let us all work through the heart...'

Unfortunately, it seemed that Katie did not return the favour. On the Thursday, Frances noticed her glancing across furtively as if she had a guilty secret. Then she was told by a stern-faced John Taylor to go and see Mr Ballard. The arch-demon was quietly spoken but nevertheless very harsh; he made it clear that he was accepting no backchat. He glared at her over reading glasses perched on his nose, directly engaging her vulnerable wide open eyes.

'What's this I hear, Frances, about you asking people whether they are happy here? You've not been in the office long and yet you want to start a little revolution, is that it? You've been at G.R.C. for some time, haven't you why choose now to cause some trouble? It's not as if your own work is that good; quite frankly, Frances, I expected more from you when we transferred you from Finance. I will not give you very long to improve. You must also stop stirring up problems where they don't exist. If I am not satisfied, then you will get a letter from Human Resources and it will be an official warning, which will go down in your file. Much more of this and I'm afraid we'll have to let you go.'

At first, Frances was surprised by her own calmness in the face of this telling off. She told herself that the 'head', aka Mr Ballard, was simply giving a panic response to the magic that the 'heart', aka Frances, was doing on behalf of the oppressed workers in the Department. She tried to stay cool and win a little victory.

'I understand, Mr Ballard, but maybe you're over-reacting. I were just trying to get to know people. And my work'll get better when I've settled in.'

From his point of view, the conversation had already finished. He hardly looked at her while replying in an irritated tone.

'Prove that to me over the next few weeks.'

He indicated that she should leave and stood up himself to rummage through a filing cabinet, perhaps in a display of indifference to her reassurances, but it gave her the chance that she had been waiting for. She needed an object that had been handled by him. With his back turned, she deftly seized a stamping pad that was lying on his desk and walked out with it concealed in her fist. This would be a very suitable object with which to do magic! It bore the seal of the company itself, so maybe it represented its power.

As she left Mr Ballard's office, she gave Katie a defiant look, as if to say 'you'll soon understand what I'm doing for you'. But, a short while later, she started trembling, asked to go home two hours early and didn't stop crying that evening. *Why am I so weak?* She then phoned in sick on Friday as she really couldn't face another day under the watchful eye of Mr Taylor without a weekend in which to gather her thoughts.

She tried to hide her discomfort on the Friday gathering at which the talk was mostly about the spring equinox/Easter weekend in Avebury. She wondered if she would have a job by then. This anxiety was alleviated somewhat by her excitement about the 'Drawing Down the Moon' ritual that Debs explained in greater detail.

'This refers to Moon Goddess. The moon is full next Friday night, one day after equinox. The rite invokes Goddess of the Full Moon and calls her down to earth into women present. They *become* Goddess, you see. In some groups, there's a High Priestess, who becomes incarnation o' Goddess. But with ours, we prefer to be more inclusive – no hierarchies, no chiefs. Just all of us together as equals in solidarity with one another.'

Jose mentioned a debate he had had with an evangelical Christian in his office about the Goddess.

'He said that God was not male or female, but the Father image was the one in the Bible and the one that Jesus used. So he argued that it is the correct way to talk about God, as it is *revealed* to us by God *him*... (indicating imaginary quote marks in the air)... self. So then I said, well maybe God was Father back then, you know. But don't you think that God, being all-knowing and all-powerful, has the right to change his – or *her* – image for a new generation. Maybe now *Mother* is the most accurate way to talk about God, or should I say, Goddess. You're crazy, he said. God is the same yesterday, today and forever, it says so in the Bible, he is constant. But, I replied, aren't we made in the image of God? It says that in the Bible too. We change, we adapt, we take account of new circumstances. Perhaps God does too. Maybe the time has come for God to want to be known as Mother. Of course my friend wasn't convinced! But I really believe it: this is the age of God as Mother, the Goddess. Maybe it's not the final answer for who God is, because God may change again in the future. But it's *our* truth in this generation.'

Nathan liked to move into rational mode when Jose got passionate.

'*However*,' he interjected, wagging his finger towards Jose; he obviously enjoyed the sport of argument 'You're just repeating his mistake, replacing one truth for another. This is not the age for *one* image of God, either Father or Mother. It is a postmodern age, in which there are lots of different approaches and we have to be tolerant of each other's. Some people say Father, some say Mother, some say neither. But they will all have to get along.'

'True,' replied Jose, looking thoughtfully into his beer. 'There are many images in a pluralist society, *but* it might just be that one of them is more powerful and more efficacious. Like, for example, when Elijah took on the prophets of Ba'al on Mount Carmel. His God, the Hebrew God, brought down fire and Ba'al was defeated. This is a symbolic way of saying that the Hebrew God had become the image of God for that time, he couldn't be resisted. In our own times, the Goddess will bring down fire of a different kind to prove herself to this generation.'

So the discussion swung back and forth, the prophet Jose against the social scientist Nathan. Debs, the Goddess-worshipping witch, might have agreed in sentiment with Jose but she was suspicious because (a) he was a man, (b) he was a Catholic, albeit a very offbeat one and (c) he kept quoting from the Bible.

'All this Goddess bringing down fire stuff, being an image for our times – it's a bit *idealist*. I mean, forgive me, I don't have any GCSEs as you might be aware, but I do know what "Goddess" means. It's a practical belief, held by women who know that they are one wi' nature, wi' the earth and so they enjoy some self-respect. Goddess is in 'em. That's all, no lady in sky when we die. Not God in a skirt but our inspiration for being women wi' dignity and solidarity with one another in a male-dominated world. Our magic does not come from heaven above, it's in the earth for our use.'

Jose tried to get her onside.

'I don't think we really disagree,' he said. 'We just have a different way of putting it, that's all.'

Debs was very effective with her 'Hmm' followed by silence, which spoke louder than words that she doubted it.

On the Saturday, Frances undertook a bit of retail therapy, an illogical but very understandable response to the prospect of losing one's income. Around £150 spent on new outfits – oops. Nice red off-the-shoulder dress and black shoes for the night out at a club with Gary. Yes, it was a successful date once again, but she noticed the first signs that cool guy Gary was getting a little impatient by her reluctance to allow him in close. He was very open for a man; it seemed easy for him to share his thoughts, feelings, hopes, fears. But she was not in a place where she could reciprocate; she felt uncertain, nervous, like something bad was about to happen. She preferred to stay with superficial banter but Gary tried to move her somewhere else.

'Come on, Frances, tell me summat more about yourself! What makes you tick? What're your main interests? What's going on in that head o' yours?'

Frances just looked away and shrugged.

'Not much at present. Just want to enjoy life.'

Yet in that head of hers, the wheels were whirling round. *Well, new boyfriend, I can't get Nathan out o' my thoughts; he looked so great last night and he always gives me that special smile. So I like you, but I'm obsessed with him! Do you really want to hear that? Don't think so. Interests? Oh yeah, I'm really getting interested in this 'spiritual adventurer' thing, but I don't know how to describe it, a strange feeling whenever I think about Goddess and weird dreams and visions. Half o' time I'm really excited about it, other half it just seems silly! Do you want to know about that? I doubt it. And if I talk about my job, I'll start crying. Do you want to spend your Sat'day night consoling a sobbing woman? No, I think not. So I'll keep all this to myself.*

Frances had been definitely going to spend the night with Gary; the taxi from town was destined for Gary's flat in Roundhay. This she had agreed earlier that evening, feeling not a little horny after some tequila amid intimate moments in the darkness of the club. Agreed, that is, until she got into the taxi and did a sudden U-turn by snapping 'Hyde Park Road' at the driver before Gary could say anything. He looked at her with a nod that tried to affirm her decision, but the disappointment was barely suppressed. Maybe the chinks were showing in his armour of laid-backness tonight.

'I'm sorry, Gary, I'm not up for it. Feel knackered all of a sudden. Next time. Don't be mad, will you?'

It was Frances who was mad, though. Mad with herself on getting back to the lonely flat, still feeling hot for some physical love. She couldn't explain what prevented her from enjoying the pleasures that she had got used to in her adult life. It wasn't some kind of hopeless romantic yearning for Nathan, either. It was more than that. A kind of feeling that things weren't worth doing unless they meant something. She was waiting for the unknown circumstances that were about to burst into her life, for good or ill, she wasn't sure. Despite all this, she did enjoy Gary's company and thought him a good sort, the kind of bloke a woman should feel safe with. *So why not, why not?!*

Oh yes, the equinox. She hadn't told Gary about next weekend's trip to Avebury, on which – she had decided – he was not invited. She had intended to do it in such a way as to make him think that it was all pre-planned and pre-booked, with limited spaces. But she just couldn't bring herself to. She would now have to do it by phone as, despite his keenness for 'a nice quiet night in wi' DVD and bottle o' wine' during the week, again she had told him that nights before work were off-limits. It was a dangerous game. He was a good catch and she was risking putting him off before the relationship had really started.

She did the deed on his call minder on Monday. Tried to make it sound casual, one of those things.

'Gary, only me. Just calling to tell you I won't be around this weekend. Going off wi' Debs and a few o' her mates, girlie weekend away – they asked me ages ago, sorry, forgot to mention it before. Will phone you as soon as I get back.'

*Oh, yeah? Girlie weekend, eh? Wi' Jose, Nathan and God knows how many other guys.*

Another truly horrible week at work had begun. Despite every evening invoking spirits to gather round a company stamping pad strategically placed in the midst of candles and thus help her get a magical hold on the Ordering Department, Frances seemed to be banging her head against a brick wall. She felt under pressure after the telling-off of the previous Thursday and she was aware just how many people, managers and administrators alike, seemed to be snatching little glances at her to see how she was doing. So while the approaching weekend had been simply something to look forward to, a chance to get away and spend time with Nathan, it now began to take on an enormous significance. Even if the little rituals at home weren't working to improve the work situation, Frances could not help but entertain the hope that the 'Drawing down the Moon' at Avebury at the equinox, surrounded by the hordes of Pagans and Goddess-worshippers, just might. It was a hope that she had to hang on to; there didn't seem anywhere else to go. The other alternative was to get more heavily into Gary, try and get him to marry her, have a couple of kids and leave work. Two things stopped this being an attractive prospect. One was Frances' gut feeling that Gary, while likeable, fun and sexy, was not Mr Really Really Right. The second was her instinct that, if she became much warmer and very dependent on a future with him, he might not stay so interested in her.

On Tuesday evening, she finally got round to listening to the *Stabat Mater* on the tape. She had put this off as she didn't want the disappointment that she expected: no feelings or visions, just a load of boring music. Indeed, nothing remarkable did happen; although she tried to visualise the woman in white, it remained an interior image and did not take on the vividness of the vision in the Town Hall. Nevertheless, the music had a mystical feel and encouraged her mood of hopefulness for the equinox. That night she had another vivid dream. She was going on a pilgrimage with unfamiliar people to a shrine on a dark mountain. The Goddess was going to be made manifest there. However, the roads became difficult to follow and the mountain seemed to recede in the distance. The excitement and anticipation of the dream journey got lost and the scene changed as the road ended in an urban street of fish and chip shops and run-down cinemas. Frances woke up feeling rather frustrated, with period pains. *But at least it's only thirty-six hours to go before we set off on our trip to Avebury!*

## 10

# Trip to Jerusalem

Avebury for Easter and the equinox celebration: what a weekend! So many new memories to cherish; interesting people to meet; strange ideas to contemplate; the long-lasting impression of feelings, sounds, sensations; the suppression of all the minor irritations and anxieties of life, eclipsed by a greater sense of purpose. Good Friday was a day off for everyone, so the weekend began on Thursday after work, rattling and rolling in Jose's geriatric Citroen as it lumbered down to Nottingham for a rendezvous with several more pilgrims, mostly female friends of Debs. Everyone stayed overnight at a large house in the suburbs owned by a woman called Alicia. A staging post for the drive to Wiltshire in the morning. Floor space only, each person bringing a sleeping bag and a blow-up bed, which they would be using on the campsite at Avebury the next night. Good fun, banter, a night out in the city centre, all crammed into the *Trip to Jerusalem*.

'It's oldest pub in England, love.'

'How do you know, Debs?'

'My mate Alicia told me. She drinks here regularly.'

'Well that must be right then. Bar prices are quite modern, though.'

Frances had perhaps rather overdone the make-up and dress; most of the women in the crowd were like Debs, with their unkempt hair, loose-fitting jumpers and old jeans. Frances stood out among the throng; with her little red number, high heels and prominent eye shadow, she looked like she was on the way to the nightclub rather than a field in Wiltshire. All this because of Nathan, who enjoyed the attention and stayed close to Frances as they jostled for position in the Friday night crowd.

'What's he perving at?' complained Frances about the fifty-something-year-old man who couldn't take his eyes off her, with not much else for eye candy in that corner of the pub.

'If you cover yourself in honey, you'll attract the bears as well as the bees,' smiled Nathan in reply.

She poked her tongue out defiantly at him and then turned and did the same to the unfortunate lecher at the bar. He looked angry for a moment but said nothing, averting his gaze. Jose showed signs of nervousness; he hated any hint of confrontation with strangers in pubs. Nathan understood and raised his eyebrows.

'Dear Frances reminds me of a girl I once hung out with,' he said, jauntily. 'She was great at picking arguments in bars but she regarded it as the man's job to do the actual fighting. She was a real liability. She always spotted Mr-Can't-Find-a-Girl-so-I'll-Get-Me-into-a-Ruck-Instead. Then she insulted him before moving quickly behind her man and pushing him forward into the firing line.'

'Which one were you?' asked Frances. 'Man in front o' girl or Mr-Can't-Find-a-Girl-so-I'll-Get-Me-into-a-Ruck-Instead?'

'No, I was Mr-Can't-Find-a-Girl-who-won't-Get-Me-into-a-Ruck-Instead.'

'Let's stop the talk about rucks,' muttered Jose. 'I played rugby at school only once. The first time they threw the ball to me, I caught it and found myself trampled on by a herd of buffalo. After that, when I received the ball, I immediately threw it up in the air at random, so that the buffalo would stampede in some other direction. So, guess what: I didn't make the team!'

Nathan was scruffy like the rest of the crowd but he looked great in everything, so it didn't stop Frances glancing in his direction whenever she got the chance. *I'm just like Mr Perv in corner there, I can't help it though,* she thought to herself. But this wasn't the night for morbid self-reflection. Frances had escaped Dracula's Castle – at least, for four days! She was gleeful and in great form. Everything was funny: Nathan and Mr-Can't-Find-a-Girl, Jose and the rampant buffalo. The alcohol, the evening and the good company began to wash over her like waves on a warm beach, drowning out the Ballards and Taylors, and sending Ordering down onto the seabed of her immediate consciousness. Vive le weekend!

In the morning, red dresses and high heels had to give way to tracksuit top and jeans as they drove off in convoy to Avebury, rather early for someone who had overdone it the night before. Debs paid Frances a lot of attention as they sat in the back together, probably feeling that her reunions of the night before had led her to neglect her new convert.

'So, Frances, what do you think of Alicia, Ceridwen and Morrigan? They've saved my life, they have! Couldn't ask for greater friends than those.'

'They seem really nice, Debs. Did you live in Nottingham, then?'

'Yeah, when I were getting away from certain man whose name I won't mention. Met 'em in refuge. They have powerful magic. You'll see when we get to Avebury.'

Lunch stop in Swindon, picking up somebody called Lazza from the station. A tall, thin lad, pale skin, ginger dreadlocks, dressed all in black, T shirt with something very rude about Jesus written on the back. Jose winced. OK for Pagan gatherings, but for Swindon station and the nearby café? No, really don't think so. He was having visions of rucks again.

Then – arrival! It was about 2 o'clock in the afternoon. The convoy stopped just short of the Avebury sign. The place was so sacred, you couldn't just drive in, Debs insisted. You had to walk past the sign, through the gate into the stone circle and go up and touch one. Frances marvelled at the sight of them, spectacular in their curved lines, each one a substantial piece of rock towering over even the tallest human being. She had been told that the circle was so spread out that it encompassed the whole village, but she hadn't been able to picture it until she got there and saw for herself. She did a funny little dance of comic joy around the first stone that she came to, a kind of cross between something that might be seen at a ceilidh and a bop in a nightclub. This made several of the group laugh out loud; even Debs wore a broad smile.

'Stone circle's made her go right loopy.'

'I'm looping the loopy,' replied Frances, already breathless.

The dancing was not just for comic entertainment, to get Frances in with the crowd, although it served that purpose well. It was also a genuine expression of her excitement; the stones seemed to symbolise the dawning of a new era in her life. She had never visited a stone circle and the fact that they existed at all had only been at the very edge of her consciousness until now.

The entry ritual over, they proceeded to set up camp between the trees in a compact meadow a hundred yards or so from the village. This was another thing outside Frances' experience. Holidays for her parents had been inexpensive B&Bs on the wet and windy northern English coast. As a young adult, when funds permitted, she had joined the Easy Jet set, flying off to cheap hotels in Ibiza, Marbella or Tenerife. So, as a camping virgin, she just held poles or fetched metal pegs while others did the organising, shivering in the cold March air. Big Tent: Alicia, Ceridwen, Morrigan, Debs, Frances. Little Tent: Nathan, Jose, Lazza. *Poo! No cuddling up close to Nathan in my sleeping bag then! Best laid schemes o' mice and horny women.* The other person least involved in camp making was Lazza, too busy making friends with those he met spread out, either across the field camping, or in the nearby car park in campervans or caravans. He made a beeline for those who had the Pagan look:

ponytails, mullets, beards, black clothes, dogs on string leads. There were many of them, given that it was the equinox; mutual recognition and common purpose made for easy community building.

Frances couldn't help but betray her eagerness to know when the Drawing Down the Moon ritual would be.

'About midnight when full moon is high up,' said Debs, giving her a little hug, pleased to see how keen she was. 'Our moon ritual tonight'll be private. The equinox celebration will be tomorrow afternoon and everyone will be there. Actually, equinox were early yesterday but it don't matter, as long as you're near the date. Sat'day's more convenient for visitors.'

'So who'll be doing our private ritual?' asked Frances, overcoming her embarrassment at her childlike nagging to know all the details.

'Just you, me, Alicia, Ceridwen and Morrigan. In our group, we don't normally include men! In early days o' Wicca, in 1950s and 60s, there had to be male and female present, to balance energies. Male high priest were considered essential to high priestess drawing Goddess down into herself. But we've changed that. We're into girl power! From time to time, we need an all-woman ritual. Drawing Down Moon is a good opportunity for it.'

*Oh. Women only. Not 100% my cup o' tea.*

In the evening, everyone piled into the pub in the middle of the village; it was as Nathan had foretold, full of the sound of pipes, whistles, guitars and constant drumming. Some Australians had brought didgeridoos, which whined strange melodies around the rhythm. It was all very *ad hoc* but created an atmosphere of festival and celebration with which Frances soon felt at ease. The Pagan groups included people of a range of ages and styles, several from overseas, and she made mental notes about them, given the difficulty of any sustained conversation above the noise. *Male, about 40. Let's call him 'Native Warrior'.* Hitting a small round drum with some vigour. Had the look of an outdoor country type, with weathered, leathery skin. Dark hair with the beginnings of greyness, tied into a ponytail. Earrings. Several tattoos on the arms, abstract designs plus two serpents and a wolf's head. A match inserted into the mouth, vacant smile, looked a bit doped out. *Female, 25 ish. 'Mata Hari'.* Gothic look, everything in black, the hair dyed jet. Her face covered in piercings, the large eyes with thick make-up peering out directly and unafraid at people, unsmiling and with intensity, as if she was trying to draw in the male of her dreams with sheer magnetism. *Couple, 30s.* Clean cut, in ordinary, casual clothes, but tapping hands with the drumbeat and nodding heads, making a special effort to show that they were into the music and atmosphere in a big way. *Bet they're lawyers on a weekend break. 'The Lawyers' it is, then.* And so on. Endless entertainment, giving out names, identities, occupations to people that she didn't know from Adam or Eve.

There didn't seem to be any strict closing time, so a little past eleven, Alicia and Debs motioned to the other women to join them out in the night air. As they went out, Frances caught sight of the full moon that had risen in the east, now visible fleetingly between the scudding, broken clouds driven along by an icy northerly wind. The scene was made especially magical by the presence of the stones – cold, silent sentinels which had stood guard over so many full moons and equinoxes. First, the women went back to the campsite to get a few things: candles, a dish, some water and crystals of various colours. Frances was somewhat embarrassed to see Alicia carrying an old-fashioned twig broomstick. She suddenly felt tense. *Oh God, tell world we're witches, why don't you!* Then they searched for a good spot, deciding on a stone on the eastern fringe of the village, where it would be quiet and the moon would be clearly visible without the interruption of artificial light. Frances noticed that her breathing was fast and her heart pounded. *It's only a little ritual to help some damaged women,* she thought to herself, *try and relax.* But this moment had taken on a considerable significance; without the meaningful experience that it promised, she couldn't see how she could face another Monday morning at G.R.C. And then the ritual began.

## 11

# Drawing Down the Moon

Alicia took the lead. Frances had begun to notice that she had a strong presence among the women: she was tall, athletic, dark-skinned with short curly black hair and strong, handsome African features, nearer forty than thirty. Her accent was northern English but not pronounced enough for her county of origin to be placed with any precision. She began by setting the scene, trying to make it clear for Frances as the newcomer.

'The Moon is important in this ritual because the ancients saw it as the embodiment of the Goddess. Although we moderns might find it hard to believe this to be literally the case, we should remember that science confirms the essential role of the Moon for all life on Earth. Anyway, the Moon is a symbol for the life of the Goddess that is in us. In 'Drawing Down the Moon', we find ourselves to *be* the Goddess. This is true on a day-to-day basis, but it is in the ritual that we fully realise it. Discovering that we have the power of the Goddess within us, we can do great works of magic for ourselves and for our sisters and our brothers too. So let's begin.'

The women, all well wrapped up in heavy coats, hats and gloves, stood in a ring with the stone at the centre, stretching their hands out towards each other, although they were too far apart to touch. Alicia left her place and walked slowly in a clockwise direction around the circumference of the circle, behind each woman. She was trailing the broom so that it swept the circle and said some words quietly to herself. Frances could just get the sense of it, that she was consecrating the circle as a sacred space for the duration of the ritual. As she did so, Frances spent a few moments scrutinising her companions. She could not see them well in the dark, but she had spent over twenty-four hours with them now and they were becoming familiar. Morrigan was small and olive-skinned with long dreadlocks died pink, green and blonde in patches, her hair swirling around in the March wind whipping through chilly Avebury. She was probably the youngest of the group, in her mid-twenties, with a serious expression that gave her a natural frown. Then Frances remembered where the women had met – in the refuge – and it caused her to wonder what history there was behind Morrigan's downbeat outlook. Ceridwen, most likely in her early thirties, was a more cheerful character, although not pretty in the classical sense. Her broad face and rosy complexion, with sandy brown hair like Frances' own, gave her the looks of someone who might be expected to be a good listener, or a caring mother. However, Frances had already discovered that there was some ice behind the smile; she did not tolerate fools gladly and had a skill in pointing out the absurdity and inappropriateness of a casual remark.

*I can't believe I'm doing this.*

Two months ago, Frances would have avoided women like the ones that she stood with now; they were not for the easy fun and superficial banter of Frances' normal social circle. But it was Debs who had first touched something in her that helped her finally to venture away from the light and harmless to the dark and challenging; away from people whose lives were focussed on hoping for an impossibly idealistic future, to those seeking escape from a real and painful past. She looked at the dark shape that was Debs. The tangles of curly dark hair flew around in the breeze like Morrigan's, in contrast to Alicia's short hair or the neatness of Frances' ponytail. She had come to like this strange woman but it was not altogether an altruistic feeling; she felt that Debs had something to offer her, a magical potion that would transform her shallow life. Maybe here and now would present the moment when the gift would be offered. She had entered the little band of witches with an intuitive sense that there was something in it for her. Witches? The word seemed so robust compared to the frail human beings that stood with Frances now, all togged up in the near freezing night air. Were there *really* ever witches who were warrior maidens with powerful wicked magic, who cackled without feeling at their victims' plight, ate children and turned heroes into small helpless animals, with snakes for hair, their ugliness portraying their inner unpleasantness? Were there *really* ever 'white' witches like Samantha in *Bewitched,* Sabrina, or the ladies of *Charmed*, whose good looks went along with a calm and confident interior, knowing that they could deal with any situation that arose, with humour and poise? Or were 'witches' simply women like those here in Avebury?

Frances' reverie came to a sudden end, as Alicia had returned to her place in the circle and they all began to sing:

'Isis, Astarte, Diana, Hecate, Demeter, Kali, Inanna!'

Frances didn't hear all the various names of the Goddess properly, but she did her best to join in. Something in her could not shake off the embarrassment factor. *I want to be here and I chose to be here. Why do I keep seeing myself through the eyes o' my old friends?* She saw herself imaged in the mocking scrutiny of Jo, Cyn, Sal, her brother Colin, the women in the Ordering office, even her parents and the elderly next door neighbour who was feeding Cass this weekend. But she forced herself to carry on despite this feeling. When they had sung the refrain a few times, there was a natural stop, and Alicia called upon them to summon the spirits of the four quarters. Having located Morrigan in the east, standing in the direction of the open country shrouded in eerie darkness, they waited for her to begin. She turned to the east and raised her hands.

'I call upon the spirits of the east, spirits of the rising Sun and Moon, of the dawn, of new ideas and enlightenment, of the soaring eagle and the beautiful Earth. Be with us in our circle and guide our ritual. Blessed be.'

She then lit a candle, placed inside a lantern to protect it from the wind. The other women echoed 'Blessed be' and then the pattern continued round to Debs, in the north, and Ceridwen, in the west, using similar formulas. Frances then experienced an uncomfortable moment as she realised that they were all looking at her.

'*You* are in the south,' called Debs.

'What do I say?' retorted Frances, sounding panicky.

'Anything you like,' came the encouraging reply. 'Don't worry, there are *no* rules. Say whatever your heart leads you to say.'

'OK.'

Frances took a deep breath.

'I call upon the spirits of the south to be with us and guide our ritual. Blessed be.'

The words came out breathlessly, at a gallop, and she had forgotten to turn to the south and raise her hands, but she remembered the candle. The others nodded their approval and the ritual continued, with Alicia again taking the lead. She gave each of them one of the small pieces of crystal to hold. This would put them in touch with the minerals and energies of the earth beneath. By the standing stone she placed the dish and into it poured water. She then raised her hands to the sky and spoke out, in a tone that was louder and grander than before.

'We call upon the Three-fold Goddess of the Moon, Maiden, Mother and Crone, to be with us in this our rite, to be around us and in us and help us manifest her glory and power and beauty.'

They all fell silent. Although earlier there had been plenty of noise coming from the village as people left the pub, all that could be heard now was the blowing of the stiff breeze. The candles flickered, causing shadows to dart across the women and onto the ancient stone placed securely in the ground between them. Frances looked at her silhouetted companions, then up at the moon, which was clearly to be seen now through a large gap in the patchy cloud cover, giving a little light onto the circle. Its reflection was caught in the water in the dish. As she noticed it there and then turned back to look at the source, something happened to her. It dispelled all the embarrassment, shyness, uncertainty and nervousness that she had been feeling and caused her to stare heavenward in rapt wonder. Then everything began to swim…

'What happened? Are you all right?' Debs was asking with some urgency as she knelt over Frances, now lying on the grass in front of the stone. 'Say something, we're worried about you!'

Frances managed to stutter, 'I'm OK. I looked at the moon and then I saw summat else. So beautiful, so beautiful…'

'Let's finish the ritual quickly,' suggested Alicia. 'So we can get Frances back to the tents, where we can see better and find some brandy or something.'

The ritual was completed hastily by the dismissing of the spirits and the closing of the circle anti-clockwise. They walked back to the campsite, Debs holding Frances by the arm. Frances later had little recollection of the walk, except for one moment, when she heard Morrigan mutter to Ceridwen as they walked together a few yards behind her:

'I saw her face in the candlelight just before she fell over. She was transformed, you know, her face was shining and radiant. Like someone in a trance.'

*Brandy. Don't really need it but I'll have some, anyway! I'm OK, I really am. Need time to try and work it all out. I can't believe what I saw. On t' other hand, maybe I'm ill. I saw John Travolta in a film about a bloke who experienced miraculous things, but really he just had a brain tumour. Maybe that's me. Frances Dryburgh R.I.P. Only twenty-nine. But if heaven's like that vision, it's OK.*

Frances' thoughts flew back and forth, as she was the only one not speaking; the women were gathered in the tent all discussing what had happened. The men joined them, squeezing into the limited space as well as they could and trying to sober up fast having heard the commotion and thinking that something bad was happening.

'Can you tell us what happened then, Frances?' asked Debs. 'Give her some room, everybody!'

'I were looking at moon,' said Frances, dreamily. 'Then it turned into a face and then face had a body. It were the woman from my dream a couple o' weeks back; difficult to describe her, her features and colours keep changing. I saw white, gold, red, blue. She came out o' moon and down toward me. She were dancing, like she were in dream, and she smiled, such a brilliant kind smile. "Let's go dancing," she says. And we blended in together, her and me. We were like one person, but she were like an energy speaking to me from inside. "Let's go dancing in office," she says. Suddenly, it were all in front o' me, my workplace and everybody there, Ballard, Taylor, Katie, Loli and all. I were in middle of 'em. And I danced for 'em all and then they applauded me. It were all so wonderful, everything were put right. That were all. Just a brilliant vision. I just felt so great for a moment, full o' good feelings.' Frances paused, but there was one last detail to describe. 'Then finally, she said as if from inside me, "I change colour but really I'm black, Frances. Remember that." Then I found myself lying on grass.'

Morrigan got emotional and started to weep and speak at the same time.

'Frances was the Goddess for a moment then. I saw her face, it was like, supernatural!'

'Well, that's what's supposed to happen to all of us,' Alicia interjected, trying to play down the more emotive interpretations of the experience. 'It was just more intense in Frances' case, that's all.'

Jose had to throw in his little bit of wisdom.

'Frances is like St Bernadette of Lourdes,' he said, triumphantly. 'She too went into really impressive trances when she saw her visions.'

'This is *nowt* to do wi' Catholicism, Jose!' Debs snapped at him angrily. 'Goddess is *not* Virgin Mary. Frances didn't see someone superior to her, putting her womanhood down and telling her to become a nun. Goddess is in us, part of us. We *are* her, not her servants!'

Jose started to say something in reply but then, realising that people weren't in the mood for an impassioned debate, fell silent and shrugged. Only Frances responded by giving him a big smile. Not that she really understood what he was on about. But his heart was in the right place. And she felt in touch with hearts just at the moment.

The group agreed to keep the experience to themselves, so when they joined the great gathering for the equinox celebration the following afternoon, they blended into the crowd. Frances was in a very dreamy state. She was going over her vision, again and again, dwelling on the details, trying to remember a bit more. *Black. What had the woman meant by that?* The equinox ritual was organised by bearded Druids in long white or black robes and was held in the north-east field next to the greatest of the stones in a pair, the 'Cove', not far from the site of the moon ritual the night before. Once again there was the establishment of the sacred circle and calling of the quarters, but it was not quiet, unlike the previous midnight. The focus was on music, drumming, dancing around in a circle, lots of hugging (*good to stand next to Nathan, then*), laughter, more cheerful than meditative.

Then the rest of the day to chill out, a chance for some shopping in the village with its New Age shops. What to buy as a memento for such a weekend? Frances saw a pack of Tarot cards, the 'Goddess Tarot'. Each card portrayed a different goddess. Could they remind her of the vision woman?

'Yes, I'll take these. About time I learnt to do a bit o' fortune-telling.'

'It's *not* fortune-telling, Frances. It's divination, a way of reading our inner lives.'

Frances made a mock gesture of impatience with Debs, always offering a morsel of corrective wisdom at her shoulder. But she couldn't really be mad, her mood that day was too light and loving.

'Well, I'd better get some, because I always get tea in bags, so there's no leaves to read.'

Nathan couldn't resist a friendly dig.

'Oh, I see you're back to your cheery self, with bad jokes and all.'

Frances tutted, with the smile barely suppressed.

'How can *you* of all people diss anyone's jokes.'

*Yes, Nathan, and I might be the incarnation o' the Goddess, but I still fancy you, my man!*

'By the way,' added Nathan, more seriously. 'You see now why I referred to you as special a few weeks ago.'

Frances just smiled. She was happy, although the attention was now making her feel just a little awkward.

'Did you contact Priestesses of Delphi, like I suggested?' asked Debs.

'No, didn't get round to it. But I will do sometime.'

# 12

# Worth It

*It feels strange now that I'm on my own again, no one but Cass to keep me company. Can't believe all that really happened; what a brilliant weekend! It were freezing cold and camping's not normally me, but I felt warm anyway! I feel like a new me has come back and old me got left behind, maybe somewhere en route. That reminds me: when we were dropping Lazza off at Swindon station, I found that Gary had just left a message on my mobile but I haven't answered it yet. 'Call me as soon as you get back, won't you, babe? I didn't text, because I didn't want to intrude on your girlie weekend, but I really missed you anyway.' Oh God. If you're going out wi' someone and you spend four days away without thinking of 'em one single time, without sending them one single text, well, what does that say? It says: goodbye, Gary. This is not the time, other things are too important, you're a great bloke but just came into my life at wrong time. I'm not in love with you, and I don't think I ever will be.*

*What happened out there, among stones? Were it a hallucination or summat? Am I ill? I don't know, but actually I don't think so. It just kind o' made sense. Goddess wants to help me live my boring life and make it better. I am valuable, despite all appearances o' crap job and no great love affair. All that advertising: spend a lot on yourself 'because you're worth it'. Well, it's not perfume and glam clothes that gives you worth. Otherwise it's only people wi' money that are 'worth it'. What about kids in back streets o' Leeds? What about people in poor countries wi' nowt, absolutely nowt? Goddess is in them too. Oh, I've gone all sentimental! Keep it under control, girl! But it's true, i'nt it? Sounds like crap but it's true. Goddess is powerful, she can choose to make people valuable when society thinks they're worthless. What about them women, from refuge? Crapped on by men, so they've turned to her for help. She makes 'em feel worthwhile.*

*Ow! Shouldn't try to pour tea while thinking deep thoughts, causes me to scald myself! God, I really should get some new china. This bloody cup's cracked; I think rest of 'em are too. No, hang on! Cracked cup's all right. It'll last a while yet. In't that what my mum always says? 'Nowadays, we live in throwaway society. When we were kids, we made us things last, because we couldn't afford owt else.' Oh, Mum! I never listen to a word you say, it's hard when you're so anxious all time. I'm sure there's wisdom in you somewhere. Why are you so scared? What are you scared of? Is Goddess a kind o' compensation for me because you can't give me strength I need from a mum? Probably, but I don't think she's only a compensation. She's real!*

*Yes, Cass, milk should be in your bowl as well as in my tea. Trouble is, I think it's turning. We'll both have to put up with it; I'm not going down to corner shop now it's getting dark. Wish Jose's family ran my local shop. Well, probably people who do are just as nice as him, so maybe I should get to know 'em better. They're not just robots who appear when you want summat you forgot to buy in supermarket. Wonder which part of India they come from? Or maybe Pakistan, is that in India? Well, I know Goa is, anyway. I should get an atlas, so I can see where all these places are. Jose's very interesting when he talks about Indian goddesses. I particularly like Kali, she's scary (not as scary as Debs, ha ha), but she's female and she's powerful.*

*Thinking o' divine beings, I should stop worshipping Nathan because he looks so great. Just an accident o' nature, he's not done owt to deserve it. He's not 'worth it' any more than anyone else. He's just a nice bloke, wi' a bit of blockage in committing himself to relationships. The 'c' word for men: 'commitment'. Who am I to talk? That Gary might want to commit himself to me! So maybe I'm like Nathan. I can't return love when it's really being offered. Maybe I've always held back, except when I'm chasing men who I know don't love me and then it's safe to love them.*

*Do I need to eat summat? Don't feel like it. Mum thinks I'm anorexic: 'Don't let all them skinny models influence you, love! They're not real people, you know, don't need to work hard and clean up and all that.' I'm not anorexic, though, it's just that sometimes, when my mind is racing, I don't fancy food. My mind's racing now, in fact it's wandering all over place! It's funny how you want to think about summat special, like my experience in Avebury, and you end up thinking about everything else. One thing leads to t' other and you're thinking about every part of your life. Let me see, can I go back through my chain o' thought? Nathan, ah yes, worshipping, goddesses, oh it's easy. No, hang on, weren't India in there somewhere? Just shows you.*

*That ringtone! It's really corny, must get a new one. Ignore it, it'll be Gary. Can't face telling him right now. What'll he say? I think he's Mr Persuader type. 'Frances, we're perfect together and you know it!' Or Mr Cool. 'Give it a little more time, Frances. I can wait.' Or maybe he'll play Mr Clown and make joke of it, hoping that'll make me like him more. Mr Angry never gets anywhere, we all know that. Nor does Mr Desperate. Then there's Mr Denial, who turns up next day to take you out as if nowt's happened.*

*Forget all that! What's this Goddess business all about? I've never really been religious, or a 'spiritual adventurer' as Nathan would say, that is until recently. But I've had weird dreams and*

*I'm sure that one or two of 'em were clairvoyant. But I were never really 'spiritual'. There were my Madonna pictures, so I suppose it were in me. Then I meet Nathan, Debs and Jose, start lighting candles and trying to do magic and – bingo – visions! Brilliant visions! Hey, I think I'll play that Plonker music in background to help me think about 'em. Salve Regina. Need some lip salve, Regina? Doing the Vida Loca. Doing the Salve Regina...*

*...Going to sleep wi' music on weren't part o' my plan! What time is it? Hell, 11.30 already. Work tomorrow. What a day it'll be. Back to Ballard and Taylor, backlog o' corrections, miserable faces o' girls in office. Then home to call Gary and end it. What a contrast to this weekend. I know I won't be able to keep good feeling I've had these past three days. Drawing Down Moon. Wish I could draw down moon into office, like in my vision. I suppose that's just another kind o' compensation for my miserable life. What can't be, I imagine it in a dream or vision. I remember Jason telling me about Freud. He thought Freud were great! 'When you dream about nice things, Frances, it's called wish fulfilment. That means you are living out in your dream what you want to happen in reality. Sadly, it's not reality and it's not likely to be.' OK, Freud! Tonight I'll dream that Gary thanks me for being honest when I dump him tomorrow and says to call him if I ever have problem, but he won't disturb me while then. Ballard apologises and says we'll do it my way from now on. And Mum starts enjoying life, Jo gets job, Cyn stops falling for clingy and boring men. And Nathan, well yes, I might have wish fulfilment dream about him too...*

*...OK, falling asleep again! Can't concentrate on trying to think it all through now, so I'll go to bed. Goodbye, good Easter Monday, tomorrow is bad Tuesday. I don't like Tuesdays, tell me why... I change colour but really I'm black, Frances. What did that mean? Black as in black people, like Debs and Jose? Is she telling me that she's a black person? One or two o' my icons are*

*black, like that Virgin of Iviron. I must ask Jose about that. Why does she dance? In dream and in visions, she's always dancing. Black and dancing. Like Beyoncé. Ha ha. Really I'm black, Frances... really black...*

# 13

# Dancing

Tuesday was just as bad as Frances had feared. It felt as if she had to pay dearly for such an enthralling weekend. The contrast between the Pagan frivolity at Avebury and the cold businesslike atmosphere of the office was a stark one. There were complaints from Taylor about last Thursday's work. She would have to stay late to make up for lost time. The task ahead was dull: writing to suppliers to inform them of new administrative processes and checking that lists of addresses were up to date. When lunchtime finally came, Sal wasn't as interested in the Avebury trip as much as Frances had expected. *Maybe we're growing apart*, she thought. Sal hadn't been as comfortable sharing tales about the new companions when she found out that they were 'spiritual searcher' types; she wanted to know details of love affairs, binges, arguments, that kind of thing. Equinoxes, visions – she didn't seem so sure. When lunch came, she changed the subject to more comfortable territory, so Frances had to listen to the story of how she had managed to convince an old friend to date a lonely colleague at work. Frances herself wasn't sure how to broach the subject of the impending break with Gary, as the reasons seemed so unconvincing in the Sal world.

Finally home and the dreaded dump by phone. Sure enough, there were already texts and voice messages from Gary on her mobile asking her to call. *Let's plan this...* Avoid 'it's not you, it's me'; while this was actually quite true, as it so often was, it was too easily read as a put-down in disguise. Other clichés that might do more harm than good: 'I'm sure you'll find someone dead gorgeous who'll really love you'; 'We had fun, didn't we?'... There was no right thing to say. Oh well, she just had to go for it. She got through quickly, as if he had been waiting next to the receiver.

'Hi, Gary... yeah, great weekend, thanks... it's so nice that you care for me but, well, how do I put this, I can't respond just as things are at the moment. I'm finding my spiritual side, you see... I don't want to go out with anyone right now.'

*'OK.' That was it? He just says 'OK' as if nothing had happened and hangs up? No arguments, no demands for more explanation? No wanting to know why I had changed so much in just a couple o' weeks? Oh God, I think he's Mr Denial. He'll be round in half an hour with a big smile, saying 'Shall we go out for a drink, or just stay in and warm each other up?'*

But he wasn't. It sunk in that that really was it, Gary's way of coping with it. No trying to salvage a friendship between two people who did have a liking for each other, after all. *If you don't want to go out wi' me, then sod you. Typical man!*

Tuesday had been absolutely crap, in every single detail, every second and every minute. Not a single moment of enthusiasm, expectation or comfort. The energy of the weekend already seemed a million years ago. It couldn't be summoned up to chase the blues away. The incarnation of the Goddess went back to being her old boring unfulfilled self and had a day that was just absolutely crap.

But it was the last blowing of the night storm before the bright sunrise and its birdsong accompaniment. Wednesday was really much, much better.

There was no hint of what was to come at 7 a.m., with the stumbling into the kitchen for tea and toast. Nor any sign at 7.30, with the realisation that necessary washing and ironing had been neglected and there were no decent clothes to wear. There was nothing obviously in the air at 8.30, as she sat down at her desk to finish off the mailing job of the day before. Still in the dark at 10.30, when she spent a few tearful minutes with Sal over coffee as she finally admitted the deed of the night before.

'He just said, "OK". Then I felt well sad and thought maybe I should've tried harder. And I also wondered whether I'd gone quite mad, because he's actually a dead nice guy. Then I wished he could have stayed friends, at least. I'm a bitch, Sal, I really am, I don't know what's happening to me!'

But then it was 11.30. Nazi Robot Woman once again played Mercury to communicate the decisions of the gods.

'Come round, everybody. I have an important announcement to make while Mr Ballard and Mr Taylor are in a meeting upstairs. There are going to be some big changes. We need to start planning a farewell collection. Mr Ballard – (correction, smile) James – told me yesterday that he has applied for and been given early retirement, so he will be leaving us on his fifty-fifth birthday next month. What a wonderful servant to the company he has been for over twenty-five years!... (pregnant pause, no expression of agreement from anyone)... However, we are not losing one good man, but two! John is moving on to a new higher post in another company and will be finishing here on the same day as James. They have worked so well together; I don't think that John could envisage staying at G.R.C. without James. So, anyway, please keep the evening of Friday April 25$^{th}$ free in your diary as the date for a special goodbye dinner.'

One more piece of information was required to make this really perfect and Frances was characteristically the one to blurt out the question that asked for it. Nazi Robot Woman did not disappoint. She was the hated one no longer.

'Ah yes, James' replacement will be Raymond Carson, that bright young man who has been doing so well in the company.

He will be interviewing for his assistant manager in the next few weeks and it could be one of you.'

Frances' eyes widened. She was trying to take this all in. Raymond Carson was a saint. He was known throughout the firm for his innate ability to put other people first. He did his own job remarkably efficiently but without expecting others to reach his own high standards. He encouraged. He facilitated. He consulted. He stood in for people. He stood up for people. He went out of his way to help people. He got in first in the morning and put the kettle on with a smile when you arrived. He replaced the sugar, milk and tea bags. He washed up. He was friendly to the cleaners. He remembered people's birthdays. He reconciled people when they fell out. What's more, he was mid-thirties and dishy, albeit in a monastic kind of way. Everybody had said what a great boss he would be. After the few seconds it took for all this to sink in, Frances felt a loud 'yes!' coming. It had to come out, a great big exclamation of 'yes!' with clenched fists and delight on the face, but so brazen an expression of pleasure at the news might spoil everything, so it came out in everything but sound. A great big silent exclamation of 'yes!' with the gestures and shape of mouth leaving no one nearby in doubt about what was not being said out loud. Loli laughed. Becca giggled. Then – good God, what a morning of miracles! – Tricia sniggered just a little bit too, trying to suppress it.

Then Frances felt tingling up the spine and a flush of excitement. *The Goddess* is *dancing here in the office, just like in the vision. You can't see her but she* is *here.* The 'yes!' of exultation and the moment of giggling evolved into a gulp and suddenly there were tears of emotion. And so she made a quick exit to the toilet, leaving others to plan collections and farewell dinners.

Sal was pleased to hear the news at lunchtime, but she wasn't the one that Frances wanted so badly to tell. Her instincts told her exactly who that was to be. After work, she didn't go home but made straight for Chapeltown by bus. She had never been to

Debs' house before, but she had the address and so she would go on spec, praying that Debs would be home. This seemed to be the right way to do things, Frances didn't know why. Spontaneity! The terraced house was a typical 1930s suburban building: unkempt and quite cracked around the edges, a bit like its tenant. The three floors of windows needed new paint on the frames and some wood protection on the sills; the pointing between the light red-brown bricks needed doing and the guttering looked near to collapse. But Frances liked the way that someone had painted the front door a bright scarlet to make it stand out and welcoming, although she wondered why the windows hadn't been done the same way to match. She knew that Debs lived with two friends. One of them answered the door, a pretty young black woman, slim as a supermodel, with long hair in ringlets. She gave Frances the friendliest of smiles and introduced herself as Lizzie.

'Yes, she's here, I'll show you through.'

'Thanks. I didn't know whether she'd be in.'

Through to the combined kitchen/dining room.

'You've company, Debs, love.'

Debs was seated perusing a magazine at a worn, scratch-marked wooden table, filling the centre of the room with all its side leaves opened out. Although still in her twenties, she needed glasses for reading. She looked up, taking them off in one motion. The immediate and – it had to be admitted – uncharacteristic broad smile showed Frances two things: one, that Debs genuinely liked her even if she didn't always show it that well; two, that she had intuited that good news was about to be shared.

'It's worked, Debs! Magic's worked! Goddess has sorted it for me! Ballard and Taylor are leaving! My vision were true! It were true!'

They danced together round the table. It was such a joyous moment that Frances refused to allow the sudden pain in her right thigh, which had caught the table corner full on, to deflect her. *Dancing whenever mood takes me – well, it's a good way to show yourself to be a Goddess person.* After a minute or two of congratulating, Debs sat her down and began to make a pot of tea.

'This shows you that Nathan were right when he picked you out, Frances, love. You've got *power*, it's in you naturally. You've more power than rest of us can dream of, not that we're jealous or owt. We're just glad to know you, really we are!'

'But surely, Debs, *you've* got power too, because you got rid o' your pimp and everything. It's not just me.'

'That took whole group o' people practising witchcraft for several months, Frances. You've been working on your own, you've seen Goddess with your own eyes and it's taken you a couple o' weeks.'

Frances had a sudden insight and looked Debs straight in the face.

'Working on my own? I've a feeling that you've been saying some spells for me.'

Debs looked embarrassed and pleased at the same time; she was clearly delighted that Frances had realised but not quite sure how to signal it.

'OK, maybe a few,' she said quietly, looking down.

And then they embraced, for about fifteen seconds, although it felt like ten minutes. It was the moment when Frances knew that Debs wouldn't ever intimidate her again or, to be more accurate, that she wouldn't allow her perception of Debs to make her *feel* intimidated. Only one thing troubled her – that she had never, until then, thought for a minute of doing a little ritual for Debs. She resolved to change that in the future.

That night, the four adventurers had a spontaneous pub session. Summoned by the victorious witches, Nathan and Jose joined them in a Harehills pub for a drink or several and the beer, wine and fruit juice flowed. Everyone knew that celebrating tonight was more important than the trouble the hangover would bring in the morning. Library cataloguing systems would break down, bus timetables wouldn't work, social work reports wouldn't get written, orders wouldn't be processed. But eat, drink and be merry, for tomorrow we make a complete mess of our work! A little voice in Frances' head made her anxious that she might be celebrating prematurely, but she suppressed it.

'Now you might believe that you're special, Ms Dryburgh.'

'Yes, Mr Smith, and for my next trick, I'm going to turn you into a frog! Oh, no need, I see you're one already. Someone got there ahead o' me.'

Nathan went along with the joke.

'What nonsense. Ribbit!'

After a good hour or so of merriment, Jose got serious all of a sudden.

'You know,' he said, with intensity. 'There might be bigger things Frances can achieve, much bigger than sorting out an office. If she's chosen by the Goddess, who knows?'

'Don't be silly.' Frances quickly became embarrassed, now that the adulation was moving away from mere banter. 'I can't do anything without you lot. It's not me, it's us. Debs admits she were working for it too.'

'OK, us. But with you, what could we achieve?' wondered Jose.

Debs had the idea. It was quite logical.

'The environment!' she exclaimed. 'You might remember I told you about political pressure building up on many governments worldwide. We must drastically reduce emissions o' greenhouse gases within a very short time. The world can't wait. They need to agree radical political steps, far more than previously proposed, which will change society radically. Strict targets. Money going into low fuel technology, solar and wind energy, better insulation.'

Frances thought of Debs' house, which looked like it was leaking heat on all sides like a misshapen teapot, but she didn't say anything.

'What's the schedule?' asked Jose, having caught the sense of urgency.

'I'm not sure, but the next big international meeting is the G8 in early July,' Debs continued. 'It's not going to be easy. The proposals demand sacrifices. Every powerful nation's worried about the cost to their economies. So there's real worries that they won't do enough and so disaster'll follow in just a few decades. Real disaster – for nature and for poorest people in world, mostly.'

'And how does this involve *us*?' asked Frances, but she already knew the answer.

'We'll do witchcraft to make them choose more difficult option and decide for environment, Frances! With you, we can do anything, I really believe that.'

There was a silence for a couple of minutes. Frances tried not to lose the good feeling of her victory that day, but she was seriously wondering if this was all going too far.

Nevertheless, one by one, Nathan, Jose and finally Frances herself came round to the idea. She wondered about the craziness of it. *It's amazing what people agree to after a few drinks and what they start to believe is possible. But Debs hasn't drunk owt, has she, and she proposed it!*

'How will we do it?' asked Nathan. 'It would have to be a very spectacular ceremony in an especially sacred place. Maybe back at Avebury? Or Stonehenge?'

Jose didn't look sure.

'It needs to be relevant, somehow. Where are they meeting?' he asked Debs.

'Japan, I think they said,' came the reply.

'Well, I don't think we can go there,' Jose concluded, gloomily.

Frances was looking at Debs, feeling a bit vacant about it all, but then words came unbidden into her head. They had been popping in and out ever since Friday night. Really I'm black, Frances. It didn't seem the appropriate time, with so much political seriousness around, but Frances changed the subject, or at least she thought she had.

'What does it mean, Jose?' she asked, looking into space. 'Goddess saying "I change colour but really I'm black." That's what she said to me in vision.'

Jose stared at her. Seeing his delayed reaction was like watching Archimedes jumping up in his bath, Newton rubbing his head after an apple fall, or Einstein suddenly seeing the implications of the light bouncing round his patents office.

'That's it! The shrines of the Black Virgin!' He was so excited that he almost hissed it and then went on with questions and answers: 'Where are they? Mostly in France! What are they? Survivals of the old Goddess religion, kept alive in Catholic Europe. What kind of Virgins? Well, centuries-old medieval statues, usually black although not always, as they have changed colour over the centuries, but they *are* called "black virgins" anyway.'

Now Frances was fully engaged.

'Then that's where we'd better go,' she agreed, with a lump forming in her throat. 'To France and shrines o' the Black Virgin.'

'It would make a great trip,' agreed Jose. 'I don't think any of us has organised a summer holiday yet.'

It was agreed that Jose should look into it. No Costa del Sol this year. The remaining half hour returned to jollity. And the evening would have been absolutely perfect had not Frances, late on, noticed a familiar face at the bar. It was a good friend of Gary's. She had met him in the club when she was out with Gary the last time. But, just as she prepared to get up from their table and greet him, he turned and slipped out. *Ah! Good one. I ditch Gary, then next day his best mate sees me laughing and joking. Do I look like I'm pining? No. Do I look like I'm celebrating? Yes. Is he going to hate me? Yes. Most definitely.*

## 14

## Mary Magdalene

'You're not trying very hard to hide your delight at the fact that we're leaving, are you, Frances?' commented John Taylor, on the Friday.

He had caught her jigging about the office in a way that would have been unheard of just one week before. There was something of a demob atmosphere starting to emerge now. The women had begun to chat to each other more and Ballard and Taylor were wearing the look of men who were set on other things; for one, the golf course and foreign beaches, the other, a new and more prestigious position, no longer merely number two. But, despite this, Taylor did not like an open display of disregard for his weakening control and he confronted Frances with an icy stare.

'I still have a month to knock you into shape. Or maybe see that you leave the company before I do.'

There was real venom in his voice. The Goddess had not won him over yet, then. Frances made an internal decision to tough it out, by accepting whatever was thrown at her for the remainder of the old regime. She could not risk them being able to remove her before the golden era of smiley Carson and his tea making and so she would put up with whatever indignity came her way. It was only for four weeks. *So, let it be, let it be, let it be, let it be, there will be an answer, let it be.* But she really didn't like the way he was staring her out today. Maybe he had cottoned on to the way she regarded herself as the agent of change, rather than a passive recipient. *You're not* deciding *to leave for new job, Mr Taylor, it's me who's* caused *you to go.*

That evening, in the pub, Jose declared that he had already carried out some investigations.

'The greatest number of black virgin shrines in Europe is in the Auvergne,' he said. 'That's a region in the central southern part of France, a mountainous area called the *Massif Central*. The Auvergne is full of volcanoes and little chapels. It's also famous for its Romanesque basilicas, that is, cathedrals in a particular medieval style, with unusual octagonal towers and rounded side chapels... (looking round at blank faces)... OK, I'll stay clear of architecture! Probably the best-known statue of the Black Virgin in the Auvergne is in a town called Le Puy en Velay. It looks really spectacular there; I've seen pictures on the web. There are other shrines we could look at, maybe the Virgin of Orcival, which is in one of those Romanesque basilicas, but I would suggest that we make for Le Puy and start from there. Maybe we should fly out and hire a car to tour round.'

'That's just great,' Debs retorted. She was regularly knocking holes in Jose's arguments, although it never seemed to faze him. 'We're going to do magic to force governments to act to prevent environmental damage and we go by plane and hire car! Oops! We'd be *adding* to pollution, so how could you expect magic to work?'

'Debs has a good point there,' commented Frances.

'But anything else would make the trip very long and probably impossible. One more plane and car journey isn't going to change global warming,' countered Nathan, balancing up the numbers in the debate.

They could count on him to bring in the rational point of view.

'It's quite logical, in't it, Captain?' rejoined Debs mockingly. 'I'm sorry, but you can't stand for one thing and do another. That's hypocritical.'

'OK,' said Jose. 'Compromise. We'll go by train, through the Channel Tunnel and onto the fast French TGV. Then when we get to the Auvergne, we'll hire a hybrid car, with low fuel consumption. There won't be buses going round black virgin shrines in the mountains.'

'Well, if there are,' added Frances. 'We hope *you* won't be doing schedules for 'em!'

The laughter brought an end to the argument. Jose's compromise was agreed.

'Anyway, we must start booking soon,' he reflected. 'July is not far away. How about we take two weeks off, just before the G8 summit? We book into Le Puy for the first few days and then take it from there. If we prefer, we can stay, or if not, move on.'

Once again, agreement. *This is going well but,* Frances wondered, *how'll we get on while on holiday? It's great, getting together in pub once or twice a week, but you find out who your real friends are when you're on holiday.* She had one or two painful memories of friendships that had gone sour, because of very different views of what to expect from hotels, how to ask for what you wanted, what kind of schedule you should keep for going to bed and getting up, what should be left lying around a shared hotel room, what should be done when someone got tired, how to agree to split up for separate activities and meet up again, how much drink to order on the hotel bill, which activities were within budget and which not, how to deal with airport delays, whether to go off to places you didn't know with guys you just met, etc., etc.

'Going to France and travelling around looking for shrines,' said Frances, reflectively, trying to be more positive and take pleasure at the thought. 'It reminds me o' *Da Vinci Code*. I really enjoyed that book. Fascinating to think that Jesus had descendants. Will we see any Da Vinci paintings over there?'

'Er, no,' answered Nathan, firmly. 'I don't think the Louvre is in the Auvergne. It's in Paris. What's more, the *Da Vinci Code* has been shown to be a load of bunkum. Historically, it doesn't stand up.'

Frances felt slightly miffed at suffering a put-down from her beloved Nathan; he was not normally someone with a superiority complex, but his scientific side was doing the talking now.

'However,' chipped in Debs, wanting to fight the men as usual. 'History's not the point. *Da Vinci Code* were popular because it told people how women had been suppressed by Christianity. It were a story but wi' truth in it.'

'Well, the *author* seemed to make a big thing of the historical aspects,' countered Nathan. 'I've seen TV programmes showing that all of his information was completely wrong.'

'Yes,' agreed Jose. 'Except for one thing. It *is* true that the Church suppressed gospels in which Mary Magdalene was more important than the other disciples. But, on the other hand, you'd be right in thinking there's no evidence that she had a child by Jesus. It seems to me that making her nothing more than a baby-carrier contradicts the claim that *Da Vinci Code* helps the cause of women. It's not true to the Gnostic texts. In them, she wasn't a mother but a spiritual leader.'

'You know, for once I agree with what you say on subject o' women,' said Debs, with a sigh, followed by a little laugh. 'It just turns her into another Madonna. Actually she was a heroine who turned her back on life o' prostitution and had the guts to visit the tomb of an executed man.'

Something connected. They all turned and looked at her with admiration and a certain amount of compassion. Jose suppressed a comment that there was no evidence that Mary Magdalene *was* actually a prostitute. Debs, the ex-hooker, a latter-day Mary Magdalene! They hadn't thought of that.

'Whose tomb will you visit?' asked Nathan, cautiously, putting a voice to the thoughts.

'Yours!' snapped Debs threateningly, then smiled to show him that it was in good humour. 'No, it's an interesting question. I think, like Mary Magdalene, I would go to tomb of a man who stood up for women when other men were attacking 'em and lose his life for it. I could believe in a Jesus like that. But not all that Son o' God stuff. God is a Father, he's got a Son and they all live happily wi' a masculine Holy Spirit in heaven. God the man rules and so men rule. It's as simple as that.'

'I not only *could* believe in a Jesus who stood up for women and died for it,' commented Jose. 'I *do* believe in a Jesus like that.'

Frances couldn't really get a foothold in this conversation; for her, *Da Vinci Code* had been a thoroughly good read, especially as it referred to art works, and she had believed every word of the history that it recreated. So she found a way in by turning to the one subject that was beginning to obsess her.

'Where were Goddess when Mary Magdalene went to tomb?' she asked.

It was her turn to get a startled silence and the full attention of the group. She could almost hear the wheels whirring as each of them sought for the most telling response to this challenging question. But Debs was first. Her answer was ready-made in her own understanding of the Goddess, forged in several years of Goddess witchcraft.

'Goddess were in Mary Magdalene,' she stated, triumphantly. 'That's one good thing about *Da Vinci Code*, it tells us Mary Magdalene is a type o' Goddess.' She shuffled and looked down at her shoes. 'Maybe rest is crap, though,' she added. 'Not that I've read it.'

'All the great critics don't read the books they write about,' laughed Jose. 'You know, I think it's time for another pint. And I think our friend the Templar knight over there... (pointing at Nathan)... is the one whose turn it is to seek the Grail.'

Late on, when getting home, Frances tried to get her dodgy computer to link into the internet, to do a search on black virgins and Le Puy. She also had it in mind that she had never found out more about the 'Priestesses of Delphi'. But computer was definitely saying no. She kept losing the link or the screen would freeze. *I must get Jose or Nathan round to fix this thing. Or maybe visit internet café. Or maybe get Nathan to find a book for me in University Library. Never mind. Life's good. Come here, Cass, time for cuddles. Do you want to cuddle someone stinking o' booze and all bleary eyed? Probably not, but it's what I give you free board and lodging for!*

On Saturday, Frances opted out of her planned shopping trip and confined herself to a stocking up of food and drink. She needed to save for France; did she really need more to wear? What about that time they moved Great Auntie Ruth as she downsized into a new bungalow? Frances had never seen so many pieces of clothing and pairs of shoes. Did Auntie Ruth really wear them all? The smaller wardrobe at the bungalow could not take them all and so Ruth had to be persuaded to give some to charity shops. Not an easy task! Frances had then vowed to keep her own wardrobe to a sensible size, but what she called the 'Auntie Ruth hoarder factor' was proving a problem; new things were important, good for the soul, but old things one had got attached to, well, the soul needed them too. So they all ended up in the cupboard. A friend of her mother's, Pat, had once remarked that she needed to throw things out from time to time and replace them, because she couldn't bear the thought of having the same possessions on her death-bed as she had had when she left home at eighteen; it would make life seem so short. 'Make sure you make changes regularly, move your house, get yourself new job, find yourself new friends and lovers. It makes life seem longer, you know.' Frances felt that she had both tendencies in her, the 'Auntie Ruth hoarder factor' and the 'Pat chuck-it-out method'. But which would prevail?

She phoned Cyn and Jo to call off the rendezvous in town. Both were in upbeat mood. Jo had had a new job for a couple of weeks now and it was going well. This helped to make the task of telling her about the coming of Carson easier.

'I don't care, G.R.C.'s really behind me now. I'm glad for you though,' she added hurriedly, as an afterthought.

Cyn had only just met her new man. She really laid it on thick. It only took a few seconds for Frances to be reminded how self-centred she found Cyn at times.

'Brilliant bloke. Ex-army; well-built, strong as an ox. Gives me owt I ask for. Good fun. And drop dead gorgeous. When'll we make foursome wi' you and that Gary?' she asked, unwittingly.

Frances sighed inwardly. *Oh well,* she thought, *I have my Goddess, I don't need bloke.* But really, she wanted both Goddess and Nathan.

That night, Frances decided to stay in and spend time doing a prolonged ritual, based on what she remembered of the equinox rituals at Avebury. It had occurred to her that she was getting complacent, as the rituals had slipped since the great news on Wednesday. Maybe she should keep them up. It was unusual, for a Saturday, not to go out anywhere, but it wasn't the spiritual adventurer night and she was really into them just at the moment. *I wonder what they do on Sat'day?* It was a kind of unwritten rule that Fridays were their gathering days, except for things like weekends out in Avebury, of course. She preferred not to step out with her normal Saturday night girlfriends and it was a good idea not to bump into Gary while out in town. Not yet, anyway.

The phone went while she was in the middle of eating, so she ignored it. No message. It went again as she started the ritual, so she ignored it again. *I'll check the caller's number when I've finished,* she thought. 'The caller withheld their number.' *Bloody cold sales again, fancy calling on Sat'day night! Must be summat they want to sell to old people!* On the third call attempt, she answered it. *I'll give 'em a piece o' my mind!* She went icy cold when she heard the voice. It was the voice of a man but muffled in such a way that you could not hear it very well, deliberately disguised. It spoke in an obviously fake posh accent in a polite tone, which reminded her of Tony Curtis doing his impression of Cary Grant in *Some Like It Hot*. But the content of the call did not have the charm or humour of a Tony Curtis or a Cary Grant. It was the most frightening thing she'd ever heard. The false politeness and lack of expletives made it even more terrifying. She would rather have met the caller in a crowded place and face him, than have to listen to him over the phone and on her own with no one but the cat for company. What was being said to her was so terrible that she froze and could neither reply nor put the phone down, but she stood there silently as every word came out, until the phone clicked and went dead at the other end. Each word went straight to her heart like a poisoned arrow and paralysed her; she felt as if her limbs were being amputated, so that she couldn't move to summon help. Sticks and stones may break my bones but words will never hurt me. These words did.

'Hello, Frances. Let me introduce myself. I'm a man who likes hurting women, really hurting them. I'm looking forward to hurting you. Women like you deserve to be hurt. Women like you need something unpleasant to happen to them and I'm going to make that happen. I'm really going to hurt you. Next time I see you, you'll find out what I mean. Until then…'

After his voice had been replaced by the call tone, she just about had the presence of mind to check the number again. 'The caller withheld their number.'

## 15

## Refuge

Frances, too shocked to shed tears at this point and shaking so much that she could barely operate the phone, instinctively called N, D and J in turn on their mobiles. They all declared that they would arrive at her flat just as quickly as they could. Nathan was on a night out in town with some University colleagues; Debs at home reading; Jose taking his turn to look after grandma. Strange that the same instrument which had carried the terror of an unknown attacker now brought the comforting voices of loyal friends. Strange too that these three people, not known to Frances only two months before, should now be the ones to whom she turned in her hour of distress. It could not be her parents, as Mum's nerves would not stand it; it seemed to Frances that more long-standing companions, Sal, Jo, Cyn, would not have offered the same empathy.

Before the cavalry arrived, she had only one thought: that the disguised voice was Gary's. Gary the good impersonator, who had made her laugh with his George Bush; Gordon Brown; Victoria and David Beckham; Ant and Dec. He could certainly disguise his voice if it were muffled. Gary the one who just said 'OK' when she told him the relationship was off – no anger, no

130     Calling

argument. Perhaps this was his way of retaliating and that's all it was. But, surely, it was much too much of an overreaction, too frightening to shrug off. How could you not take it seriously? *Gary the secret psychopath? Oh God, no!*

Nathan arrived first, as his gathering was not too far away and he ran; Jose next, because he came in the dilapidated Citroen; Debs last, as Chapeltown was too far to walk and so she had to wait for a late bus before walking from town. Each heard Frances' description of the call. Each had her or his own way of responding.

'This is terrible but we must look for the positives,' said Nathan. 'The fact is that, if he were going to harm you, he would have done that by now. He wouldn't have warned you. He's just trying to frighten you. It's awful but that's all there is to it. I'll stay here tonight and as many nights as you want me to.'

'We must make sure he's arrested immediately,' said Jose. 'People like that need locking up for a very long time, so that they're no longer a danger to others. Poor Frances! How could anyone do that to you?'

'You must get out of here,' said Debs. 'I know a refuge house, hidden away in back streets o' suburbs. They'll take you in while this is sorted out. Threats against women are more common than people realise. Don't worry, Frances, I know all about this and how to deal with it. These kind o' men are weak, in actual fact.'

Then the police arrived an hour after Debs. They had their response too.

'We'll have a word with this Gary first thing tomorrow,' said the policewoman, looking to her male colleague for confirmation. 'But there's nothing we can do unless we have proof. You'd better change your number and go ex-directory.'

'Surely you can do *something* to protect Frances,' argued Jose.

The policewoman shrugged.

'Well, I'm afraid this type of call happens all too often and so we have to be convinced that the caller represents a real threat. If anything happens to suggest that, we can install an alarm system or try to get him to phone again and trace the call. But these things are expensive.'

Frances started to get tearful and upset.

'Expensive? Isn't my safety worth anything to the police? Isn't that what I pay my taxes for?'

The policewoman looked as if she were used to that kind of reaction.

'Experience tells us that these threats are very rarely realised. I repeat: if something occurs to suggest that this man will actually get violent, we will step up our response. Have you someone to look after you for the time being?'

It was decided, somewhere amid all the urgent voices speaking, that Nathan should stay the night with Frances and answer the phone if it rang. The police officers gave Nathan a hotline in case he needed to use it. They agreed to interview Gary the next day at his home and would then report back by telephone to the flat. When they had done so, Debs and Frances would go down to the refuge house with enough in the way of clothes for Frances to stay away for a few nights. Nathan would continue to sleep in the flat and see if there were any more calls or whether anybody came round. In order for the possibility of his talking to the caller to find out more, they wouldn't change the number quite yet. Then, if there happened to be no arrest, Frances would come back with Debs and pick up more things and stay at the refuge for longer. It was going to be carried out with military precision; Nathan wrote it all down. Frances was the only quiet one, nodding from time to time and only speaking when she was asked a direct question. The police wanted to know as much as possible about her relationship with Gary. Was he the only partner in her life at the moment? 'Yes.' How long had she been going out with him? 'Just a month or so.' Was there anyone else just before that? 'Not for a few month.' Did he show any signs of violence? 'Not really, but he looked like he were trying to suppress his anger sometimes, like when I didn't want to sleep with him.' Had she done anything else to upset him, other than ending the relationship? 'No. But his friend saw me laughing and joking the day after I ended it.'

Everyone but Nathan finally left. Frances now achieved the goal that she had secretly harboured since mid-February: to have Nathan all to herself overnight in the flat. But she hadn't wanted it *this* way, she being terrified and he sleeping on the sofa. *Funny how prayers get answered,* she thought. *You get what you wanted, literally speaking, but not how you wanted it.* She remembered that old Edgar Allen Poe horror story, *The Monkey's Paw*. An elderly couple are given a magical talisman, a monkey's paw and are told that they can use it to gain three wishes. They wish for a sum of money but only receive it in compensation for the death of their son, mangled in a factory accident. And so it goes on. Moral of story: wish carefully. Pray carefully. *'Goddess, please let Nathan stay overnight wi' me in flat.' Sorted! Oh sorry, Frances, you should have mentioned that you didn't want a terrifying phone call to be the means by which it happened! Can't change it now, they won't re-package answers to prayers at the factory. No refunds.*

A long night, no sleep until a series of dozes from about four o' clock. Nathan snores. *How can he sleep while I'm in danger?* Then bad dreams: everyone in the Ordering Office is receiving death threats by phone from the Yorkshire Ripper. Jose crashes a bus into the River Aire. Mum cries into the phone and Dad shouts 'They're going to hurt you! They're really going to hurt you!' Gary in prison but there are no bars to keep him in.

In the morning, breakfast for Nathan alone as Frances couldn't eat anything, despite his encouragement. He did his best to reassure her: this sort of thing happens all the time, 99.9% of cases are empty threats, ignore him and he'll get bored. *Why don't you put your arms around me,* thought Frances, frustrated. *That would make me feel better, not these matter-of-fact statements.*

Debs and Jose came round mid-morning.

'He'll be down at police station right now,' said Debs, looking her most scary.

'Don't suppose he'll admit it,' replied Frances, gloomily. 'There won't be any evidence and he'll be allowed home to do it all over again.'

'If he does, I have some friends that'll pay him a visit,' said Debs, quietly but with menace. 'Girls can be heavies too, you know.'

Jose shuddered at the talk of violence. Nathan looked at football results on teletext. Debs finally persuaded Frances to eat some toast and drink tea.

Lunchtime. Still no call from the police. 1 p.m. Debs calls police station. No, the officer dealing with that isn't available right now. A message can be left. 1.30. She tries again, same result. 2 p.m. Debs falls foul of the police receptionist after trying to be forceful and is warned not to call again but to wait for a reply. 3 p.m. Debs shouts and starts to storm around the flat. Jose has to stop Debs and Nathan arguing, as Debs cannot take his attempts to soothe everyone any longer. Frances falls asleep, exhausted.

'Best thing,' all three say in unison, sharing a grimace between them.

Frances slept until 4.17, when she woke with a start. The phone was ringing in her dream, but it turned out to be real. Debs got there first.

'Yes, I see... Couldn't you have pressed him harder?... OK. Sorry... Yeah, OK. I'll take her to refuge now.'

She put the phone down.

'They've interviewed him but he's not owning up. They had to let him go. They'll keep in touch, they've got our mobile numbers. Don't worry, I'll not let owt happen to you.'

Then Frances' mobile went off. Gary's name appeared on the screen. She didn't answer it, just started to sob and threw the phone onto the sofa. A minute or so later, beeps told them that a text was coming through on it.

'What does it say?' asked Frances through her tears.

'I'll read it word for word,' answered Nathan. 'Frances, surely you can't believe I'd do that to you. Please ring me. I'd never harm you. Gary.'

'Bastard!' cried Debs. 'They always turn to sweet talk after they've made threats.'

Frances now wailed uncontrollably for some minutes and buried her head in the sofa. When they finally got her to say something, it was blurted out with a hammering of a fist into an unfortunate cushion.

'It weren't him! It weren't him! What have I done to him? Of course it weren't him!'

'How do you know?' asked Jose, until now unnaturally quiet.

'He only knows my mobile number. Why would he use land line? He never uses land line. It can't have been him last night!'

'Are you sure?' asked Nathan.

'Yeah, I'm sure. I'm sure. What a fool I am. Of course, it were that John Taylor. He hates me, he made it clear last week.'

'Does *he* know your land line number?' continued Nathan, rather cautiously, aware that his questioning might lead to grief from either of the women who, from his point of view, just seemed to 'know' things rather than attempt any proper analysis in situations like this.

'No, but he could have looked it up,' said Frances, sniffing, tears pouring down her cheeks. 'My name's not very common.'

'Well then, so could Gary,' said Nathan, ever more softly each time he talked.

Frances had a logic all of her own.

'But Gary knows my mobile number. And now I just know it weren't him. I can tell from his message. I'd better phone him.'

'No, you mustn't.' Debs was firm but gentle. 'He's manipulating you, can't you see? You've dumped him, so he's frightened you; now he's going to play the injured party to get you back. But he's shown his true colours. You must avoid him now.'

Frances was extremely apologetic for getting them to believe her accusation against Gary, but she had changed her mind and she was adamant. It wasn't him. She phoned and started by asking him if she could keep the call brief, she was so upset. Then she told him that she was sorry, so, so sorry.

'I were frightened, Gary. I saw your friend watching me in pub other night when I were enjoying myself. But I were only laughing because my boss is leaving next month.'

'None of my friends has said owt to me, Frances. I don't blame you for ending it, it's your right. No one can demand that anyone be in relationship with 'em, I've always said that. I don't hold it against you and I'd never threaten you.'

'I know. Thanks, Gary. Look, I'll call you in a few weeks when all this is settled, OK?'

Then she ended the call and turned to the others: Debs unconvinced, Nathan pensive, Jose uneasy.

'We'll have to tell police it were John Taylor,' she said.

'Frances, you can't just keep...,' Nathan began, but she was already phoning.

Fortunately, the policewoman was in. Frances blurted out the change of chief suspect. The policewoman finished what Nathan had begun to say.

'You can't just go from one suspicion to another and accuse everyone on the way.'

But, having heard Frances' description of the events in the office of the week before, she agreed to interview Taylor.

'But he'll be the last man we talk to without really good evidence,' she insisted.

Frances packed a bag. Jose drove her and Debs to Middleton, where the refuge was situated. He had to drop them several hundred yards away as no man, not even a timid gay one like Jose, could know its location. They scurried through the streets, mostly in silence except for a brief exchange. The house that greeted them was a sizeable but shabby detached, two semis having been knocked into one hostel, but the purpose of the house was deliberately concealed to the outsider. The double garden was full of shrubs and wild flowers. They went up the few yards of the path with Debs trying to get Frances to walk alongside rather than behind her. She knocked on the door; there was no bell and the knocker was missing. After the sound of running feet, it opened: a brown-skinned child, about eight years old, stood there. With big dark eyes and curly hair, she looked up at them.

'Hello, Lucy,' said Debs, although the little girl made no sign of recognising her. 'Is your mummy home?'

The little girl ran from the door without inviting them in, and they could hear her shouting, 'Mum-my!' Debs slipped through the open door and beckoned Frances through. There was a musty smell of old carpets which needed replacing; the pale yellow wallpaper patterned with blue pansies had seen better days. The smell of cigarettes hovered in the air; someone had clearly ignored the ban on smoking in public places. A hostile-looking short-haired young woman covered in tattoos came out of a door at the other end of the corridor, saw them, then turned and disappeared again. Frances wondered whether she had left the frying pan for the fire.

But then she met Irene. Clearly, Irene was well suited for the role of welcoming anxious women and children into the initially unsettling atmosphere of the refuge house. Her smile was as warm as a crackling fireplace in a comfortable country pub; everything about her was maternal and soothing. A tall woman with a broad, bonny brown face and dark hair tied back, she looked about forty, with the signs of someone growing from slim young adult into a more portly middle age. She wore a blue V-necked pullover with the sleeves pushed up, and black jeans. A silver locket hung around the brown neck, with its several moles and freckles. As she and Debs exchanged words of greeting, she took Frances' bag in one hand, her arm in the other, and led her through to a small living room, its shabby three-piece suite squeezed in next to a rather battered wooden dining table in one corner.

'Sit down there,' she said, with softness in her voice showing concern. 'I'll make you a cuppa.'

Frances began to weep while she was out of the room and the tears were not stemmed by the sight of Lucy peering round the door. The combination of anxiety, the loss of her home comforts and Irene's kindness were too difficult a combination for her emotions to handle. Debs put an arm round her shoulders as they both sat together on the small sofa.

Irene remained caring but was businesslike as she came back into the room with tea and chocolate digestives.

'Lucy,' she said. 'Go up to your room and play with your dolls for a few minutes. Mummy's got to talk to this nice new lady.' With Lucy gone, Irene began to set the scene for Frances. 'Debs phoned me about you this morning. Luckily, we've got a small room free at present. You can stay as long as you like, although Debs said it might only be for a few days. There's two other women and they've two children each, plus my Lucy and me, and my co-worker who's off duty tonight. We're an annex attached to the main Leeds refuge and operate for clients who would benefit from a more intimate community and domestic routine. There's just three rules, which are very important. First, don't talk to anyone outside about this house, its whereabouts or its occupants, not even to friends and family. Second, no contact with anyone who has potential to hurt you or anyone else. Third, no drugs. I would also add: don't try to force women here to open up about their past unless they volunteer it first. I hope you see why those things are necessary.'

'Yeah,' nodded Frances. 'I'll stick by 'em.'

'OK,' Irene continued. 'Have some dinner tonight and I'll introduce you to the others. Debs, you'd be very welcome to stay too. For the time being, Frances, regard this as your home. Most important of all, I'm here to talk if you want me. Anytime, I really mean it, anytime.'

Frances, still accompanied by Debs, was shown to her room, tiny but homely. Someone had placed a vase containing a variety of fresh flowers on the windowsill and there was a picture of a river scene above the bed, restful to the eyes. Before they returned back downstairs for the meal – by now they could smell cooking – Debs opened up a difficult topic.

'What about your work, now that you suspect one o' your bosses?' she asked, gently. 'You can't go back in those circumstances.'

'I've been thinking about that,' replied Frances, sombrely. 'I'll take tomorrow off ill because o' shock. But I must go back in Tuesday, that's the way it has to be.'

'How come?' queried Debs, unconvinced.

'Well, because... one, I've had too many sickies off and I've been told that there's a limit. I need to save for France and they might hold my pay back.'

'Couldn't you stay off on grounds o' harassment?' suggested Debs.

'I won't be able to prove harassment unless Taylor admits it, so that won't help me. They can sack me. I'm already under a warning, you know.' Frances sounded a little calmer now and more focussed. 'And two, what were my victory o' last week worth, if I can't go back in and face him?' she asked. She turned her head so that the grey-green eyes blazed at Debs, who for once had to concede to a more intense gaze. 'Goddess is on my side, so I must go in. Or it were all for nothing. I've decided. Yes, I must go in Tuesday.'

# 16

## Fool's Day

The refuge children, all being Lucy's age or under, ate before the adults. However, none of them found their way to bed before the evening meal, so they were very much in evidence as the cooking and eating took place. There was a two year old, looking every bit the little urchin, feet blackened by playing outside and a constantly runny nose. He was gaining little words and phrases all the time and the older children delighted in teaching him things that he shouldn't say, so as to cause offence to adults. His elder sister was about four and very boisterous; she expressed her affection by jumping at people and hitting them wildly before being yelled at by her mother, Hannah, only about twenty, fair-skinned and blonde like her children, with prominent cheekbones and a freckled nose. She was the woman they had seen in the corridor and had worried Frances the moment she saw her; thin and gaunt, almost emaciated, chain smoking, with a hostile demeanour that suggested fearful anxiety.

Danny, another four year old, was generally subdued and sullen. It was difficult for him to make his mark on the small community with the antics of the little girl dominating the scene and with an extrovert six year old brother, Jake, who aspired to adult conversation and constantly fed the newcomers pieces of information about his friends, toys and things that he'd seen during the day. He was very friendly and likeable, but there was something about him that made Frances uneasy. Both boys had dark curly hair and a stocky build. Their mother, Kelly, sat in the corner of the room, a squat, broad-shouldered woman with shoulder-length nut-brown hair and sallow skin, seemingly a few years older than Hannah. She was chatty, although without Irene's warmth, and she tried to give the air of someone very confident and sorted out.

Among all these, Irene stood out like a Mother Teresa amongst the needy, doing most of the cooking and asking only a little help of the others, although Debs was keen to demonstrate her professional presence by helping out. Irene answered Lucy's questions with great patience; the little girl tried to establish her seniority by getting her mother to admonish the other children when they stepped out of line. But Irene, though attentive to her, was concerned not to take away parental authority from the other women, and she was able to establish a measure of order by saying only a little now and again to achieve it.

As they all sat in the cramped space for dinner, a spag bol hit the table with plenty of grated mild cheddar cheese and a leafy side salad.

'Black pepper?' smiled Irene, mimicking an Italian waiter, suspending a large grinder over the table.

'Go on then,' replied Debs and, turning to Hannah, tried to get into conversation with her. 'How are you, Hannah? Any news on that flat?'

Hannah just shook her head without looking up from the spaghetti that she was cutting into small pieces.

'I'll have a word with council first thing in morning then,' said Debs reassuringly.

'Best not bother'. Kelly came in. 'They made right mess o' my cousin's flat. She were top o' waiting list, then some bugger made balls up and she ended up on bottom.' Then, without warning, she turned to Frances. 'What're you here for, love? You don't look like battered wife type to me.'

Irene reinforced house rules.

'Now, Kelly, you know we don't go round asking people about their situation.'

'Well, I don't mind telling you,' said Frances. 'I'm receiving abusive phone calls from someone who's threatening me.'

'Phone calls!' retorted Kelly sarcastically. 'That's nowt. I wish I had phone calls. Better than the bastard actually hitting you.'

The following day, Frances phoned in sick and then went back to bed, where she remained until lunchtime. She dozed off repeatedly and, in the waking moments, tried to concentrate on invoking the Goddess to help her. Irene brought up tea and biscuits. Debs called to take her out for lunch and tried to dissuade her from going to work the next day.

'You can't go, love. If it's Taylor, he could be dangerous.'

'I'll tell Security to watch out for me. Anyway, he won't do owt whilst he's at work, he's too bothered about his new job.'

'Are you sure that it *is* him, then? Gary's still my number one suspect!'

'No, I just know it weren't him. I made a mistake, that's all. But Taylor hates me, he senses I forced Ballard out. But he'll not touch me at work. I've got to go in, Debs. Otherwise what? Day after day under bed sheets in refuge?'

Debs sighed, then she reached down and pulled out a card from inside her bag. On the front was the outline of an angel, a misty figure in blue on a white background. As she looked at the image, Frances felt a sudden tremor, as if a slight gust of air had blown through the café.

'Did you feel that, Debs? A wind?'

'No. We're inside and the door's closed. You're imagining it. It's quite understandable. You're frightened, but you don't need to be, Frances. We're all with you and we won't let harm come to you.'

142   *Calling*

The support was confirmed by the message inside the card: Debs had written words to the effect that Frances would never be alone, and she had got Nathan and Jose to sign it.

This helped Frances get through the afternoon.

Midway through the long evening, Debs called to say that the police had called her. Frances had accidentally left her phone switched off and they couldn't get through. The news was that the police had interviewed Taylor but, as with Gary, he refuted the charge adamantly and there was no evidence. They had asked how he would manage to work with Frances given the seriousness of the allegation, but he had countered that he was not going to be there for long and he wouldn't let it interfere with their working relationship. Debs tried again to persuade Frances not to go to work. But Frances thought that the police's involvement ensured that he wouldn't do anything. He was too much a career man.

'How do you know he's not a psycho?' asked Debs, grimly, before dropping the subject.

And then Tuesday morning, April Fool's Day of all days – back to Dracula's castle. It had become a sunny place over the last week, but now it recovered its former gloom. Frances imagined dark towers standing like ghoulish shadows against the scudding clouds. The bats were squeaking again, the nails had been prised off and were no longer keeping the coffins shut. The endangered heroine tried to make the best of living out of a suitcase (although she had played the distressed daughter role well enough to persuade Irene to do some last-minute ironing for her). And so, Fräulein, into Jose's coach and four and off into the Transylvanian mountains…

…And through the office door. John Taylor came straight over to speak to Frances the minute she came in. She trembled inwardly on seeing him and almost passed out but, determined not to cave in, she just sat impassively as he pulled a chair over and began to talk to her quietly, almost under his breath, in the somewhat vain attempt to prevent others from hearing. He knew better than to ask her to step into a private office. But, although upset, he was not at all aggressive; consequently, Frances was a little thrown by his attempt to be reassuring and reconciliatory rather than confrontational. Being Frances, the resolve with which she set out to dismiss his overture soon became shrouded in doubt.

'Frances, the police have been to see me. They said you think I have been threatening you on the phone. I need to assure you and convince you that I would never ever do such an awful thing. I understand why you might suspect me; I haven't been easy on you since you came here. But I have never used threats of violence against anybody and certainly would not do so against you.'

'You were very angry wi' me on Friday,' Frances whispered back defiantly. 'To say you've not been easy on me is an understatement, you've persecuted me. You want to hurt me because you're leaving and you've got no power over me any more.'

'I thought your work needed sorting out, that's all,' replied Taylor, trying to keep the calm and friendliness in his voice. 'I think that, for a senior clerk, you could achieve a great deal more than you do. But that doesn't mean that I hate you or that I would do anything so terrible as abusing you on the phone.'

'You're a control freak,' retorted Frances. 'What about my friend Jo? She had to leave and needed counselling. There's no humour in this office. And I were beginning to bring some fresh air into place, so you couldn't take it.'

John Taylor took a deep breath, as if he were preparing a major speech. He continued in a low but urgent voice.

'Let me explain things. When I started in management, Frances, I was only a young man. I was perhaps appointed a little too early. As you can see, I hardly overflow with charisma. So I didn't find it easy to get the clerical workers to take me seriously. The girls used to chat about their nights out for the first hour of the day, they had long coffee breaks and there was plenty of horseplay in the office. The work didn't get done. My own boss was a weak man, nearing retirement and suffering bad health. The management couldn't do much with him, so they put me under pressure to improve the place. But I found it too difficult. I had plenty of sleepless nights in those days, I can tell you. I might have hoped to be promoted again in a few years, but it didn't happen. And then the old chap got his golden handshake and they brought in Ballard. He was a strong man and that inspired me. It was his philosophy that the work had to be a priority and only if it got done could the employees start relaxing. It's tricky, Frances, managing young people who have no interest in the business, only in their wage packet. So I adopted Ballard's approach – strong authority and no nonsense. He helped me cultivate it. And so I started getting good appraisals and once again set my sights on higher things. But certain people, who came along from time to time, threatened to put me back to square one. People like your friend Jo, for instance. Look, Frances, do you want a coffee? I'll bring one over. Milk, sugar?'

Frances nodded, grimly.

'White, no sugar, thanks.'

She felt bad. How easy it was to gain her sympathetic ear; she now felt guilty and foolish. Who else would she accuse? She looked down, dimly aware of the growing interest in the little tête-à-tête. Becca, Tricia and Katie were straining every sinew and ear muscle to hear what was going on. They found it hard to believe that John Taylor was making coffee for one of them; it should be the other way round. Was it an April Fool's joke, or maybe the Carson era was here already? But, no, there must be something wrong, something had happened. Taylor had been called away from his desk yesterday morning and had returned looking ashen. Yes, something *had* happened. But what? As for Frances, the unease deepened as it suddenly struck her: if not Gary, if not John Taylor, then who? And then Taylor came back with the coffee.

He sat down and inhaled another long breath. It was clear that he was keen to get things off his chest. The visit from the police had shocked him into needing a cathartic experience. Anyway, he was leaving the company soon.

'OK. I was talking about Jo, wasn't I? Well, Jo – I'm sorry, I know she's your friend – was one of the worst clerical workers we'd had for some time. She really wanted to chat all the time, she was sloppy in her work, she had no regard for authority. It wasn't that she was insolent or rebellious, more that her head was so much in the clouds that she didn't *realise* she was obstructing the work of the office. I said, let's see if we can move her on to another department, but Ballard would have none of it. He has principles about that sort of thing. No, he said. Why should it become somebody else's problem? We'll just have to clamp down on her.'

'She were really upset,' interjected Frances. 'Maybe you didn't see her soft side. Actually, she's all soft but people don't realise it, because she's so dizzy. She likes to flirt and play; she's always surprised when people get mad at her.'

'Maybe you're right,' conceded John Taylor. 'Perhaps we went too far. But for me, it was life and death. I had to gain the upper hand, or see my management career go out of the window. The others were fine, we could get them to work OK. But Jo threatened to turn everything upside down. So we put her under a strict regime.'

'Well, you succeeded in getting rid of her,' said Frances. 'But I see what you're saying. I suppose it were just a case o' misunderstanding on both sides. But what about me?'

'Ah,' sighed Taylor; then he grimaced and nodded his head. 'We'd been told that you were all right. We needed someone badly and Finance were overstaffed. But we like to run a tight ship and it was obvious in a couple of days that you weren't quite the experienced administrator that we were looking for. I'm sorry to say this, I don't want to offend you, but you seemed very immature for your age. You didn't seem to want to do your work properly. So we decided we needed to put a bit of pressure on you too. We wanted to have a good ending here. I knew that Ballard was going to take early retirement and I was looking for jobs elsewhere with more responsibility, now that I felt more confident. We didn't want to end in disruption; we wanted to hand things over to our successors in good order. I wasn't going to compromise all that by being friendly with someone so obviously young at heart as you. Mind you, I have realised in the last few weeks that there's more to you than I first thought. I began to sense that you might have the power to influence people and so I guess that made you even more of a threat. But even then, that would never provoke me to criminal or abusive behaviour like the phone call you received.'

Frances had switched off a sentence or two before and so she didn't appreciate the compliment. Her heart was sinking fast, even lower than it had reached with all the weight of threatening calls and two nights in the refuge.

'So when did you decide to leave?' she asked, with a certain desperation. 'And when did Mr Ballard decide to retire?'

'Some months ago,' replied Taylor. 'As soon as I heard, I started to look for more senior jobs and finally I got one with my third interview.'

'OK,' said Frances. She now needed to end the conversation, so she decided to accept the conciliation. 'I'm really sorry I accused you; I didn't know where else to look and maybe I misjudged you. I suppose we'll not be working together that long, so I just wish you well in your new job. I'll try to do my work properly in last few weeks and hopefully you can come to like me after all. Thanks for telling me your side o' things. Do you mind if I go outside for a few minutes to get some air? It's been a difficult time.'

John Taylor smiled in agreement, showing warmth that she had not seen in him before. He slipped away from her desk, all the eyes following him as he went. *Nowt as queer as folk: who'd have thought it, Taylor being nice to me?* But it didn't compensate for the despair that she was feeling and which she needed to face on her own. So she snatched her bag and made for the door. She needed a little walk.

The day was grey with a mist that hung stubbornly in the air, resisting the spring sun that vainly tried to peer through at the creatures enveloped below. The company resided in a shabby urban street, with a fence one side, covered in flaking posters, a derelict garage next door, the forecourt bare with its pumps removed, fag ends everywhere and waste paper blowing about in the wind. This all formed an appropriate backdrop for Frances' agonised walk to nowhere. The one thing that had kept her going since the call, in all the chaos of the refuge, was the belief that the Goddess had got rid of her tyrannical bosses for her. She had come to depend on her conviction that the Goddess had brought in a new era because she cared for Frances, heard her prayers and responded to her magic. But now the awful truth was: she hadn't. Ballard and Taylor had already decided to leave before Frances came to Ordering, started the rituals, went to Avebury, had the visions. It was all just coincidence. She had been wrong about everything, absolutely everything. Wrong about the effect of the rituals. Wrong about Gary. Wrong about John Taylor. Could the abusive caller be Ballard? No, she knew that was wrong too. The situation was even worse – some completely unknown stalker was phoning her in the middle of the night. Perhaps a serial killer who picked people at random out of the telephone directory? He could be close at hand, lurking round the side of the deserted garage building or on the other side of the fence, staring at her through one of the many gaps and splits in the corrugated iron. Frances shuddered, her desire to walk suddenly over. She went back into G.R.C. It was safer inside. Dracula was outside the castle, after all.

# 17

# Spirits of the East

Frances had arranged to meet the adventurers in the pub that night as a follow-up to the events of the weekend. She was desperate to see them, yet she felt uncomfortable. How could she face them and admit that she had over-hyped the effectiveness of the ritual magic? How could she confess to them that, for the second time in just over two days, she had reported a man to the police for making malicious phone calls and then completely absolved him on the strength of one conversation? She would have to throw herself on their mercy. Would they see through her at last: the fake visionary? The so-called 'special' one who was just a bit dippy and weak and had blundered into being a victim, at the hands of she didn't know who. Maybe Nathan or Jose? Frances groaned inwardly. She was getting into a paranoid state where she blamed everyone.

Well, at least she could rely on Debs to be sympathetic, however things turned out; Debs was always on the side of a woman suffering the threat of violence. And it was Debs who met her from work to take her straight into town for an early drink and something to eat before they met the others in their usual haunt. Debs sensed that Frances was not in the mood for much talking, so she just slipped her arm into Frances' and nothing was said until they sat down in the rather-too-brightly-lit city centre café. The first news was not good: it deepened the gloom.

'I have to tell you, Frances,' said Debs quietly. 'That there's been another call, last night at your flat. Nathan listened at first then interrupted, giving him a warning. Caller hung up.'

'What did he start to say?' asked Frances, very wearily, hardly wanting to know the answer.

Debs grimaced and looked awkward. She felt impelled to tell the truth, but she knew that Frances would get even more depressed on hearing it. She sighed.

'Summat on lines that him not coming round yet didn't mean he were giving up and going away. But it means nowt, Frances, I'll not let him hurt you.'

Frances slumped onto the table, her head on her arms.

'You order,' she mumbled, 'But not for me – I can't eat and I can't drink. I might as well be dying.'

'Please don't say that,' replied Debs, trying to sound encouraging. 'It'll work out. He's all talk, this bloke. Believe me, I've seen and heard it before. We're all with you on this. You *must* eat to keep your strength up.'

'OK,' agreed Frances, her head remaining down. 'Just plain omelette and salad. Wi' coffee, black. But there's summat else really getting to me. The rituals didn't achieve owt. Ballard and Taylor were already planning to leave before I met you and the guys. It were just lucky coincidence, not Goddess.'

Debs thought for a moment, then reached over and shook Frances by the elbow quite vigorously in her disagreement.

'No, you don't understand. It don't work like that. Fact is, is you found out about it right after you did ritual, didn't you? So your magic worked. You did it and then things got better... well, apart from calls, but your magic weren't about them and we'll soon sort them out. Anyway, what if Ballard and Taylor had changed their minds and not gone after all? They could've done at any point up to when they announced it to staff.'

Frances sat up.

'Maybe,' she said. 'But it's still not same as it were last week.'

Debs was keen to persuade her and kept shaking her by the arm, leaning over the table in her fervour.

'Look, look,' she argued. 'You did magic and then got the news you wanted. That's all there is to it. How it came about, who thought what when, that don't matter. Keep doing magic now and you'll see what I mean. You'll get rid o' mystery caller as well. Don't you see, it's all just means by which Goddess shows you she's with you. Those calls are right scary but they're probably part of her plan. One, you learn what world's like... sadly. Two, you come to know you can call upon your magic to help you in any situation.'

Frances was lost in thought now. The idea that it was all a learning experience was very attractive, but part of her felt that believing it was just another futile and superstitious effort to avoid the harsh reality of life. Life as an urban woman in a modern city: a soul-destroying job, men who wanted to take advantage of her and, in some cases, hurt her. But, gradually, the thinking developed in a more optimistic direction: *well, maybe Debs is right, Taylor might not've got that job, it were his third try, after all. So maybe it weren't settled until I started my rituals. Fact is, Ballard and Taylor are going, Carson's coming.* The omelette came. She managed to eat it slowly as the nausea began to subside. Debs remained silent and looked steadily at her, concerned about her friend but not wanting to disturb the process by which Frances was trying to make sense of the situation. Eventually, nearing the end of the omelette, Frances restarted the conversation.

'So, do you think Goddess is leading me in a certain direction?' she asked. 'Even though it's not a very nice one?'

'Yes, I do,' answered Debs with conviction. 'Your magic is like a conversation between you and her. So keep talking, that's what I say. Change is painful, but you have to face it. That's not to excuse bastard who's phoning you. But maybe he's calling *you* instead o' someone else who he could've called. Someone who would've been destroyed by it. He's being led by Goddess in bad direction for him, because *you're* the one who's going to be strong, *you've* got magic, *you've* got friends. So he'll end up screwed. We'll do that together, Frances, through magic. Let's do a ritual wi' lads tonight. Back at your place, where it all took place. We'll defeat him together, that's what we'll do.'

Nathan and Jose were at the pub, bang on time. They were keen to show their support for the beleaguered Frances and hugged her warmly on her arrival, asking how she was bearing up at the refuge. Both men, unsurprisingly, accepted Debs' reading of the situation.

'The world of the spiritual is not to do with "a causes b", "b causes c",' stated Jose, firmly. 'It's to do with your experience. You carried out an equinox ritual at a sacred stone circle, had a vision in which you saw the work problem solved and then it was! That's very powerful, Frances. What led up to it is not the point.'

'That's exactly what I said,' added Debs, keen not to be upstaged.

'Yes, and I like your idea that Frances is being tested,' said Nathan. 'If she holds firm – and we're there to help her – her spiritual journey will be strengthened by all this. This is going to be a great spiritual adventure! We are the adventurers, after all.'

'Great,' responded Frances. 'I get victimised and for you it's some great thrill.'

But she smiled at him nevertheless. Although to some extent she was resisting it (she'd got used to wallowing in misery over the last three days), the excitement was infectious and she was catching it too. *Goddess won't let me down.* And so they left the pub with a vigorous sense of purpose, almost buoyant.

'We're like d'Artagnan and the three musketeers,' exclaimed Nathan. 'Have at you, sir! You'll feel the sharp point of my sword, that's a fact. That's for the phone call, you scoundrel!'

They all walked briskly up the hill past the University and down the main road to Hyde Park Corner, the long way round, as it was best to avoid Woodhouse Moor with psychopaths about. Frances was desperate to see Cass again.

'Has he been feeding you, my love?' she asked her, when they got in. 'What's it like, living wi' smelly man instead of a nice lady?'

Her repartee was coming back, thought Nathan. Must be a good thing.

'She's having the life of Riley with me in charge,' he countered. 'Alone with a handsome man who gives her chocolate and beer.'

'You'd better not be, it's bad for...' started Frances, but Nathan interrupted, pushing her head to one side playfully.

'Joke!'

'Oh, OK, ha ha. Well, Mr Joker, I see you're allergic to washing up.'

'Yes, it's a problem I have caused by deep childhood trauma. We had a drying up rota at home, terrible thing for a young boy who needed to be outside playing football. I have a profound terror of sinks now.'

While the banter went on, Debs had begun the business of setting up the ritual. She rearranged Frances' candles around the living room, a couple left on the mantelpiece, one on the small coffee table that she pushed to one side, one on each of the two windowsills, one on the TV. Then five on the floor, equally spaced out in a circle in the middle of the room between the armchairs. They were all carefully placed and then lit. She went to the kitchen, found a brown bread bun in a packet that Nathan had bought and put it on a small plate. Then she opened a bottle of Rioja, also acquired in Nathan's shopping trip. A search of a top cupboard, requiring a considerable stretch, revealed a set of wine glasses, cheap but nevertheless elegant with spiral patterns on the bowls and slender stems. All these she carried back into the living room and placed in the centre of the circle. Then she stopped the chatter between the others, which had carried on regardless of her preparations, by insisting that they all sat down on the armchairs.

'We'll get ourselves ready,' she said, 'By doing a little meditation. Try to clear your minds of everything, all your problems and hopes and fears. Just centre on Goddess. Use *that* if you want.'

She motioned to the picture of the Sistine Madonna, which still had prize of place after Frances' Saturday night ritual. She couldn't hide her distrust of the figure of the Virgin Mary being used as a symbol of the Goddess: the Virgin, humble servant of the Father God of Christianity, the role model for downtrodden mothers and nuns, the one who worshipped her own son as a god. She had told Frances that one day she would take her out and help her buy some stronger and more independent images of the Goddess: maybe horned Isis; the terrifying Kali with the many arms and knives; Demeter of the corn harvest; Athene the warrior maiden and wise one with her owl. Yet Debs had also observed that behind these goddesses in the myths stood even more powerful male deities: Osiris; Shiva; Hades; Zeus. Were there any images which captured the awesome wonder of the One Great Goddess, above and beyond all patriarchal religions and present in all women? Even those New Agey attempts to configure her had a sugary frailty about them. She wanted to find a picture of Brigantia, ancient goddess of northern England.

Debs' attempts to meditate on the Goddess were interrupted by a realisation that time was moving on. She stood up to cast the circle, using Frances' broom with its plastic handle, not much like a witches' besom.

'It's the symbolism of sweeping our sacred space clean that matters,' she said.

Each of the four of them knew enough to improvise the calling of the quarters and spirits. Debs had her own interpretation of the relationship of quarters to elements.

'It should link to place where we live, Britain. Water's to our west; fire to south because o' the heat o' southern lands; earth east, that's land mass o' Europe and Asia; air north, the windy North Atlantic.'

Frances liked how Jose's invocation of the East related to her situation.

'We call upon the spirits of the East,' he intoned in a relaxed and even rhythm. 'Spirits of the rising Sun, the Sun which throws its rays on hidden things and brings dark evils of the world into the bright light of day. Be with us and inspire our rite. Reveal to us who is causing this harm to our friend Frances. Blessed be.'

Frances concentrated as hard as she could on the Goddess who would care for her in the crisis and lead her through it into the daylight of knowing who was threatening her, thus stopping it from happening. They shared bread and wine as the fruits of the harvest, gifts of the Goddess who was in and of Nature.

'Just because Christians do it don't mean we can't,' Debs said. 'Consuming food in ritual is ancient and you can find it everywhere. It's pre-Christian.'

They made invocations and transferred positive energies around the circle. Then they came to a point where Debs would have suggested drumming and invoking the names of the Goddess, but there was no drum, so they had to clap instead. As the clapping started, Frances began to feel a little strange, a little light-headed. She looked over at the picture of the Sistine Madonna and then stopped moving. She stared into the air for a few seconds. Debs noticed first but continued to clap, sensing that this was one of Frances' trance moments. Then, with a little cry, Frances swooned and slipped into the armchair behind her. Once again, as at Avebury, they rushed over to help her. However, instead of anxiety there was a mood of anticipation and excitement: Frances had had another vision! She was still staring into space with a rapt expression, apparently at peace, although her body was contorted. Her head had fallen awkwardly on the side of the chair and one arm was tucked underneath her. It took more than a full minute before she was able to straighten up and began to speak.

'What happened?' asked Nathan. 'Did she come to you again?'

'Oh, yes,' replied Frances, breathlessly, almost in a whisper. 'She came to me again, all right. It were wonderful, wonderful.'

'Let's give her some wine,' suggested Debs. 'And give her time too, to compose herself.'

It took another few minutes of Frances sipping Rioja before she could articulate what she had seen.

'The Sistine Madonna came out o' wall,' she said, stopping every few words. The others could see that she was still in a state of wonderment. 'She came into our circle and started dancing in middle. Then she pointed to floor, and there on carpet were corpse that I saw in my dream, the one that said she were killed by sins. The Madonna raised her hand and, when she did, corpse stood up. She were alive again and so happy; then she thanked me and called me by my name. I tried to say, it weren't me who saved you, but no words came out. The Madonna seemed to have gone and it were only me and the woman. Then she gradually disappeared too while looking at me in a real loving way; that were it.'

Then the phone rang. In the hushed and reverent atmosphere of rituals and visions, it sounded like an air raid siren. They all looked shocked for a second before Nathan rushed to get it.

'Stop!' cried Frances. 'Let me, let me!'

Nathan was standing with his hand outstretched towards the receiver. He tried to protest.

'It might be...'

But Frances grabbed the phone and put it to her ear.

'Yes?'

It could have been Mum, or Dad, or Jo, or Cyn, or Sal, or a wrong number, or a cold sales call, or a cousin she hadn't seen for ages. It was none of these. It was the mystery caller, with his same mock politeness of three days before.

'Frances! Glad you're in. I didn't want you to forget how much I'm going to hurt you. I'm just waiting for the right moment. It's ...'

Frances interrupted, firmly but without shouting. The caller fell silent.

'You don't understand, do you? This is *my* moment. I'm in charge, not you. Or else you wouldn't have chosen this moment, *my* moment, to call. And now you're trapped, because you've walked into sunlight, you vampire, and if you don't know now, you soon will.'

The line went dead. He had nothing to say in reply.

The others were full of admiration.

'You were so calm.'

'That's thrown him now – he might have expected "Who are you?" or "Please go away", but you said much more than that. What a genius you are!'

'You had no fear a' all.'

'I did have fear,' replied Frances. 'But I'm also confident that my vision was telling me that lunatic can never hurt me. Now let's finish the ritual, shall we?'

The rite was completed. The spirits were given leave to depart, with many words of thanks for the inspiration that Frances had received and for her ability to remain calm in the face of danger. There were also many prayers for her safety. When it was all over, they noticed that it was 1 o'clock in the morning, on the eve of a workday. Time to go. Debs looked at Frances.

'Well, I don't know if you want to stay home now, seeing as you've got rid o' your fear,' she said, watching for Frances' reaction.

It came with a little ironical giggle.

'Debs,' she said. 'There's some maniac out there who might want to kill me and maybe I had a nice comforting spiritual experience but I haven't lost my sense o' self-preservation. Take me to refuge, please!'

Debs smiled.

'You're right, Goddess gives us strength, but she doesn't want us to be stupid. Jose, let's get Miss Dryburgh back.'

'Certainly, Ma'm,' replied Jose, bowing with a sweep of his arm indicating that they should follow him down to the car that had been parked outside several hours earlier for just this purpose.

# 18

# Mothers

Having taken a selection from the several enticing tapas dishes onto her plate, Sal stopped for a moment and looked up at Frances.

'So you're still at refuge. How long's it been?'

'Just over three weeks,' Frances replied.

'How can you stand it there?'

'I hated it at first, but now I've kind o' got used to it. It's OK, really. And I can't go home while phone maniac is still out there.'

She was catching up with Sal who, apart from snatched moments during work breaks, had taken a bit of a back seat in her life over the last month or so. One day in mid-April, they agreed to meet up after work at a tapas bar in Greek Street. The conversation caused Frances to reflect on the period since she received the phone calls.

First of all, she felt stronger. The vulnerability she had experienced on entering the refuge had lessened with the daily coming and going into the house. Irene had proved to be the rock that she seemed on first impressions; strong, steady and reliable, she soon encouraged Frances to leave the comfort of her room and take a hand in helping with the running of the house. Little Lucy, it turned out, had been adopted by Irene a couple of years before, an abandoned six-year-old urchin from somewhere in Bradford. It took all of Irene's emotional strength and patience to keep Lucy stable; her early life had left its legacy. She was the kind of child who slipped back into turmoil at the slightest reproach. Irene had a condition that meant she could not have children of her own. She said that this had caused difficulties with relationships in her twenties; one or two bad experiences led her to accept that life was better on her own. She ventured instead into putting all her energies into caring for young women at risk and, eventually, into running the house as a refuge overflow with a council grant.

Hannah and her children left the house, much to Irene's regret, as they were going back into the situation that had caused harm in the first place. Kelly, Jake and Danny remained. At first, Irene had had to protect Frances from the aggressive Kelly but, as time wore on, Frances began to get the measure of her. Kelly's normal mode of communication was confrontational; you just had to work with it. Jake was much more difficult; his friendliness masked inner disturbance that led him to seek out younger children or animals to torment when no one was looking. This sickened Frances. She couldn't bear to contemplate the idea of any kind of creature, from cats to insects, suffering cruelty from human hands. She was constantly on the look out for Jake when he made his frequent forays out into the back garden and down to the alleyway. Danny avoided being alone with his elder brother and clung to his mother wherever possible, a whimpering, frightened child, always under adults' feet, therefore attracting irritation and the occasional slap. Irene always confronted Kelly gently when she lost her temper, trying to remind her that the little boy's behaviour was a consequence of the fear of violence and that further physical punishment would do no good at all. Kelly did not acknowledge Irene's corrections or seem to accept them explicitly, but it was noticeable that she refrained from hitting out for a day or two until her temper got the better of her again and the cycle was repeated.

Two young women had moved into the house, Leanne and Kat, both no more than teenagers, both addicts who had to be reminded that they couldn't take drugs in the house and certainly not in front of the children. 'They'll close us down,' said Irene, looking anxious, as if a council officer was about to step over the threshold at any minute, as the substance in a smoking cigarette gave off tell-tale odours from a bedroom. Leanne, a tall, spindly lass with fair skin and red hair, came and went unpredictably. Kat, on the other hand, a small, dark mouse of a woman, who peered out fearfully from a curtain of black hair, spent a lot of the time in her room and needed regular consoling from Irene. Frances' relative stability amongst all these characters made her a natural lieutenant for Irene, and she did her best at comforting, encouraging, organising. Within a week, it seemed not so much that she was a refugee herself but rather a co-worker without pay. Yet she adored Irene and was only too pleased to support her. She began to notice that Irene's patient calm was a cover for considerable hidden anxiety; she was emotionally involved in the lives of her tenants in ways that could only cause pain, given their backgrounds. She caught her at unguarded moments, looking nervously into space or talking under her breath to herself, quickly regaining her smiling composure as she noticed Frances' presence.

Just as Frances began to provide backup for the ever-busy Irene, so Debs was a regular support for her, calling in every couple of days, making sure that she never went out anywhere alone. She asked Jose if he would drive Frances to work and back every day; he accepted gladly, joking about the bus service ('no good going by bus; who in the hell schedules them? – oh yes, it's me!'). The police seemed to have dismissed the phone call case as insignificant; without any sign of physical threat, it was not high on the priority list. Anyway, the calls had now ceased, as Frances seemed to have frightened off her tormentor.

Frances also became familiar with the workers that came from the main refuge to the annex house from time to time. Child workers and counsellors were on hand for appointments and family work; Irene always encouraged the residents to take full advantage of their services. Advocates supported the families when they returned to the community at large and so became involved just before the point of departure. A volunteer, a woman in her fifties whose family had grown up, came in on a part-time regular basis to help out. The support network was impressive; for Frances, it was all eye-opening as until then she had had no idea that such a world existed.

In the third week, Frances, feeling by now quite settled in the refuge, raised the question of the women doing magic together. She only did this when she was sure that the two boys were asleep. Kelly's instant sceptical and snorted response was quite predictable, Kat said 'yeah, sounds great' in the same flat way she replied to anything unthreatening. Leanne had just gone out. Irene asked Frances to explain a little more.

'It's a way of taking control o' situation when you didn't think you had any,' Frances said, a little nervously, but she was determined to try and articulate what she meant. 'You ask Goddess to help and she puts her power into you. She comes right into you; I've had the experience myself. You feel stronger. It's been done in refuges before.'

'It's not black magic, is it, Frances?' asked Irene, fearing another reason for the council to shut them down. 'You're not asking us to put curses on men who've done us wrong?'

'No, absolutely not,' said Frances, trying to reassure her. 'We're just taking control for ourselves. It's up to Goddess what happens. I've never known anyone get hurt by it.'

She felt a little foolish at this point, realising that she was claiming expertise in something that was new to her only a few weeks before. But confidence was the best policy.

'OK, show us,' said Irene, looking straight into Frances' eyes in order to warn her that she had to be careful what she said and did, given the vulnerability of the other women.

'We need to light some candles. I've brought a picture of the Madonna wi' me, which I use to visualise Goddess. I'll bring it down. And then we summon spirits and ask Goddess to come into us and make us strong, give us control.'

The four women sat together, Kelly folding her arms and looking very cynical but persuaded by Irene to stay in the room and give it a try.

'We should do this together,' said Irene. 'Or not do it at all.'

Frances had to say all the parts herself, as none of the others knew the first thing about it. She asked them to help her light some candles in front of the powerful-looking Iviron Madonna. She created the circle and welcomed the spirits of the four quarters. Then she uttered prayers into the silence.

'Come into us and make us strong, Goddess. Come into Irene and Lucy, Kelly, Jake and Danny, Kat, me and also Leanne, although she's not here now. We've all been hurt, each in our own way, some more, some less, but we all need your strength in us. We all need each other and we need you.'

During the silence that followed, Frances didn't dare look at Kelly, as she was sure that she would be badly put off by the dismissive expression on the stocky woman's face. Kelly did not seem one for the sentimental moment; the only time that Frances felt that there was any communication between them was when they chatted about practical matters or talked critically about councils, employers, or men. But, finally, as the ritual progressed, she couldn't help but sneak a look in her direction. She was astounded to see tears on Kelly's face, welling up in her eyes; she was weeping silently. Frances tried to look away to spare embarrassment but Kelly had seen her.

'It's my Nan,' said Kelly, her emotion forced out through loudly spoken words which cut through the quiet. 'She were Catholic. When we were little, she took us to church to light candles for everyone in family. Then she died; I were only six. Without her, family fell apart, my mam couldn't cope without her. It were all crap from then on. All this reminds me it were only good time in my life. Nan were best person in my life.'

Irene and Frances both recognised that an over-reaction to Kelly, by way of comforting and hugging, would spoil the moment. Instead, Irene just reached out and took her hand for a few seconds. As she watched them, Frances thought about how mind-blowing the changes were that seemed to come about through rituals and prayer to the Goddess.

The ritual over, Kelly and Kat retired to their rooms, Kelly because she didn't know how to converse normally after allowing her defensive façade to slip, Kat because she hadn't had a surreptitious fix for a good couple of hours. Frances felt very pleased with the success of the ritual that she had suggested, so she was alarmed to see that Irene, uncharacteristically, was having trouble making eye contact and had started to busy herself with an unnecessary tidying of the little living room.

'Were that OK?' asked Frances, concerned. 'Is there a problem?'

'Not at all,' replied Irene, still looking everywhere but at her. 'It were very moving. We must do it again.'

'You seem unhappy,' insisted Frances. 'If I've done summat wrong, please tell me. Irene?'

Irene looked back at her. For the first time since the beginning of the ritual, their eyes met. What Frances could see was not anger but tenderness. And then she realised what was about to happen.

'Can we sit down?' asked Irene, gently yet with more than a hint of nervousness in her voice.

Frances later realised that three contrasting responses were going through her head in that moment. The first was the instinctive one when, on a couple of occasions, women had made a pass at her. She wasn't a lesbian, she was sure of it, and she didn't want to go there. So the first possible reaction was: No way, goodbye! The second one came from somewhere deeper. When she looked at Irene, at the attractive forty-year-old woman, with the reassuring broad smile and beautiful brown skin, there was just maybe something in her that could have responded. *Why not? Relationships with men haven't worked out too well, have they?* She looked at Irene's arms and wondered whether she would want to be held in them, to feel them all over her body. They were always bare from the elbow down, well-proportioned but with some width and muscle, seeming to have the strength and comfort of a peasant mother reaching out for her children. However, the skin was smooth and flawless, with regular moles and freckles, more like that of a Mediterranean lady. Yes, one had to admit that she was beautiful. She looked back up at Irene's warm dark eyes and pleasant round face. And she knew that she did indeed love Irene and wanted those arms about her, not as a lover but as a child comforted and reassured. She wanted to be kissed by her, not with tongues meeting in a passionate embracing of the lips, but tenderly and with maternal compassion. That was the third response: it was the true one.

As Frances sat down, she smiled reassuringly at Irene and waited for her to speak. She remembered all those times that she had been in the reverse position, hoping for a positive response from the men in her life including, most recently, Nathan, and she resolved to give as caring a response as she possibly could. Irene began, after biting her lip.

'Frances, I really hope this doesn't upset or embarrass you, but I've got to say it. Tonight, I knew for sure that I loved you, that I knew what had been going through my mind the last couple o' weeks were right. I shouldn't really do this and in normal circumstances I wouldn't. Women here are vulnerable and I wouldn't ever compromise them, but you seem strong. I love you and, well... I'm in love with you. That ritual's finally pushed me to say this. You seemed like you were shining with some beautiful power.'

She reached out and held Frances' hand, stroked it and looked deeply into her eyes for the second time that night. She was waiting for the answer. Frances took a deep breath and tried to find the right one.

'I love you too, Irene. But... I'm sorry to have to say that I want you, not as a lover, but as a kind o' mother. I don't think I can do the woman on woman thing, it's not in me. But I think you're one o' the most wonderful people I've ever met. I know maybe you need someone to help you too, because everyone looks to you for support. And I do, ever since I came here in a right mess. Each day at work, I can't wait to come home and see you and when I do, I know that you care for me. To me, you're nearest thing to Goddess that I've ever seen in a real life woman.'

Despite the knock-back, Irene didn't stop smiling, and now the eyes were steadier as she looked back at Frances. Then she glanced down and answered her, thoughtfully and with the sad but slightly relieved calm that comes when someone knows that passion will not follow.

'Funny thing is, Frances, although I'm disappointed, I think you're right. Our relationship isn't about sexual love, although I have to admit that I do fancy you. I do need help and you've given me that since you came here. Everybody looks up to me because of the state they're in when they arrive, but I also need someone to look up to. Tonight, I realised that I really look up to you. You might be younger than me, but I think you're a kind o' mother to me too!'

Then they both laughed. Irene continued to clutch Frances' hand and squeezed it with a mock aggression, as if to release some of the pent-up sexual energy; Frances responded by grabbing her arm. Then they embraced, staying that way for several moments.

'OK,' said Frances, when they finally released each other and began to sit up. 'We can be mothers for each other. Your turn first, I'll have cup o' tea and two chocolate biscuits.'

Irene laughed again and then went off in the direction of the kitchen, but not without making a loud and very rude raspberry noise at her newly found 'daughter'.

But Sal didn't hear this part. It got heavily edited and ended up being a description of how Irene had confided in her that she needed more help. The relationship between Frances and Irene was too wonderful a thing for it to become an 'I got hit on by a lessie' story for the prurience of less discerning friends.

# 19

# Queen of Swords

Throughout Frances' time at the refuge, there was no indication that the police – or anyone else – had come anywhere near to identifying the phone caller. Debs suggested two magical approaches to this problem: firstly, spell-making designed to force him to reveal his name. She didn't know a traditional formula for this so together they made one up, involving a ten-inch-high model soldier in combat gear that one of the children had left lying around in the refuge. They placed a hankie over the soldier's head then, summoning the spirits and the Goddess to help them, pulled it off ritually so that the soldier's face could be seen. Frances had hoped that she might go into some kind of trance at this point and see the face of the man but it didn't happen.

The second tactic was the use of divination and, in Debs' bedroom, Frances pulled out her brand new Goddess Tarot pack for the purpose. Debs suggested a 'runic' spread, which consisted of drawing three main cards. The first one to emerge at random symbolised the immediate past, insofar as it formed the basis of the present situation; the second, the present situation; the third, the future about to unfold. If any card remained unclear, you could draw up to two further cards after each one to supplement it to try and get more information, giving a maximum of nine.

The first three cards were difficult to interpret; all Debs could say about the 'immediate past' was that the cards made her think that the man had been badly emotionally scarred at some point, whilst adding quickly, in case Frances saw this as a reason for somehow blaming herself, that this couldn't excuse him. The 'present situation' started with major card number sixteen, 'Oppression', which didn't make Frances feel very optimistic. Debs read out the guide book interpretation for this card.

'During the Dreamtime, the Australian aboriginal sister goddesses, the *Wawalak*, were swallowed whole by *Yurlungur*, the Great Rainbow Serpent.'

'Oh,' exclaimed Frances anxiously, applying this to herself. 'Did they get out?'

'Yes,' said Debs, tapping her chin thoughtfully. 'Although there is no detail as to how and when.'

The first card for the 'future' yielded number twenty, 'Judgement', associated with the Welsh goddess of the sea, *Gwenhwyfar*.

'It was believed that no man could rule Wales without her by his side.'

This seemed to provide confidence in a good outcome. Frances was further cheered by Debs' comment that in her own Tarot pack, this card was known as the 'Last Judgement' with the dead rising from their graves. This reminded Frances of the vision in which the 'sins' woman was resurrected. But there was nothing in the cards that gave them the remotest of clues as to the identity of the caller.

Frances did not meet the spiritual adventurers in the early evening as usual on the fourth Friday evening of her time in the refuge. She was instead due to be at the dinner to say goodbye to Messrs. Ballard and Taylor. The last three weeks had been quiet ones at work; John Taylor had made no further attempt to engage Frances in conversation other than brief instructions, which he imparted with a bland friendliness. Frances, for her part, tried to be more attentive to detail. She was a responsive person; if someone was nice to her, she would repay them with what they wanted. But it usually needed them to make the first move, or Frances could be quite stubborn and remain defensive and sullen. Ballard she had hardly seen; he spent his last few weeks mostly out of the office. Whether he was sneaking off to the golf course or frantically going round suppliers to leave everything in good order for the next incumbent, Frances neither knew nor cared.

The finale came.

'So what am I going to wear for goodbye party? Maybe dress down, no desirable man's going to be there. But then, on t' other hand, I can't resist making Taylor and Ballard look at me on their last night. So plenty o' make-up tonight, maybe loads of eye shadow for a witchy look, mysterious and sexy. I'm going to turn their heads, I really am! I want 'em to grow old thinking of me!'

Irene smiled.

'Well, even if they don't, I will,' she said, with fire in her eyes. 'Will you let me help you get ready?' She winked mischievously. 'In a maternal way, of course! I'd *love* to play my part in your final victory over office bigwigs.'

'I wish you could come,' replied Frances. 'But they're not allowing friends or partners.'

Irene played her part. Frances got into the Jose limousine looking as near drop-dead gorgeous as it was within her powers to do. Her hair was done up like a Greek goddess, maybe Aphrodite, queen of sexual attraction; the strands of the pony tail that hung from high on the back of her head were wound round each other in sweeping curls. The top end was tied in a black band. She wore an orange dress that complemented her hair colour, short-sleeved – so that she could display a pretty silver bracelet or two – and quite high in the skirt, showing a good length of her shapely legs in their stiletto heels. She had used the few sunny days of April getting something in the way of a light suntan, which cheered her up in the bad moments in the refuge. The dress had black hems round the neck, sleeves and skirt, and it was drawn in at the waist, so that no one would be in doubt that one of her attractive features was a trim figure.

'Hello, Cinderella,' said Jose, greeting her with a toothy smile. 'Now then, you're making me reconsider my sexual orientation. Make sure you're out by twelve. The car turning into a pumpkin will be the final straw for this dodgy gearbox.'

'I've no intention o' staying beyond ten,' replied Cinderella/Aphrodite as she squeezed into the old Citroen, politely removing yesterday's *Guardian* onto the back seat. 'There'll still be time for a drink or two wi' my fellow adventurers. Anyway, I'll call you as soon as I can get away.'

'There's something in there about the G8 summit and its likely approach to the environmental problem,' Jose commented, pointing to the discarded *Guardian* as he slammed the reluctant gear stick into first.

'It's really important,' said Frances. 'We must try and help 'em make up their minds for sake o' Mother Earth. It's now or never.'

Her growing confidence about using magic was counterbalanced by the fact that she felt awkward about her total lack of knowledge on the subject of the environment, having very little understanding of the scientific and political issues.

The 'carriage' drew up outside the *Bojangles* restaurant. Cinderella/Aphrodite got out, but the aura of her loveliness slipped a little as her dress caught on the car door handle and she uttered a swear word or two in her concern for the expensive garment, the buying of which – a few months before – had put nights out on hold for a week or two.

'Careful,' called Jose. 'This car's sensitive; language like that and it might refuse to take us home.'

Frances looked apologetic as she looked back into the car, not because of the cursing but due to a thought that Jose's comment had provoked.

'Jose, I'm really sorry that you can't enjoy yourself on a Friday with a few drinks. It's so kind of you to drive me about. I really do appreciate it, you know. Hopefully, it won't be for much longer.'

'However long it's needed, I'll be there and so will Chitty Chitty Bang Bang,' replied Jose, with a reassuring smile.

He managed to convey to Frances in that short exchange just how important it was to him to be needed, and how much he empathised with her as a victim of threatened violence. Her intuition told her that he had some experience of this himself.

Cinderella/Aphrodite floated into the restaurant, intentionally a little late in order to make a grand entrance. *Pants!* Everybody else had had the same idea; the only members of the party present at the bar awaiting the table were Loli, Becca and Nazi Robot Woman (to whom Frances' internal voice referred using her first name, Jane, now that she had become a 'goodie'). So it had to be awkward small talk, awaiting the arrivals of others. Loli complimented her on her appearance; the praise was returned mutually, of course, then the same with Becca and Jane, but Frances knew she was the belle of the ball for once. Becca could have looked pretty but was fairly nonplussed about a night out with the oldies and wore nothing different to her everyday office attire.

Then John Taylor appeared. *Yes, he's looking at me,* thought Frances. There was a real pleasure in being admired by one who had struck such terror in her just a few weeks earlier. Then the remaining women arrived including Katie and Tricia, both dressed up but neither exuding the glow that Frances felt; the impending change of management had not succeeded in transforming them – at least, not yet. Finally, into the restaurant came the retiring boss himself, James Ballard. Frances knew that Ballard's attention was inevitable and not to be counted as a great victory. The slick, silver-haired fifty-five year old had a bedside manner when dealing with attractive women and liked to court a lady looking at her best. However, he acted – it seemed – virtually on autopilot, leaving the overwhelming impression that it was his own ego that remained the object of his admiration. His attentive remarks were smooth and well practiced but rarely spoken from the heart; there was always a distance in him and he couldn't avoid a patronising edge to his flattery.

So when, after a few minutes of greetings, he sidled over to Frances, she was not surprised, although she couldn't help a wicked feeling of self-satisfied pleasure. However, she was not expecting what followed.

'Frances, could you come away from the group for a minute or two?' he asked, in a low voice, speaking directly into her left ear and taking her by the elbow. 'There's something I must say to you tonight before we say goodbye.'

They moved to the corner of the bar. For the second time in a few weeks, Frances felt the women's eyes on her, wondering why the male bosses wanted to speak to her privately. It wasn't entirely a pleasant feeling. She was worried that they might think she was prostituting herself with these older men.

The loud singing of 'Happy Birthday' from a nearby table allowed Ballard to open the conversation without fear of being overheard. He asked her a very surprising question.

'Frances, are you a witch?'

How on earth to respond?

'Well... well...'

How did he know this? Had she said something to Katie or Tricia?

'Come on, Frances, I know I'm right.'

'OK, Mr Ballard, I *am* interested in witchcraft and all that, but I haven't gone through any initiations or owt and so I wouldn't count myself as one.'

'Aha! Well, it wouldn't surprise me if you had done a few spells when we had our... er... little falling out, eh, Frances?'

Frances tried to smile, but out came a grimace. She decided to come clean.

'Well, if I did, it were only so's we'd all get on with each other.'

Ballard chuckled.

'Ah, yes, a white witch. No, seriously, you could become a powerful magician, my intuition tells me. I must confess that I know something about the subject myself. Frances, I hope you'll keep this to yourself – and I will deny that I ever said it if you don't. I am a member of a centuries-old secret order that has a good deal of experience with magic and the occult. We would really welcome someone like you, someone young with potential. We could help you develop your skills and channel your energies.'

Jane came over and interrupted.

'Come on, you two,' she said, firmly. 'Everyone else has sat down and if we don't order soon, we won't eat tonight!'

She tried to sound cheerful, but an edge to her voice suggested that she was quite thrown by the fact that Ballard would engage in private conversation with one so lowly as Frances. She had probably decided that the only reasonable explanation was that he was coming on to her in a final fling as her boss. As they walked to join the others, Ballard said the very thing that would have confirmed this suspicion.

'Let me know what you think by the end of the evening and give me your number. We can then arrange something.'

Jane glanced at him, then threw Frances a look that was murderous. This aroused Frances' suspicions. *Nazi Robot Woman and Ballard? Has summat gone on between them two?*

As she ate, Frances thought furiously whenever she got the chance away from the table banter. Her first instinct was to avoid Ballard, to be glad that he was soon to be out of her life forever. On the other hand, she was flattered. *I'm going to be a powerful magician, and he's recognised it. I've won over Taylor and now Ballard. Goddess has given me power, so why shouldn't I take advantage of it? The secret occult order has come across my path for a purpose, so why not go wi' flow? Try it and see, if it don't work out, I can leave. But... I don't know.* Frances realised that she had to make some kind of decision tonight, here and now. *I wish Debs were here to talk to!* Then she remembered that the Goddess Tarot cards were still in her bag.

Frances went into the ladies' toilet. She found a cubicle in reasonable order and pushed the seat down to sit on. She then pulled out some paper towels and placed them on the floor, to protect the cards from dirt. *Can't be too long. Just a three card spread, no supplementary cards. Ask a question: should I take up Ballard's offer?* Shuffle three times, cut three times. Deep breath. Peer between legs at the cards as they are placed on loo floor. The immediate past: Ace of Pentacles. 'The beginning of a new phase of life that promises prosperity, fertility and generosity.' *Yes, that's true.* Second card, the present: Seven of Cups. 'Daydreams. Time to wake up and rejoin the world.' Hmm. Third card: the future. Queen of Swords. 'Brilliant and strong, the Queen of Swords is the woman (maybe an older woman) to consult when confused because of her willingness to tell it like it is – even to the point of sometimes being a little harsh.' *Oh. Where does that leave me? OK, I've an idea. Get phone out. Call Debs? But she's not older, is she? OK, plan B. Please be in, Irene.* Bang in number. *It's ringing.*

'Brill, Irene, you're there. It's me, Frances. Listen, I'm phoning a friend; I've only got thirty seconds. Big boss, you know, Mr Ballard, wants me to join his secret occult society that'll help me develop my magic gifts. He thinks I've got real potential. What do you think?'

'What kind of secret society, Frances? I'm not with you.'

'I'm not sure myself, to tell truth.'

Irene snorted.

'Well then, how gullible are you? He's only brought you misery. You're about to get rid of him, now a bit o' flattery and you want to spend your spare time with him. Get real, lady!'

It was as abrasive as Irene ever got.

'Thanks, Irene, that's the right answer and now, thanks to you, I've won a million. Bye, love, see you later!'

Frances took only a few seconds to make her final decision. Witchcraft was about freedom, adventure. It was for ordinary people like Irene and Kelly. It was not to be dominated and kept exclusive by a centuries-old secret society. Taylor, it turned out, had some redeeming features. Ballard, however, was a manipulative bully, only nice to people when he wanted to use them. All this was now clear to her. Frances folded a paper towel, put it in her bag and went back to the table. At the end of the meal, she summoned Jose by text and then made an excuse to leave. She said goodbye to John Taylor, gave him a flashing smile and a hug. Then James Ballard, the same, while he looked into her eyes expecting her to say something significant. She slipped the folded-up paper towel into his hand, turned tail and left. As soon as he got the chance, he opened it up to see what she had written there. Seeing all this out of the corner of her eye, Jane sighed in disgust. What is it with middle-aged men and young tarts, she asked herself. Ballard read the paper towel. The writing was in orange lipstick. 'BYE MR B GOOD LUCK.'

Outside in the cool late evening air, Cinderella/Aphrodite, grinning from ear to ear and leaving no glass slippers behind, got into the carriage. It was still two hours away from transmogrifying into a pumpkin.

## 20

## Calling

According to Nathan, there had been no communication from the mystery caller since Frances had challenged him that night in the flat. Perhaps there was no need to change the number. Maybe the whole thing had fizzled out. On the Saturday after the farewell dinner, however, there was a development. While trying to cheer up Danny by playing games with small plastic zoo animals, Frances received a call from the policewoman with responsibility for her case.

'Frances Dryburgh?... Good. Frances, I'm afraid to have to tell you that your mystery caller has branched out. Two other women in the Leeds area have suffered similar calls; from their description, we think it's the same guy. We need to ask whether you know either of these women. First: Claire Robinson?'

'Er... No, I don't think I know a Claire Robinson,' replied Frances, carefully.

'All right. Second: Vanessa Fairclough?'

Frances was disappointed. This was an opportunity to resolve the issue but, as much as she searched her memories, she could not recall anyone of that name either.

'No... I don't think so. Damn!'

'Look, don't worry about it, you either do or you don't. If you recall anything that can connect someone to yourself and these two women, let us know immediately. OK?'

'Yes, OK,' agreed Frances, a little despondently.

'One more thing. To date, not one of the three of you has suffered any harm or come into face to face contact with the caller. Based on psychological profiling, we feel *reasonably* certain that he will not go beyond making threats. While this is not a 100% assurance, we would advise that you may be able to go back to your house, as long as you remain vigilant at all times. That must remain your decision, of course. Please let us know immediately if you have any problem or anxiety connected with this case.'

'OK, thanks for the information.'

Frances phoned round her friends, but no one else knew the names either. She then called Nathan for advice about moving back into the Hyde Park flat.

'Yeah, sure, why not? I suspect the police are right; he hasn't done anything except phone. Look, I'll stay there with you until the whole business is sorted out. I can go with you to work and back.'

'But it's out of your way! I go to other side o' town and University's just up road.'

'That's what friends are for, isn't it? It won't be a bother, but it might mean we have to leave a little earlier than usual.'

'Right then, that's great. Home it is! I really miss Cass.'

'Oh, she loves me now! I've adopted her.'

'Shut up. She might love *you*, but you probably give her cold shoulder!'

'Ouch,' said Nathan, spotting the autobiographical reference. He switched into serious mode. 'Friendship can be a warmer thing than relationships, you know. More faithful, less stressful, more long lasting.'

Frances didn't want to hear this, so she stayed at the banter level.

'You're right. Cass'll probably prefer friendship. She can't settle down wi' someone who sleeps at night and doesn't want to run along alleyways chasing small animals!'

Raspberry, came the stern reply. It reminded Frances of Irene, another phantom raspberry blower, who would not be ecstatic at the thought of Frances returning home.

'OK, must go, Mr Smith. Thanks for everything – I'll take up your offer. It's really kind; I really do appreciate your friendship!'

Irene came into the room. She had overheard. She smiled, but it couldn't hide the fact that she was crestfallen.

'I'm sorry, I wouldn't normally listen in but I just had to when I realised what you were talking about. Of course, you have to go back to your flat, Frances. How could I stand in your way? It's *my* fault for getting so dependent on you in such a short time.'

Frances stretched out and, clutching Irene's upper arms, spoke fervently, not breaking eye contact.

'I'll not go while tomorrow, Irene. It's not surprising you needed someone, everyone depends on *you* all time. It's just that I'm not your normal refuge dweller. They've all got too much hanging over 'em to think about helping you. Kids, drugs, violent partners. I was free enough to be able to muck in and give you support. But this is not goodbye! We're right good friends, aren't we?'

Frances thought it ironic how, in just a few minutes, she had had the friendship discussion from opposite perspectives. If only Nathan and Irene could coalesce into one being! How intensely she would love such a person!

'Maybe I could get a few hours away to help you move back,' said Irene. 'Then I could see your flat, meet your cat and know a little bit more about the Frances who lives in Hyde Park.'

'What a good idea,' agreed Frances. 'Tomorrow afternoon then. And you'll probably meet Nathan too. I don't think you've seen him yet, have you?'

*And that'll test you to see if you really are a lesbian,* she thought. *If Nathan gets off with you, I'll kill you both, then myself and save mystery caller the trouble!*

She needn't have worried. There was no flicker in Irene's eyes at the sight of the blond bombshell on Sunday afternoon, as she and the adventurers helped Frances reinstall herself in the little first floor flat. The elderly man next door was very intrigued to find out what was going on; no one had told him about the calls, the refuge or Nathan staying. Frances felt guilty as usual, so she tried to explain the situation with the least amount of complexity.

'You should've told me abart it,' he said, in his South Yorkshire accent. 'I'd have given him right seeing to!'

*You've missed point already,* thought Frances, irritated. *He weren't there to be seen to!*

Neither was there much of a firestorm in Nathan's eyes when he first saw Irene. *I should've realised, men seldom go for older women, even attractive ones, when they've started putting middle-aged weight on. God, only ten year or so to go for me and I haven't got head start like bonny Irene! Hello, Cass! Oh yes, treat me cool like I were never away, why don't you? Cats! Bad as men!*

Irene didn't feel she could stay long, as a new family was moving in that evening, so with hugs, kisses and dire warnings about not keeping in touch, she left them. As soon as the four were alone, with bags unpacked, tea made, Debs opened up a new line of discussion.

'What about Beltane?' she asked. 'Only one week away, what're we going to do? We've a long weekend to play with!'

Frances had not fully digested all the Pagan terminology. She had a blind spot when it came to details. She was better at impressions, emotions and people. It was only her feelings about art that had got her through the degree, as the history bit was definitely not her strong point.

'Now remind me, what's Beltane?' she asked.

'May Day,' said Jose. 'The great festival that celebrates the beginning of summer. Maypole dancing, crowning the queen of the May, all that kind of stuff. It's even more important than the equinoxes for modern Pagans, Witches and Goddess worshippers. It doesn't have to be celebrated on 1$^{st}$ May exactly, just around that time. The first May bank holiday weekend provides the perfect opportunity. The thing is, the car's playing up and it won't get very far. Avebury's out this time.'

'OK, then the Dales,' suggested Nathan.

'Yeah,' Debs agreed. 'We can have a practice for our trip to France.'

'Are there any black virgins in Dales?' asked Frances, in all seriousness.

Nathan returned an expression that said, er… no. Frances shrugged her shoulders and held her hands up with a grimace, as if to reply: how was I to know?

'No, don't think so.' Jose paused and frowned, as if he were just checking through his memory, to make sure. 'We don't need a black virgin on this occasion. Just pretty hills and rivers and a nice outdoor space.'

'OK, we'll leave it to you,' said Debs. 'We can't stay away from home, as we need all our money for France. So it's just day trip wi' picnic, shall we say Sat'day?'

Later that evening, Frances found herself on her own with Nathan again. All the excitement of the last few weeks: the hothouse atmosphere of the refuge with its broken women and disturbed children; the anxiety about whether the mystery caller would somehow carry out his threats; the coming changes at work; the ambivalent relationship with Irene – all this had made Frances feel more horny than ever about Nathan. She had suppressed her urges with Gary, because she was sure he was not the 'one', but Nathan – charming friendliness, wicked sense of humour, common interests in things spiritual, very good looks – was a different matter. She was so frustrated that it made her whole body tremble as she watched him sitting there, reading a book on cosmology that he had bought the previous day. *How many months have gone since I had sex?* She had to express it somehow. With no warning at all, she suddenly and impulsively threw a glass of water all over him. He jumped up.

'What're you doing?' he said through his teeth, trying to keep from shouting.

She ran over and embraced him. The tears started.

'What *am* I like? You do so much for me, you stay in my house to look after me and I do that to you. I'm so sorry. Everything's got on top o' me and I just want to reach out and grab you. It's driving me mad. I'm so sorry, please don't leave me, I won't do it again.'

Nathan looked awkward, then cleared his throat. He was about to say something momentous. 'Look, I think you're really nice. If you want to sleep with me, OK, then let's do it. We're here all on our own. It must have been a terrible time and you need some comfort, I can see that.'

Frances had calmed down. She stared at him but without the emotional response that he was expecting. She was getting better at reading situations and making decisions. A few years or even months ago and her clothes would be off by now.

'Please don't get me wrong, Nathan. You're a wonderful person and I want to stay really close friends with you. But I don't *need* owt. A needy woman's not normally an attractive one, is she? What I *want* is to find someone who wants me in return, who chooses me from other options, who hopes for me, who sighs about me when he's alone. And that's not you, is it? Now you must get dry. I'll not forgive myself if you die o' flu or summat.'

Nathan returned to the living room, having sorted himself out. Frances had poured them both a vodka and coke. He sat down, picking up the cat and placing her on his lap.

'OK, I don't have the feelings that you want me to have,' he conceded. 'I was offering to sleep with you because I wanted to help *you*, not for myself. The truth is, Frances, I don't have those kind of feelings for anyone at the moment! In a way, I *was* choosing you, because I wouldn't have done that for anyone else. You've become my dear friend and you *are* attractive. But I don't know what I want; all I do know is that it's not sex and hasn't been for a year or two now.'

Frances sipped the vodka. The water-throwing incident had rid her of pent-up energy and she felt calmer now. After all, he was here, wasn't he? At least he wasn't with some bimbo. And tomorrow was the beginning of the Carson era. And the weekend was that Beltane-thingy, the start of summer. There were plenty of reasons for feeling upbeat. But try as she might, her reflections still came out a tad mournful.

'So, four of us. One doesn't know what he wants but it's not sex or any intimate relationship, another's gay but can't find a partner, another's too damaged by sexual relationships to even contemplate them, and then there's me – twenty-nine and nowhere near finding a proper relationship. We're a bunch of saddos, eh? Maybe it's right what some people say – what we call 'spiritual' is just a compensation for failures in other parts of your life.'

'So you've been reading psychology books, have you?' said Nathan, knowing full well that the answer was no. 'Well, there are several ways of looking at it. One, as you put it, spirituality's a compensation for saddos. I don't buy that. Religion has been too powerful a force in human history. Two, the opposite view – spiritual people don't easily find fulfilment in one-to-one relationships because their horizons are broader. I don't go along with that, either; there are many people in strong committed relationships who *are* highly spiritual. No, the answer is that we four hang around together because we're single *and* spiritual. We're birds of a feather. But there's no necessary connection between the two.'

'Very deep,' commented Frances. Yet, having known Nathan and Jose for a few weeks, she was getting far better at interpreting their cerebral flourishes and knew what he meant. 'You're right, though. Perhaps if we were to get together, it wouldn't be good for Jose and Debs. Anyway, I'm going to become a dyke. That Irene really fancies me and I think she's quite gorgeous too, don't you?'

'She's an attractive woman,' agreed Nathan. 'But if it's not in your nature then it would be quite hard. I think you regard her too highly to experiment on her, don't you?'

'That's quite perceptive – for a man! Of course I wouldn't. I want her to be my mum, actually, or maybe big sister that I never had.'

Nathan suddenly moved the subject into strange territory.

'Have you ever thought about celibacy? You know, like Catholic priests, monks and nuns? You don't have to want to be a Catholic to think that there might be something in that idea. Keeping yourself free of relationships to be available to a spiritual way of life.'

'Making a virtue out o' necessity, it's called,' replied Frances, after a couple of seconds of thought. 'You don't like commitment, so you start thinking about celibacy.'

'Touché!'

Frances frowned.

'Trouble is with celibacy, half of 'em are paedos.'

'I don't think that many of them are. I know why it looks like that. A: it gets in the news when one of them is caught for it; B: celibacy in an institution like a church *will* attract such people, who might see it as a cover for what they do. But that doesn't mean there isn't something far more profound and healthy involved for many others. It's a kind of calling.'

'Calling? Did you *hear* call to celibacy, then? Do you have visions, like me?'

Nathan smiled.

'No. I'm just wondering if it's where my life is taking me, that's all.'

'My visions haven't included owt about celibacy,' said Frances, as she thought about it. 'But maybe they *are* a calling.'

It was a good thought with which to go to bed. Frances reflected on the friendly intensity of the conversation and conceded to her inner voice that it was still a good thing being with Nathan, sex or no. Accepting him for who he was might just be part of the deal. *OK, Mother,* she said to the Goddess in her final thoughts before sleep. *You've given him to me just as he is; if he weren't like that, he'd already be married wi' three kids. It's Nathan as Nathan, or nothing. Good joke. Nathan or nothin'.*

# 21

## Beltane Fire

For someone who didn't want a relationship, Nathan was very insensitive to the effect on Frances of a week of intense conversation, laughter, banter and being close to one another morning and night. It was like being in a live-in partnership, without the sleeping together. She was getting too used to him. She walked into the front room on a sleepy workday morning to be greeted by the kind of remark one would get from a grumpy husband:

'Look at the mail! It's all advertising. I thought that you were supposed to have rubbish taken away, not delivered!'

'It's Cass' fault,' quipped Frances, drowsily. 'She savaged postman and now I don't get any proper letters.'

'In a world of mobile phones and internet,' said Nathan, 'Do we *need* letters?'

'Oh, yes,' replied Frances, slurping tea. 'We can never abandon the *letter*; it means a lot when someone takes trouble to write instead o' just texting.'

'Hmm…'

Nathan had the embarrassed look of someone who hadn't written a letter since the stamps bore the head of the previous monarch.

'So when did you last get a letter that wasn't a bill, Frances?'

'Given kind o' phone calls I get, I'm better off without letters!'

'Thus contradicting what you just said.'

'Pardon?'

Rational conversation with someone staring into space and occasionally sucking in hot liquid was not such a good idea. Nathan laughed to himself and wandered off into the bathroom.

Nathan at home, Carson at work. Not a bad combination. The new boss soon made it clear that his philosophy was something along the lines of: workers feeling supported and encouraged equals efficient and hard-working office. With the changed atmosphere at work and the fact that the phone calls seemed to have dried up, it was hard at times to remember that a threat remained in the background. True, it wasn't completely out of her mind. Frances resolved to do some more magic at Beltane to try to force the mystery caller to reveal himself. She was in an optimistic mood which made her feel confident that it would work this time. But events in her life seemed to provide a counterbalance to whatever had been going on just before. If it was going well, then a shock occurred; if badly, then a nice surprise. The good week should have been a warning. And the problem half of her life made its re-entry in the pub on Friday with the non-appearance of Debs.

'It's gone nine,' said Jose, sombrely. 'She's not answering her phone. I think we should get round there.'

'But she were only on phone on Wednesday, chatting away,' replied Frances.

'Maybe, but I still think we should go,' repeated Jose.

He looked at Nathan with a fervent glance that told Frances that the two men had been here before.

'What's wrong?' asked Frances. 'What aren't you telling me?'

'Debs has periods of severe depression,' answered Nathan. 'They come on suddenly. There's never any warning. She tries to battle on without asking for help then goes under before you know it.'

Frances felt her stomach invaded by several hundred angry butterflies.

A bus ride into Chapeltown, then the three of them stood at the bright scarlet door in the darkness of late evening. Lizzie opened the door with the chain still on. Recognising them, she nodded, let them in and indicated that they should go up the stairs. Debs was lying face down on her bed, an old-fashioned monster with an iron bed-head. She was still wearing her work clothes, a blue levi shirt and black jeans. One weak lamp shed poor light across the room, a small plant next to it casting macabre shadows on the opposite wall.

'Debs!' called Frances, signalling her alarm at the melancholy scene and moving towards her.

The body on the bed turned round very slowly. Her dark eyes were barely open, as if she could not spare the effort to look at anything.

'Hi,' she said, listlessly.

Frances sat next to her and put her hand on the slumped shoulder.

'What's up, Debs? Why weren't you in pub tonight?'

She knew the answer by now, but it seemed rude to confess that they had talked about nothing else but Debs and her depressions since leaving the city centre. She wanted to hear it directly from the subject herself. But the answer took an age in coming. The men, familiar with this state of affairs, said nothing but waited, almost reverently.

'I just can't stop thinking about taking hard drugs,' she said slowly, licking her lips regularly. 'It never left me, you know. It does some people. But not me for some reason. Whenever I get down, these urges come back. I start to think about drugs. I mustn't take any, or I'll lose everything. So I just have to lie here while it goes away.'

'Then we'll stay here with you,' said Frances, with determination, the tears gathering in her eyes.

'That's right good of you,' replied the prone figure. 'How long have you got? Last time it were three weeks.'

'Well, we've certainly got three days for the bank holiday weekend,' said Jose. 'We can take you to the Dales and remain with you all the time, at least until we have to go back to work.'

'Then we could take turns to take days off,' suggested Frances, defiant in the face of this new challenge.

Debs could not really respond to this show of friendship. It was as if the emotional energy had drained out of her.

'Whatever,' she said. 'I'll not be good company, I'll tell you now. Just let me sleep as much as possible.'

She then turned back onto her left side and closed her eyes.

'I don't understand,' whispered Frances, weeping by now. 'Is she still an addict?'

'Probably not, in the true sense of the word,' said Jose. 'She hasn't taken any regularly for years. But there have been a few lapses, not that we should let her employers know that. It's all tied in with depressive illness. When she goes under with that, it seems to manifest itself in drug cravings.'

'We'll stop here for the evening and discuss tomorrow's trip,' said Nathan. 'Then, maybe it's best if you sleep here overnight, Jose. There's only enough room for one on that small settee in the corner. I can then stay with Frances as usual.'

'No,' Frances protested. 'I can stay here. There's enough room in the bed for two of us, so it can be me who stays.'

It felt strange saying this. She would never have imagined herself suggesting it a few months ago. She was comfortable enough with the touchy-feely nature of friendships with women, but she had never shared a bed with one, not for any reason. The boundary lines between intimacy and unwanted sexual liaison were not established securely enough, somehow. Yet there was

Beltane Fire 191

something about the new experiences of the year so far that caused her to have a rethink. Debs, the witches of Avebury, the phone calls, Irene: all these had inculcated in her a feeling of solidarity with other women. This made her more confident that she was able to get really close to a woman without feeling awkward and compromised.

It was agreed. The rest of the evening was spent in quiet discussion about what they were going to do the next day. When the men left, Frances encouraged Debs to put on more comfortable attire for the night and settled her in. Then Frances herself stripped off. She needed to shed the evening clothes, just a little too damp from sweat after rushing round to the house. She showered quickly, found a long T-shirt of Debs' to wear, turned off the lamp and got in beside her on the left side behind Debs' turned back.

'I'm not leaving you,' she said to Debs gently, as she made herself comfortable.

It took Frances a while to get to sleep. She thought back over the last few months. From the perspective of, say, last Christmas, being in this ex-prostitute's house, lying with her in her bed, looking after her illness as if she were a sister or childhood friend was totally unbelievable. *I can't believe I'm here. Getting to this strange place makes me feel like I'm on a journey. A journey into uncharted territory. I'm getting brave in my old age. I'm like a heroine going into a forest on a great mission, like Xena the Warrior Princess. Xena looks tough, she's got a big sword and a PhD in stunt fighting. But inside, she's just a bit more nervous than she looks. Don't let the enemy know. Forests, deserts, oceans, mountains. Here she is, on her journey. Xena's got travelling companions and occasionally she has to look after 'em. Then, when she's wounded, they look after her. One day, they'll get to big walled city. Then they'll have to work out how to get in...* When she dozed off into dreamland, the walled city was there but not Xena. Instead, she was just herself, walking through streets on which drug addicts lay left and right, stretching out to beg for alms that would fund more drug-taking. Then in front of her, she saw another wall and realised that inside the city was another, smaller citadel. And in this citadel?... As was habitual, Frances woke ten minutes or so into her first dreamy descent into sleep. How long it took her to fall asleep again varied. On this occasion, thanks to the surroundings and Debs shifting about every couple of minutes, it took some considerable time...

The next day, they all sat in Jose's 'limousine' as it left the city of Leeds in bright sunshine.

'I'm making for Almscliffe Crag, if that's all right,' said Jose, as the aged Citroen chugged along north on the A61. 'It's not too far and it overlooks Wharfedale. Nice view. The way the crag sits on the top of the hill there reminds me of a nipple on a great breast.'

'The milk of Mother Nature, eh?' replied Nathan, looking oversized as always in the front of the small car. 'That does sound a good place for a Beltane ritual.'

The women in the back contributed far less to the conversation than they normally did. Debs just stared through the window, eyes down, and Frances, after a poor night's sleep, had her eyes closed.

When they left the main road and started up the hill towards Almscliffe, Jose spoke encouragingly to the car, convinced as he was that its demise was not far off. A drive up even a relatively gentle gradient with four people could be its death warrant. He seemed highly relieved when he parked it at the side of the road with the crag in view. It was a prominent outcrop on a small hill rising steeply away from the open fields. They couldn't get close because of the number of cars parked along the narrow country road.

'We'll walk from here,' stated Jose firmly. 'Good exercise.'

Frances finally stirred. *OK, let's go! I'm glad to see that guys are carrying rucksacks. Don't feel too energetic today. They're not bad are they, doing all food between 'em. Wonder what they've put in? A couple o' six packs and no lunch? Probably. Come on, Debs, love. She's not looking good! Today we'll do a ritual for her before we do one to reveal caller. She's more important right now.*

'We'll need to find a good space,' said Nathan. 'Somewhere a little way away from the general public. But there are so many people up there on that little group of rocks. The weather's not bad and it's bank holiday weekend. Couldn't we find somewhere more secluded?'

Jose frowned. He was feeling got at for his choice of destination. The only time he had come here was in the winter, when it was less crowded. He hadn't anticipated the numbers of day trippers.

'I'm not driving any further,' he snapped. 'The car really wouldn't like it.'

He looked as though he wondered why none of his friends had got a car of their own. His face fixed in a frown, he puffed a little as he limped up the hill with his rucksack, stepping awkwardly over puddles in the grass. Then he became more positive.

'I'm sure we'll find a little corner that we'll make our own. That's the Pagan way. A place is sacred because you make it so, just for the moment, not forever as in the building of a church or temple.'

'Do we *make* a place sacred?' asked Nathan. 'Don't you think that everywhere in nature's a sacred space in its own right?'

Jose nodded breathlessly.

'Can we stop for a moment? Yes, I suppose you're right, we're just tapping into that sacredness for a few moments. It becomes sacred for us during the ritual, but it's already sacred then and forever. The point I was making is that we can choose where to get in touch with the holiness of nature. Not always here, not always there because the Church says so, but maybe somewhere that's not been chosen before.'

'A landscape full of shrines,' Nathan proclaimed, leaning against a fence by a stile and looking across the rolling fields with the hills beyond, as if he were in wonder at the beauty of a Gothic cathedral.

Frances arrived at the stile, having drifted a few yards behind with Debs.

'Listen to these guys,' she laughed. 'They think they're poets, just because they walk uphill in the countryside.'

She glanced anxiously at Debs, who gave a wan smile by way of trying to please her.

On the crag, there were several trainee rock climbers and families giving the children and dogs a run out. They had to walk some yards away to find a quiet space. There was a dip hidden by a muddy ledge in the lower ground as it sloped from the summit, where cows stood around a small pond which had formed from the spring rains. The herd moved reluctantly as they climbed down and then turned round to stare. Debs asked if she could just sit to one side on a prominent flat stone, but the others insisted that the circle pass right through where she was seated; even if lacking in the energy for active participation, she was not going to be allowed to opt out.

'We'll channel Goddess down for you,' said Frances, sympathetically.

'What makes you think that a depressed person cannot be a channel for the Goddess themselves?' asked Jose.

'Yeah, good point,' said Frances, quickly. *Best to concede when you haven't thought it through yourself.*

As they had found shelter from the persistent wind, Nathan was able to light a small Beltane fire to celebrate the beginning of summer. He was well prepared with wood and fire lighters in the rucksack. He had also brought a bodhran, a small Irish drum with beater, to enhance the atmosphere of the ritual. And so it began with the calling of the quarters. Frances had moved on from her stammered first attempt at Avebury to a new confidence in speaking out prayers and invocations. She called them out in clear speech with no fear of being overheard by nearby hill walkers.

'Goddess, mother of the Summer, come and dance with us as we celebrate... Give Debs your life, your health and your strength... Reveal to us the identity of the caller, let me see him face to face...'

Occasionally, passers by, hearing the drum and loud voices, peered over the ledge hiding them from the crag but quickly moved away again, made uncomfortable by the sight of the makeshift ritual. Frances, facing that way, resolved not to let it embarrass her. *We'll never see 'em again, so what's the problem?* She tried to focus and looked up at the top of the crag, visible above the ledge. All that she could hear was the wind and the bodhran. Utter stillness for a few seconds...

A figure appeared high on the rock with what seemed to be a pet of some kind. *I can't make them out, it's all blurry. Someone wearing a hoodie and walking a dog? Oh wow, they seem to be stepping off crag into the air and floating down towards me. Wearing a golden cloak with a hood? It's her! She's coming nearer! That's not a dog, it's a lion! I can't believe all this! Oh God, I can't believe that this is happening again! It's Goddess, like in Leeds Town Hall and at Avebury! I know it's her!...*

'It happened again, didn't it?' asked Nathan, as he helped her up from the sodden ground. 'What did you see?'

'Goddess.'

Frances' words came in gasps.

'She had a lion! She were in complete control over it. It shows how powerful she is. Everything were weird, like in a dream, but then it were very real too. I can't explain it.'

'Did she say anything?'

'She came close, but the wind made hood swirl in front of her face, so I couldn't see her properly. I just heard her say: "It'll be OK, Frances." Then that were it – I blacked out.'

Someone shouted out from the top of the ledge: 'You all right down there?'

'Yes,' Nathan called back. 'We're in control. It's OK, she just stumbled.'

The man stayed watching for a few seconds and looked on very suspiciously. Two men supporting a woman covered in mud and another staring into space, seated on a rock. A drum lay nearby, a fire was just going out. Cows looked on. All very odd. But he shrugged and wandered off.

'What's the point of challenging someone if you allow yourself to be fobbed off with an excuse?' asked Jose, crossly. 'If we really were attacking you, what good would he have been?'

'I think he got spooked; it all looks a bit strange,' replied Nathan. 'Anyway, I'm glad he's gone. Let's get Frances and Debs back to the car.'

Jose looked at the mud on Frances' clothes and covering all their shoes, associating this with his car interior. He sighed inwardly but decided to let it be.

*It'll be OK, Frances.* Simple words, but Frances kept repeating them in her head as they drove off to try and find somewhere they could eat their picnic. She looked at Debs. Was it her imagination, or did Debs look a bit brighter now? She had prayed for two things on the crag, for Debs' health and for the end of the threat of the mystery caller. Maybe if one of them was being granted, so would the other. Debs started to speak now and again.

'You know, the Goddess controlling a lion is on one of the Tarot cards, the card called "Strength". That's a good sign is that, Frances.'

She definitely looked a bit better, not 100%, yet not absolutely down. It'll be OK, Frances. Debs' salvation and her own seemed inextricably linked. Having realised that, Frances desperately wanted her to get well.

## 22

## The Lion Goddess

Debs had company for every moment of the bank holiday weekend. Her contributions to the conversation were even more infrequent than usual so, as words were hard to come by, Frances could not resist making a good deal of physical contact with the patient, a lot of shoulder rubbing, arm holding and sitting close. She was surprised by how much Debs' depression affected her. Probably, if it had happened to a girlfriend in the past, she might – while outwardly responding with concern – have been a little suspicious of the demands that were being made on her, as if they were not totally genuine. In Debs' case, she had no doubts that the illness was real and severe. Along with the anxiety about her friend's health, she felt hopeful about its resolution, her optimism brought on by the apparition of the lion goddess at Almscliffe.

Jose had his own opinion about the significance of the lion.

'People say that we have just moved into the Age of Aquarius the Water Bearer. This is because the constellation that the Sun is in when it crosses the equator at the spring equinox has been Pisces for 2,000 years but it's now Aquarius. Pisces was the sign of the fish, the secret sign of early Christianity, but apparently we're headed into a new age, because we're now under the sign Aquarius. That's all very well, but I ask why we only concentrate on the *spring* equinox? The constellation that the Sun is in when it crosses the equator again at the *autumn* equinox has changed too, from Virgo to Leo the lion. These are the signs directly opposite to Pisces and Aquarius. So the Virgin, Virgo, is being replaced by the Lion, Leo. Maybe now a new image of the Goddess will become prominent: the Goddess of Leo, the Goddess with the lion.'

'OK, I see the logic,' agreed Nathan. 'But while the image of the Virgin has been prominent for centuries, I can't think of any examples of the Goddess with the lion, can you?'

'Well, yes – the Hindu goddess Durga,' replied Jose, with barely hidden triumph. 'In the ancient world, there was also Inanna. And, as Debs said, there's a Tarot card with that image on. *Plus* I can see another possible link in Roman Catholicism. The sign Leo is associated with the lion but also with the Sun. The connection between the Virgin Mary and the Sun has become important, particularly since the apparitions of Mary at Fatima in Portugal in 1917, where thousands thought that they saw the Sun falling towards the Earth. There were healings. Even atheists were converted. I was brought up with that story, you know, living in a one-time Portuguese colony. Goddess and Lion; Mary and Sun; a new age of Aquarius and Leo. Perhaps Frances' vision will be the inspiration for a whole new set of Goddess images! OK, it's just a theory!'

On Monday evening, Frances was left alone to potter around the flat and attend to housework that had long been neglected. Jose stayed with Debs; Nathan was meeting some work colleagues for a drink. Frances always felt a pang of jealousy when he did that. In any group, there was *bound* to be one really attractive lady that was after him, wasn't there? So she took it out on Cass, moaning as the cat sought attention as she tried to dust.

'You don't want me normally, do you, smelly cat? It's only when I'm busy that you want me to fuss wi' you! Shouldn't you be out, catching mice?' That made her laugh to herself; it reminded her of people getting annoyed at policemen when being pulled up for a traffic offence. 'Yes, Cass, you should be out there, catching real mice criminals! It's mice what's running vice rings and stuff, but here you are giving me a ticket for dusting. Anyway, can you prove I were dusting over speed limit?'

The silliness of her humour made her relent and she dropped the duster to pick up the imperturbable cat, oblivious to the nonsense being spoken at her. It was at that moment that there was a loud knock on the flat door. As Frances' flat door was not open to the street, it had to be the elderly neighbour, rather forgotten over the last few weeks.

'Oops, it's Mr Miller. Sorry, Cass, I have to give him some attention. He must be really lonely with everybody else enjoying bank holiday.'

She opened the door: sure enough, there was Mr Miller, but behind him was a familiar face, although the name wouldn't come.

'This young man wants to see you but he rang wrong doorbell,' explained Mr Miller, seemingly glad to be of some use. 'Anyway, I'll let you both get on and talk.'

He then shuffled away toward the stairs, leaving Frances to let her visitor in. *Now who is this guy?*

Frances couldn't remember the young man's name, but she knew she had met him a few times. Before she let him over the threshold, she made a questioning gesture, as if to say: remind me what your name is and what do you want? He responded. He was tall and thin with a large mop of brown straight shoulder-length hair, which partly hid his face, pale but quite handsome; however, the demeanour was downcast and anxious, his thick eyebrows knitted in a deep frown.

'It's Jonathan,' he said. 'I used to go out with Cyn. I wanted to ask you, Frances, how is she? She won't reply to my messages. I know she's got a new bloke, but I still care about her and just need to know that she's all right.'

'OK, come in,' said Frances, having got used to her counsellor role that she was developing of late. She felt a rush of pride; she was clearly someone whom people felt they could talk to and get help from! 'Sit down. I'll make you a cup o' tea but I can't guarantee being able to help. I don't see so much o' Cyn these days.'

She went out to the kitchen to make some tea. She was humming contentedly as she reached up for a highly coloured mug, one that might have helped to cheer him up. She was just thinking: *how weird it is, Cyn's ex-boyfriend coming round*! Then she made a sudden connection, which came from nowhere. One word hammered into her consciousness: 'Cyn's'. That was a word that had an association. It sounded like 'sins', the one word spoken by the corpse in the nightmare as she tried to identify her killer. Frances mulled over this as the kettle heated up. Normally, she would have gone back into the room to talk to a visitor while she awaited the noise of steam, but she was now standing by the sink, deep in thought. 'Cyn's' – 'sins'. What if the word were a kind of prophecy? What if Frances had misunderstood this word? Then she got goose bumps. What if the corpse were trying to say 'Cyn's ex-boyfriend, Jonathan' but only had life enough for one word? As Frances poured the tea into the old pot with only a saucer for a lid, she recalled the voice of the mystery caller. Some while back, she had given up trying to place it; having first accused Gary, then John Taylor and afterward hearing the resonance of the voice in every man she encountered, she had decided that it wasn't a successful strategy. She had mentioned the difficulty of identifying that 'something' in a spoken tone – that made it distinct – to Nathan, who had replied with a silly joke: 'The timbre of his voice caused trees to fall on your head.' This had made her mad at first, because it seemed that Nathan wasn't taking it seriously but, a minute or two later, she was giggling about it. But now: Jonathan? Well, yes, he did fit the bill, actually. The speaking pitch was slightly high for the average man and had a nasal quality as if a cat was quietly purring in the background. Although the mystery caller disguised his voice, there was an unmistakeable similarity between the two. *OK, what if it were Jonathan? Maybe Goddess has set up this meeting in response to my prayers and rituals and I'll be OK, remember? Take a deep breath and see it through.*

As she re-entered the room, Frances decided to do two things, but she was badly flustered now and got them horribly in the wrong order. First, she tried a test. The names of the other two phone call victims were indelibly etched on her memory.

'Oh, by the way, Jonathan, I saw Claire Robinson the other day. You know her, don't you?'

Jonathan all but leapt out of the armchair.

'Oh, well, yes, but I, er… didn't know *you* did.'

Frances wondered at how her voice or hands didn't tremble so violently that she was given away, but somehow she managed to keep her act together. The effort was excruciating. She felt a terrible pressure in her chest and stomach. The possibility that someone quite evil and unpredictable was in the room effected every sensation, as if the room itself had become corrupted.

'Yes, a little. Remind me – how do *you* know her?'

'She's a colleague at work,' answered Jonathan, looking down at his cup. 'I don't know her that well, she's in department next door to me.'

It would have been better if Frances' next action had been carried out before she had made Jonathan suspicious.

'Before we go on, I must just call my friend Nathan,' she said, trying to keep the breaths even. 'He said to call before eight.'

But both the mobile phone and landline were on the other side of Jonathan's chair, on the coffee table. As she moved towards them, he reached out and impeded her path. He then picked up her mobile and gripped it.

'Please,' he said. 'Can you leave that, just for a few minutes? I must talk to you.'

'Oh, OK, but quick then,' replied Frances, deciding not to protest but looking straight at him with some defiance and trying to remember the lion. 'What did you want to say to me?'

Jonathan couldn't return the stare. He looked down again and started to mumble.

'You don't know what it's been like. I really loved that girl. Why did she do that to me? I always knew that, if I fell in love, someone like Cyn would do that. So I tried not to. But she were so... so *wonderful*, you see. I couldn't not fall in love with someone like her.'

The passion of his last remark caused him to look up, push the hair back and look straight into Frances' eyes for the first time. His eyes were wide open and wild; he seemed spaced out. Then something else dawned on Frances. *Oh yeah, the first call came at about the same time as Cyn's new relationship, didn't it?*

'Jonathan,' she said firmly. 'We all suffer from losing out in love. It happens to everyone. You know that old saying: better to have loved and lost than never to have loved. I've missed out several times. But you can't...' Frances took another very deep breath. This was the crucial moment and it took a lot of courage. She kept trying to focus on the lion and uttered repeated internal prayers to the Goddess. 'You can't take it out on *others*,' she said, the trembling in her body and voice now unmistakable.

Jonathan glanced at her, back at his cup and around the room several times before answering in a low voice.

'What do you mean?'

'It were you who made them calls. Yeah, it were, weren't it? I realised it a few minutes after you came in,' announced Frances, with some boldness. 'You're like a criminal who has to return to scene o' crime, aren't you? You have to see what damage you've caused. Well, it did cause damage, but I didn't go under, you know. Maybe Claire Robinson and Vanessa Fairclough did.'

Jonathan just stared into space.

'OK, but you don't understand,' he said, very slowly and deliberately. 'I were just so mad at Cyn. But I couldn't hurt her, so I just phoned other women I knew a bit and took it out on *them*. I were just so angry. I called women without any connection to each other, so they couldn't trace them easily to me. Disguised my voice: good actor, aren't I?'

He gave an uneasy laugh, but there was no humour in it, not even of a malicious kind. It was full of bitterness and desperation. Frances tried to take control of the situation.

'Please give me my phone. I need to call my friend.'

Jonathan ignored her and kept talking. He was responding to her verbally, but his body language and distant stare showed him becoming scarily disconnected from the reality of the situation.

'It's not such a big deal. I just needed to get my feelings out. You must know that I wouldn't really hurt you.'

'That's just the problem,' replied Frances, betraying her agitation. 'I didn't know that. How could I, wi' some mad person saying terrible things on phone? Men do hurt women, you know, every day, thousands o' them. How were I to know that you wouldn't come here to harm me? How do I know that you won't hurt me right now?'

Jonathan had now got past the point where proper dialogue was possible. He was raising his voice.

'Let's forget it! You must tell me about Cyn. How is she? Is that bastard treating her right?'

He then started to sob violently, still holding the mobile so that Frances couldn't make a call. *I know why you're here,* she thought. *Goddess has led you.* She pictured the lion once more; in her faltering attempt to summon up more courage, the image of Xena came back into her mind.

Frances and Jonathan sat for a few minutes without speaking, he in the single armchair with his head in his hands. Frances was now convinced that he was high on hard drugs. She sat perched on the edge of the settee, stroking the apparently unconcerned Cass and just looking vacantly at her unwelcome visitor while trying to keep her nerve. She was trying to think what to say and eventually she broke the silence, fighting to overcome the panic in her voice.

'You *must* seek help,' she said. 'And you *must* tell police, so that the whole thing is resolved and Claire and Vanessa know everything's OK.'

Jonathan began to talk to himself quietly through the tears. It was difficult to make the words out. There was a mention of Cyn and 'that bastard', but other than that it was unintelligible. Frances struggled on, attempting to find the right words.

'OK, what if you agree to go to a psychiatrist and promise never to make calls again? On second thoughts, we won't go to police. That wouldn't help any of us, would it? Then you wouldn't have to face Cyn finding out.'

Frances disliked the thought of lying to him, suggesting this while intending to phone the police after he had gone. Yet, despite her belief that she was being protected by a divine hand, she was getting desperate. With Jonathan not responding to her idea, still looking into his hands and weeping, she decided to try and edge towards the landline phone. She uttered a particularly intense internal prayer to the Goddess, put the cat aside and moved quietly towards the little table by the door. But Jonathan suddenly came to life. He sprang up, blocking her way. There was no contact but only inches between them. He was about six foot and, while not bulky, loomed large over her in the small room. The staring, tearful eyes were now really frightening; there was no reason in them. He then switched to the fake telephone voice with his eyes steadily fixed on her.

'I'm really going to hurt you, Frances! Really going to hurt you! Unless you do things my way. Stay where you are!'

The scare tactic worked. Frances sat down and then so did Jonathan. She was now terrified and shook violently, no longer trying to disguise the fact. Tears appeared in her eyes. There was silence between them, although he continued to look through her. The atmosphere in the room was now unbearably intense. It reminded her of the scene in a television serial which had so frightened her as a child: Jane Eyre in her bed late at night, surprised by Rochester's mad wife, who had escaped from the attic, broken into Jane's room and was now standing in there laughing demoniacally. The distortion of the familiar living room by the presence of evil was extreme; nothing looked right, not the furniture, carpet and curtains, ornaments, television, not even the cat. The madness and the terror permeated all of these things; they all seemed to swim in it. Although the lights were on, there was an apparent darkness. It was as if Death itself had arrived on the scene, speeding in from the remote future on receiving the signal that it might be called upon prematurely to take Frances. She looked up at the only items that might have somehow kept their shape of normality. The Madonna pictures. Jonathan saw her staring up at the wall, followed her eyes and his gaze too fell on the Madonna of Iviron. They were both entranced for a second, each perusing the icon from totally different perspectives. She saw Jonathan looking but could not fathom what his understanding of the image might be. The moment was so powerful and dreadful that, strangely, neither of them heard the turn of the key in the lock until the flat door was well and truly open and someone was coming through into the little hallway which led into the living room.

## 23

## White Charger

Jonathan and Frances turned their heads from the Madonna icon to see Nathan's tall frame in the living room doorway. Frances gasped. Life was becoming unbelievable; it was as if she had been transported into the movies. Nathan seemed to be entering purposefully like a saviour figure, transforming the room to its former status as a refuge of homely comforts and casting out its evil. In actual fact, having no idea as to what was going on or who Jonathan was, he gave a sheepish smile and shrugged as if to say: sorry to disturb you, I know you weren't expecting me home so early! Immediately, Jonathan got up and, with some determination, pushed past him towards the flat door and the stairs. Frances signalled to Nathan with an open hand held up: let him go. Her anxiety for her own safety was now transferred to Nathan, as even a big bloke like him would have trouble with a drugged-up madman. Before Jonathan could even have reached the street, she was on the phone to the police. They heard the front door slam. Then they phoned Jose. Then she hugged Nathan in a silent iron grip until Jose, Debs and the police all arrived at the same time. 'You were lucky that a patrol car was nearby, ma'am.'

The end of the mystery call saga was just like the beginning: late evening at the flat, a policeman, a policewoman (albeit not the same personnel as last time), all the adventurers summoned and Frances shaky in their midst. But this time, no mystery, instead – revelation!

'I think you'll find there *is* one person who knows Claire Robinson, Vanessa Fairclough and me,' declared Frances to the police, so pleased to be able finally to say these words. 'He doesn't know any of us well. That were his plan, to express his anger without being suspected. His name's Jonathan, I don't know his surname or address, but Cyndi Hogan will do. I'll give you her number.'

Frances looked at the cat, still lying on the sofa. Not much seemed to have happened in the cat world; she might have detected some tension among the humans, but nothing had been thrown and the raising of voices had been minimal.

'Incidentally, for what it's worth,' added Frances, tentatively. 'I think he's on drugs. You can tell by the eyes, not to mention his weird behaviour.'

'Ah right,' said the policeman, knowingly.

He was a young man who made Nathan and Jose look middle-aged, with spiked up short dark hair and large blue eyes that didn't help him to look authoritative. The policewoman nodded and shut her notebook. She was a blonde, athletic woman, also young but with a more mature demeanour, exuding a sense of purpose and dynamism.

'We'll get back to you the moment we have information,' she said with a sense of closure for the evening's business. 'Thank you for all your help. I assume that someone will be staying with the lady tonight?'

Nathan replied with a firm yes, then the two of them were on their way.

After they had gone, Frances began to tremble uncontrollably and said that she needed several measures of stiff drink. Nathan's special ten-year-old single Irish malt whisky was opened, like the celebratory killing of the biblical fatted calf. Jose immediately launched into talk about how amazing it all was, given the apparition at Almscliffe; even Debs was shocked out of her languidness by the realisation that Frances had been in such danger.

'Don't worry about me,' she said. 'There's no better remedy for depression than knowing a good friend desperately needs you.'

'Goddess sorted it,' breathed Frances, combining fatigue with exaltation. 'She took control and made things work out OK.'

'Yes, but only through you and Nathan,' said Debs. '*You* took control with her help. How did you cope, knowing that a dangerous man had got into your flat?'

'It were lion,' replied Frances. 'It gave me courage.'

'The Age of Leo has arrived for you, then,' said Jose, with a broad smile. 'Oh yes, there's a third symbol for Leo besides the lion and the Sun. The heart.'

'Working through the heart,' murmured Frances. 'But, Nathan, love, why did you come home so early? Did you have an intuition that I were in danger?'

Nathan looked down at his feet and chuckled.

'Yes, that's it. I heard a voice telling me to come home on a white charger. The horse is outside, tethered to the lamppost.' Then he looked up apologetically and grimaced. 'OK, the truth then. I got the wrong pub. I must have misheard where my colleagues agreed to meet. I looked all over town but couldn't find them. Forgetfulness even happens to librarians, you know. I wasn't very pleased with myself while I was walking back home but now I see that it was a happy accident.'

'No accident!' interrupted Jose and Debs, speaking at the same time. 'Divine providence,' added Jose, as if anyone needed the explanation.

The next morning, a sickie off work was needed, a really genuine one, although Frances felt quite elated. Her sense of being in the care of the Goddess was growing very strong. During the Beltane ritual, she had prayed that the mystery caller be unmasked, then he had walked right into her living room. When things started to get out of hand, she had looked up at the Madonna and, at that moment, back came Nathan unexpectedly. *Thank goodness that he had a key! But then no, thank the Goddess, actually.* Through the pain of the headache, Frances smiled. Goddesses sorted out threatening lunatics but they just didn't do the curing of hangovers. That was your own fault; there could be no overturning of the ancient law: alcohol in excess equals next day, bleah! As she slumped back into the sofa, her body's balance mechanisms all apparently having shut down, she glanced back up at the Madonna of Iviron in her silvery metallic cloak. It looked like the armour of a warrior maiden, more Athene than Mary the peasant mother from Nazareth, an Athene harbouring a secret love child that compromised her famed virginity. A super-Xena. The Madonna warrior Goddess had given her command, sent her messiah Nathan into the crisis and the flat was a safe place once more. The corpse woman had been, in a symbolic sense, Frances herself. Her life had been destroyed by 'Cyn's ex-boyfriend' but she had been resurrected here in the flat, just where the vision foretelling this had occurred. It all felt good; Frances enjoyed reflecting on it and playing with the ideas with plenty of coffee to help the brain work.

There was just the mopping-up to do. She awaited the call from the police to tell her that Jonathan had been arrested and could do no more harm. Instead, a call from Cyn sounding a bit agitated.

'Why do the police want to know about Jonathan? They said you gave them my number!'

'Well, you know I told you about them calls a few weeks ago? Well, it were him.'

'Jonathan? No! He's boring, screwed up a bit maybe, but harmless.'

'Apparently not, Cyn. He admitted it to me last night. He were angry at you, going out with your new guy.'

'Why couldn't he have phoned me personally?'

'I don't know, Cyn. Maybe you should ask him, although on second thoughts, I would advise you to leave him well alone from now on.'

'You shouldn't have got involved, Frances.'

'What! I didn't choose to, you silly cow!'

'Don't get overwrought. Anyway, he didn't hurt you, did he?'

'No, but only because Nathan came back early! Couldn't you be a bit more sympathetic? It were your mess in first place.'

'OK, if you're going to be like that, I'm going to ring off. I'm at work, you know.'

Slam phone down. *Grrr! How quickly some people drag you down from a spiritual high to being your stupid old irritable, everyday self. Try to regain composure. Uh-oh, a ring at the door. I'd better not answer it without checking, Nathan's at work. I can't rely on miracles two days in a row. But I can't see front door step from up here. I'll go down and ask who it is through letter box. That Mr Miller had better not open it again! I'll have to tell him about that.*

She breathed easy again when she discovered that it was the policewoman who came the first time a few weeks ago. Frances asked her in, but she declined the cup of tea.

'It's about Mr Jonathan Barwell,' she said. 'The man you complained about. Well, he seems to have left the city. We went round to his place in Gipton in the early hours o' the morning. Landlord let us in. He's taken a few possessions and left rest. We've put out a call to pick him up and circulated his car registration.'

'Good!' exclaimed Frances, beginning to get anxious about this but trying to maintain her optimistic mood. 'So it'll not be long, then?'

'To be frank,' replied the policewoman, without any emotion, 'All we have is a few nasty phone calls and a suspicion o' drugs. He's not really going to be a priority, I'm afraid. All I can say to reassure you is that we have no reason to believe he will hurt anyone. We'll grab him when we get chance.'

'But he's terrorizing women,' complained Frances, experiencing a sinking feeling. 'He threatened me in my flat. I'm sure I read that violent crimes are often preceded by warnings, like threatening behaviour or summat.'

'In a few famous cases, yes,' agreed the policewoman, her body language suggesting that she was trying to balance an urge to get away to more urgent tasks with the desirability of completing this one. 'But it's not a general thing. Some people are all bark and no bite, I'm glad to say.'

That had to be that. The policewoman left. Frances was not pleased. She had thought that she had finally achieved liberation from weeks of looking over her shoulder and that Jonathan would be getting the help that he so clearly needed, under the restraints necessary for the safety of others. But not yet. Would there be any end to it?

A call to Irene reminded Frances of the conversation in the toilet prompted by the Tarot cards. She decided to consult them again, to see if they could reassure her about Jonathan. *Will he get caught and stop hurting people, that's my question.* OK, shuffle three times, cut three times. Immediate past. The Moon. Goddess: Diana. 'Support of women who truly care for you. Intuition. Intense dreams.' *Well, yes, there doesn't seem to be any need to ask further about that. The Jonathan situation has brought me into contact with Irene and it has made me understand women's solidarity more. What's more, Goddess herself cares for me. Let's do present:* Judgement. *How strange! This were future card in reading of a few weeks ago and I linked it to resurrection of corpse woman. That were in future, now it's the present. Will Jonathan be judged, in court? Let's ask for further clarification.* Three Cups. 'Three women dance in a circle, celebrating the round of life. A celebration involving women.' *Wow! Three women: Claire, Vanessa and me! I think the answer has to be yes, he will be caught; we can then all relax and celebrate. So: the future.* Take a deep breath. Eight staves.

'Sudden communications – unexpected telephone calls, surprise letters.' *Oh no. I don't want any more unexpected calls, do I?*

She told Nathan about the policewoman's visit and the Tarot reading when he came back from work, as they both settled down for something to eat.

'I'm sure he will be caught and face judgement,' she declared.

'You really are a witch now,' said Nathan 'You can tell the future. Did you ever check out that Priestesses of Delphi?'

'No, I keep meaning to, I must do that sometime,' replied Frances, with her mouth full of tagliatelle.

Then the phone rang. Ever since that Saturday night, the landline phone had taken on a new personality of its own: shrill, demanding, menacing. Yet despite this, Frances got there first.

'Hello, is that Frances Dryburgh?' It was the policewoman from the morning.

'Yes, hello. What's happened?'

'I had to tell you before going off duty. A couple of hours ago, Mr Barwell phoned the police in Sheffield. He had gone there to stay with his sister, but she persuaded him to give himself up and seek help. So he's down there, talking to our colleagues and we will keep you informed as to how it goes. It seems I was wrong this morning; things have been resolved pretty quickly and I'm really pleased to be able to say that. Only thing is, we will probably need all three women who received these calls to testify in court. It won't be for a few weeks. We'll let you know.'

She rang off.

'You and your prophecies, you really are scary,' said Nathan, as the whisky came out again and he held it up with a questioning expression. 'Do you want some? Not so much "hair of the dog that bit you", more "locking yourself in the kennel with a pit bull terrier".'

Frances nodded, with her characteristic 'relaxed and relieved' giggle.

'Yeah, unexpected call weren't the one I received but the one that Jonathan made to police. Nobody could have expected that.'

'I can't believe that you have foretold things so accurately. I will definitely come to you when I want something answered.'

'Who's to know whether I can do it for other people?'

'Well, it is worth trying one day. Of course, there is one consequence of that call this evening. There is now no reason for me to stay here. I'll pack my stuff up tomorrow and go back round the corner to Springfield Terrace.'

'Couldn't you stay anyway?' said Frances, not needing Tarot cards for the answer.

'No, I couldn't. What would it say if I were to live here in a one-bedroom flat without a reason? Anyway, that sofa's seen better days.'

*You didn't have to sleep on it,* thought Frances. *My bed's king size. Typical, in't it? Life always seems to throw up a silver lining behind every cloud but then also a cloud behind every silver lining. Maybe I'll not drink that whisky after all, can't test Mr Carson by taking another sickie off tomorrow!*

## 24

# Twelve Moons

The next few weeks were all about preparing for France. The arrangements were altered by a dream that Frances had a few days after the visit by Jonathan. It was so striking that she felt she had to try and respond to it. The Jonathan incident had confirmed her as a prophetess amongst the other adventurers and they were highly receptive to anything she had to say. 'We'll have to be careful, we're beginning to treat Frances like an infallible guru,' Jose said at some point, light-heartedly but with the sting of truth that made Frances uncomfortable. However, the dream had already shaped their plans by then.

There was much about the dream that Frances couldn't remember, but the most memorable 'scene' came, as usual, just a little while before waking. It showed a beautiful young woman with long black wavy hair and fair skin, clothed in a red cloak, seated on what looked like a lotus plant in the middle of a small lake. Next to the lake, on the right, was an oak tree. Behind the woman in the distance were mountains. She looked like an ancient Celtic priestess, a raven-haired Morgan le Fay. Her body was framed by an oval-shaped mandala, made up of twelve moon shapes (Frances just knew that there were twelve without counting them). The figure held nothing and did nothing, simply looked out at Frances from the oval. A voice said, 'That's what it takes'...

'Mountains may indicate area o' France where we're going,' said Frances to Jose and Nathan. The three of them sat together in the pub during the following Saturday lunchtime. Debs still felt too low to join them but had insisted that they go out and leave her. 'What do twelve moons mean, in your opinion?'

'Twelve moons in a year, one for each month,' replied Jose. 'That's what the months are based on, the cycle of the moon.'

Frances thought for a while and then – despite not having joined the Priestesses of Delphi – gave a sibylline interpretation.

So I say that when we're in France, we have to do twelve rituals, one for each cycle o' the moon in a year. That's what it'll take to make powerful enough magic to influence G8 summit, see? We'll have to find twelve shrines o' the Madonna, that's how I understand it, anyway.'

'Twelve!' exclaimed Jose, sounding concerned, by nature the cautiously practical one of the four. 'I know of only two in the Auvergne region so far, Le Puy and Orcival, although I can look for more on the web. What worries me is how long it will take with a ceremony at each one. We've only booked two weeks.'

'Fourteen days, twelve shrines,' said Nathan. 'Sounds OK to me.'

'No, hang on!' Jose was not happy. 'Over twenty-four hours to get there, twenty-four back. That means at least one shrine and a ritual per day, plus travelling. No time to breathe; we might feel like doing nothing some days, it *is* a holiday after all.'

'OK,' suggested Frances. 'Let's go for three weeks instead.'

Jose winced. Debs' insistence that they went by train had already cost them a good deal more than a cheap flight would have done. Now more tinkering could increase the bill.

'I wouldn't normally go along with so much disruption to well-made plans,' he sighed. 'But one thing sways me. I noticed that we would be travelling on the night of the summer solstice, so we wouldn't be in a very good position to celebrate it. If we went a week earlier, we could include the solstice in our schedule more easily.'

'That's it, then,' said Frances. 'Now we've got Carson in charge, I feel confident that he'll let me add a week to my leave. He's kind o' bloke who'll find a way to do it when he knows your request's genuine. I'll just have to work harder between now and then.'

It was agreed; within a few days, all four had reported success in getting an extra week. They would go on Friday evening, 13$^{th}$ June, and return on Saturday, July 5$^{th}$. The G8 summit in Japan was to be held the week after they returned. There would be twelve rituals at separate shrines of the Madonna, where they would do magic that would contribute to the most powerful nations deciding in favour of a radical approach to the environmental issues facing the world. A few days later, Jose volunteered to research into possible shrines and working out a pattern, but Frances stopped him.

'We'll start at that Le Puy place, like you suggested, but let's go wi' flow after that,' she said. 'I like the idea of being spontaneous; I'm getting used to Goddess guiding me.'

Nathan nodded his approval. Jose the bus timetabler could get a bit control freaky about schedules. They would spend three weeks looking at their watches if they weren't careful. Jose stayed relaxed, laughed and nodded an OK, conceding to the prophetess and her devotee. *He'll be privately deciding to check the area out anyway*, thought Frances.

Those weeks in May and early June were good. Debs began to look better and gained more energy; she admitted that the resolving of Frances' situation had helped her move out of the worst of the depression. As for the calls, Frances made another statement to the police and was briefed about her role in the court case. She worried that it might disrupt the holiday; no, said the prosecution lawyer, the case wouldn't come up until mid-July at the earliest. She saw Irene a few times. Even Cyn had phoned up to restore contact. Work was OK, still dull but so much easier since the change in management. Sal was bored and looking elsewhere for work. Frances began to think how she could retrain for a more fulfilling career but no thoughts came. There was one other blot on the landscape: her feelings for Nathan. She saw Gary once or twice, but it was clear by now that their relationship was not going to go any further. Gary himself seemed to have accepted it and moved on; he was now pursuing a recently divorced woman who was new at his work. 'Yeah, she's got a kiddie, but I'm ready for that now. I could handle it.' But passion for Nathan still burned in her soul. She kept thinking of that song: *Isn't he good, isn't he fine, isn't it madness that he won't be mine?* It did seem like madness; they got on so well, their conversations fluent, their interests convergent. They had similar tastes in music. So why not, really why not? None of Nathan's previous reasons for keeping distance made sense. So she sought a conversation about it with the re-energised Debs, who popped round one weekend.

'Debs, he *does* fancy me, I know he does. I can see it in everything he does when we're together.'

'Maybe, Frances, but it's common for people to see their own passion reflected in the one they fancy. They feel what they feel so strongly that it seems like it *must* come from other person. Men are particularly prone to this, often on a very basic physical level – she looks sexy, I fancy her, so she must fancy me – but women suffer from it too.'

Frances bit her lip.

'I'm so stupid, aren't I?'

'No, it's quite understandable, we've all done it one time or other. Important thing is not to expect yourself to be perfect but to understand yourself.'

'You're right. He doesn't fancy me then. So where *is* he coming from?'

Debs took a deep breath. She wanted to help Frances and get the facts right. But it needed frankness.

'As far as I can see, Nathan's in love with *ideals*. He does volunteering work wi' people who have learning difficulties but he doesn't mention it to anyone. That's another ideal: keeping it hid. You didn't know it, did you, even though he stayed in your flat wi' you? He's deeply committed to freedom of all kinds; he were quite political in his university years. But his project over last few years since going to India has been *spiritual* freedom. That's what brought him to us, Frances. He loves seeing people exercise their right to be spiritual in whatever way they choose and to grow through it. He's happy to take part in that but any deeper romantic involvement would make it messy for him. It would make him uncomfortable and then not relate so well to us.'

'Didn't he ever fall in love then?'

'I suspect no, not with a real woman. But maybe with an ideal woman, a goddess. I think, from time to time, he *has* fallen for someone but always a woman who were unlikely or just unavailable. For that reason, they remained ideal and not real. It's as if his goddess follows him about, peeping out from behind bushes; as soon as he gets a brief glimpse of her, she's gone.'

Frances frowned, with a sceptical expression.

'Unavailable to someone as drop-dead gorgeous as Nathan?'

'Well, he's an odd character. You're so besotted, you haven't seen him as he really is. I think that, when beautiful girls have been interested and gone out with him, they're quickly disappointed and have given up fairly soon, leaving him to remember 'em as his ideal, never giving him a chance to discover their weaknesses too.'

'Why can't I be his ideal?'

'I think you're too real for him to dare to put his feet in water where you're concerned. But he does have one great talent. He prefers to influence people rather than get too involved with 'em personally, so he *does* see and encourage potential in others. He made friends wi' Jose and me because at that time we were loners and needed company to bring us out a bit. This year he saw you. What intuition – especially for a man – to walk into a pub and see a woman and sense that she were just ready to go on great spiritual adventure! And because he's so attractive, people get drawn to him, but he stays one step away, causing 'em to reach out, overbalance, and by way o' compensation, find the spiritual freedom that he wanted 'em to find. That's a great gift, I suppose.'

'Are you saying he's a kind o' spiritual bait?'

Debs gave her an appreciative smile.

'That's a good way o' putting it.'

Frances frowned. She really needed to get to the heart of her Nathan bug.

'Well, he does inspire me. It's true. I read it somewhere, it's not so much that you like people for who *they* are, but more that you like people who make you feel good about *yourself.*'

'I agree wi' that,' nodded Debs. 'I hope you don't hate me for saying this, but you and he have a lot in common. You too are a charismatic person who's chasing ideals, aren't you?'

'Ideals? What, being a priestess o' the Goddess?'

'Well, yes, but I didn't mean that. No, I meant chasing *him*. He's your ideal, in't he? You're not unattractive, are you? How many men've looked your way since Nathan came along?'

Frances didn't take long to think.

'Well, no one apart from Gary.'

'You're quite wrong there, Frances. Your antennae just aren't functioning since you met Nathan. Gary were cheeky enough to walk straight in under radar screen, but he only got away with it for a short while.'

'Yes, Debs, but Nathan's not just an ideal, is he? He's real, he's close and I love him.'

'Sadly for you, if he remains true to the person I've come to know, he will remain an ideal, at least as far as a one-to-one relationship is concerned.'

'Well, if I'm chasing an ideal, I'd rather do that than settle for summat that I don't really want.'

Debs laughed out loud. She hadn't done that for so long, it was welcome to Frances, even if she didn't like what she was hearing.

'That's just what he would say! So you are alike, then. Two idealists!'

'Pooh,' said Frances, frowning.

She then smiled broadly to show Debs that she didn't resent it and hugged her to convey gratitude for the straight talking that only a good friend could do.

And so the countdown brought the 13<sup>th</sup> June nearer. Frances went through the normal holiday traumas of deciding what and how much to pack. How hot would it be? *Probably quite hot, although it's up in mountains.* Would it rain? *It probably would.* Will there be an iron in the room? *Probably not, we're only staying in cheap hotels, arriving on the off chance. I always forget one thing when I go on my holidays, I wonder what it'll be this time. Last year, camera. Year before, my small bag to carry things around in during day. Before that, sun lotion. No wonder airport shops do so well. But this year, we're not travelling by air!*

# 25

# A Town Ruled by the Goddess

And so – the journey! Departure Friday night, 20.40 from Leeds station, London King's Cross train. *Workday, so had to pack last night. I'm very tired! But we're off to France and shrines o' Black Virgin! Sitting opposite Nathan, good! He looks so cool, even in travelling mode. Blue T-shirt and white shorts go so well with his blond hair and tan! How come he's still so blond at his age? Wow! Steady. Remember, it's spiritual friendship! Debs looks better health-wise these days, but she never loses that messed-up look. Is that a hairstyle? Is it, heck! Just long frizzy strands hanging down with a white ribbon unevenly tied on each side to keep hair off her face. Like a rag doll. No point in telling her though, is there? I don't like it when people say things to me. She's quite big in the upper arms and shoulders; you don't normally see them. Mind you, that white looks good next to her dark brown skin. She makes my little tan look a bit weak. We've both got white vests – spiritual sisters dress alike! Except she's gone for red cotton slacks, whereas I've got khaki shorts. Now, Jose looks like bit part character from fifties thriller. Short-sleeved white shirt, grey cord trousers – why do those two wear trousers in weather like this? Other people are strange. Now train's moving out o' Leeds; we're all excited, can't stop smiling at each other but no one can think of owt to say right at the moment. Hang on, Nathan is about to say summat momentous.*

'Flat shoes, Frances? Haven't you got your high heels this time?'

'No heels in French mountains, Nathan, love! It'll give me more space in my luggage.'

*Debs is coming in.*

'Great, then we'll be the same height for a change, won't we?'

*She's fully back to normal, in't she?*

As the train slowed into Wakefield, only a few miles from Leeds, Jose stretched out his arms wearily but then the yawn turned into an excited smile.

'This is tremendous. We're doing something about the state of the world at last. It may be an odd something that we're doing but it's our contribution. You never feel you can achieve anything, do you, in the world of big business, transnational companies and all? You just sit and watch while other people screw up the planet.'

'It's going to succeed,' exclaimed Frances. 'Our magic's going to succeed. I just feel it.'

Then the magician piped down, as she had said this rather loudly during a lull in the conversation of the people opposite, who looked over curiously.

'Beware, weirdo on train,' said Nathan, in a low voice only audible to Frances. 'Conductor, please remove the weirdo woman at the next station.'

'And remove man who got me *into* this fine weirdo mess,' riposted Frances in a whisper.

23.45 The train pulled into King's Cross, a few minutes behind schedule. They had not planned to stay anywhere in expensive London as they were catching the 06.25 from St Pancras. Waste of money to get rooms, Nathan had said; they could doze on the station. So they stayed up as long as possible and sat in a large, light and airy hotel bar, rather empty at the late hour. Jose wanted to talk about the Catholic Church; he had seen two priests in their dog collars walking across the platform.

'It's supposed to be the Church of Christ,' he complained. 'That's what we were all taught when I was at school in Goa. Christ rules it, runs it, sacrifices himself for others in it, teaches through it. Yet now, whenever I look at the Church, all I see is Caiaphas... (acknowledging puzzled looks)... the corrupt High Priest who helped to crucify Jesus, you know. He stayed in power longer than any other High Priest. Why? Because he was in the pay of the Romans! The Catholic Church is full of priests who keep the tradition of Caiaphas going rather than that of Christ. They put their own comfort above the needs of the poor, the dull weight of doctrine and the fine rules of ritual above the truth of the Gospel. They are the scribes and Pharisees that Jesus railed against in his lifetime.'

'You *have* got a bee in your bonnet,' commented Nathan.

'Good for you,' added Debs. 'A Catholic who saw the light.'

'They would really hate us if they knew what we were doing,' continued Jose –he was in full flow now. 'The Churches, both Catholic and Protestant, exalt the male leader. Christianity, apart from a few brave souls, is a religion which idolises male leadership. Protestant Christianity has simply replaced the dog collar with the suit and tie. Have you ever seen a Televangelist or Evangelical Church leader without a suit and tie? Christianity, the religion of male executives! The worship of the male: Father, Son and Male Spirit. God in a dog collar or a tie. That's why they hate – and I mean really hate – any spirituality that challenges that way of thinking with a more feminine image. Witchcraft! It makes them tremble and spit! They would burn the lot of us were it not for the secular world in which we now live.'

'Well, burning witches stopped well before the world became secular,' interrupted Nathan, who couldn't resist pointing out weaknesses in arguments.

'True,' said Jose. 'They had to, or there wouldn't have been any women left. But witchcraft was still technically illegal until 1951.'

'Like homosexuality,' added Debs, who could see where the real tender spot was. 'That weren't legalised until the sixties.'

'Yes, and the irony is that most priests *are* gay,' sighed Jose. 'But they idolise maleness so much that they have to suppress both homosexuality and femininity in themselves. They deny sexuality, but in secret they… well…'

Jose was so pent up all of a sudden that no one felt able to comment apart from nods of agreement; another short silence fell. *It's funny what conversations you have when travelling late at night, excited about your holiday,* thought Frances. Then Nathan broke in.

'Talking of priests, I met this friendly vicar in the University Library the other day, told him something of what we were up to and he just laughed and said, "The unbearable lightness of alternative spirituality"! Then he rushed off before I could reply.'

Frances raised an eyebrow.

'What did he mean by that?' asked Debs, frowning.

Nathan replied after a moment or two looking thoughtful.

'I suppose that he regarded our rituals and ideas as not having much in the way of an established tradition, just superficial and faddish.'

'We do have a tradition,' stated Debs, firmly. 'For centuries before Christianity came, Pagans of all kinds across the globe practised earth magic and celebrated the seasons. They also cared for wildlife and the natural world.'

'OK,' said Nathan. 'I'm with you there. I'll tell him next time if I get the chance.'

And then all the talk about Christian priests put an uncomfortable idea into Frances' head.

'I suppose these Black Virgin shrines we're going to… they're Catholic, aren't they?'

Jose, having by now calmed down, looked straight back at her and smiled.

'Yes, that's true. We'll see quite a lot of Catholic priests this holiday so I had better get myself under control. But Black Virgin shrines are mainly sanctuaries of the ordinary people; they represent a popular tradition that goes back centuries. They are echoes of a pre-Christian Pagan goddess cult, maybe Isis, who was often depicted as black. Mind you, Black Virgins aren't always literally black, but that's what they're called. 'Black' signifies a special power more than a colour. Those who say they're goddesses under a Christian veil – well, they're right. Le Puy's cathedral was built over a temple to… now which goddess was it?'

His musing was brought to a halt by the sound of Debs gently snoring, having found a way to prop her head on her rucksack.

'The Goddess of Sleep?' suggested Nathan.

'Yes, Alice, Goddess of Dreaming and White Rabbits,' said Frances, who was beginning to wonder how she could get her head into that position too.

Memories of the night soon became a blur: the bar closing; moving into a waiting room; occasional snippets of conversation as they stirred between dozing, leaning against their packs; the night air causing Frances to decide that Jose and Debs were sensible to wear trousers after all; the clock ticking round so very slowly; a coffee machine that didn't work; finally making their way to the train through the airport-level Eurostar security; Nathan making those jokes that come out of the hysteria of tiredness, only funny at the time; everyone hoping that the motion of the train would send them to sleep; it doing so; finally the Channel Tunnel itself and then, just after 8.30 French time, the train pulled out into France. The sight of the French countryside, soaked in morning sunlight, had a strange effect on Jose. He became animated all of a sudden. He stood up, stretched his arms out and, swaying with the motion of the train, said in a loud voice,

'La belle France! The country of Francis Poulenc!'

He then blew an extravagant kiss into the air. *Not like Jose to make a scene in public. He must be excited!*

Nathan, still in a joke-a-minute mode, repeated the actions but switched from classical music to football.

'La belle France! The country of Thierry Henry and Arsene Wenger!'

Frances felt impelled to join in. The onlookers round about were expecting it now.

'La belle France. Country o' Black Virgins and bucketfuls o' wine!'

Debs smiled but didn't get up. Much more quietly but loud enough for them to hear, she added,

'La belle France. Country o' very stupid and embarrassing English tourists!'

Paris Gare du Nord. A metro trip. Some uncertainty about how you got a ticket, then the need to ask for directions followed by a surprising revelation! Supposing that they would be the ones to deal with such things, Nathan and Jose attempted to communicate with a passer-by but, seeing them struggle, Debs cut in. Her French was perfect. Frances couldn't pick out any words; like most young English urbanites, her foreign travel was limited to a few package holidays to places where you didn't need to speak the lingo. She had some French from school, went to Normandy on a school trip and had valiantly tried on a previous visit to Paris. But French was a language of which she could make out some words on paper but, spoken, it was near unintelligible to her. Debs, on the other hand – well, she was a natural.

'Where did you learn to speak French like that?'

The men looked a little outflanked. Despite all the gender equality rhetoric, it was always assumed that, in matters requiring head knowledge, they were the ones to lead the way.

'At school like everyone else,' replied Debs. 'I struggled to do stuff like Maths and History, partly because I were hardly *at* school, thanks to my dear Mamma. But, for some reason, I can do languages. Some people are like that. Thick at everything bar languages! Just a few lessons, a short holiday, and I've got it sorted.'

'You never mentioned it.'

'You never asked me!'

'Well, it's going to be really helpful,' interjected Frances, trying to bring some resolution to the slight tension that had crept in among tired comrades. 'But I'm sure we'll *all* get a chance to try it out!' she added, aware that a good French-speaker in the group inhibited everyone else.

The men shrugged and nodded agreement. Then it was off to the Gare de Lyon.

Exciting, the TGV. So fast and sleek! Paris to Lyon in under two hours. Polite smiling at French people. *It's their country we're in now!* A middle-aged dark-haired man with greying temples got very interested in the Goddess book that Debs was reading.

'You do this?' he asked, in tentative English.

Debs replied in her fluent French, at which his eyes widened. He looked very impressed both at her ability to speak his language and at what she said. He replied in kind. Assuming that Frances also understood, he addressed both of them, not noticing Frances' blank look.

'What were that about?' asked Frances.

'I were saying that, yes, we did do Goddess rituals, to make good things happen. We believed in the strength o' women and power o' Goddess, which we could channel when it were important to help people. And then he said, he completely agreed. It's about time, he said, that the power o' the feminine was recognised in religion.'

Lyon, a fast food lunch – it was 13.30 now. The car hire pick up point was not far, but it seemed a bit of a walk when carrying a rucksack. Lyon, a large, crowded city, had become quite hot and Frances began to worry that they hadn't booked a B&B in Le

Puy; it was all down to being lucky and finding somewhere. It'll be OK, the men had said, no problem, it's not the French school holidays yet, we'll go to a hostel if we have to. But why not book forward, using the Internet? No trouble, nothing to be anxious about if there were any delays. She was about to complain when it suddenly struck her. *Who wanted to be spontaneous? Frances Dryburgh? Yes, it were. Who said that Goddess would take care o' them? Frances Dryburgh? Yes, it most certainly were.*

'What were you going to say, Frances?' asked Nathan.

'Erm... just that we'll have to be careful when crossing road, what wi' traffic going wrong way,' said Frances, coming up with the first thing that came into her head.

'You mean with us *looking* the wrong way,' Nathan replied.

The little exchange amused him greatly and he sniggered for some minutes. *What did I see in him?* Frances asked herself, a bit cross with her own confusion and irritated that Nathan should derive mirth from such a small thing. But she began to sense that Nathan's laughter came from the hysteria of tiredness, a thirty year old beginning to find that overnight travel wasn't quite as easy as it used to be in his teens. As they saw the car hire sign, he began to look a little uneasy that he had volunteered to take the first driving shift to Le Puy with four lives in his care. Frances noticed him taking some deep breaths in readiness for the responsibility of driving a strange car in a foreign land.

Nathan climbed into the driving seat of a hybrid Honda, a saloon absolutely stuffed full of people and rucksacks. He wasn't going to let on, but he really looked exhausted now. He grinned as if to make out he was OK. Only about fifty miles to Le Puy. Which gear is that? Ah, the car's gone backwards and bumped into that bollard behind.

'Only slight, no damage,' he said, getting back into the car and trying to look cool and confident to the worried people inside.

'So why didn't we get that extra insurance?' asked Jose, sounding anxious. 'We have to pay for any scratches that we cannot blame on someone else.'

'It was too expensive,' replied Nathan, firmly. 'That'll be the last time I do it, I assure you. Just getting used to the gears.'

Pulling out into the street – ooer, he nearly drove up the left. Just caught himself in time. He didn't think anybody noticed the hesitation. And then he saw Debs and Frances, their piercing eyes looking straight at his in the rear view mirror.

'We want St Etienne and then the N88,' said Jose, sitting next to him with the road atlas on his lap.

'Eighty-eight, two fat ladies,' laughed Nathan. 'They're in the back.'

A joke or two was his way of trying to convince them he felt OK. The rear passengers looked at each other and sighed; they would just have to trust that some divine hand would help with the steering.

When she looked back, Frances' memories of the car journey were as hazy as her recollections of the night on the station. After a motorway stretch, they passed onto main roads through pretty hills covered in trees and villages. Frances dozed on and off, with the men exchanging comments about the route in the front; Debs was quiet. Exotic town names going by, one stuck in Frances' mind: Monistrol-sur-Loire. Seemed a scary name. She was on an adventure where maybe she might have to fight monsters. In a doze dream, she saw a kind of Loch Ness monster surfacing in a river. The real monster came along in the form of the beginnings of travel nausea. Would she make it to Le Puy? She did, sucking a peppermint and taking long breaths. A long downhill section before crossing the Loire and entering the outskirts of Le Puy. It was just another urban sprawl at first. And then the fairytale began.

'Look!' shouted Jose. 'Wow!'

Frances looked, and then she gasped. The nausea disappeared. Le Puy was a town in a dip surrounded by hills. In its midst was a great rock, on the lower levels of which the town climbed upwards. A great cathedral stood high up, just underneath the rock's summit, placed on the top of which was a colossal russet statue of the Madonna and Child. The Madonna stood tall and proud while the Child clung to his mother's right arm with one hand and held the other out in what seemed like a greeting to newcomers. Near the great rock was a smaller one, a thin column on the top of which perched a chapel. It was difficult to see how anyone could get up there, let alone put a building on the summit. A miracle! The whole vista breathed an aura of strangeness, of being a place where myths came true and the ordinary dullness of life had no place. A town ruled by the Goddess, who stood imperiously overseeing it. Their journey, which up to then had been trains, timetables, cafés and car hire offices, was now passing into a new phase as they entered a magical country. Frances stared in wonder as the car moved into the town centre, which had the air of normality – shops, businesses and traffic lights – but the giant figure above contradicted that impression.

The Goddess had influence over the town's tourist accommodation too. A friendly man on the main street suggested *L'Hôtel Compostelle* and gave Debs directions. The proprietor of the *Compostelle*, a thickset man with grey hair and a bushy moustache, looking over his glasses in that fifty-something authoritative kind of way, said: how lucky, it was quite busy this time of year but someone had cancelled and some others had just checked out. Not too expensive, yet it was two star, looked comfortable, near the middle of town. How many nights? Let's say five, suggested Jose, we can use it as a base.

Holidays were great when the travelling was over and the rooms sorted out. Suddenly tiredness evolved into curious expectation and, with it, the need to go out, eat, drink, talk excitedly, reflect on the silliness of the journey, which could no longer cause anxiety, and laugh. Through it all, Frances could not get the image of the great Virgin and Child out of her mind. They would go up on the rock tomorrow, but the thought of the Goddess' guiding hand made visible in a huge high statue filled Frances with an excitement that she had only just begun to anticipate at Avebury and Almscliffe. There, she had seen the

Goddess first in the moon and then on the crag. Her own idiosyncratic experiences. Yet, at Le Puy, it seemed that generations of French people understood because they had seen the Madonna high on the crag too and so built her image for everyone to share.

'This is fantastic,' she whispered to Debs, across the gap between their beds in the twin room.

They had finally collapsed under the single thin cotton sheets, as much as one needed in the summer night air, with the pleasant taste of dry white wine, goat's cheese and fresh herb omelette, finished off with fresh fruit salad, so evocative that Frances brushed her teeth without paste so as not to spoil it.

'I can't wait for tomorrow, Debs.'

## 26

## Black Virgin

Morning – the *Compostelle* supplied hot drinks, croissants, butter and jam with no plate, just a knife and several paper napkins.

'What does *Compostelle* mean?' asked Debs, knowing that Jose would know the answer.

'Compostelle is the shrine town of Santiago de Compostela on the Atlantic coast of Spain,' replied Jose. 'Santiago, in English, is St James, the brother of John and one of the twelve disciples. He's the patron saint of Spain; his body is supposed to lie in Compostela, translated as the "field of stars". Medieval pilgrim routes stretch from France across Northern Spain to Compostela. Le Puy is one of the traditional starting points, which is why this hotel has the name that it does. The footpaths are still crowded with pilgrims, walking or cycling. It takes about nine weeks walking from here.'

'We'd better get going,' quipped Nathan. 'Nine weeks' walk and we've only got three. Where do we start from?'

'The Cathedral at the top of the town,' said Jose. 'They'll give you bread and a copy of the New Testament if you're a genuine pilgrim.'

'How do they know you're genuine?' asked Nathan, mischievously. 'Maybe we could get a free lunch and reading material for the afternoon.'

Jose raised his eyes to heaven but he had a smile on his face. On mention of the Cathedral, Frances' heart leaped. She could not wait to get up that hill; she had been quite restrained the evening before when the others had said that they were too tired. Frustratingly, everyone else wanted to wait half an hour or so, with various things needing to be done, extra coffee required to kick-start the day. So she decided to set off alone. *It's not a bad thing if we have little spaces on us own*, she thought. *Three weeks is a long time together.*

'I'll see you in Cathedral,' she told them.

'You're keen,' said Nathan. 'No probs, we'll see you up there. Wear a red rose.'

Frances turned up her nose at him playfully. A little quiet time on her own, a walk through an interesting town, a mysterious Cathedral, then a reunion with Nathan – it didn't sound a bad proposition. She stood up.

'Quelle direction à la Cathédrale?' she asked the proprietor in her clumsy French.

'Là-haut,' he replied in an offhand tone, pointing towards the top of the hill and, seeing her blank stare, continued in strongly accented English. 'Up there. At the top.'

He perused her over his glasses as he placed a replacement coffee down for Nathan, who interpreted for her.

'He means any road going up will take you there.'

'Sounds like my doctrine of religion,' added Jose. 'Any faith, as long as it doesn't abuse people, will take you up to God.'

'That's the trouble with *your* doctrine,' countered Debs, ever ready for a religious argument. 'God is up *there*, rather than down *here* with us. Goddess is in us, all round us, walking up with us.'

'So is God, properly understood!' protested Jose. 'It was only a metaphor!'

Frances said 'Bye', waggling the fingers on her right hand, and left them to it. She took her little shoulder bag, remembered this time. She was wearing a clean vest, yellow with white trim, white shorts and trainers without socks. She had covered her head with a white baseball cap through the back of which the mousy brown ponytail popped out. A narrow street seemed to go upwards from the far right corner of the square on which the hotel was situated. Frances took it. There was an interesting variety of shops on each side of the road beneath tall terraced buildings, their slatted shutters still drawn for the Sunday holiday. She continued her climb up the hill. Not many people around, still only nine-fifteen. As she crossed the road, a bicycle came from nowhere and whisked past rather close. 'Attention!' cried Frances, rather relieved that the boy didn't seem to hear her poor pronunciation as he sped down the hill. More streets – houses now rather than shops; the hill was more residential as she went up. She kept looking forward and upwards to see if the great statue would emerge, but there was no sign; the buildings were three or four storeys high and the gaps between them yielded nothing. Then a point at which she had to make a decision – which way to turn? Ahead stood a pretty garden and a curious Labrador behind a wire fence and neither way, left nor right, seemed to continue up. For some reason, based on the vaguest sense of direction, she chose right. This didn't seem to lead anywhere – the streets coiled round and round and began to descend. The sun was getting hotter in the clearest of blue skies and Frances, leaning against a low wall, applied some cream to her face, shoulders, arms and legs. Which way? Occasionally, there had been a passer-by, usually a mature person, the young still sleeping off the Saturday night activities, she supposed. It was time to ask.

'La Cathédrale?' she enquired of an elderly plump lady struggling along in a thick pink cardigan and heavy black skirt, neither of which seemed the right thing to wear in Southern France in June.

The lady merely grunted, swung her wicker basket and, in doing so, pointed Frances back towards the T-junction. So her original intuition was completely opposite to the right answer as usual! She was famous for it.

As the lady disappeared, Frances was alone again but became aware, out of the corner of her eye, of a figure that seemed to be shadowing her at a distance. She turned just in time to see a teenage boy slip into a side alley. As she continued along the road, she kept glancing back. There was no doubt. She was being followed by two or three tall and athletic-looking teenage boys, who seemed to be sizing her up. She looked down at her money belt containing her passport, train ticket, money and bank cards. It was prominent; Frances wore her vest fashionably with her midriff showing and the shorts low on her hips, so there was nowhere to hide a belt. *This is going wrong.* The boys were quickening their steps as if closing in on a vulnerable prey. There was still no sign of the statue and the T-junction was not coming into sight; Frances wondered whether she had taken a wrong turn, as this winding street did not look familiar. Why weren't there more people about? This was a town, even though it was a Sunday morning. The answer came to her: in bed, at home doing chores, or at Mass! This wasn't Leeds. *This really is going wrong.* No travelling companions, why had she assumed that she could go out without them? Where was the Madonna, wasn't this the hill? If she shouted and assistance came, the boys would pass by and she would appear a lunatic. If it didn't, it would prove her helplessness to them. Anyway, she had no proof that they were stalking her. Was it worth running? To where? Frances became a little frantic as she walked faster and faster, but she was getting nowhere. She was lost. She looked back; they were close now and they still had the look of hunters closing in, waiting for the right moment. Last month, Jonathan in her flat, now this. Wasn't a woman safe anywhere? Couldn't she walk the streets untroubled as a man the height of Nathan would? *This really, really, really is going wrong.* In desperation, near to sobbing, she uttered a little prayer internally. *Madonna on the hill, where are you? Please protect me. I'm lost in your town. Goddess, please help me again as you did before!*

Everything happened very fast. She could hear the boys breaking into a run. At the same moment, from an alleyway on the left, people suddenly emerged. The boys ran straight past, laughing and jeering, but they left her alone. She would never know if they meant her harm or simply enjoyed watching her sweat. Frances gave thanks in her relief, but she knew she needed to stay with people now. There seemed to be several elderly women and men in a group. They had the look of tourists in various kinds of headgear to keep the sun off, with cameras on straps around the shoulders or hanging off wrists. She turned to them and tried her ropey French again.

'S'il vous plait, où se trouve la Cathédrale?'

It came out in a muddle and so she tried to say more about needing company, but her brain was scrambled with the fear that she had felt. Nothing would come. A tall, elegant woman wearing a cream-coloured silk scarf skilfully wrapped around her head spoke to her.

'Anglaise? You English?'

'Yes... oui,' replied Frances, all flustered.

'Ah... attendez. Way Chee!' called the woman back down the line of people.

They stood back as an East Asian woman in a yellow blouse and white slacks caught up with the leading group. She was tiny, stick thin and wore a straw hat, so that it was difficult to see her face properly in the shade; she walked up in little bird steps that reminded Frances of geisha girls and bound feet. She looked up into Frances' face so that her own could be seen. It was small and delicate with leathery light yellow-brown skin covered in lines, but there was a youthful brightness in the dark brown eyes despite the signs of advanced old age.

'Hello, are you English or American?' she asked in an East Asian accent yet with clear pronunciation. 'I can speak English. Where are you going?'

Frances, still overwrought, just managed to prevent herself weeping.

'Yes, I am English. My name's Frances. I'm trying to find the Cathedral. I... I hope you don't mind, I need to stay with people for a bit. Can I walk with you?'

'Of course. We too are going to the Cathedral. My name is Way Chee. We are visiting here, a party from Paris.'

'Are you Japanese or French?' asked Frances.

'Actually Chinese, although I was born and grew up in Vietnam.' Way Chee smiled. 'But I've been in France many years. Now, let's go. We will talk as we go up to the Cathedral.'

Way Chee had such a vulnerable and unassuming air, walking rather unsteadily, that Frances soon forgot that she had been the one to be rescued. She found herself assisting the little Chinese woman as she stepped on and off kerbs. As they passed the T-junction, this time taking the other turn and now entering a flat stretch through the narrow streets, Frances and her companion found out more about each other. The French people, feeling uneasy about speaking English, left them to it, while nodding and smiling politely whenever Frances caught an eye. Frances found out that the woman's name was spelt Wei Chi. She had managed to emigrate during the Vietnam War, travelling by boat to live with relatives in Paris. She had lived there in the suburbs at Poissy for forty years or so. As for this trip, she didn't know her travelling companions well as most of her close friends and family of her own generation had died, so she took holidays with a company that organised tours for older people. But Wei Chi was reluctant to say any more about herself and wanted to ask about Frances: whom was she travelling with, had she come there before, etc.? Frances answered her but baulked at telling her everything about the rituals and the G8 summit. This didn't feel like something you told a stranger.

Frances had been so attentive to Wei Chi that scanning the hill for the great russet statue had slipped her mind. Suddenly, it appeared through a garden doorway, perfectly framed by the arch and larger now that it was so much nearer. It faced her directly.

Frances gasped and came to an immediate stop. Seeing it, overawed and still upset by the earlier events, the long-delayed tears started to come. Why had she doubted? She stared at the giant Madonna and her Child, still waving obliviously as if nothing had happened since she first saw him in the car, driving from the Loire into the city. She felt a touch on her arm. It was Wei Chi, whose dark brown eyes stared straight up into her own with concern. She didn't ask Frances to explain her emotional state and continued to hold her arm as they walked. Across a square, a right turn and there was the great Gothic Cathedral up a cobbled street in front of them, a large gaping dark door awaiting those who climbed the hill. It formed a perfect archway, around which were a series of regular brown stripes on a light beige brick background. Above the door was a smaller tier of arched windows, then a row of open arches and, at the very top of the facia, little triangular turrets.

Wei Chi stopped and turned to Frances.

'Did you know that the Cathedral of Le Puy was meant to have been dedicated to the Virgin Mary by angels?'

Frances shook her head, but the mention of angels brought with it the sensation of a gentle gust of wind, resulting in a shiver down the spine. *Where does that feeling come from? There's no wind today. It must be my imagination.* The feeling of awe remained as they approached the grand entrance. The steps up to it and into the cathedral interior were steep and the group of elderly people did not find them easy. They went in via a dark antechamber through an inner door, around which squirted shards of light from the great chamber of the cathedral. Inside, the French group and Wei Chi crossed themselves with water from the stoup. As she looked ahead towards the nave, Frances saw many people sitting or kneeling in the pews, quietly praying, with their attention forwards. She craned her head to the right to see what they were looking at and she gasped. There on the high altar, resplendent in a great halo of red candles, was a statue of the Madonna and Child, covered in blue robes with a gold lining. They were framed within a grand, decorated throne structure, at the top of which was a gilded eagle. The child's head protruded through the robes directly below his mother's. Both figures were crowned and they had been sculpted from dark brown wood. It was the Black Virgin of Le Puy.

Frances' response to the great red Madonna on the hill had been one of joyful recognition as of a child to a kind mother, but she experienced something deeper and more intense on seeing the Black Virgin in her regal austerity. She demanded respect; this figure was one to be feared. It was as if, in that instant, Frances saw generations of pilgrims on their knees before this mother, terrible and awe-inspiring to those who had climbed the hill to be in her presence, all their emotions and superstitions inside out, raw, tender. They would have cried to her for help in all their ills: plague, poverty, serfdom, conflict. For a moment, she felt a slight revulsion, as if the gentle Mother Goddess had been supplanted by this... by this what? She searched for a word and then it came... this *witch*. But this instinctive response caused her to reflect further. 'Witch' was a word that had changed its connotations for her since the nightmares of early childhood. The terror of the witch she now saw as an irrational and unfounded fear of the feminine, of the women in the refuge, of the women amongst the stones at Avebury, of strangeness, of dark people from other lands with unusual beliefs. Of Debs. But she was not fearful of these – at least, not any longer; indeed, the last few months had taught her to love them. And then she looked again at the Black Madonna, had an intuitive sense of the presence of the great Goddess whom it represented, and she loved her too. And then she recalled the words. 'Really, I'm black, Frances. Remember that.' That's why they had come here. She felt strange, as if she were going into a visionary trance again. But someone caught her eye and distracted her. It was Wei Chi, who had moved towards the chairs to sit down after her arduous ascent. As she sat there, she looked, not at the Black Madonna with everyone else in the pews, but directly at Frances, studying her in that moment of rapt concentration on the statue. Frances gave her a weak smile of acknowledgement; Wei Chi responded in kind. Then someone dug Frances in the ribs and she squealed, trying to suppress it because of the quiet sanctity of the place. The someone laughed. It was, of course, Nathan, who had just arrived by the direct route with Jose and Debs. And the tension of the last half-hour, plus the way his light jocular greeting had disturbed the intensity of her thoughts, caused her to give him the fiercest and sternest glare that he had ever experienced from her.

## 27

# Notre Dame de France

'It makes me uncomfortable,' commented Debs in a near whisper, as she surveyed the statue. 'I can imagine all those generations o' people on their knees before it while Church takes their money and enforces its own warped morality on 'em. And what is it, actually? Just a doll, dressed up like Barbie. A fetish object. An idol.'

'I know what you mean,' replied Frances, also hushed. 'I had that feeling when I first came in. But then I caught a sense of her power. Even kings and lords had to bow to that power, you know. Look, there's a painting of 'em venerating the statue over there on the wall.'

'The fact that she's black does make it interesting, I'll give you that,' conceded Debs. 'So many statues of Jesus and Mary are white. In actual fact, Jesus and Mary would've been quite dark brown coming from Middle East.'

Jose came over. He had been on a private tour of the various hidden corners of the cathedral.

'I've found another Black Virgin in a side chapel. It's a copy of the original that was destroyed during the French Revolution. And there's an ancient healing stone over there to one side of the altar. That confirms the close relationship between popular Catholicism and its Pagan predecessors. Now, Frances, how do you think we're going to carry out the ritual here? We can't do it inside. Maybe we should look for somewhere more amenable up the hill.'

Frances didn't answer. Something had distracted her. All of a sudden, she moved away quickly and trotted towards the door to the stairway exit.

'Wei Chi, wait,' she called, while waving.

The little Chinese woman was on her way out with the rest of the group of elderly tourists. As she waited momentarily in the queue for the stoup, she had looked over towards Frances. The glance had been enough to attract the younger woman's attention.

'I don't want to lose touch with you,' said Frances breathlessly, having reached her by the door. 'Are you staying in Le Puy? Maybe we could meet up. I'm sure you would enjoy meeting my friends.'

'I don't know…' Wei Chi seemed hesitant.

'Please!'

Frances was insistent. She gently put her hand on Wei Chi's shoulder to demonstrate that she was genuine. There was something about the Chinese lady that she really liked, although it was difficult for her to put her finger on it. She just couldn't let it go. Yet Wei Chi continued to argue.

'I'm really so very much older than you and your friends. I wouldn't be good company.'

Frances sensed that her reluctance was only a show.

'What's age got to do with it? Anyway, you've got a great life story to tell. Come on, I'm sure you'd like to meet us, at least just the once.'

'OK, yes, I would,' agreed Wei Chi, nodding and giving her a gracious little smile that added a few more lines to her wrinkled face. 'At the moment, we're on a programmed tour and we're going on a coach trip this afternoon. Why don't we meet this evening in the *Restaurant du Cloître* in the square down below the Cathedral? It has a good menu, not too expensive.' She drew up close to Frances and whispered. 'By then, I will be happy to leave this group for a little while!'

'Great,' said Frances. 'Seven o'clock?'

'I will see you then,' replied Wei Chi, as she was involuntarily ushered away by the line shuffling through the exit.

Frances told the others about the arrangement; there was immediate approval from everyone. They left the dark cathedral by its opposite door out into the bright sunlight and walked up the winding path that led to the great red-brown Madonna at the top of the hill, each of them taking in the view across the slopes of the Velay region and the awesome sight of the nearby column of rock, 'L'Aiguille' – 'the Needle' – and its precariously built chapel of St Michael. Debs suggested that they should sit for a while on a long wooden seat to enjoy the vista for a few minutes. Jose took the opportunity to share a memorable experience.

'I've always liked Chinese people,' he said. 'When I was a little boy, my father tried to set up a business in Singapore. He took the whole family. We lived there for three years but it didn't work out; we had to return to Goa. However, there was one incident in Singapore that I will never forget, when I was about eight years old. My parents had enrolled me in a Cub Scout group. They're all over the globe, in Singapore and in India too. We were all taken off by the cub leaders one evening to a big campfire somewhere in the country. Lots of singing, plenty of noise and larking about. I was small and limped, so it was easy to leave me out. My own fault, I suppose. So, pushed to one side in the crowd, I became panicky. I got it into my head that it was getting late and my parents would be worried about me. Given that I was already in safe hands, supervised by adults, it was irrational, but that's how I felt. I didn't have the courage to approach anyone; instead, I ran out into the night. It had just got dark. I started to walk down the road away from the field where we were; as I did so, it dawned on me that I didn't know how to get home. As far as I was concerned, I couldn't go back; something was driving me away from the campfire. So I kept going along the road. I seemed to remember that we had come from that way and there was a village quite nearby. However, as we had come there by coach, I had no idea how far it was to my home. As I realised the hopelessness of my situation, I began to cry. The road was deserted and I was alone. I had heard a rumour that Singapore was a bad place for child kidnappings; that too came into my mind and increased my terror. In the opposite direction, a Chinese man came into view; he was the only person in sight. I began to feel frightened of him, but I felt I had to keep going, so he got nearer. He was probably about as old as we are now, around thirty. I'll never forget him. He saw me in my cub uniform, by now weeping buckets. "What's the problem, little chap?" he asked in English. In desperation, I informed him that I was trying to go home and told him my address. "Don't worry, I'll help you," he said, turning so that he was walking with me back in the direction from which he had come. I had no option but to trust him. When we got to the village, he led me towards a bus that was waiting there. He paid the driver and instructed me where to get off. Then as the bus pulled away, he stood there waving benignly. I got home without any difficulty, beginning to feel foolish. I didn't tell my parents that I had come home under my own steam and I wasn't missed at the campfire, so it was all forgotten. No one knew but me – and him, of course. A crazy evening. I don't know what got into me. I never did it again. But I'll never forget that man and, as I grew up, I wished I could see him again and thank him. I started to think that he was some kind of saint that I'd met and that I'd been driven from the campfire so that I would meet him. I would like to help a Chinese person one day and, in some way, return the favour.'

The passion with which Jose had spoken, plus the evocative power of the view, halfway between the Black Virgin in the medieval cathedral and the great red-brown Madonna of the hill, caused an awed hush. Frances broke it.

'You won't find it difficult to be kind to Wei Chi,' she said. 'She's a really sweet old lady.'

The huge Madonna and Child was known as *Notre Dame de France*, 'Notre Dame' meaning 'Our Lady' in French, a title of the Virgin Mary; she was therefore 'Our Lady of France'. A plaque told them that the statue had been made from captured Russian cannons at the end of the Crimean War, in the 1850s. It bore a resemblance to the Statue of Liberty. Through a door in the back, a steep, narrow spiral staircase coiled its way up the Madonna's body inside, ending on a landing from which a few steps, hardly easier to climb than a ladder, ascended towards the top. On the inner walls, large bolts could be seen holding the various pieces of bronze together. The shape of the Child was imprinted inside out in the metallic superstructure.

'The mid-nineteenth century was a great time for large statues, particularly of the Virgin Mary,' Jose informed them, puffing with the effort of ascending the stairway. 'You can see them on hilltops all over France. I suppose it was an attempt on the part of the Catholics to demonstrate their faith in a time when the country was becoming less and less religious. So the bigger the Virgin Mary, the better. She was seen as the guardian of the faith and protector of the people in the town below. It's a kind of evangelism by statues.'

Frances peeped out through a small window in the Madonna's head; the sight was dramatic. Miles of hilly countryside could be seen, with the sun's rays dappling the fields and small villages nestling in its warmth. Frances went into a dreamy state. It wasn't quite right being a tourist in such a magical place, she wanted to disappear into an otherworld.

'Let's do the ritual soon,' she urged. 'No more history, facts and figures, or viewfinders. I just want to breathe in the spirit of the place.'

'Well, maybe not in here, exactly,' said Nathan, rather asking for trouble. 'There are too many visitors coming up.'

'No, not *in* here,' snapped Frances. '*Around* here somewhere.'

Like Almscliffe Crag, the hilltop was full of summer visitors. In looking for a quiet spot, there was no alternative but to descend back down the winding path. Part-way down, a small fenced garden next to the rock and just off the main path allowed some privacy. It was pleasantly laid out, a small area of lawn bordered by a lively cluster of petunias, which added a pleasant lilac colouring to the predominant greens and browns. A densely leaved plane tree afforded shade; ivy and ferns adorned the rock face. Forming a circle, each of the adventurers in turn summoned the spirits of the four quarters, then the energy of the volcanic rock up was called up before prayers were offered for the world's environment. Frances knew that she was going to have a vision. She had felt strange on seeing the Black Virgin in the cathedral, with that pleasant – if giddy and faint – feeling coming over her and it had almost happened then. As they stood there, halfway up the great rock, with a light summer breeze making more bearable the heat of the midday, Frances recalled the crag at Almscliffe. There she had seen a Goddess on bare rock; now the statue stood at the summit, providing a visual stimulus. She looked up the rock face; the Virgin's head and the Child could still be seen facing her, a colossus towering over the little garden. She took a deep breath. And then…

*Sun's appearing above rock, it's going high up and now it's coming down, on top o' Madonna's crown. It's huge! Rays are streaming out from crown and from Child's head. It's so beautiful. Look down, Frances! Oh, thousands o' pilgrims. They're coming out o' cathedral towards statue. They're the generations of ordinary people, who've prayed here for centuries. They're coming closer! So fast! But they're not French. No. Some are Chinese, wi' coolie hats and peasant dress, carrying those yokes wi' baskets, and they've got wounds. Oh God, they're all covered in blood and terrible burns. Then there's Africans, naked apart from small loincloths, men and women. They're covered in whip marks, lashes across their backs. Indians too, limping like Jose. They look ill, disease-ridden and in dire poverty. Thousands of 'em, Chinese, Africans, Indians marching up to statue. They must be in agony, but they're singing and looking up to statue. And the Sun's still up there, right on Madonna's crown and Child's head. They're all going up into the Sun, that's where they're going! That's where they're going... That's where...*

Frances came to in Nathan's arms. He had held her to stop her falling. When he saw that she was back in the everyday world, he smiled.

'Whatever you experienced there, Frances, it was very powerful. You were moaning in a kind of ecstasy! Now relax, I'll let you sit down.'

Frances blinked at them as she recovered. She looked back up at the statue; everything was normal now. After a couple of minutes composing herself, she described the vision. Nathan spoilt the moment with some amateur psychology.

'It's like a waking dream, isn't it, Frances? All the components of the dream can be explained in what we've been talking about today. We mentioned the many pilgrims of the past, Wei Chi is Chinese, then we were remarking on the blackness of the statue, which explains the Africans. Then Jose told us his childhood story, which is why the Indians were in there.'

Frances looked at him. He really was being annoying today. Can she have ever thought that she loved him?

'Yes, maybe, Nathan, but that don't explain the Sun coming down over statue and the fact that they were all walking up into it singing, despite their wounds '

'You got that from Fatima,' remarked Jose, almost dismissively. 'That was the vision in Portugal where the Sun came down, remember – I told you about it.'

Et tu, Jose?

'OK, OK, maybe visions are like that, made up o' things you've experienced recently. But my interpretation is that Goddess were telling me that she were here for suffering people o' the world. She takes them into herself.'

'That's very nice, but religious consolation can sometimes stop people from rebelling against the causes of their suffering,' commented Debs.

Frances frowned and looked round at each adventurer, stunned. They had been supporting her in her visionary journey up until then, but now here they were explaining everything away.

'You lot crack me up,' she said, without any hint of laughter. 'Are we here to do rituals and me to have visions, or what?'

'We're sorry,' said Jose, giving her a warm smile. 'I hope I'm speaking for everyone else when I say that we really do believe in you and in the magic that we're doing, with you as the focus. But we're also thinking people; we like to look at these things scientifically as well as emotionally. Your experiences are very interesting, you know. I've heard so much about famous apparitions and never had a chance to see them for myself firsthand.'

'That's right,' agreed Nathan. ''We're behind you all the way. What you say about the Goddess being for the suffering is absolutely right.'

Debs didn't add anything, just took Frances' arm and helped her to her feet, then pushed up close to her as they walked back onto the path. Frances felt reassured to some extent, but the visionary experiences made her emotional and it was difficult to field searching questions. She decided to put her discomfort aside for the time being and hope that the adventurers would be gentler next time.

A little way back down into the town, with no one saying much, they came to a small shop with stands placed outside under the awning, selling all kinds of souvenirs, gifts, small statues, postcards and local produce stocked inside – a variety of liquors and jars of pickled fruits and vegetables, in particular, the famous Puy lentils. A woman sitting at the entrance worked with lace, a well known local industry, in the hope of attracting tourist interest in the finished articles. Frances and Debs stopped for a while; the men walked on for a few yards before they realised.

The women looked at the merchandise on sale. There was a small replica of the Black Virgin of Le Puy, which didn't quite have the awe-inspiring presence of the original, the faces of the figures being too saccharine in their friendliness. There was one of the red *Notre Dame de France*, which turned out to be thin plastic when picked up, rather overpriced. Frances was just about to give up on the small market, telling herself that it was better not to buy trinkets when she would only have to carry them back on the train, when she noticed that some of the postcards were of Madonnas. She picked one off the stand. Bells rang inside her head.

'That's it,' she said suddenly to Debs. 'Wherever this Madonna is, that's where we're going!'

The Madonna pictured on the card was seated on a simple throne, holding the Child on her lap. The Child held up his right hand in blessing and carried a book in his left. There were no ostentatious robes; the clothes of the figures were etched into the wood of the statue. They were faded blues, greens and reds, the garments intricately carved. The Madonna's face stared impassively forward with a stern expression. There was something slightly manic about the eyes, full round irises etched into wide almonds.

'I just have a feeling, Debs,' continued Frances, answering her friend's curious look. 'This is where we're supposed to travel to next.'

She found a couple of other Madonnas and handed the cards to the saleswoman, a dark gypsy with wild black hair, who grinned showing several gold-capped teeth. She had seen Frances intensely perusing the card.

'C'est une Vierge en Majesté, Notre Dame de Saugues,' she said, by way of information, and then added something else that Frances didn't understand.

'What did she say?' Frances asked Debs, as they walked away.

'It's a Virgin in Majesty, Our Lady of Saugues,' replied Debs. 'She's the Virgin who has to protect Saugues from the

Beast o' Gevaudan. Beauty and the Beast. In French, La Belle et la Bête.'

'See, I told you we had to go there,' said Frances, triumphantly. 'The Virgin who fights beasts, that's some lady worth visiting!'

'If you say so!' Debs nodded in mock excitement, chuckling. 'But she's not black, more a kind of nut brown.'

'Jose said Black Virgins aren't always literally black, so it don't matter,' replied Frances, with assurance. She called over to Jose and Nathan, waiting a few yards further on down the cobblestone road. 'We're going to see Beauty and the Beast!'

## 28

## Tay Bac

That evening, they walked up the hill towards the *Restaurant du Cloître* under something of a cloud. There had been an argument just before they left the *Compostelle* after showering and changing and it left a bad taste. Frances was downcast. It was not so easy to shake off. *Surely not disagreement so soon, before end o' first full day in France!* Jose had looked up Saugues, using his phone to connect to the internet, and found that it was only fifty kilometres away. They could stay in Le Puy and go there and back easily on the Monday. But, he said, it was lucky, because they couldn't go traipsing about back and forth across the Auvergne just because of Frances' intuitions. There had to be a plan. Frances, feeling the criticism quite deeply yet, trying to stay calm, had gone back to her theme of being open to the Goddess and trying to be spontaneous. Jose hadn't replied, his way of sticking to his original argument. What disappointed Frances was that neither Nathan nor Debs had come to her aid. Debs had shrugged; Nathan had made a comment to the effect that they would have to see where Frances' inspirations led. There were no leaders; it was all down to consensus. That had to mean that he agreed with Jose. Frances had looked at a map of the Auvergne and suggested that nowhere was out of reach of a good drive from Le Puy. Jose had said that he thought they wanted to cut down on fuel consumption. And then quiet descended, because it was all going absolutely nowhere. Frances felt mad with Jose and this was now added to her earlier frustration with Nathan. She would like to have clung onto her friendship with Debs, but Debs seemed keen not to take sides and went into a typical Debs silence, which meant not allowing eye contact.

*They don't share my belief in Goddess, that's what! They're interested in me because I have visions, but for them it's just an experiment. They put my vision this morning down to a 'waking dream' in which I just regurgitated all the conversations that we had earlier. That's not true – had we been talking about lions when we went to Almscliffe Crag? And going back further, what about Goddess dancing? When had I discussed that? OK, I saw office in my vision, which I'd been worried about, but that's because it were a prophecy. No, they're not into it like I am.* Frances wished she could stop negative thoughts but, when they came, they circled round and round in her brain. And so it was; she tried a false smile or two to try and break through the mental barriers, but nothing would work and that's how it stayed until they filed into the *Cloître*. Neither the striking variety of colours of the five storey buildings around the square – walls of almond peach; ochre; terracotta; slate grey; cream, and windows adorned with shutters of chocolate; pearly grey; charcoal; white; cornflower blue; olive green – nor the pretty fountain at its centre managed to cheer her up.

The restaurant was cool and dark, a relief from the bright sunshine of the summer's day. In the far corner of the dining area, Frances saw a lone figure seated at an oblong table. It was Wei Chi. They smiled at each other. Frances was surprised at how glad she was to see an elderly lady whom she had met only that day. The inner turmoil began to abate.

'Hello,' said Wei Chi, struggling to her feet. 'It's good to meet you all.'

She was slightly hunched and looked up at them from a face that sloped down to a receding chin. Clearly, she had dressed up for the occasion. Her tightly drawn-back mop of grey hair had been fastened at the back with a white clip shaped as a butterfly. She wore a white long-sleeved blouse open at the neck and beige trousers. This went well with the sallow skin, although it was pale with age. Frances noticed again how extraordinarily thin she was. Jose, keen to show the others that he had meant it when he said he had a special affection for Chinese people, was the first to shake her hand, wrinkled and delicate with signs of arthritis. However, it was Debs who gave the diminutive old lady the warmest greeting. She saves it for vulnerable people, thought Frances. If it'd been a businessman in a suit, she'd have been cold as ice. They sat down; Wei Chi opened the conversation with some tips about the best and most reasonably priced items on the menu. After the niceties had been gone through, Nathan tried to find out more about her.

'Now, Wei Chi,' he said. 'What long road has led you here to Le Puy?'

'The story's a little too long to tell,' replied Wei Chi, with a little laugh which was followed by a short cough.

Frances noticed once more that the English was smooth, the Chinese accent forming only a surface gloss.

'OK, in brief, then,' agreed Nathan, with a broad smile.

'The quick answer is: on holiday. But what about you: you look as if you're doing more than touring around looking at mountains.'

'We're spiritual adventurers,' answered Jose, with some pride. 'We want to know whether, by our being here among the shrines of France just before the G8 summit is being held, we can influence its decisions on the environment by channelling our spiritual power,' he said, summarising it the best way he could.

Wei Chi's eyes widened.

'What a wonderful idea. I wish I had thought of it. And in such a spiritual place too.'

Frances was impressed that a Chinese woman could say 'spiritual' without too much difficulty. Just as she was thinking of commenting on it, Nathan came in.

'I sense that you're *also* here for spiritual reasons,' he suggested. 'I can tell by the way you reacted then.'

He dropped his voice for the last few words and smiled broadly at the small, round, sloping face. Wei Chi responded instantly.

'Yes, I'm a spiritual adventurer too.' Wei Chi laughed with some delight at this and clapped her hands, although it cost her another cough or two; clearly, the docile, vulnerable look hid a bright personality. 'I have always been one. Even my name is taken from the *I Ching*, the ancient Chinese book of changes. I wasn't born with it.'

'Why did you choose it?' asked Debs.

'I adopted the name as I was leaving Vietnam in the 1960s to escape the war. I needed to start a new life, so I took a new name. When I consulted the *I Ching* about which name I should choose, the coins indicated "Wei Chi", which means "Before Completion". Appropriate just as you are leaving on a great journey, isn't it?'

Frances thought of her Tarot reading and felt excited. *What a fantastic person to meet!* She could sense the sudden leap of interest in the other adventurers too.

'What was your original name?' asked Nathan.

'It doesn't matter, does it?' answered Wei Chi, looking straight back at him. 'You will never meet the person that I was back in Vietnam and so the name might as well no longer exist.'

Wei Chi was proving to be more formidable in conversation than the little hunched figure had suggested. Nathan, tongue-tied for once, was rescued by the arrival of the waiter with a basket of bread and a notepad for orders.

There followed a friendly battle in which both sides demanded to know more about the other, so as not to dominate the conversation with their own stories. Wei Chi won. So she heard a potted history of Jose's life in Goa, Singapore and Yorkshire before the arrival of a carafe of white wine and a delicate canapé as a *mise en bouche*. Then Nathan continued, recounting his journey in India and his spiritual quest. *Hors d'oeuvres*: a couple of minutes passed in silence, as people began to tuck into what was really quite delicious French *cuisine*. Wei Chi had only a small appetite and pushed food onto Nathan's plate. Debs kept her part of the storytelling to working for women in refuges and avoided her earlier history. Frances felt that her autobiography was not as interesting as the others, so she kept to recent events too: the threatening phone calls and how she had discovered that the Goddess was with her in the crisis. There was mention of rituals, witchcraft, Drawing Down the Moon. Wei Chi was a good listener and convinced them of her genuine interest and approval. Then part-way into the main course, Frances, remembering Wei Chi cross herself at the stoup in the Cathedral, asked her whether she was a Catholic.

'Does some o' what we're saying make you uncomfortable? Maybe it goes against what you should believe as a Catholic.'

Wei Chi refuted this with a firm gesture of the hand accompanied by a shake of the head and a smile. It was clear that she had the gift of mildly rebuking without giving offence.

'Didn't you hear what I was saying earlier, Frances? I told you that I was a spiritual adventurer, too, that I named myself after an *I Ching* oracle? Would such a person object to others who set out on their own journeys? I am a Catholic now, it is true; I began to attend Mass soon after arriving in Paris. But Catholicism was only a vehicle for me, not an absolute truth. I came to love its folk tradition, which reminded me to some extent of my childhood in a multi-ethnic region before the Vietminh came and discouraged popular religion. I came to love the cult of the Virgin, its flowers, its processions and its rosaries; I came to love the power of the Mass and its great sense of the presence of God.'

During the cheese course (*is it possible to get it all in? – but it's so delicious*), Jose expounded his theories about the Catholic priesthood. He did so with considerable excitement, hands waving in the air, sipping his wine frequently and then pouring out another glass, offering the bottle to the others, of whom only Nathan was ready for a refill. Frances tried to suppress the thought that, if the boys were going to drink three times the amount of everybody else, they could pay for it. However, all of that suddenly paled into insignificance. Debs called out in panic, interrupting Jose in mid-flow.

'Wei Chi! Are you all right?'

The little Chinese lady had slumped backwards and was holding her side. She was clearly in some pain.

'Please take me to the ladies,' she whispered.

Frances and Debs returned to the table with Wei Chi looking a little better. She had taken a strong painkiller from a little pillbox in her handbag.

'I'm really sorry,' she said. 'It suddenly comes on. I shouldn't have met you and subjected you to this. You're here to enjoy your holiday. Let me finish my dinner quickly and then I'll go home and leave you to it.'

'No,' insisted Debs. 'Whatever your problem is, let's share it. We're big enough to do that. Only a few weeks ago, these good friends o' mine were standing round my bed, looking after me. They're not my childhood friends, but they're the ones who care for me now. I met them once as strangers, just like you've met us today.'

'Well said,' agreed Jose, and the others threw in their own statements of commitment.

'*Whatever* it is,' added Frances.

They all looked attentively at Wei Chi. The little colour she had began to return to her cheeks, but her breathing remained shallow.

'OK,' she agreed. 'I'll tell you. But I must insist that you do not spend your entire holiday worrying about me.'

The dessert was now on the table but no one started on it. They were all looking at Wei Chi and wanted to show her that they were serious. There was nothing for her to do but tell them the facts.

'This area of France, the *Massif Central*, consists of miles upon miles of beauty. There are mountains, rocky crags jutting into the sky, river valleys, lakes, pretty villages, little bridges over streams, animals grazing on high slopes, wooded hillsides, wonderful viewpoints, splendid sunsets and refreshing winds. It reminds me of my home, the Tay Bac region of Vietnam just near the Chinese border. I had to leave Tay Bac, but I never forgot the countryside that was my first love, you know. So I am here because it makes me feel as if I am there. And I want to be there because I am dying of cancer and now I have only days, rather than weeks, to live. I don't want to die in the suburbs of Poissy but here in the mountains. So I have come here on a tour. But unlike the other holidaymakers, I have no intention of going home. I will stay here in this region until the moment when I draw my last breath. When it gets near, you begin to sense it, you know, and it is very near.'

Looking round at the startled faces, she picked up her spoon and, finally, so did everyone else.

'In your situation, some good friends are what you need,' said Jose, with plenty of emotion in his voice. 'And here we are! Just one evening in your company and I'm in no doubt at all. I want to stay with you until the end. Then you can pass on some of your wisdom before you leave for Tay Bac for good.'

Jose was finally going to get to pay back the Chinese people kindness for kindness in full measure.

# 29

# Beauty and the Beast

After getting a grunted agreement from Debs, still snuggled up under the single cotton sheet, Frances pulled back the faded green shutters of their east-facing bedroom to allow light to flood through the windows of the *Compostelle*. Her first realisation about the new day was that it was raining hard. Splashing on the tiled roof above, the sound of little streams forming on the road below as the water sloped off the camber into the drains. Raining hard! Could this be sunny southern France? She had heard that, in the mountainous *Massif Central*, long dry spells were unusual, but Frances still hoped for a torrent-free vacation. The Goddess would arrange it, surely?

'I can't believe it, it's pouring down,' she remarked out aloud.

Debs was already awake in the bed nearby, facing upwards with her head just resting below the bolster.

'Well, what of it?' came the dismissive reply. 'We'd all die o' drought if we didn't get rained on sometimes. It's Mother Nature's way o' feeding us, you know.'

'Yeah, I know,' said Frances impatiently, feeling defensive given that she seemed to have been accused of the greatest blasphemy: insulting both Nature and the Goddess at the same time. 'It's just that, with all that rain last year, I thought we were due a dry holiday!'

'I understand what you're saying.' Debs turned her head towards Frances to look out of the window. 'But English people always talk about "bad" weather. French do too: "il fait mauvais"! Yet, in England and France, we have two o' the most beautiful and green countries in world.'

Frances started to jig across the room and chimed into a sarcastic little song.

'You're so right, you're so very, very right, you're the rightest person in the world!'

Debs just stared at her. *OK, thought Frances, we'll stop the silly stuff. Miss Serious doesn't want to muck about.*

Apart from her irritation at the rain, Frances felt an uncomfortable mixture of emotions. First, excitement! After yesterday looking round Le Puy, today the plan was to drive the fifty kilometres to the old church at Saugues, where the Virgin on the postcard resided, and to discover what was behind the mystery of 'the Beauty and the Beast'. Secondly, anxiety. Wei Chi's news had caused Frances' stomach to churn; whether it was straightforward sympathy or the fear of being with someone as they exhaled their last breath, Frances wasn't sure. Thirdly, guilt. Frances could not believe that she had entertained such negative thoughts about her friends on a day when the Goddess had paid her the privilege of appearing to her yet again, high on the *rocher* overlooking Le Puy. Even if it *were* a creation of her imagination, that didn't change the powerful insight that she had had. The oppressed peoples of the world, those that Europeans had enslaved and belittled – those were the ones taken up into the sun-filled world of the Madonna-Goddess. It was a true and powerful revelation and therefore not one worthy of being followed by agitation and resentment against those who had shown her such friendship and affection over the last few months. Frances sighed.

'What's up, Frances, love?'

A muffled voice came from under the white sheet. Its owner had disappeared back under it.

'Nowt. I just sometimes realise what a fool I am.'

Debs popped her head out again.

'Well, what brought that on? Aren't we all fools? It's part o' being human.'

'Yeah, I suppose. But Nathan and Jose pissed me off yesterday and I shouldn't have let it get to me. Then when we met Wei Chi and heard about her illness, it all seemed so trivial.'

'They're men! It's their job to get on your tits. They annoy me all time.' Debs spoke sleepily between yawns. 'When we get to Saugues, you, me and Wei Chi'll go off to see Madonna and send lads off to meet Beast!'

'Good! We'll let beasts of a feather flock together!'

'Very witty. Now let's get showered and go and have some brekkie.'

Breakfast was somewhat subdued. Wei Chi was on their minds. She had agreed to travel with them to Saugues. 'La Belle et la Bête! Sounds interesting.' Her hotel was not far away and they drove the Honda Hybrid up the narrow streets for the first time since arrival in Le Puy. Wei Chi looked smart and not a little refined in a black trouser suit, underneath which she sported a light yellow blouse, with a silk scarf of darker yellow and a black hair grip which matched the suit. *How can a dying woman bother to dress up?* wondered Frances. She imagined herself as a seventy or eighty-something year old, no longer wearing baseball caps and short vests but seeking out more stylish and mature attire. It didn't seem such a bad prospect, as long as she had Mr Right and was a proud granny by then. But terminal cancer? No, that wasn't part of the dream. She helped Wei Chi dodge the puddles as they made towards the car.

Stuffed to the gunwales with five passengers, the Honda set off west. Through the intermittent rain, the countryside was pleasant, with rolling hills, farms and villages mixing old and new: smart modern functional white or yellow houses with neat red roofs, in which one imagined busy family life, alongside older, taller, less robust-looking, dark brick buildings, tiles missing and some windows shuttered, with an air of semi-residence. The conversation was light and expectant. No one mentioned cancer, visions or global warming, just remarked on the views and speculated on the mystery of the Madonna and the Beast. Jose, at the wheel, had the look of someone who had already researched everything on the internet using his phone, but he judiciously stayed quiet. However, he was given one chance to show off.

'What's a Virgin in Majesty?' Frances asked Jose.

He had been doing his homework as usual.

'It's a style of Madonna and Child statue dating from the Romanesque period, the eleventh and twelfth centuries. The Madonna sits on a throne. It's known as the Throne of Wisdom.'

The road twisted round bends and between dense woodlands towards a village called St Privat d'Allier gathered round a strange-looking long, thin chateau, next to a church with its pyramid of a red tower. As the rain had abated, Jose suggested that they stopped there, as his guide book noted that the church stood on a spur of rock which served as a viewpoint.

'It's said that no one stays the same after seeing the Allier Gorge,' remarked Wei Chi, finally ending the lacuna in which words were replaced by gasps at the beauty of the deep and extensive wooded valley, at the high point of one end of which St Privat stood in regal splendour.

'Had you already seen it?' asked Nathan.

'No, although at eighty years old it's not too late to be changed forever,' replied Wei Chi, with a disarming smile.

Frances marvelled at the thought of someone so near to the end of their life being transformed by a view, even one as magnificent as a French river gorge. She walked off lost in thought. The church door was open; the space inside, cool and shaded, broken up by sturdy pillars, created a sense of quiet stillness. The old church had a modern stained glass window;

Frances recognised it as a depiction of the apparition of the Virgin Mary to St Bernadette at Lourdes, something in which she had taken an interest since Jose mentioned it. Exactly 150 years ago. *So, you saw a Goddess too*, she thought, addressing in her head the kneeling image of the teenage peasant girl in the glass. *What were she like? Did she make you feel better about yourself? Did you have any idea that, because of you, millions would come to Lourdes in search of healing? You and me, Bernie, love!* Then Frances shuddered, not at the cool of the church interior but because her moment of hubris had spooked her. The thought that millions of people would someday be moved by the story of St Frances Dryburgh the visionary made her uncomfortable. She had been brought up a Yorkshire Englishwoman, for whom fanciful flights of self-importance were followed by fear that something bad would happen to put you back in your place. She decided to go back outside and admire the gorge once more.

They drove on. The road wound down into the deep valley and through the village of Monistrol d'Allier, low down by the river. Monsters again. It crossed the Allier, alongside which a picturesque railway ran, and meandered up the other side. After many bends on the steep wooded climb, the journey resumed on the high plateau once more; Saugues was only a few kilometres away, the road passing across farmland. The way ahead opened out into a wide valley and, as the descent began, a strange sight came into view on the right hand side of the road. A large wooden figure of a wolf, standing stiff with its head forward as if ready to pounce, threatened from on high the inhabitants of the town that came into view below. Jose stopped the car so that they could inspect the site in a lay by provided for the purpose and a hundred yards or so to the right along the hillside, they saw a large statue of the Virgin, standing upon a grey stone arch. She was smaller than *Notre Dame de France*, white marble rather than red bronze, but still grand enough to dominate the view of the hillside. She had no Child, so her arms were free to be outstretched by her sides, the hands open in a gesture of maternal protection towards the valley. La Belle et la Bête, Beauty and the

Beast, figured in wood and marble, the drama of the battle displayed in great sculptures, visible for miles. Debs translated the plaque on one side of the wolf.

'This is the "Beast of Gevaudan",' she informed them. 'It were supposedly a vicious creature that terrorised the Gevaudan region in which we now stand, during eighteenth century. It were first of all reckoned to be a huge wolf that devoured several victims over a large area, but legends began to spread that it were more than a wolf, a kind of satanic monster. Local people were repentant, believing it to be some kind o' punishment, and prayed to God or Mary to protect 'em. It were so notorious that King of France himself sent marksmen to kill it. However, it were thought to have been finally dispatched by a local hunter. Its widespread fame meant that it's never been forgotten; it's been mentioned up to present day in books, novels and films.'

So, that is what the stallholder in Le Puy had been referring to: two great statues on the hillside overlooking Saugues. The story was fascinating, but Frances felt some disappointment that there was not a greater element of mystery. They continued on down into the town and found a parking space in the marketplace next to the medieval church with its hexagonal Romanesque tower. The rain began pouring again.

'This is what we've come to see,' said Frances, 'Notre Dame de Saugues.'

As at St Privat d'Allier, the church interior was dark.

'I can't see a thing in here,' complained Nathan.

'Try taking your sunglasses off,' suggested Debs, with a little mock tut of disapproval. 'I don't know why you were wearing 'em in the rain!'

The Virgin in Majesty of Saugues was not prominent like her sister on the high altar in Le Puy, as she was situated in a little alcove in one wall behind thick glass, with a light switch for anyone wishing to view her. The statue was about eighteen inches high, richly painted at one time but now in fading colours. It was clearly very old. What most held the attention were the wide eyes and large round irises.

'It's even worse than Le Puy,' said Debs. 'Another fetish object to frighten locals. See those staring eyes and that grim expression. It's difficult to feel owt else than fear and revulsion when looking at it.'

*It's not unlike you then,* thought Frances, giggling to herself.

'I don't agree,' she whispered, trying to establish an atmosphere of devotion. 'It's beautiful, noble and serene. A masterpiece, in fact.'

The conversation ended as they suddenly realised that Wei Chi had slipped away from them unnoticed. She was sitting at one end of the church, scrabbling for her little pillbox in the shoulder-bag. As they rushed towards her, she signalled them away.

'No, you can't worry every time I feel pain. It will happen every day,' she said, struggling breathlessly for the words.

Frances went back to Notre Dame de Saugues and sat in front of the glass. She put the light back on and quickly became conscious of the fact that she felt utter fascination with the statue. After all, they were only there because she had been drawn to a photograph of it. She was entranced. Everything was becoming blurry. The charismatic power of the statue seemed to be triggering a vision. Did it matter that it was happening before any ritual? Frances allowed the trance state to continue sweeping over her...

It was as if the whole scene: church, friends, statue, had all been raised to another level, a kind of higher floor in the same building. What's more, she seemed to have become detached from her own body. In the vision, she had moved to the other side of the church and was looking back at herself sitting in front of the statue. Yet it was no longer hidden by the alcove, which had disappeared, allowing Frances to view the statue directly. Notre Dame de Saugues was now life-size and, it would seem, lifelike, although she and the Child continued to stare ahead with their fierce glazed expressions. Frances then saw Wei Chi sit beside that other Frances. Both of them looked up devotedly at the

Virgin, who was looking over their shoulders with her fixed stare. What was she staring at? Frances looked to the left of the seated figures and froze. Both she and Wei Chi were being threatened by a dark shadow moving slowly towards their backs. There was something indescribably awful about it, a truly nightmarish being far more terrible than any wolf creature. Frances shuddered; there was a horrible sick feeling inside her. It came right up to the seated women and it seemed inevitable that it would engulf them. However, its progress seemed to be stopped by something; from somewhere in the shadow came an impatient hiss. Frances looked back at the Virgin. It was her strong glare that held it back. The tableau was set out in front of her, as if in suspended motion: the shadow; herself and Wei Chi; the staring Virgin and her Child. Nothing moved...

Then it all disappeared and she came to, swaying on the bench. The Virgin was back behind the glass; Wei Chi was at the west end of the church where they had left her. Frances had returned to the ground floor of her psyche. She summoned the others from different parts of the church.

'She don't look like that to frighten locals,' she said, dreamily.

'Pardon?' asked Nathan.

'Summat Debs said,' answered Frances. 'But the point is that the Madonna's fierce because she's enemy o' the *Beast*. It's him who she glares at, to keep us all safe. She's looking over our shoulders at Beast who's like a dark shadow creeping up behind us.'

Debs was quite pleased with that explanation, as the idea of a woman keeping male beasts in their place appealed to her, but Jose saw a flaw in the argument.

'The statue comes from the High Middle Ages,' he pointed out. 'It was sculpted several hundred years before the period when the Beast terrorised the local populace.'

Frances frowned.

'Well, maybe there were other beasts back then,' she suggested, without much conviction.

Debs came to her rescue.

'If the Beast is like a shadow, it represents death, I expect. That's always terrified people. And we are all moved by hearing about Wei Chi's illness. That's what the vision is about.'

Frances looked anxiously at Wei Chi; to liken her situation to being threatened by a shadowy beast might not have been very diplomatic. But Wei Chi was equal to it.

'The beast is not death,' she said, firmly, once again able to sound strong despite the frail voice. 'It's the *fear* of death. There is nothing terrible about death. It only becomes terrible when we allow it to frighten us.'

'We'll have a ritual later,' suggested Nathan, searching for something more positive to talk about. 'Let's get outside, it's so cool and dark in here!'

As they wandered out into the bustle of the market square, people trying to avoid the rain but continue the daily business, Frances began to experience feelings of unease. She usually felt upbeat after her visionary experiences, elated that she had been visited by the Goddess; there had never been ill effects. But this time, things were different. At first, it was a vague sense of physical discomfort. But quite soon, she realised that she simply didn't feel well. A pain engulfed her neck and ran down into her left arm. Her left leg didn't seem to want to move with its usual fluency. It felt as though something was about to snap inside. This went with a nagging thought. She could understand the vision of Wei Chi being threatened by the shadow, but why was Frances also in that situation? She wasn't close to death too, was she? The pain in her left arm caused her to think of health warnings about heart attacks, so she felt her pulse. The rhythm seemed steady but felt as though it was laboured and about to break down. Then there was a sudden quickening that made Frances quite frantic. Her breath didn't seem to want to function as easily as it normally did, either. Perhaps Wei Chi wasn't going to be the first to die, after all.

'Where shall we go?' asked Jose. 'Maybe we could do a ritual up near the great statue of the Madonna, as we did in Le Puy.'

They looked at Frances, but she was staring at the flagstones of the pavement.

'What's wrong, love?' asked Debs.

'I don't feel very well,' replied Frances. 'Perhaps I could just sit down for a bit.'

'OK,' said Nathan. 'Let's find a café. There's bound to be one in the town.'

The first place that they found was a small bar on the high street that sold hot, cold or alcoholic drinks and provided '*sandwichs*'. It was a rough and ready little place with a few locals propped up at the bar and telling each other in-jokes. Frances didn't say much. Occasionally someone asked her how she was. However, she was not keen to give details, as it was difficult to pin down exactly what the problem was. Her arm? Her neck? Her leg? Her breath? Her heartbeat? There was an overwhelming sense of something very bad about to happen in her body that was hard to describe. In her thoughts, she swung from rational explanation to inner panic. Rational explanation – *yes, it must be moving from brightness of the day into dark church.* Or – *visionary trance probably can have an effect sometimes, especially when it's so scary, but it'll pass off.* Or – *it were just worry about Wei Chi.* Or – *French food, I'm not used to it.* Or – *I'm ill and that vision has just told me that I'm about to die. Wei Chi and me. She in all her experience and wisdom might be able to overcome fear but I can't. Not even with Goddess on my side. I just can't stand the fear, just can't stand it. No, come on. This isn't first time me or one o' my friends has had a bout o' hypochondria. I'm becoming just like my mum. Just try to relax. Oh, God, my heart just jumped again.*

'Are you feeling any better, Frances?' asked Wei Chi.

'I'll be all right, just give me time.'

'Why don't I get you a brandy?' suggested Nathan.

'OK.'

*Alcohol might just calm me down if it's just anxiety. And if it's not, then I don't think a brandy's going to make it any worse. So, yeah, OK, I'll have one.*

A double brandy made Frances feel much better, but she was also drunker than she normally would have been after that amount. She went all floppy and couldn't bring herself to speak much. She was fairly hopeless as they tried to carry out a ritual by the Madonna up on the hillside. Furthermore, the wind strengthened along with the intermittent raindrops and it was difficult for them to hear each other. Not a ritual with which to present spiritual adventuring to Wei Chi for the first time! So they left, went back to the car parked by the wolf and returned to Le Puy. There Frances retired for the whole late afternoon and evening, eating nothing, scared to join the others in a meal out in case the nasty feeling came back as the alcohol wore off. *Best to stay in and recuperate. I'll be better tomorrow. I will, won't I?*

# 30

# The Water Bearer

The hired car made its way out of Le Puy up the hill westwards; after five days in Le Puy, they were on their way to a new base at Massiac, on the river Alagnon. Including the extra traveller, Wei Chi, made space difficult, so the passengers had to sit with bags on their laps. Jose, who was driving, had assured them that it was not too far to Massiac via Brioude. There was silence in the car; ten o' clock was still sleepy head time on holiday. Frances looked out of the window for a last look at the red-brown Madonna high on the rock but seeing her – the Child seeming to wave a farewell – did not bring comfort. She was still feeling ill and suffering inner turmoil. She thought back over the three days that had passed since the visit to Saugues.

The symptoms had not subsided; if anything, they had worsened. Sudden, though elusive, pains in her neck and arms; irregular heartbeats; a feeling of paralysis in her left leg, which made it feel as though it was dragging; breathlessness after any small exertion. Had she slowly been succumbing to a deadly disease these last few months? That might explain the visions.

She only felt some relief after alcohol, which knocked her out so that she was unable to socialise with her usual gusto. The fact that all of these experiences came and went intermittently, there being no one fixed problem, convinced everyone else that Frances was suffering neurotic hysteria that was perhaps an unavoidable aspect of being a visionary. Frances therefore kept her ups and downs to herself and feigned gradual recovery, so that people had ceased to ask her how she was, with the exception of Wei Chi who had fished for some answers the day after the visit to Saugues.

'Are you afraid of death, Frances?'

'Yeah, I suppose so, I don't really like talking about it. The thought o' not being alive for ever and ever terrifies me.'

'At your age, such fear is understandable. You are imagining death from the perspective of being young and healthy. It would be a terrible disaster for you, so you don't want to contemplate it. But when you are older like me and feel tired by life – you've done everything you needed to do and those things you haven't done were probably not yours to do – then death is no longer frightening. It's like a release, a state of peace.'

'But, Wei Chi, not being forever wi' no waking up, how can you face it?'

'That depends on whether you believe in eternal life, Frances.'

The conversation reminded Frances of the discussion in the pub in Leeds in which death was likened to a birth into a new world. But it had been more palatable, as then she had been talking about death without this awful feeling that it was just around the corner.

Wei Chi was worried that her terminal illness was causing Frances to have empathetic feelings, so she tried to turn down insistent requests that she spend each day with the young pilgrims. However, she had become a *cause célèbre*, particularly for Debs and Jose, who were determined to stay with her to the end. She had become more important for them even than rituals and the G8 summit as the reason for this touring journey. So Wei

Chi had to accept that, without her, the four of them would do nothing; she had to travel with them. However, she insisted on there being no summoning of doctors or visiting hospitals, however ill she became.

She entered enthusiastically into the rituals as far as her weakened body would allow.

'I have an idea. Let's build five altars of flowers, four for the elements and quarters; we will create them just when we call the spirits and disperse them when we dismiss them. The fifth altar will symbolise the Goddess at the centre. The four and the five will bring together the western and Chinese symbolic systems, as the Chinese have five elements, you know.'

Incorporated just as eagerly as Frances had been a few months earlier, Wei Chi was now one of the gang.

The next two apparitions had both occurred on the last full day in Le Puy. In Saugues, Debs had had a brief conversation in the bar in French with a local man, who told them of other shrines in the Saugues neighbourhood. There were two he particularly recommended, in places of extraordinary natural beauty. So they returned to the area two days later. The informant had been right: the views were stunning despite the clouds and frequent showers of rain. Deep in the countryside, the chapel of Notre Dame d'Estours stood on a rocky promontory halfway down a very steep wooded gorge, in which the river Seuge flowed between Saugues and the Allier. It was a delightful grey-bricked building with red roofs and a rounded apse that was face on as one approached the chapel; at the far end was an open three-bell mounting, standing as a narrow tower. The entrance was locked and a notice declared that the medieval statue, too valuable to be entrusted to the remote chapel, was now protected in a caged alcove in the church in Monistrol d'Allier. According to a medieval legend, it had been found by cows behind a rock in the gorge.

'*Beugler*,' said Debs. 'It means to moo. That's a French word I didn't know. The cows mooed to tell cowherds that they had sensed a hidden statue.'

As there was no one else in the vicinity of the remote chapel, the ritual was held outside it. There was a space for outdoor services, with a large modern marble statue of the Virgin standing high on the rock above a stone altar surrounded by a low wall. Frances was feeling quite queasy after the long clamber down to the chapel, breathless and nauseous, so she was happy to go into the trance state that soon followed the beginning of the ritual...

The promontory over the gorge was suddenly standing on its own in space, it seemed; Frances was alone and looking down from it upon a wide lunar landscape, bare with scattered rocks and meteor craters. The cloudy sky was replaced with blackness studded with a legion of stars. Her eyes were drawn to a bright object far away low near the horizon on her right hand side, and she saw a huge heavenly Madonna in the sky holding the Child on her left arm, clinging lovingly to her cheek. Both were radiant in yellow light. On her right arm she held a great wicker basket, in which Frances saw two fish and several loaves of bread. The figures were like the ever-present statues in France, serene in their immobility. However, the whole tableau moved downwards and began to disappear behind the hills in the distance...

Frances once again came to in the attentive Nathan's arms, but the first thing she saw was Wei Chi in her broad-rimmed straw hat sitting on the wall hunched over, looking rather the worse for wear and reaching for her pills. This caused the peaceful feeling that she normally had after the visions to evaporate quickly back into breathless anxiety. In trying to get a rational perspective, she thought that maybe it proved there *was* a link between Wei Chi's illness and her symptoms. Frances and Wei Chi sat together while the others completed the ritual, using flowers that they had bought for the purpose from a little shop in the square by the *Compostelle* in Le Puy. They surveyed the beautiful view together: *why can't I enjoy it,* thought Frances, still fighting for mental control over the rising panic. Afterwards, Jose was the first to comment on Frances' description of the apparition.

'It signifies the end of the age,' he pronounced calmly, as if it were the most obvious thing in the world. 'Do you remember – we talked about it? The Age of Pisces and its opposite sign Virgo. Jesus was represented in the early Church by the Fish of Pisces, whilst Mary is the Virgin, the Virgo. In the basket there are the loaves and fishes of the New Testament miracle, the symbols of the harvest sign Virgo and the fish sign Pisces. They are setting on the horizon; the age is coming to an end.'

'No more Christianity?' asked Nathan.

'Not necessarily, but maybe it'll take new forms now,' suggested Jose.

'Good riddance, if it does decline,' said Debs, harshly. 'Patriarchal claptrap.'

Jose answered calmly, but he was clearly suppressing irritation.

'No, not completely. There are wonderful treasures in it, you know. I still regard myself as a Christian.'

'So do I.' Wei Chi came into the conversation. 'But I don't suppose either of us see it as the only true faith, do we?'

'You're absolutely right,' replied Jose. 'The trouble with Christianity is that it hasn't really been tried yet! Not bigotry but unconditional love and acceptance of all that is good and wholesome, like other cultures and their faiths and people in mature homosexual relationships.'

Frances kept relatively quiet in the discussion about her vision; the experience for her was more emotional than philosophical. It had left her fatigued and not far from tears, which she suppressed, as she was by now employing a strategy of trying not to allow her nervous health to disrupt the holiday.

Wednesday night was the full moon and it was decided that they would celebrate it with a second ritual late in the evening, a 'Drawing Down the Moon' as at Avebury. The location was discovered in the afternoon: another pretty chapel, this time low down in the river valley by the side of the tree-lined Allier just a few kilometres from Estours. The shrine of Notre Dame des Chazes. The sandy brown brick chapel, with its tall pyramid-roofed open tower, stood at the bottom of the gorge by a large rock, which gave the building a dramatic relief. This time the chapel was open. A photograph of its valuable medieval statue, taken away from the chapel into private hands to protect it, had been placed on the altar. It was another Virgin in Majesty seated on her customary throne, with the Child this time leaning forward as if eager to meet visitors. As with other statues, he had the appearance of a small perfectly formed adult on his mother's lap. The Virgin was unusual in that her head was bare; both she and the Child had centre partings in silvery blonde hair making them look, according to Debs, like pop stars. The figures' skin was painted pale olive green; the search for the Black Virgins had opened out into a discovery of the many-coloured Virgins in Majesty. The mother's hands were poised to support the child, an inch or so from his body. Frances tried to relax, as she sat quietly by the rippling eddies of the Allier, trickling down from the mountains of the *Massif Central* to join the Loire on its way to the Bay of Biscay and the Atlantic. It was strange. Debs with her tendency to depression and over-seriousness; Jose with his frail body and worried caution; Nathan with his emotional distance and bad jokes – all of them seemed so calm and at peace in the pretty French countryside compared to poor Frances, for whom a couple of days of high anxiety had seemed like an eternity. It was as if she had always been the unfortunate member of the group and so she almost resented the *joie de vivre* exhibited by the others, complemented by the outlook of their new elderly travelling companion, apparently sanguine on her impending demise. Frances had got used to the pounding of the inner hysteria so quickly that it seemed as though it must have always been part of her, a hidden monstrous butterfly larva waiting for its moment to hatch and fly around in her stricken body.

They returned to Notre Dame des Chazes after a meal in Saugues. A pleasant breeze along the Allier gorge cooled the evening air; the clarity of the night sky, the occasional clouds a welcome contrast to the overcast day, allowed a whole panorama of stars to be presented. The full moon was just rising above the high cliff at the top of the gorge's rocky and part-wooded embankment behind the chapel. The sense of being alone with nature was greater at night than it had been earlier in the daytime; Frances almost had a sense of vertigo in reverse as she looked up at the star-pricked sky. The ritual began; rocks were used on this occasion rather than flowers, as they suited the terrain. Frances did not dare look up at the full moon for the first part of the ritual; she knew what the likely consequence would be and something about it now terrified her. The visions had, until this last couple of days, been a wonderful and benign addition to her relatively humdrum life, a source of comfort; now they were becoming sinister, as if she were opening some kind of Pandora's Box into a dark region full of unknown terrors. But that's why they were here in the Auvergne, to use her magical and visionary powers to help bring about an important change in the world. She had to keep going, take the plunge. So, when it came to the moment of the Drawing Down, Frances – despite a strong feeling of revulsion and fear – forced herself to look up at the moon. As she saw it, she felt the rush of the trance state, a kind of pleasant tingling throughout the body, as if she had heard some beautiful music, then a letting go akin to fainting…

Although they were deep down in the gorge rather than on a high platform as at Estours, Frances was transported to the lunar landscape for the second time that day. This time the bright light was high above her in place of the full moon, rather than setting on the horizon. In the light, she saw the cloaked woman of Almscliffe with her lion in a still life portrait. She had several cups in front of her into which she was pouring water from a large urn, with the lion looking on as if she were feeding milk to a cat. Her demeanour was benign, but for some reason it only added to Frances' discomfort, she felt oppressed by it…

The next moment, she was back once more with the ritual gathering in the moonlight by the side of the Allier. She began to cry.

'She's beautiful and kind, as always, but she's so *powerful*,' she blurted out. 'I can't stand it, it's killing me.'

The others looked stunned and anxious, and so it was left to Wei Chi to speak her words of wisdom.

'Of course, she *is* powerful. And it's hurting you. But it's the unknown and new that's terrifying you, not any evil. We'll keep watch over you while you go through it. You're being prepared for a revelation of some kind, I'm sure.'

Frances, soothed a little, managed between sobs to tell them the content of the vision.

'Earlier, Pisces and Virgo setting,' said Jose. 'Now Aquarius the Water Bearer and Leo the Lion high in the sky. It shows where we are now in the great cycle, in the Age of Aquarius the Water Bearer.'

The ritual over, they drove back to Le Puy. Jose asked Wei Chi the question that had been troubling him for some time.

'What has the Water Bearer got to do with today's spirituality? The symbol isn't anywhere to be seen in the modern world, unlike the Fish and the Virgin in early Christianity.'

Wei Chi swallowed and licked her lips while she reflected on her reply.

'Well, I can give you my opinion, but it's not necessarily a definitive one,' she said. 'Each person must find their own answer. In eastern cultures, these images don't resonate with our traditions anyway, so we're only talking about a western phenomenon. OK… my view is that modern spirituality is to do with everyone finding their own path and creating their own relationship with the divine. The Water Bearer has the spirit of life but pours it into a great number of cups. The cups are each one of us. The cups have varying shapes and sizes, and so the spirit that is poured out looks different for each person. As long as love and justice are the chief elements, there are no rules as to how you conceive of it. But it is the same spirit nevertheless. Water takes the shape of its container, but that doesn't make it any the less water, does it? So spirit is still spirit in all its various guises.'

'Ah,' said Jose. 'I like that answer. I'm glad we met you!'

And now on the route west towards Massiac, a few hours and a sleep later, Frances contemplated the new developments in her journey. She was tired; they had stayed late in the gorge and this was followed by checking out of the hotel the following morning. They were moving on. This had been decided on Frances' instigation; she had asked Jose to look up other rural locations for shrines of the Madonna. She wanted to stay away from urban centres and instead remain in modestly sized towns, villages or the countryside; the statues had to be many centuries old, either Virgins in Majesty or Black Virgins. The visionary was becoming something of a *prima donna* – when she sensed that something was right, that's the way it had to be. Jose found locations north-west of Le Puy towards the heart of the old Auvergne, where the central chain of volcanoes, no longer active, ran north to south. He suggested staying in Massiac, a small town next to the *Méridienne* motorway that would afford easy access elsewhere and which stood in the middle of Madonna country. Despite the prospect of this enticing destination, the continuing rain showers matched the gloominess of Frances' mood. Whenever things got better, they immediately became even worse. Somehow it was easier to deal with an external threat, like a mystery caller, than an internal one. No police force in the world could be called upon to manage the threats from inside the body or mind. No friends could turn up and drive the problem away. Where was it coming from, this overwhelming feeling of being ill at ease, of being at odds with your friends and yourself, alienated from all the things around you? And worst of all, she was suffering a sense of separation from the Madonna Goddess who had emerged in the last few months as the very goal of her existence and who now seemed to be powerless in the face of the encroaching shadow that sucked out life itself from her soul. The Goddess' constant presence, as evidenced in the apparitions, only seemed to bring the shadowy beast closer, but there was no turning back. Frances had to trust that she would redeem her, and soon.

# 31

# The Mountain

The cathedral town of Brioude lay upon the plain through which the Allier flowed after it emerged from the gorges. As Brioude and its great basilica came into view across the flat country, with the hills now in the background, an idea came to Frances.

'Wei Chi, you know you said about that *I Ching*? What is it?'

'Yes, well, it's like other types of divination. In the randomness of the oracle, the gods or spirits speak to you, as in the drawing of cards. In China, the oracles of the *I Ching* were traditionally cast using yarrow stalks. You can also do it with coins, which is more convenient!'

Wei Chi knew what was coming.

'Can you do it for me?'

'Yes – OK, Frances. Tonight.'

Frances had the Goddess Tarot pack with her but, in the last few days, her brain was scrambled and the readings did not make sense. They could be interpreted according to her mood, gloomy or desperately optimistic, swinging backwards and forwards. She needed someone else to consult an oracle and interpret for her.

They stopped in Brioude town centre for lunch and admired the twelfth century cathedral with its octagonal tower and layers of rounded walls and side chapels, distinctive in the Romanesque style. The basilica's most intriguing and unique artefact was the *Vierge Parturiente*, a medieval statue of Mary reclining while giving birth, the emerging infant said to be hidden under the folds of her long white dress. As the sculptor had assumed the ancient tradition that she had suffered no pain while giving birth to Christ, the Madonna looked quite casual as she leant back, propping her head on her right hand with the left hand laid on her belly, presumably to feel how the progress of the birth was going underneath the fabric.

'Looks quite easy, don't it, childbirth?' commented Debs. 'At least when you're an impossible creature like Mary, divorced from the reality o' women's lives.'

'Yes, and maybe not as difficult as the labour you're going through now, Frances,' said Wei Chi to the rather subdued visionary. 'That's what your anxiety is, you know, just pangs of the birth of a new period in your life.'

'I'm OK,' murmured Frances, attempting to deflect attention and trying to summon interest in the wealth of old treasures on display in the cathedral.

The several Madonnas included two standing Virgins, one carrying a child Jesus holding a bird, the other made out of volcanic lava; there was also a seated Virgin in Majesty, in a striking array of colours, red, blue and green, albeit rather battered and scarred, entitled *Notre Dame de Laurie.*

'Where's Laurie?' Frances asked Jose.

'Don't know. I'll look it up later.'

'OK, do. I'd like to go there. I just feel that it's right.'

Jose nodded without any trace of real enthusiasm. Over the last few days, Frances' intuitive decisions, delicate state and reluctance to enter into any sustained dialogue had made her come across as rather dictatorial.

A few kilometres on, the car pulled into Entremont, a pretty little farming village in the rolling hills above the flat plain of the Allier. It comprised several stone buildings two or three stories high, mostly with the red roofs numerous in the scattered communities of the Auvergne. Entremont had the look of a village that had moved on from the rundown buildings and rough sheds that must once have been ubiquitous, although they were still in evidence here and there. Most of the dwellings looked sturdy, as if restoration work had been carried out in the recent past. At the centre of the village was a little stone church, not much bigger than a chapel, with a single bell in the narrow open tower. This was to be the next rendezvous with the Madonnas of the Auvergne.

At Entremont, several attempts were made to check out whether Frances was up to going through yet another ritual and possible apparition. Wei Chi and Frances waved away doubts on the subject, Wei Chi because she was convinced that Frances was undergoing a spiritual transition that was uncomfortable but necessary; Frances, because she had reckoned that if visions were to be such mental agony, she might as well get as many of the twelve out of the way as early in the holiday as possible. Le Puy; Saugues; Estours; Chazes – only four so far and almost a week gone. The church in Entremont had a locked door; however, in a village, it was worth seeking out the key. Whilst the others knocked on doors, Debs took Wei Chi to one side.

'I'm concerned for her, Wei Chi. She's not herself at present. Maybe we should leave visions for a few days.'

'She's OK, really. With good friends around like you, she'll get through. It's obviously important to her.'

The confrontational side of Debs' character came out, without her intending it to, in front of the frail old Chinese lady.

'I wonder how much you care for Frances and how much you're in a hurry to see what comes out o' her revelations. After all, you've not long, you say so yourself!'

Instantly, she regretted it. But it didn't faze Wei Chi at all. Her response was kind and calm.

'You may have a point, Debs, thank you for being honest with me. Yet I really do believe that Frances is safe from harm and that she came here to undertake a task, which isn't going to be as easy as she thought. Debs, I wouldn't keep her in this anxious state if I could help it, but delaying the process won't make it easier. She's got to go through it.'

Debs gave a grim smile of acceptance. She would allow it to go on for a little while longer. But she was too used to taking care of women in distress to feel comfortable about it. And knowing her own depression, well, she wouldn't wish that on anyone.

A friendly elderly woman in a sturdy looking farmhouse produced a large iron key while her two collie dogs looked on with distrust. The chapel door yielded to a firm yank of the lock and they stepped into the space of the interior. The chapel was small but light and airy. To the left was the main altar and, near the door, a standing Madonna and Child. However, directly ahead on a side altar sat the Virgin in Majesty of Entremont, in the blues and reds of the carved clothing familiar by now, the Child in green with his mother's large hands protectively holding him perched at the front of her lap. While the others looked round, Frances – somewhat obsessively – went straight to the statue. Strangely, the face of the Madonna, while from the front view seeming unattractive and downcast, was elegant and noble in profile. So Frances silently prayed to her from the right hand side of the little altar. *Please make me feel better, please don't let me die now, at my age. Am I doing wrong, seeking out these visions at your shrines? Are you punishing me for being so arrogant? Give me some reassurance, let me know I'm on right track.* She imagined the large hands of the Madonna around *her*, keeping her safe. But a feeling of pins and needles in her left arm, sure signs of a heart attack according to something Frances had heard from somewhere, sent her into a new panic and she started to tremble. The tingling went when Frances felt a hand on her arm; she jolted in alarm. It was Wei Chi, keeping a regular check on her protégé.

'Stay with it, Frances, it'll be OK. Trust in your Goddess, that's what you have to do.' Wei Chi continued as she looked up in wonder at the statue. 'Amazing, isn't she? Full of dignity, calm in the face of all the terrors of the world.'

Debs, coming over to the altar, overheard.

'Yeah, dignified, sorted out, not a real woman a' all but a fiction. Children don't look like that, they scream and struggle, that's what they do. It's a myth, just like Madonna giving birth without pain.'

Wei Chi shook her head.

'That's one way of looking at it. On the other hand, maybe she represents what we'd all like to be and, somewhere inside deep down, we *are*. Somewhere beneath all the worries, anger and confusion, we are serene like her but we have to reach down to find it.'

Debs looked at her with a sceptical frown, but it was nevertheless the look of someone who wasn't entirely confident in her own objections. Wei Chi didn't say much but, when she did, somehow it had a ring of authenticity, something worth considering seriously. As she dispensed her few words of wisdom, she always remained as calm as a warm summer's evening.

The ritual took place during the late afternoon in a pleasant hillside grassy field a kilometre or so from Entremont. The wet weather was continuing and there was no point in waiting for an elusive sunny spell. Frances' discomfort steadily deepened. The depressive anxiety was getting worse and worse, throwing up new and unsettling symptoms at every turn. She felt that she couldn't breathe, her throat felt blocked. She glanced at Wei Chi, looking fatigued, seated on a plastic mac laid out on the grass. *She's eighty and dying, but I've got no more energy than she has.* As she fretted, the altars of flowers were prepared.

'Look at this beauty around us,' declared Nathan, addressing the circle. 'It will all be destroyed if the environment is not protected. The rain we are experiencing this week will gradually recede. The fertile French countryside will suffer more and more droughts and begin to resemble North Africa. The great rivers like the Allier will dry up and the vineyards will no longer yield. That's why we're here, to make magic together to force the world's governments to take decisive action. Let's really concentrate today; don't let this become just a routine.'

He then began to call the quarters. Frances really didn't want to enter the trance state at all; it was more terrifying than ever. There was something to be encountered and she didn't feel up to facing it. Although she had only seen the shadow once, at Saugues, it was as if it was still behind her, coming closer and closer with each apparition. But the more she resisted, the stronger the urge to enter into the dream world of the vision, like a patient facing a dangerous operation, who has already received the anaesthetic and tries in vain to prevent unconsciousness...

Again, for the third time, the moonscape. Its darkness contrasted so strangely with the brightness of the day. This time, Frances' attention was drawn to the horizon on her left hand side. She felt a chill passing through her. There was a great black mountain there, blocking out what lay beyond. Around the edges of the mountain was an eerie blue light. Frances felt certain that whatever emitted that light was about to emerge over the top of the mountain to threaten her...

That was it. No message of comfort from the Goddess, no symbolic tableaux, just a rocky terrain and a 'something' terrible about to appear over the horizon. The apparitions had turned from hopeful and bright to cold and menacing. Why had this happened? Despite the beauty of the countryside all around as the group moved on, all Frances could see in her mind's eye was the bleak moonscape. She was disturbed to see mountains not far off as they approached Massiac: the Cézallier region, said Jose. For her, mountains suggested that she might be nearing the climax of her nightmarish vision.

'Do we have to go to a mountainous area, Jose?' she asked as the car approached Massiac.

'We're not far from Laurie here; that's in the mountains and it's where you said you wanted to go. Remember the statue in the basilica in Brioude?'

'Yeah, OK, but I'm not so sure now.'

'What were in your vision?' asked Debs. 'Why won't you tell us?'

Frances described the moonscape in a flat voice.

'Well, you've seen the image of the Age of Pisces setting, as it's now in the past, and the image of the Age of Aquarius high in the sky, representing the present,' said Jose. 'Now you're about to see the Age that is to come, the Age of Capricorn.'

'That's 2,000 years away!' protested Nathan.

'True, but we will begin to see its influences emerging soon,' said Wei Chi, in a voice that seemed more feeble and breathless as the day wore on. 'Each age contains the seeds of the next.'

Jose found the hotel in Massiac, the *Maison des Gorges*, which he had located in advance. The accommodation was comfortable and spacious but not unnecessarily luxurious, therefore not expensive when shared rooms were taken into account. The remote and rural Auvergne had not, fortunately, caught up with northern Europe on prices. The hotel was run by a couple in their forties, both of whom seemed to wear permanent but genuine smiles. The outlook was pleasant too, Massiac being hidden in a cleft among the hills; the back of the hotel stood close to the bank of the river Alagnon and on each side of the valley there were two high gorges overlooking the hotel, on each a small chapel.

In the hotel, Frances stayed with Wei Chi as the others walked down to the river to explore. She was keen for her to cast the *I Ching*. Wei Chi agreed, but she looked frailer than ever as she lay on her bed and her hands trembled as she took out three copper coins from a box. Each had a square hole in the centre.

'These are about 150 years old,' she said feebly, handing them to Frances. 'Now we will sit for a moment in prayer, while you ask your question. You needn't tell me what it is. As you do so, roll the coins backward and forward in your hands so that the throwing is random. When you're ready, throw the three coins six times; we will record how many heads and tails there are on each occasion. This will make up what is called a hexagram, with six lines.'

Frances silently asked the Goddess to confirm that she was still being helped and guided and also to indicate what was going to happen next. She then cast the coins onto the bed. It was up to Wei Chi to decide which were heads and which tails on the old coins, as all Frances could see was worn Chinese writing.

'Two heads and a tail: Yin... again, Yin... three tails: Yin changing to Yang... again, Yin... Yin... Yin. OK, Frances, that's it. It's not difficult to see what the first hexagram is: all Yin, so it must be *K'un*, "the Receptive".'

Frances was in a very negative and pessimistic mood. Everything that Wei Chi said caused her to conclude that things were not going well. Didn't three tails together suggest some dark future?

To interpret the oracle, Wei Chi referred to a leather-bound volume that she unwrapped from a burgundy-coloured silk cloth; clearly it was something she cherished.

'The hexagram *K'un* means great success and you will do well if you persevere, it says. Follow like a patient mare; do not lead. Find friends to help you but at the important moment you will be alone with your god. The hexagram *K'un* and the mare both represent the Earth.' The effort fatigued her. 'There you are,' she breathed.

'OK,' said Frances, relieved that there was no presage of disaster. 'The Earth's what we're here to protect.'

'Exactly,' agreed Wei Chi. 'But there's more in the oracle.'

She was clearly struggling; Frances felt a pang of guilt but was too desperate to know the meaning of the divination to allow her to rest straight away.

'Please go on,' she said. 'Let's just finish the interpretation and then I'll let you get some sleep.'

'A deep sleep would be nice, but it doesn't come often enough these days,' sighed Wei Chi. 'Well, the moving line, the three tails, means that you should complete your task in the service of others. You have to follow where the Goddess is leading you, however difficult it may seem.'

'That's fine,' said Frances. That's given me some encouragement. Now you can go to sleep.'

'Not quite,' said Wei Chi, barely audible now. 'The changing line means that *K'un* transforms into another hexagram, which is the answer to this question. It's *Ch'ien*, "Modesty".' Frances was by now opening a bottle of vodka to have with some lemonade. 'Stop drinking, Frances, it won't help.'

'I can't help it, I really can't.'

Tears began to course from Frances' eyes as she waited for her interpreter to take one of her pills; a few more moments elapsed before Wei Chi regained her strength to speak. Finally, she came out with it, in no more than a hoarse whisper.

'In this hexagram the lower half changes from the Earth... to the Mountain.'

It was the word Frances didn't want to hear. It took her back to the menacing vision. She sobbed. Wei Chi just managed a few more words.

'Yes, *Ch'ien* is the hexagram in which the Earth is above the Mountain.'

Wei Chi slipped, exhausted, into a breathy sleep. Frances, her eyes and cheeks wet, just stared into space and kept glugging the vodka.

# 32

# Scary Mary

*Friday, June 20<sup>th</sup> – it's not been a good day. Woke up, felt terrible, sick in pit o' my stomach, limbs dead, almost like being paralysed. Wei Chi looked bad too, she couldn't get up.*

*Made a decision after the others finished breakfast (couldn't eat any myself). Got them together in foyer. They were worried, what wi' Wei Chi and me both being so ill.*

*I say, 'I'm sorry to have to tell you all, but I have to go home today. There's a station in Massiac; I don't care how much it costs, I'll find my way back across France to the tunnel and home.' 'That's crazy,' says Jose. 'You have to see it out. It's the solstice tonight, just after midnight. Wei Chi thinks it might be the turning point for you.' 'No,' I say, 'My mind's made up. I can't take any more, I really can't face it.' 'OK,' Nathan says. 'It's your decision. Just go and see Wei Chi before you leave.'*

*Crafty! He knew she wouldn't agree wi' me going off. She were still lying in bed under a thin sheet, sweat trickling down her face. She could hardly speak. She says, 'Don't go, Frances.*

*Please stay with me until I go. It won't be very long now.' 'How can I?' I answer. 'I can't stand another day and you might be here for weeks yet.' 'No.' She's insistent. 'I really only have hours to live.' 'One more day, then.' I agreed to stay one more day only, absolutely no longer. 'I'd love to stay with you, Wei Chi, but I'm dying too.' 'OK,' she says. 'One more day.' That's it, she couldn't speak any more and she closed her eyes. The others were pleased I weren't going straight off, but they were still really worried.*

*We left her asleep and went to Molompize. It were still raining, every day rain, might as well be in Leeds. Molompize is a small town just five kilometres from Massiac. There's a Virgin in Majesty there. Oh no, I thought, not another vision. When blue light emerges from behind mountain, I'm finished, I know I am. I just know.*

*We went into church; a parishioner were just tidying up inside and kept door open for us. Madonna in a glass box behind altar were quite unusual, hard-looking. Colours very faded. Really like a witch this time. 'Scary Mary,' Debs calls her. I couldn't manage a joke, what wi' waiting for last breath to arrive each minute. Debs saw how unhappy I were and gave me a hug, but that made me feel worse, as there's something wrong wi' my stomach and she caused me to squeeze it.*

*I can feel everything I touch for several minutes. A door handle, it feels like I'm still holding it a while later. I can feel cold o' different objects I touch and sensation stays with me. My muscles ache; pains come and go. A really bad one in right side o' my head and then it's in my neck; I'm sure there's a blood clot, as it goes hot, then cold. I wait, because I'm sure I'm about to collapse, then it passes into my mouth and my teeth ache. Where did I read that heart pain can be transferred into your teeth? Now and then my throat is constricted; I can hardly breathe.*

'We can do a ritual by the chapel at Vauclair,' says Jose. 'That's where this Virgin comes from, she's Notre Dame de Vauclair. It's only a couple of kilometres further down the main road.' Off we went. Chapel has recently been restored; it's on the site of what were once an abbey. They've got a replica of Scary Mary in there. It's by side o' Alagnon river, same one as at back of our hotel. Pretty place low down in high wooded valley, but I were too desperate to care about view. All I noticed were railway running alongside through valley; why didn't I go home while I had the chance?

We found a space. It were quiet. I were really breathless, although we'd only walked fifty yards. It were quite warm, yet I were trembling wi' freezing cold. How can that be? I remember my grandma feeling cold in boiling hot summer, just before she died. Must be summat to do wi' blood.

Rituals. They're killing me, why am I joining in? I let the others do it; I just sat on a pile o' rocks and watched. They used some stones to build altars. Spirits of the east (save me). Spirits of the south (save me). Spirits of the west...

I went into trance as usual. No stopping it. Moonscape again. Same oppressive atmosphere. Same mountain. Same blue light, except brighter. Whatever is coming over mountain top is about to appear. I'm sure the beast is behind me, I feel a prickling sensation up my back. That's it, nowt more to it. First time a vision has repeated itself. It's like my imagination is dying along wi' rest o' me. No goddesses, not even any movement. Nowt comforting. I just know that blue light contains summat terrible. Why did I come to this place?

The others were keen to hear about my vision in case it contained some hopeful message. No. Nowt. Just same as yesterday. I think that Jose must be irritated. I'm spoiling holiday, I'm sure he thinks that. Debs is really caring today. She *thinks it's a depression like she has, but I think I'm physically ill. Nathan – can never tell what he's thinking. He's kind, though sometimes I wonder if it's all a front.*

*I keep feeling that a hair or some insect has touched my arm, but there's absolutely nowt there. My nerves are all over place. Then I feel wet, but I'm bone dry. Maybe it's a kind o' Parkinson's disease.*

*Back to Massiac. How could I eat lunch when I couldn't swallow and hardly breathe? Sometimes they make me angry, these friends o' mine. They don't seem to get it. I'm really ill. I can't be 'cheered up' by a piece o' French bread and some Auvergne cheese.*

*Wei Chi were awake and strong enough to talk for a few minutes. Silly conversation. They were trying to decide on the most basic human experience. Wei Chi starts to lecture as far as her strength will allow. 'Human living is ultimately characterised by the dilemma. In everything we do, we experience the dilemma. Nothing's ever straightforward. We can't escape facing dilemmas, although we want to live without them – if we try, we become self-deluded, or ignorant, or cruel. Dilemmas are the stuff of our lives; how we respond is the crucial thing.' She's right. I wanted to come here, I followed guidance o' Goddess, now I want to go home but I can't because I don't want to leave Wei Chi. Another dilemma. I don't know what I'm doing any more. I haven't got strength to make a choice.*

*Then the conversation tired her out. She's really weak. I want to lie down too. I'm feeling her illness in me. I can't believe it. We've only been in France a week and known her five days. It feels like an eternity. She's like a grandmother who I've always known. It's weird, really weird.*

*We watched her for an hour or so; the others were still talking about dilemmas. Then she opened her eyes. She says, 'Where will you celebrate the solstice tonight?' Nathan says, 'I'm not sure. Any ideas?' Wei Chi whispers, 'Why not go up to the top? Up there on the gorge.' She's looking through window to top o' high cliff. 'The chapel of the Magdalene.' 'Yes,' says Debs. 'It must be a great view from up there, even at night.'*

*Jose had been gathering information again. 'The chapel of the Magdalene – in French, Madeleine – on the top of the gorge at Chalet, has a wonderful legend. It was where a St Madeleine stayed as a hermit. This was Mary Magdalene herself, or maybe someone named after her, I'm not totally sure. On the opposite side of the gorge, there was a hermit called Victor and so over there is St Victor's chapel. Victor and Magdalene together guard the Alagnon valley, keeping a spiritual watch high up on either side of it.' I like that idea. I feel so vulnerable, that idea o' someone strong guarding valley appeals to me. Maybe they'll keep guard over me.*

*'Carry me up with you,' says Wei Chi. 'What?' replies Nathan. 'Are you well enough to go up to the top of the gorge at midnight?' 'There's a road almost to the top,' Wei Chi says, 'I asked the proprietor about it'. 'Even so,' says Nathan, a bit rattled. 'You're really ill, it wouldn't be right.' Wei Chi were really weak but determined. 'Carry me up. I came with you to take part in your rituals, didn't I? You knew I would get worse.' 'OK, let's do it,' says Debs. She didn't want Wei Chi to get upset in that state.*

*So we had dinner in town in fancy hotel, although it weren't that expensive. Wei Chi stayed behind in our hotel. I didn't eat much again, but I felt a little better wi' some wine. 'Don't drink too much,' says Jose. 'You need to have your wits about you; this is the big one.' 'I'd rather be pissed,' I say back to him. We didn't want to stay out too long, wi' Wei Chi being so ill, so we went back to hotel as it were getting towards time to go up to chapel o' Mary Magdalene. She lived there, that's what legend said. Victor on other side o' valley. That gives me hope. They might look after me. Nathan had to carry Wei Chi into the car. She looked really bad. The hotel manager were really worried as she watched us go out.*

*I thought Wei Chi were asleep in the car, so I says, 'She probably wants to come with us because she's frightened of dying alone.' Oh God, she heard me! I felt even more terrible. Her eyes opened immediately. 'No,' she murmurs, 'It's not that. People say that dying is the loneliest thing you experience. But they're wrong. We all die together. Each and every one of us will go through it. When we're dying, we're finally one with the whole human race.' You can't keep her down. Until the very last, she wants to impart her wisdom of eighty odd years.*

*Now we're up here. We had to walk last hundred yards or so, too rough for car. Not raining any more, quite clear with only a few clouds. It's still light round about ten o' clock. I feel terrible but it's not tiredness, so staying up won't make any difference. Chapel's right on end o' cliff next to huge drop over gorge, so we'd better be careful. Jose says let's do ritual at midnight, then stay up here while solstice at two o'clock. Nathan's carried Wei Chi here and now she's sitting on a wooden seat so she can see view o' valley. Lights o' Massiac, and our hotel's in view. It's fantastic but I'm really scared, because being up here reminds me o' moonscape in my visions; there's hills all around.*

*OK, midnight, so we're going to start ritual. I'll try and take part this time. I've got to make an effort. I've had this feeling for several days and nowt's happened to me. Maybe it's not going to. We've got candles and a drum. There's no one about, thank God – they'd think we were mad. Do they do the solstice round here? We've started. I'm going to concentrate on Mary Magdalene protecting me. She's a kind o' Goddess, in't she? She'll protect me from blue light. Oh God, I feel really scared now! Why do I have to keep thinking o' that blue light? Mary Magdalene... Mary Magdalene... Mary Magdalene...*

# 33

# Falling

Moonscape again. Rocky terrain. Jet black sky overhead punctuated by stars. On the left, the great dark mountain. *I'm trembling* A wind circulating. *I'm really afraid. I can't bear to look at the mountain but I must. Please, no.* The blue light beginning to move. *It is, there's no doubt about it.* The terrible being casting that light now stirring from sleep. *It's beginning to climb over the mountain peak.* Real fear. *I want to scream but I can't.* A gigantic blue sphere edging out, starting to rise into the sky. *So full of light and energy, an encounter with such a thing is too great for a mere individual to stand. I have to cower before it. What is it? Why a moonscape? Now it's clear. What would be in the sky if you were on the moon? What great blue sphere would dominate the sky? It's the Earth! But it's filling the sky so much more than I've seen in photos from the moon.* Only a portion risen above the mountain, but even that completely fills the left horizon. *Of course, the Earth. The Earth above the Mountain.* Already the power and presence of it unbearable. Not the romantic, homely globe of space pictures but a truly monstrous being. It's still climbing and climbing, slowly but unstoppably. *The sheer bulk of it. Unbearable.* Not just a large bundle of minerals and liquids but a living entity. Not the Earth of a single snapshot in time but the Earth through aeons, the whole Earth. Centuries and centuries. This whole great Earth is pouring forth its history all at once. History darting out from the blue and falling onto the moonscape, tableaux of humans and animals struggling for life, conflicts, battles, suffering. Ancient spearmen; medieval knights; modern green bereted soldiers; cavalry; cannons; nuclear bombs. Humanity as if it were one complete and wounded creature, its individuals joined together through time, all part of the terrifying, intelligent animal that crawls upon the Earth in its fragmented agony. One being, yet fatally divided in itself. *I can't stand it anymore. No more. Unbearable.* Huge blue Earth still climbing into the sky. Higher and higher. More energy streaming out onto the lunar surface, the light fiercer and fiercer. Visions ever more frenzied: buildings, cities, civilisations rising and falling. Rituals; coronations; funerary processions of the great and revered; hopeful new initiatives, doomed soon to fail; discovery provoking unexpected disasters; invention of devices that brought wretched misery with them: weapons, instruments of torture, machines that spit pollution into the air. Animals and humans beaten, confined in tiny spaces, abused, destroyed. Invasion; conquest; subjugation; rape; domination. Violence upon violence. Zeppelins and trenches; mass bombings and concentration camps; small countries used as pawns in a great war and burnt up. Hitler, Stalin, the great, the powerful, the terrible. All the while the beast that is humanity rolls its body back and forth with all the inner conflicts of its being, causing smaller and less powerful species to scuttle off into the undergrowth. A dreadful, screaming creature spinning a vast web of rubbish, waste, pollution. Life struggling to breathe, caught in the sticky tendrils. *I'm going to have a breakdown, it's too much for one person to take in.* 'But it's already part of you' – a voice from nowhere, from the ether. Another voice: 'You're made of this stuff, it's the very fibre of your existence.' *No, my life's not just about battles and tragedies. There's love and gentleness and happiness there too!* A third voice: 'At whose expense? At whose expense?' Then sweat shops; smoky factories; plantations with near starvation wages; women labouring all hours at home while trying to keep and feed a family; unjust trading deals; supermarket shelves bulging with ill-gotten produce. The great Earth rising in its totality above the Mountain and releasing the agony of human existence. Questions – of history, of pre-history, of civilisation, of society. *Why ask me? I'm barely able to look at it.* The magnificence of the heavenly orb now filling the sky. *I'm just one person. Why ask me and why now?* A voice: 'You get asked every day. Didn't you know?' *The questions are too overwhelming, I can't answer them. I don't know what to do, what to say, how to make sense of things. The world is too complex.* Another spirit: 'You cannot escape, you must face it.' Each statement and question coming from a new voice, there's no fixity or stability to these spirits. *They speak from here, from there, tearing me apart.* The Earth has released demons into the cosmos. Breakdown. Something's going to give. A terrible noise emanating from the giant blue globe above, an agonisingly loud cracking sound as if it were a gargantuan thunderbolt. *Look up. No, it's impossible.* At the centre of the Earth, a great gaping wound that seeps red blood across the blue and white of the sphere. *I'm sobbing.* The awfulness of the vision. A great purgation: flood upon flood, wave upon wave. Washing the world in great libations. Getting rid of the pests and parasites that prey upon the surface. Cleansing itself of humanity, the greatest cancer of all. Flooding. No ark, just floods, floods of blood. The end of everything. Ripped apart. *Look down, it's too awful...*

...Another voice, softer this time: 'The labour is over.' A horn sounding the reveille. *Look up.* The massive wound healing, the blood disappearing, demons vanishing. New visions, heart-gladdening comforts: favourite friends; good moments with the family; beautiful views; unexpected gifts; the ecstasy of a dance; the intimate sharing in a love affair not yet gone bad. The great blue Earth pouring out tenderness – yet, just as the conflict had been, the tenderness is almost too awesome to take. Shattering love. Love that goes to the heart of your being, judges you.

*Unbearable.* Encountering the Goddess again, but she is so many times more powerful and vibrant than before. *What can you do? Try to send love back. I'll try. My efforts are paltry.* Now a new, strange, unsettling feeling. *Until now I've been secure in my position. But the Earth's gravity's so strong. Feeling myself lifted upwards.* The Earth had been up, but it was turning into down. Vertigo at the thought. The pull of the Earth is too great to resist. *I can't fall that far! I'll be killed!* Yet another spirit voice: 'Why can you never trust?' *Stretch out my arms like a diver. Throw myself into the air as if freefalling from a plane. Now I'm plunging towards the massive blue expanse, the moonscape and mountain becoming smaller – I'm leaving them behind. Plummeting up. Free. Into the Earth I fall. Everything is blue.* Suddenly a most wonderful peace inside. The peace after childbirth; the stillness of the armistice morning; birdsong after the storm. *I'm falling home, home is embracing me with her big blue and white arms, drawing me ever inside herself.* Back into the womb. Into the placenta, to re-experience the time before the Earth went bad. When Mother Wisdom ruled. *It's a feeling I never, ever want to end. Never, ever...*

But it did end, at the entrance of the stony chapel on the top of the gorge above Massiac. Frances was kneeling on the ground, the three adventurers looking down at her, mesmerised.

'That was the most intense trance yet!' stammered Nathan, excitedly. 'You were calling out, then murmuring, then groaning as if you were in ecstasy.'

'My God,' breathed Debs. 'You were transformed. I really saw it that time.'

'Yes,' said Jose, awestruck. 'Like a great spirit was coming through you.'

She looked up at them, still at peace in herself; it was like greeting long-lost friends. Since coming to France, she had inexplicably become alienated from them. Without her *joie de vivre*, she had not been able to love them, not even Nathan. She smiled.

'You're better, aren't you?' The question came from Debs, who grinned back with the recognition of one who had woken up from depression herself.

'You won't believe what I've seen,' replied Frances, speaking slowly, still in the languor of the trance-state. 'I can't tell you everything right now, but Wei Chi were right – I were like someone in labour, on verge o' giving birth. But now it's done.'

'Wei Chi!' called Jose. 'You were right. The solstice was the turning point for Frances.'

There was no answer from out of the dark. They looked across the several yards of rocky ground towards the grassy bank against which Wei Chi's seat was placed. The chapel was lit up spectacularly at night, spotlights facing straight at it, which made peering any distance away all the more difficult.

'She's too weak to answer,' said Nathan.

He moved away from the group towards her.

'Are you OK, Wei Chi? Wei Chi…?'

Nathan disappeared into the dark and then re-emerged, looking stern.

'She's not where we left her.'

'She has to be,' said Jose, looking baffled. 'She was too weak to have gone far.'

Jose and Debs joined Nathan in scouring the top of the cliff. Frances pulled herself up to a standing position. She felt exhausted. The peaceful feeling at the end of the vision had soon been clouded by the unease of this new mystery. She tried to fathom it. A light wind stirred across the crag top and disturbed the still warmth of the night. The moon, a couple of days past full, was now rising above hills to the east. And then, with her friends searching further out from the chapel and calling into the darkness, it became a mystery no longer. Frances knew and her heart leaped. She stood up, walked uncertainly to the edge of the sheer drop from the gorge top and tried to peer over. It was an impossible task to see down properly. She looked across at the chapel of St Victor, lit up on the other side of the valley. The awareness of the great drop in the open space between the chapels made her shudder.

'Oh, my God,' she murmured to herself, slowly. 'The great fall into the Earth in my vision weren't mine after all but Wei Chi's. She's thrown herself over the edge.'

It was hard convincing the others.

'No, I can't believe it,' cried Debs.

'It's only a few yards,' replied Frances, with a resigned look on her face. 'While we were doing ritual and I were in my vision, she could've dragged herself there to end her suffering once and for all.'

'Oh, God,' gasped Debs. 'I think you're right.'

Frances could not bring herself to feel anguish over the probability that Wei Chi had either slipped over the edge or thrown herself to her death; the fact that the fall in the vision had been so peaceful and wonderful made her believe that it had been the right thing to happen. It was a release; probably she had only a few more hours of agony to endure. Perhaps she had chosen this moment, high over the valley by the beautiful chapel at the time of the summer solstice, the time associated with light, merriment and celebration. Why not? Didn't a person have the right to choose the time to die? Frances was free of neurotic symptoms for the first time in several days; if this coincided with Wei Chi's death, then it all made sense – she had been suffering empathetically and Wei Chi wanted to release her. She realised that she hoped it was true, despite the desperate looks on the faces of the other three. Nathan decided to call the police on his mobile. Debs took the phone to speak French to the gendarme at the other end. The only words that Frances understood were 'Massiac... la chapelle Madeleine à Chalet... en haut... nous croyons... elle a tombé.'

'The police will come up as soon as they can,' said Debs, after completing the call. 'They'll also send someone down to the bottom to see if they can find her.'

And so the night went on... the police arriving... the discovery of the body at the foot of the gorge... the waking of the hotel managers... the questions... the need for coffee... the stupefaction of tiredness, shock, the seriousness of the situation, having to speak to strangers in the early hours of the morning. No one would ever know for sure how it happened. When sleep came, it was sudden, deep and dreamless. The last thing Frances remembered was contemplating the empty bed in the adjacent room where Wei Chi had spent most of her last hours. *Goodbye, Wei Chi,* she thought. *Just six days, but I don't think I'm going to forget you! So you were right: the Earth above the Mountain. You were right about everything...*

## 34

## Ace of Cups

Saturday breakfast didn't happen until the early afternoon. The hotel manager on duty had kept some back for them: the usual welcome selection of cereals, yoghurts and croissants with the option of ham and cheese. They were all hungry; the shock hadn't curbed their appetite but it did kill the conversation for some time. Finally, Nathan asked Frances about the vision.

'So what is the Goddess of the Age of Capricorn like?'

'It were just amazing,' she replied. 'She's the Earth itself, a living Earth full of energy, conflict and love. It were terrible and wonderful at same time.'

'Interesting that Capricorn is an Earth sign,' commented Jose. 'Perhaps in the future people will once again worship the Earth as they did centuries ago.'

'And the other sign?' asked Nathan. 'There are always two opposite signs, remember.'

'Cancer is the sign of the Mother,' replied Jose. 'Astrologically, Cancer is ruled by the Moon, of course. The Earth and the Moon are one system. Frances saw both in her visions. Together, they're our Mother.'

'Seems logical,' commented Debs. 'The Earth's everything we know and it's what we should be looking after. Watching out for an old man in sky's just a waste o' time. Only by keeping our feet on planet Earth will we sort out the mess we're in.'

'Wasn't Wei Chi an incredibly interesting person?' said Nathan, suddenly, voicing what had been avoided so far at the table. 'I was interested in her name, you know, and I managed to find a book in French on the *I Ching* in a bookshop.' He indicated a page that he had marked. 'Debs, what does it say about Wei Chi, "Before Completion"?'

Debs perused the book, concentrating hard.

'The gist of it is that, leading up to a time of transition, one must prepare very carefully.'

'I suppose Wei Chi had important transitions in her life,' said Jose. 'Travelling to France from Vietnam. Becoming a Catholic. Preparing herself for her death.'

Another quiet period followed.

'Oh, my God,' exclaimed Frances suddenly. 'What about the funeral? Where will it be? Hadn't we better inform Wei Chi's friends and relatives in Paris?'

'The police will have done that,' said Nathan. 'They have her belongings. Perhaps we had better just slip out of the picture quietly.'

'No.' Debs disagreed sharply. 'Let's ask manager. We should see it through, this whole meeting wi' Wei Chi, right through to its end. It's become an important part o' what we're doing here.'

'OK,' conceded Nathan, graciously, with no hint of being put out by the rejection of his suggestion.

The hotel manager was helpful, as if she had been waiting for this question. She said that the police had found a letter in Wei Chi's handbag. In it, Wei Chi had indicated that she was terminally ill and would die in the Auvergne. She had written the telephone number of a contact person in Poissy. The police had undertaken to communicate the news, but the manager hinted via Debs that it might be a good thing to follow this up with a more personal call from friends. The name given was not Chinese but

French: Madame Dominique Bousset. Debs called on the hotel phone. They left her to it for a few minutes.

Frances followed Nathan, who was walking out through the automatic glass doors at the front of the hotel and staring up at the Madeleine chapel. She had some catching up to do with the object of her desire; their relationship was based on repartee and wicked humour. However, it had been left on the back burner for the last few days. Jose joined them; they all stood on the hotel forecourt, staring into the sky with dark glasses on to lessen the brightness of the early afternoon. The day was clear and scorching hot, a contrast to the week that had gone before. It was as if Wei Chi's death had cleared the air of its humidity.

'The sun's really high up in the sky this far south,' said Jose, having not much else to say in that thoughtful moment.

'No, sun's not up, it's down,' replied Frances, absent-mindedly.

'What do you mean by that?' asked Nathan, his gaze staying on the chapel on the cliff top.

'Well, according to direction o' gravity, sun's at the bottom o' things, in't it?' stated Frances, as though it were obvious. 'We're looking down a deep well at it. It's only Earth's speed what's keeping us up here.'

The men looked at each other. This was their territory, quasi-scientific nonsense, not Frances' area at all.

'I'm gob smacked,' said Nathan. 'You're quite right.'

Frances smiled. In her trance state of last night, on the moon, the Earth was up, but really it was down because of its greater gravity. On the Earth, however, she now realised, the sun was down. So there were revelations in her visions, after all. It wasn't all rehashed conversations.

'What's more, it's made me feel quite strange,' said Jose. 'I never thought I'd get vertigo thinking about the sun.'

Debs came out.

'Yeah, police have already phoned her,' she said, putting her sunglasses on. 'She were expecting it. Wei Chi told her what she were doing. They said goodbye in Poissy a week and a half ago.

Guess what? Our Wei Chi's a celebrity among some people in Paris. Gave talks on philosophy o' the *I Ching* and other spiritual topics. Right up to a few month ago. Then she were diagnosed terminal and she stopped doing it.'

'It doesn't surprise me that she's well-known,' reflected Jose.

Debs continued.

'Yeah, well, Madame Bousset wants us to go to funeral in Poissy. It'll probably be in a few days time. It'll be a requiem Mass.'

'Let's do it,' said Nathan. 'Paris it is. We'll ask the hotel manager if we can stay here until the day before.'

Frances had decided to take a few days off visionary experiences. The night before had left her with a huge sense of relief that the threat had turned out to be only the apprehension of a wholly new and powerful experience. However, she felt drained. The others agreed to leave the rituals for a while. She went for a walk alone, down to the river. She hadn't told them that she was still suffering the strange symptoms, because it was different now. They didn't scare her anymore. The events of the solstice night had finally made her believe that they were all in the mind. They were pangs announcing the vision of the great Earth and physical expressions of empathy with Wei Chi's death. Probably they would go on for a little longer while her body adjusted. Anyway, the feeling of paralysis wasn't really that; it was a kind of light-headedness, probably caused by muscle tension. The pains in the throat and left arm were not actually that intense when she thought about it. What about that bad neck she had suffered a few years ago after walking out by the sea in December? What about the broken wrist of her schooldays? Those were occasions of real pain, on reflection much worse than this. It was just the equivalent of seeing through a hangover, or the end of a cold. There were odd moments when she almost lapsed back into panic, but she stopped herself. How could the Goddess who had given her such a powerful vision allow her to die here, at the age of twenty-nine? No, it wasn't going to happen; it was time to pull herself out of negative thinking.

Frances' self-absorbed reverie by the river Alagnon was interrupted by the sight of a familiar figure walking towards her, with tousled hair and ill-fitting clothes. It was Debs, attentive as usual to the possibility that a woman needed support. Frances looked up and smiled so as to invite Debs into her private space. They gave each other a warm and welcome hug, something that had so far been missing but was needed after the trauma of the previous night.

'We women need some time together,' said Debs, tentatively, as if she weren't sure of the right words. 'Time together to do some grieving. We only knew Wei Chi for six days but she'd become one of us. Women should gather to mourn when a woman passes.'

'I know what you mean,' replied Frances. 'Gather like we did in our little circle at Avebury. We need to do a little witchcraft right now. But what shall we do?'

'How about this?' suggested Debs, as she began to pick out small twigs from among the trees by the river: alder, maple and rowan. With some long grass to tie them together, she started to make a small figurine. Frances looked on attentively, occasionally putting her hands forward into the air as if to try and help, but Debs was adept at the spontaneous craft work and there was no need. When the twig figure had been made, Debs held it up.

'This is our friend, Wei Chi,' she announced. 'She had a long hard life, but she learnt a lot from it. She were courageous; she faced death without flinching. We want to help her cross over.'

She looked at Frances. Clearly, she wanted her to say something.

'Goodbye, Wei Chi,' Frances called into the air. 'You drew me into dying with you and taught me to face life without fear. We both fell into the great blue Earth and it took us into its heart, where there is peace. Thanks for letting me share it.'

After a short silence, Debs tossed the figurine into the middle of the Alagnon. It floated out of sight on the rippling stream.

'Goodbye, sister,' said Debs, softly. 'May Goddess go with you.'

They sat together watching the river. Apart from the occasional passing car on the road fifty yards or so away, the only sounds were made by the trickling of the water. It was a sacred moment. Then Debs spoke.

'I really feel I know you now,' she said, turning her intense stare towards Frances. 'I know you wouldn't have wished it on yourself, but that anxious depression o' yours were final step in our bonding together. Only you and I know what it feels like when everyone tells you to pull yourself together. It's not possible. It has to pass of its own accord.'

'Yes, I've been though the initiation now,' agreed Frances. 'It's not pleasant, although I don't feel I suffered as much as you do. Only five days. I guess it might come back one day, but I hope I'll be ready for it.'

She then remembered that she had put the Goddess Tarot cards in her bag.

'I brought these out here so I could do a reading. Let's do one together, Debs.'

'OK,' agreed Debs, her solemn expression giving way to a more relaxed look of genuine interest. 'What question shall we ask?'

'You, me and Wei Chi,' replied Frances. 'That's what we'll ask about.'

*Shuffle three times, cut three times. Ask Debs to do same. Then draw top card and lay it out on the dry ground, where it's flat. Open little book o' meanings.* The past: Juno. Tradition. 'Juno was honoured as the patroness of marriage and other traditional rites of passage in women's lives. This Roman goddess was believed to watch and protect all women – from their first breath to their last.'

'That's clear enough,' said Debs. 'Our reading's working out. The death of Wei Chi is now in the past. The rites o' passage for Wei Chi's last breath – that's what we're here for.'

*OK, no need to draw extra cards of explanation.* The present situation: Lakshmi. Fortune. 'The Hindu Goddess of fortune and prosperity...The ability to be open to abundance. Positive expectations.'

'Well, I suppose we *should* be positive,' mused Frances. 'But about what?'

Card for illumination: Two of Staves. 'Beginnings of a business venture. Possible partnership. New ideas that transform lives, bring inspiration and energize people.'

'Very exciting,' said Frances 'But what new ideas?'

Debs didn't seem to know either, so – another card. Ace of Staves. 'Beginnings of a focused, creative period, inspiration that inspires action.'

'That's a powerful and positive card,' declared Debs. 'It's all on same theme: we're at a point of opportunity. Maybe it means some kind o' creative business partnership between us. Two staves. Two of us.'

'I'd love that,' said Frances. 'It'd be great to get away from office and do something creative.'

'Reading Tarot cards?' suggested Debs. 'You'd be good at it. Visionary who helps people by reading cards for 'em.'

'Clairvoyant?' replied Frances. 'Not sure. But what about you; isn't this supposed to be about a *partnership*?'

'Well, I'm not so keen as you to give up my job but part-time – yes, why not? You could be full-time partner. A little consultancy, using divination and good wise advice to women.'

'Maybe men as well.'

Frances wasn't into the women-only stuff as much as Debs.

'OK,' laughed Debs. 'But only nice blokes.'

They shook hands, then hugged again. *It's serious, this! The Tarot cards have inspired it. When we get back to Leeds, a little business venture. Witches Inc. Divinations R' Us.*

'We're forgetting summat. The future,' said Frances, suddenly. She drew another card. *Wow! Another Ace.* Ace of Cups. 'Great emotional satisfaction. Beginning of a new important relationship.'

'Is that our plans for partnership again?' asked Frances.

'No,' replied Debs. 'It's the future. We've already established our relationship in the present. Cups are to do wi' romantic relationships, not business partnerships. One or both of us is going to get into summat interesting, no doubt about it!'

She laughed again. Frances was about to draw a card for explanation, but Debs stopped her.

'No, leave it there. Let's just see what future brings. Lovely card, the Ace o' Cups. Lots of happiness. A good card to finish reading. Just leave it at that.'

'OK,' agreed Frances.

They went back to their silent thoughts, listening to the lapping of the river against its bank. The cards remained laid out on the ground, a T-shape with three cards in a row and two below the middle one. *A new romantic relationship. Maybe wi' someone I already know. It's not necessarily a stranger, is it? Well, it's not likely to be Debs who gets into one, is it? She's not into that kind o' thing, she don't like men and don't seem to be into women either, not in that kind o' way. No, it's got to be me, they're my cards. Of course, I needed to go through all the Wei Chi and death stuff before I got my reward. It's just a question o' time. Nathan's mine; he can't hold out any longer!*

'Come on,' said Debs. 'Let's go back and join others. Time for some dinner.'

Frances gathered up the cards. She felt slightly guilty that, after all the excitement about a new business partnership, the drawing of the Ace of Cups had made her forget it quickly in favour of dreaming about a blossoming love. *Oh well, you can do both, can't you? One helps the other: romantic and business relationships all at same time. Cups and staves. Sounds like a good combination to me.* She looked up at the crags. The Mary Magdalene and St Victor chapels stood in their sentinel positions overlooking the valley as the summer evening wore on. *Mary Magdalene, cups; St Victor, staves. New love and a new career. Yes, I like that idea very much.*

# 35

# Sun-Drenched Hills

'No, Wei Chi's her *name*.'
It was very difficult explaining an edited version of the tumultuous events of the last ten days to Mum and Dad in Leeds over a crackly mobile. With a sigh of relief now that was over, she then tried Irene. Surely she of all people would understand? However, Irene was keen to share her own story about a drugs raid on the main Leeds refuge by women police officers and the arrest of several people. It was all very tricky. There were three options. Imprisonment of mother – children into care. More disruption when she comes out in a few months. Anyway, the prisons are full. Rehab for mother – it's already been tried, so why repeat the cycle when the addict isn't really interested? No action against mother – condoning the habit with the likelihood that it would be passed on to children. And so on. *The dilemma*, thought Frances, without voicing the word. A long conversation before she was able to talk about her own experiences. So, she just left it at:

'There were this really wonderful old Chinese lady that we met, but she died. So we're going to funeral in Paris on Friday. I'll tell you all about it when I get home.'

The date had been confirmed: it was to be Friday the 27$^{th}$. Madame Bousset had offered them accommodation in Poissy for two nights and so they would travel up on Thursday, returning to a new place to stay on the Saturday.

The events of the solstice had opened Frances up and left her wanting to reach out. She began to appreciate things around her again: the roses in full scarlet bloom at the front of the hotel, the red poppies punctuating the yellows, greens and browns in the fields and on the riverbank. Great philosophical thoughts about the Earth came intermittently but didn't last long; a relationship was uppermost in her mind. She was in the mood for a confession and grabbed Nathan for a walk to an old chapel as Debs and Jose sat enjoying the late afternoon sunshine in the pretty village of Blesle, with its old buildings, abbey church and gurgling stream a few kilometres from Massiac.

'I were going to say sorry to you, I weren't myself last week. I expect you noticed.'

'Well, yes, a bit, but it wasn't really a problem,' said Nathan, insensitively.

*Not for you, maybe, but no… hang on, Ace o' Cups and all, this guy's going to be my partner, let's be patient.*

'Well, I suppose I kept it hid. Fact is, at times I were harbouring irritations and bad feelings towards you and the others too. But it were just depression, it made me hyper-anxious and my tolerance levels were low.' *OK, now your man o' the future thinks you're a hysterical manic depressive.* Change tack. 'Of course, it were just the Wei Chi thing, I think I were kind o' going through death with her. I don't normally have acute anxiety; I'll probably never have it again. I don't like to have bad feelings inside against people I love.'

'It doesn't really matter, does it?' commented Nathan. 'What you feel inside, I mean. It's what comes out that counts. In your case, no malice came out, so there's no harm done. Sometimes people say to me, "Express your feelings". And I agree with them only if my feelings have been thought through and stay in proportion to the situation.'

Frances looked puzzled. *Will we really be sitting by fireside as old people, talking like this?*

'I don't get you.'

'In other words,' Nathan continued, trying to explain. 'If I'm in a mood, there's no point expressing it, because I've probably got it out of proportion. I might feel differently tomorrow. Only if I feel something for several weeks, because it's really an issue, and I think it through – only then is it worth saying something that might hurt someone else.'

'OK, that's noble but it sounds very repressed,' said Frances, attempting to be honest without coming across as argumentative. 'Part o' friendship is talking about your feelings and they won't always be positive. So friendship has ups and downs, that's what makes it. And when you get it wrong like I did sometimes last week, you need to say sorry like I'm doing now.'

Nathan opened the chapel door with a squeak. It was small and bare inside, except for the mandatory statue of the Madonna and Child above the altar.

'I see what you mean,' he said, looking round, 'But in actual fact you didn't say anything terrible last week. You just looked a bit quiet, that's all. The main thing was that you were still having these fantastically interesting visions. That's what this is all about, isn't it?'

Frances left it there. This was a sensitive time. *No point in blowing it all by saying: no, surely that isn't all that I mean to you, I'm not just a spiritual freak show. If you'd have behaved like me, I would've been upset and worried. But that's just you, in't it, Nathan? I have to accept you as you are if it's going to work out between us. Stay patient.* She thought back to that evening in the flat and Nathan's offer to sleep with her. There didn't seem to be much hope after that conversation, so why was she resurrecting it now? Ah, the Ace o' Cups. One Tarot card in the right place, now it all changes. Was she fooling herself? *No, don't give up on it, hold on to it,* she decided. *There'll be other chances to make connections.* Another aspect of the conversation left her wondering. Did it matter what you thought inside about people and situations? Did negative thoughts somehow harm people you loved, or were they meaningless if they never got expressed, just an inner battle that you had to go through? The main thing was how you acted. Frances couldn't help disliking the theory: it sounded rather male and stoical. Maybe all that repression could make you ill. *On other hand, people who always say exactly what they think and when they think it face a life of argument and conflict. Unless, maybe, they're expressing love. But that can lead to misunderstandings too.*

Three days after the solstice, Frances felt a renewal of old energies at last.

'What about going to Laurie today?'

'Not a bad idea, 24$^{th}$ June's the traditional midsummer's day,' Jose agreed.

'OK, prima donna visionary's ready,' replied Frances; a little comic self-deprecation seemed a good idea right now.

With Nathan at the wheel, they drove out of Massiac into the sun-drenched hills to the west of the Alagnon. No more worries about mountains, which had returned to their former benign splendour, the flowing bosoms of Mother Earth. Frances began to realise that the solstice vision had changed her perspective on natural beauty. She remembered the great blue sphere, how it presented itself as an integrated being with whom one could communicate, to whom one could relate, on whom one could rely. Living on it day by day was mundane – literally, that was what the word meant – but seeing it from outside, like the astronauts had, transformed one's viewpoint forever. Returning, one's eyes were opened to its wonder. Folds upon folds. Greens and browns of every possible shade, punctuated by a striking red or yellow here and there where nature had painted it. Every possible hiding place for people; animals; organisms; plants. Life burst out from the picturesque landscape that greeted them as the car wound up the gorge on the St Victor side and then cruised over and away into the Cézallier. For the first time in over a week, Frances began to look forward to the possibility of new revelations. The Beauty had reasserted her command of the Beast; the Goddess had tamed the lion; the shadow had melted away. Pretty, sleepy villages were passed, with little bridges over brooks, church towers protecting a higgledy-piggledy collection of old houses, only the odd car giving any clue as to the century in which one was viewing them. Each settlement had seen so many decades of evolution and slow growth that they seemed to fit exactly in their environment, crafted that way as if some divine hand, rather than the serendipity of human movement, had designed them to be there.

Laurie was one such, a compact village high up on the mountainside with a sweeping vista over the plunging valleys below. To Frances, it was a delightful place; it made her heart leap with gladness. A herd of cows caused a welcome delay as they drove in, giving more time to enjoy the view. The brown and white stone-bricked church, with its grey tower, was high up in the village next to the small *mairie*. It was open and inside was Notre Dame de Laurie, in a glass case with a tall conical gilded top. The interior was dark but a switch yielded a swathe of light on the altar. The statue was in better condition than the copy in Brioude, mirroring the improvement in Frances' inner disposition since she had seen it there. Notre Dame was seated on her throne, a small but matronly crowned figure dressed in red, the Child in blue and green on her left knee. Laurie was a well known local pilgrimage centre, explained Debs, having read an informative plaque. People had travelled into the mountains since the eleventh century to pray there. All four of them sat down on pews and spent several minutes without speaking as if in respect to all those previous visitors. Each was sure that the others were remembering Wei Chi. There was a strange quality to her memory, Jose had said the day before, which made you feel you were in touch with several cultures, several philosophies, several religions, several decades and several powerful experiences all at once. She was a woman who had reached out, beyond the confines of her own rural background in a troubled country, to embrace the global village in all its variety and turmoil.

At the shady tree-lined edge of a cornfield dotted with purple cornflowers and red poppies a few hundred metres above Laurie, with a spectacular view over the mountains, they held their eighth ritual of the holiday. It was slightly sombre, the first since the solstice. Knowing nothing of the little figurine on its way down the Alagnon, until this point the men had not seen the need to create a rite of passage for the passing of Wei Chi, but now they entered into it with intensity, calling upon her spirit in the mountain breeze.

'I think she's gone back to her first love: the mountains of Tay Bac,' declared Jose, with some emotion in his voice.

'Well, high up here is probably the best place to remember her,' added Nathan, holding his hands up into the air like a charismatic at an evangelical rally.

Frances was intrigued to know what kind of vision could follow the amazing revelation of Saturday morning. In actual fact, the trance was brief and not particularly intense, as if the solstice had drained all the visionary energy out of her...

Again she saw the great blue sphere and the moonscape as if she were in a third place viewing both of them from a distance. This time the Earth, on her right, did not have its crushing presence of Friday midnight. Instead, framed in it sat the dark-haired woman in red that she had seen a few weeks before the holiday; she understood that this was Mary Magdalene, how she did not know. The woman smiled at her and indicated the Moon on the left, on which Frances saw an old bearded hermit in a ragged brown cloak with a staff. It was clear that this was St Victor. The Earth and the Moon were like the twin crags of Massiac; she looked up at them as if she were back at the *Maison des Gorges...*

That was it. No voices or powerful feelings this time.

'Could Mary Magdalene really have lived in Massiac?' she asked Jose, as they drove further on from Laurie through the mountains. The heat of the day was beginning to become oppressive even in the cooler areas high up, and so the air conditioning was full on.

'Probably not,' replied Jose, with a hint of lamentation in his tone that suggested he did not enjoy deconstructing the myth. 'When Christianity spread across Europe and Asia, there was a tendency for people in those countries far from the Holy Land to claim that they had been visited by one of the figures from the Bible. This made the story more real, I suppose. In India, there was the belief that St Thomas had taken the gospel there; in England, Joseph of Arimathea was meant to have visited Glastonbury. Some argued that Christ himself had gone to England, hence William Blake's famous words, "And did those feet in ancient time walk up on England's mountains green?" In France, the legends centred upon Mary Magdalene, Martha, her sister – as it was believed – and their brother Lazarus. Mary was supposed to have preached across parts of the south of France until she retired from public life to live as a repentant hermit at St Baume in Provence. So there are many chapels of the Madeleine in these regions; maybe some of them are claimed to have been founded by the lady herself, including the one at Chalet above Massiac. It's good old-fashioned legend making, very stimulating but historically not very likely.'

'Ah, but we've just been saying that the spirit o' Wei Chi's here in Laurie and also in Tay Bac,' Debs chipped in. 'Could not the spirit o' Mary Magdalene have touched crag above Massiac in a special way?'

'Maybe,' replied Jose, giving a little laugh. 'But is the fact that a powerful landowner demanded that a chapel be built to bolster his public esteem the same thing as the place being visited by the spirit of Mary Magdalene?'

'Yes,' suggested Frances, back to her old passionate talkative self. 'For poor people who prayed there, she came. Her spirit were summoned by landowner, but she didn't respond to it for his sake but for theirs.'

The day was like a holiday should be: chatter; laughter; stopping for soft drinks and refreshing ices in Allanche, a town in the midst of the mountains; touring the high plateaux with lots of peering at road signs and maps, first the Cézallier and then moving across the heart of the volcanic Auvergne into the mountains of the Cantal; the oohs and aahs at the magnificent peaks around the great Puy Mary; a walk up a grassy slope when the afternoon got a little cooler; driving back to Massiac down the upper Alagnon valley; Frances waving at the Madonna standing aloof above Murat, a picturesque town with a café in which four plates of *croque monsieur*, the French cheese on toast, filled a hole; the beautiful villages standing on outcrops of rock; the forested banks of the steep valleys; recognising the chapel of Vauclair as they approached Massiac, with Frances remembering how troubled she had been on their first visit there. *Funny thing, illness. One yearns for it to end but when it does it's gone before you notice it. You hardly realise that you've reached the point that you've been so desperately waiting for.* As if to prove that she was fully recovered, she decided to make some mischief. She was sitting behind Nathan, who was in the front passenger seat. She pulled at the neck of his vest.

'Nathan, you've got a two tone body; there's a line between tan on your neck and fairer skin on your back! Are you sure it's your body? Maybe your head's got stuck on someone else's body! Strange things happen in these hills, you know! Somewhere else, there's a man with a light-skinned head looking down and thinking, where did I get this body from? It's darker than mine and podgier, as if its owner's been out drinking too many pints in Leeds pubs!' She giggled. Nathan grinned sarcastically and raised his eyes; she could see him in the mirror. Unchecked, she went on. 'I think that hotel manager's got the hots for you, Nath! Her husband's jealous. But when she finds out that you've got someone else's body, it might put her off a bit!'

She looked round at Debs to share the joke. But she met only a piercing stare. At the wheel, Jose said nothing and continued to concentrate on the road. *OK! For five days I were out of it and all of you were joking around! Now, I'm full of it and you're all looking depressed! I can't win!* She grimaced.

Perhaps the best way forward was to return to more serious conversation. She thought back again to the vision of Mary Magdalene framed in the Earth.

'About Mary Magdalene again. Do you think that she's a kind o' goddess? If Jesus were God, couldn't Mary Magdalene have been Goddess?'

This stirred Jose out of his silence. Clearly he had already thought about this one. He gave a little sermon, as his hands continually adjusted the position of the wheel.

'People associate God with the things they value most,' he said. 'Jesus was male, a leader. He preached, taught and interpreted the Jewish Law in powerful and radical ways. Christians therefore value those activities. However, the women around Jesus said and did comparatively little, according to the gospels, that is. They stayed in the background and supported Jesus in his ministry. Well, if we were to place a higher value on people in the background, those who help others to make things happen then, following the logic, Mary Magdalene could be regarded as the Goddess.'

There was a pregnant pause as the others tried to take this in. Debs came in first.

'It's people who help out without expecting to be in limelight all time that make the world a better place. Women do that naturally, because they've been told to stay on sidelines. But in my work I see what they do without any recognition.'

'Apart from someone like Princess Di,' interjected Nathan. 'She sought the limelight and got a cult following.'

Frances tried to suppress another giggle. She could still see his neck low down beneath the label on the vest.

'Well, I suppose so,' answered Debs. 'Royalty's the exception, along with Hollywood. But you have to be beautiful to be a prominent woman! Everybody thought Di were great. She breezed into wards and care homes; everybody said how wonderful she were. Easy to pop in! What about the people who care twenty-four hours a day? Nobody worships *them*, do they? That's the problem wi' society, we gather round rich and glamorous and forget real workers.'

Frances saw the vision of Mary Magdalene in the Earth on the next day too, in woods near St Gervazy. This village was north of Massiac, situated in the rolling hills of the Dauphiné further down the valley, near the confluence of the Alagnon with the Allier. They had visited the Madonna and Child in the parish church, large and stern in black wood, the straight lines of her carved cloak making it look as it she were wearing armour, reminding Frances of the Virgin of Iviron. She was placed in a rectangular theft-proof thick glass box on a pillar. The whole edifice looked like something out of the space age, the centre column of the Tardis perhaps, commented Nathan. Jose suggested that it was about to take off or maybe had just landed. He shut up as an elderly lady walked in, smiled broadly at the visitors and proceeded to tell Debs the whole story about the statue, not letting them leave until she had revealed every last detail. It all boiled down to the fact that the medieval statue had been stolen in the 1980s only to turn up in an auction in Madrid and was eventually returned, to the joy of the local people.

The vision was the same one as the day before... Mary Magdalene in her red cloak framed in the Earth, St Victor the hermit on the Moon. It was more vivid, however. This time, between the two spheres, the Alagnon valley stretched away into the distance and, far off, Frances saw an arched and ancient door. The valley led down to the door. Mary Magdalene and St Victor were indicating that she should walk towards it down the riverside in the direction that the figurine of Wei Chi had floated, the way that they had come that day to St Gervazy along the picturesque wooded gorge of the Alagnon with its castles and churches. In the vision, however, the valley had an uncanny, mystical quality... What was behind the door? It was the next stage of the journey. Three visions to go. Frances would soon find out.

## 36

# Romantic Paris

The Église Sainte-Agnès in Poissy, near Paris, was unlike any of the old, architecturally impressive churches and chapels of the Massif Central. It was large and square, spacious but dark because of its high windows, with a wooden ceiling shaped as if to represent the pendulous roof of a large marquee. Built in the mid-twentieth century as a functional place of worship to serve the expanding population of the Paris suburbs, it seemed a strange home for the Chinese lady of the mountains. Although only a few blocks from the river Seine in one direction and the open space of the Forêt de St-Germain in the other, by Auvergne standards it was lost in the concrete jungle of suburbia. Yet Poissy did not suffer the drab uniformity of a British urban scene. Debs and Frances were enthralled by the way that every house, with its own tight and busy garden, bore the stamp of individuality: various shapes, sizes, colours.

'There's summat about the French,' reflected Debs. 'They love to be different from each other, don't they? A nation of people expressing themselves.'

Frances was in a thoughtful mood too.

'I could live here, couldn't you?'

In Poissy town centre stood modern black metallic sculptures: three tall, spindly, stylish angels. Like the great Madonnas overlooking the towns and villages of the Auvergne, the angels suggested to Frances that suburban Poissy was being cared for too. As she wandered round the white block on which they were placed, the sensation of rustling wind came again just when there didn't seem to be any disturbance in the air at that moment. Frances shuddered despite the warmth of the day.

The adventurers all felt a little weary after the long journey of the day before and the crawl through the Paris rush hour to find Poissy. We were foolish timing it to arrive at 6.30, Jose had said, over and over again. After several frustrating circles in heavy traffic, they had finally met the friendly, elderly Dominique Bousset in her strange-looking house: a tall, many-roomed, three-storied, beige brick building joined in a semi-detached arrangement to a shorter, two-storied, grey stucco neighbour. She had made them really welcome with a late meal and generous amounts of red wine topped off with a large port. She spoke English; her reminiscences of Wei Chi kept them going until the early hours. Debs asked her what had happened in Vietnam to cause her to leave. Dominique took a deep breath and exhaled a long sigh before replying.

'In 1967, Wei Chi was a little under forty years old. She had a husband and a family of four children, two girls and two boys, between the ages of ten and seventeen. They ran a small farm in Tay Bac and their produce was important to the war effort, but the farm began to fail, so the government instructed them to move to Hanoi and work in a factory. On the road, the bus they were travelling in got caught in an American air raid and was struck by a bomb. Wei Chi had walked up front to say something to the driver, so she was the only member of the family to survive. When she recovered from her injuries, a few weeks later, she begged the government to allow her to leave Vietnam and stay with relatives in Paris who had left the country a few years before when Vietnam was a French colony. She could not bear to stay, given the circumstances. On compassionate grounds, they allowed it. One of her cousins paid for the journey. Ironically, she arrived in Paris in the middle of student riots. But there was no napalm here and she settled down. She worked for her cousin in his laundry until she retired.'

Many seconds of intense silence followed this revelation. Uncovering Wei Chi's tragic secret was like trespassing on holy ground. Yet Dominique hadn't finished. She spoke more softly now.

'For Wei Chi, the one thing she couldn't accept was the fact that her children would not be around her as she died. That was not how it should be for a mother, she said. She kept repeating that 'the Spirit', as she called it, whispered impossible things to her, telling her that during her final hours her children would be there after all, how she didn't know but it would happen. And she believed it.'

The silence resumed. The near still life scene of silent people seated round an old oak table, the remains of a generous feast scattered upon it, was one which Frances could only glimpse uncertainly through a curtain of tears.

Now, as they all entered the church just before noon the next day, Dominique smiled to make them feel welcome, revealing the missing eye teeth that on first meeting Frances couldn't help identifying as her most prominent characteristic. Otherwise she was a white-haired pensioner of medium height and weight, with fair skin and big owl-eyed glasses. She wore a smart black trouser suit on top of a new white blouse. She indicated a pew one row from the front.

'Maybe further back?' asked Frances. 'So that the family and close friends can sit nearer the altar?'

'You are special guests,' replied Dominique, reassuringly. 'The last to see Wei Chi before she died. She telephoned to tell me about you. In just a few days, you had become important to her.'

Introductions followed: one by one the Chinese contingent, younger cousins first and second times removed, came to meet the 'special guests'. Soon, faces were aching from smiling. None of the relatives was Catholic and so they were new to the church too; however, there were also some Vietnamese in Poissy, one or two who were parishioners. One tall, remarkably slender elderly man called Ho seemed to be in charge of the organisation of the Requiem. This was an unmissable opportunity for Nathan, who tried to inject some humour into the solemnity of the occasion.

'He's so thin, you could get three of him into one Santa Claus,' he whispered. Frances saw it coming. 'Ho Ho Ho.'

She shushed him crossly, desperately trying to suppress the giggles that bubbled up and surprised her, as she had thought that laughter would be off-limits for a day at least.

Only Jose the Catholic would have expected the coffin to be already in the centre of the church where it had lain overnight. This caused a few tears. It was the first time they had been close to Wei Chi since seating her down near the Madeleine chapel overlooking Massiac. The fact that the coffin was closed gave rise to an uncomfortable suspicion in Frances that the fall from the gorge top might have disfigured the body. She kept this to herself; if anyone else thought it, they were not voicing it either. Jose alone understood the sequence of the Mass in French and what was happening in it; Debs alone understood anything of the long eulogy delivered by the priest. Nathan and Frances were left with their thoughts. Frances looked round. The church was absolutely packed; people were forced to stand despite the large number of seats. It was clear that many people towards the back had little or no experience of a Catholic Requiem Mass, although they were absorbed in the eulogy. She remembered what Debs had reported: that Wei Chi was popular for her talks on spirituality. Maybe these were the people who had admired her as a freethinker. Frances wondered what the Catholic priest thought. Would he frown on all that alternative stuff? Surely, being a priest in the conservative Catholic Church, with its dogma and strict authority, he would?

After he had finished speaking, she asked Debs in a whisper, 'Did he say owt about *I Ching* and all that?'

'Yeah, he seemed to think Wei Chi were a great teacher. I think he were pretty supportive, based on what he said. Maybe he's a liberal.'

'Look at crowds in here.'

'Yeah, it's really amazing. She were quite a character, weren't she?'

'Yeah, a real character. I'm glad we were lucky enough to meet her.'

'She were lucky too! She met the great visionary Frances Dryburgh.'

Debs said this with a mischievous smile. Frances screwed up her face in mock disgust. But, although she knew that Debs was being gently sarcastic, the comment still thrilled her and the hairs on her arms stood on end as she contemplated the excitement of being part of the spiritually adventurous international jet set. Here was the great and celebrated visionary in Poissy, Paris, at the funeral of her renowned friend, the extraordinary, gifted Chinese teacher Wei Chi.

The party went to a nearby cemetery after the Mass. Wei Chi had requested burial, not cremation. The coffin was lowered while something was read; Debs said it was from one of Wei Chi's own books. A long silence followed before the relatives were invited to throw the first earth down, watery eyes and downcast looks everywhere amongst the large gathering. Frances remembered how the solstice vision included the great fall into the embrace of the Earth; now Wei Chi was deep inside its heart. She felt glad about it all. Wei Chi had had a long and partly tragic life; now she was at peace. Before she had gone, she had imparted a little of her wisdom to Frances and her friends, young people at the beginning of a spiritual journey. Frances' tears were warm and not grief-stricken, tears of awestruck emotion, of feeling blessed, of being in touch with a great spiritual reality. Wei Chi had believed in it – in *her*, the Goddess – and now Frances was a believer too, an apprentice who would take away many lessons from the last two weeks. The Massiac vision once again came to mind. Remembering the encounter with the whole Earth and its history now gave Frances the insight that, at a funeral, one experienced a whole, larger than life human being, somebody greater than the person one met in the normal everyday contacts of a single slice in time.

Deep in her daydreaming, Frances had not noticed that the ceremony was over. Someone tapped her shoulder. The realisation that it was a stranger made her start. It was Ho, the one third of a Santa Claus. *Damn Nathan's jokes!* Now the poor man would always be associated with that puerile quip. Ho was worth more than that; despite the gaunt visage, his dark brown eyes sparkled with warmth and intelligence as he spoke for the first time to Frances. In her mind's eye, particularly active today, she thought she saw the Tay Bac mountains mistily haunting him.

'Perhaps you like this, to remember Wei Chi?'

He held out a book.

'It's an English translation. For you.'

'Oh, thank you,' replied Frances, giving him her most affectionate smile.

He then slipped away into the crowd of Chinese and Vietnamese mourners. In East Asia, they were two nations; here in Paris they looked to the European like a single one, exiles a million miles from paddy fields, rickshaws, sampans and the regional struggles of the twentieth century. Frances looked down at what she was holding. The book was authored by Wei Chi. It carried her photograph on the back, a younger Wei Chi looking sublimely wise and inviting the reader to revel in the treasures inside. On the front was a picture of a flying dove with an industrial scene in the background. It was titled, *Before Completion: Spirituality in the 21$^{st}$ Century.*

There was no reception. Dominique informed them that because there was likely to be such a large number and, as it was a work day with many people unable to take the whole day off, the local people had come to the view that it was impossible.

Probably the relatives would have their own gathering. However, for the rest, that was it.

'Maybe you should have an afternoon in Paris?' she suggested.

Jose suddenly brightened up. The scheduler had been doing some research in the area of 'what's on in Paris'.

'There's a performance of Poulenc's choral music in the city centre in the early evening,' he said. 'Frances and I can go to hear it. The others, too, if they like. But I suspect that they'll prefer to do something else.'

'Yeah, maybe something else,' laughed Nathan. 'Anything else!'

Frances' heart sank. Why would she want to spend an evening in romantic Paris with Jose when her beloved Nathan was there? *Plonker again!* But the excuses for not going to the recital wouldn't come. They stopped in her throat. The concert in Leeds had been the gateway to a new life, hadn't it? When she was kind to Jose by staying, that had occasioned the first vision, hadn't it; the visions had led to welcome changes at work and dramatic new spiritual experiences, hadn't they? To turn him down this time, would that be like throwing away a lucky talisman? Throwing back into the waters of fate the good that had come out of it? And would she really want the slightly built, vulnerable Jose to be on his own in Paris?

'Yeah, OK, Poulenc it is,' she heard herself saying with some conviction, as if in some dream where the enlightened Ms Jekyll had taken over, leaving Ms Hyde and her lustful desires on the sidelines.

'Fine, then we'll go exploring,' agreed Debs, addressing Nathan.

The parting of the ways came in central Paris at the Opéra Metro station. Frances looked longingly as Debs, in light mood, led Nathan away in the direction of the Seine. They made an odd couple as they disappeared through the thronging streets: Debs with her dark hair flying, having escaped all the attempts to tie it into some sort of shape for the funeral, Nathan looking particularly tall, handsome and debonair. They were slowly enveloped in the sea of the Paris urban mayhem: people touring, delivering, gesticulating, standing, running, disagreeing, laughing, cars hooting and changing lanes unexpectedly, taxis picking up and setting down fares in the worst places, buses blocked by myriad obstructions from transporting their passengers with any speed. Tall buildings; shops and offices below flats; plane trees battling for space; the insertion of bus shelters and lamp posts causing uneven flagstones in the pavement; litter, especially cigarette ends; the smell of smoke, sweat and vehicle exhaust hanging in the air – the epitome of the global city. Adverts rotated in what looked like miniature mosques: pillars with onion domes on top, the wayside shrines of the cult of the free market. A giant anthill with an incredible insect activity; if looked at from above, the human motions much less predictable and purposeful than their ant counterparts. Jose smiled; Frances responded with surface warmth. She couldn't let him see how regretful she was about the pairing off. For the second time that year, Jose and Plonker were to be given some of her valuable time, whatever her inward feelings were on the subject.

As for the concert, it could have been in any city. Square modern building, light, airy foyer, decorative chandeliers, advertisements for forthcoming performances. Then music, the international language, the European idiom now dominant across the globe: black and white uniform, conductors with batons, tuning, bowing, applause, encores. The wonder of Poulenc's sacred choral repertoire: *Gloria. Stabat Mater. Quatre Motets de Pénitence. Quatre Motets de Noël. Salve Regina.* No vision this time. *O Magnum Mysterium.* Frances found herself thinking, *Well, I have to admit that this is actually quite inspiring.* The music took her back to the mountain valleys of the Auvergne, to the gorges of the Alagnon, Allier and Seuge, the territory owned by the Virgins in Majesty; it seemed to be sung in their honour. As if to prove the point, the concert ended with the *Litanies à la*

*Vierge Noire*, sung by the women alone. But inside Frances' head there was a counterpoint to her enjoyment and growing appreciation of the music. *I mustn't like it because it's taking me away from Nathan. Oh, what am I saying, it's only one evening; yeah, but it's Paris, in't it and we're going back to the Auvergne tomorrow. But Goddess is going to give me Nathan and I'm doing this for her and for Jose, so it's good. Just relax, Frances, love, it's going to be OK.* Ms Jekyll aka Goddess, speaking at one moment, Ms Hyde, aka Frances in love, the next.

Jose was full of it as they left the building.

'Poulenc... and in *Paris*,' he grinned. 'A stroke of luck. And what a brilliant set of performances. I bet you enjoyed them too, didn't you, Frances?'

Nod, give affirming smile. *Yeah, not bad at all, but do they make up for an evening without your future love, Jose? Wonder what he's doing?* They'd decided to meet Nathan and Debs back at Madame Bousset's. So it was straight to the Metro and return to Poissy. Frances was listening to Jose's bar by bar analysis of the choral music when, out of the corner of her eye, she saw them. In Leeds, she had an instinct for spotting them in good time to keep out of the way but this was Paris. They were lads. English lads, sounded like Londoners. Lads out on the booze in a foreign city, probably on a stag weekend. They were drunk, noisy and coming across them suddenly was like bumping into a belligerent herd of wart hogs in the growing darkness of a forest evening – no one knew which way they were going to charge. But one thing was clear; they had seen Frances and were now fixated on her lithe body emerging from the tight yellow vest that she had donned that afternoon after taking off the one blouse that she had brought with her and worn at the funeral. It was enough for them. Just how beautiful she really was or wasn't meant nothing to the beer-soaked pack.

'Hey, honey, come on over 'ere!... What a little darling!... Oi, babe, ditch the Paki and get yourself some English beef!'

'Let's keep on main road,' urged Frances, quickening her pace.

Big mistake. One of them was close enough to overhear.

'Wow, the babe's English! Don't ignore us, love, we don't fucking like it!'

The nearest lad, a guy with a shaved head and portly in a football shirt, twenty-something but with a beer belly big enough for several midlife crises, started to trot and made a lunge towards Frances, paying no attention to Jose's close proximity. The little limping man was of no consequence...

Seconds later, they were gone. They went because Jose was now stretched out on the pavement and people were beginning to mill round. Somebody was calling the police on a mobile. Time for the 'lads' to make an exit, back into the shadows of the Paris side streets. Time to find another bit of fun and plenty of alcohol somewhere else. Jose was lying on the pavement because Mr Six Bellies had knocked him there with a flailing blow to the head. He had done this because Jose had stood between him and Frances, preventing him from reaching her. Frances was very distressed. She could think of nothing worse than sensitive, frightened little Jose being assaulted by a bunch of louts. It was his worst nightmare. And all on her account. Strange then that he was smiling as he sat up, firstly at her and then around at the gathering group of Parisians and tourists.

'Are you OK?' asked Frances with urgency, kneeling down and helping him sit up by holding his right arm and shoulder. 'Why'd you look so happy about it?'

'Well, I don't think I'm hurt, really,' replied Jose. 'He was too far gone to do any damage.'

'You were protecting me, weren't you?' Frances shouted above the crowd, part-happy about Jose's friendship and part-guilty that she had been pining so much for Nathan.

'Yes, I suppose I was,' Jose responded; he was now beginning to laugh with relief that it was all over with.

The crowd began to melt away and some were tutting. Jose's laughter was giving the impression that it was all a prank between stupid young English people. But Monsieur with the mobile stayed until the gendarmes came and insisted that they did too. It turned out to be a good decision, as it meant a lift in a French police car all the way back to Poissy. And, as they made the journey from city centre to Paris suburbs, Jose, the assault victim, had the air of someone who'd won the lottery.

'The point is, Frances, when you're small, partly disabled and Indian and you live in Britain – well, you're going to get hit one day by somebody like that guy. It's inevitable. But it never happened to me until now because I was always hiding to make sure I avoided it. I dreaded it; I was in mortal fear of it. Just now, I stopped hiding and ducking, and it happened. It's happened and I'm OK after all. I feel liberated!'

# 37

# The Dragon

Sunday morning was pleasant; scudding clouds tempered the heat of the late morning. Frances felt content as she lay face down on a blanket, carefully placed across a rough patch of grassy earth. The only sound was the trickling of the Couze Pavin, a narrow river that flowed near to Besse-en-Chandesse. Besse was a small town with modern houses surrounding a medieval centre where the *Comte de la Dauphiné* hotel, little more than a bar with B&B, had been chosen as the fourth and final base of the holiday. Besse nestled in the folds of hilly country north-west of Massiac and afforded sweeping views across the Parc des Volcans, the telltale flat tops of several hills revealing the volcanic origins of the whole range. Frances wanted to go as far as possible into the chain of volcanoes; somehow this seemed to be the right direction. The vision at the Madeleine chapel above Massiac had suggested to her that to be somewhere linked to the very core of the Earth was the place to be. Above Besse, the ski village of Super-Besse was to be found, with its monstrous hotels seemingly out of place in the quiet countryside; the slopes led up to the highest mountain in the Auvergne, the Puy Sancy. All around there were open pastures with cow bells sounding day and night, more fortunate for the sound sleeping lover of the rural idyll than for the insomniac.

A black Madonna inhabited the church in Besse; she was to be taken up ceremonially to her shrine on high ground at Vassivière on July 2$^{nd}$, the following Wednesday. This annual transfer probably originated in a movement of the herds further up the mountains for the summer. It had been decided, therefore, that the pilgrimage day of Notre Dame de Vassivière would be a fitting focus for the twelfth and final ritual, three days before they departed. For the intervening period, Jose had located two famous pilgrimage centres within easy reach: Ronzières and Orcival.

As they walked towards the car, Frances glanced across at Nathan. His easy gait and relaxed smile mirrored her own inner sense of peaceful contentment since they had returned from Paris along the A71. He had been more attentive to her and seemed to connect with the others better than he had hitherto in France, engaging in close conversation and cutting down on the throwaway jokes. She looked forward to the time when he would open up and allow her in; surely it couldn't be long now. But, given their past history, she was reluctant to make the first move; she would stay cool and remain assured that it would work out. Perhaps the holiday, with two other people close at hand, was not the best time. What had Wei Chi said that Chinese proverb was? 'If your horse runs away, do not chase after it. If it is truly yours, it will return to you.' Jose, on the other hand, gave the impression of being quietly ecstatic. His characteristic nervous anxiety had receded; he was clearly enjoying his new role as the have-a-go hero. The drunken blow had not really hurt him, which seemed to confirm for him that the world was not the dangerous and threatening place that he had always perceived it to be. Debs, too, was on the top of her game. She had purchased some new clothes in Paris, dragging a surprised Nathan along to a boutique or two, not an activity that one would expect to be involved in whilst with Debs. She sported a pink top with short, braided sleeves;

this made her look girlier and prettier than the customary summer vests did. Her hair had been tidied up as well; it was smoothed with gel and carefully tied back so that random strands of frizzy hair didn't stick out all over the place. Frances marvelled. *What's going on, has everybody been liberated? What's she done to us, that Wei Chi?*

Driving to Ronzières took the hired Honda down the river valley back towards the lower country nearer the Allier. Great wooded gorges gave way to more gentle rolling hills: eye-catching swathes of colour across the farms, cereals in yellow brown; bright greens, unlike any seen in Britain; the dazzling yellow of rape fields. Single lumpy volcanic hills stood out from the patchwork as if some giant had pushed his knee up beneath bed sheets; each one was populated with a picturesque village that sprawled on its slopes. The Romanesque church of Ronzières stood on one such bump, its silver-domed roof topped with a Madonna statue visible for miles around. A splendid view across the fields and hills greeted those climbing up, although its isolated location in a small village suggested that it would seldom be overflowing with visitors. Inside, the Virgin in Majesty sat behind a heavy wrought iron gate for security, so that it was almost impossible to see both Madonna and Child at the same time through a gap in the curled pattern. She was another 'Scary Mary'; while her head was covered in a type of tight skull cap, making her look young, the fierce gaze had the unnerving intensity by now familiar. The Child raised his right arm in blessing. A switch allowed the visitor to light up the shrine altar on which her throne was placed. Swallows flew around chirping high inside the empty, gloomy church interior, adding to the mystique of the place.

A plaque outside gave some indication of the area and its legends. Debs translated with a hint of 'this'll interest you more than it does me'. Apparently, the site had been founded by a St Baudîme. He had defeated a dragon that terrorised the neighbourhood; as it was being vanquished, the dragon had disgorged part of the hill of Ronzières, dragging it down while falling. St Baudîme had also discovered a holy well and he established a shrine there. When the shrine was destroyed during the French Revolution, the statue had been lost but was later found buried a short distance from the site of the well by cows pawing fervently at the ground. A familiar legend for a pastoral sanctuary.

'Where *is* the well?' asked Frances. 'That could be a good place for our ritual.'

'Yeah, good point,' agreed Debs, and she proceeded to call out to a passing woman of about sixty years, who – without any bag or coat – looked as if she were local. She replied in very friendly terms and began to walk back up to the church, beckoning them to follow.

'She says it's in woods behind church,' said Debs. 'She's only found it once herself, as she only lives here for part o' year. But she'll go with us to find it, because she'd quite like to see it again.'

Their guide led them into the dense vegetation of the woodlands, where a narrow track snaked down the hill across its rolling contours. As Debs talked to the Frenchwoman, Nathan lagging behind studying the flora, Frances asked Jose a question.

'How many saints have fought with dragons? That seems to be a common legend.'

'Yes,' answered Jose. 'St George is the obvious one. St Michael conquered the dragon who was also the Devil. And here we have St Baudîme, whoever he was.'

'All o' them are men,' mused Frances, stumbling over a tree root.

She tottered for a few steps, which caused the following Nathan to snigger and she couldn't stop herself smiling in response. *Men! They fight dragons but laugh at people tripping up. They fart and they drink too much. What kind o' dragon would allow itself to be defeated by one o' them?*

'Well, there was one woman saint who defeated a dragon,' said Jose. 'Martha! In legend, she came to France with Mary Magdalene and conquered a dragon.'

'Good,' replied Frances. 'She must have been quite a lady.'

As she considered that, suddenly there was the well, a skillfully erected pile of stone slabs surmounted by a concrete cross, surrounding a trickling water source that was caught in a hollowed-out stone. The well was deep in the woods; behind it, a young ash tree leaned over precariously, growing at forty-five degrees to the ground. There were many objects left on the side of the small basin: a tiny Virgin Mary, the odd wild flower, strips of coloured rag and some writing on scraps of paper. It was clearly a shrine in current use, a place where pilgrims came to leave prayer requests.

They thanked their guide as she left; it would not have been possible to locate the well without her. This was about as perfect a place as they had found for a ritual. The well served as an altar; they could stand around it and call the quarters. The silence of the woodlands, except for the occasional birdsong, created an atmosphere of reverence for nature and for the visitors of the past. When the vision came, Frances was fully expecting to see a dragon. So often, the apparition experiences repeated themes in her recent thinking...

But instead she returned to the dark corridor between the Earth and the Moon and found herself in front of the once distant doorway. She saw ivy crawling in and out of the gaps in the crumbling stonework of the archway, then the door opened smoothly of its own accord and she seemed to float in. The interior was extremely bright compared to the night sky on the outside; Frances' eyes went straight to the source of the light...

She described it afterwards.

'Wow! It were Goddess, seated like Madonna in Majesty statues, but there were no Child. Like before, her features, skin colour and clothing were not very distinct; she constantly changed, and she were never one thing long enough for me to take in one clear image. She were dancing woman; she were Black Virgin; she were pale Mary Magdalene in red dress; she were big built like an Earth mother; she were slight and fairylike; she were young and beautiful; she were old and wise. She were crowned, then bareheaded, then wore a cap like Notre Dame de Ronzières, then horned headgear like Isis in Tarot pack. One thing I did know: her eyes were fixed on me. It were really, really amazing. She seemed to say: "Come and sit on my lap." I did. Touching her strange body made me feel absolute peace; she were like a wonderful alien being who's come to help the world. Her voice were crystal clear, yet it's difficult to describe: gentle; firm; friendly; powerful, like a queen. "Thank you for coming," she said. "I couldn't do anything else – you summoned me," I said or, rather, I thought, as my ideas seemed to take on form o' speech. "We summoned each other," she replied. I said, in my head, "I'm so glad to have you on my side, you've supported me, haven't you?" She then said, "Of course. I always will. It'll be OK, Frances." A conversation were taking place between us, but it were like no ordinary conversation. It weren't one comment coming logically before another. It were more like a sharing o' thoughts and feelings. It were, like, emotional and intuitive rather than intellectual. "What should I call you?" I asked. She said, "I have many, many names. In the ancient world, I was Isis; Cybele; Demeter. For Christians, I have been Mary, or Mary Magdalene. For modern people, I am the Earth, Gaia, or simply the Goddess. But names never capture who or what I am." "No, you're different from age to age," I said, remembering visions o' Pisces, Aquarius and Capricorn. She suddenly announced: "You will see me again and I will reveal more of who I am." Then my vision were over.'

Frances' sense of well-being after the apparition, in contrast to the anxieties of the week before last, was profound. They found their way back out of the woods; Frances stopped to spend a few more minutes in front of the statue of the Madonna of Ronzières. She then went outside and gazed at the view for a few more minutes. It caused her to think of the great Earth vision, which associated itself in her brain with the story of Wei Chi's family. So much violence in the Earth; she had seen wars and bombings: the Vietnam War, of course, that was a good example. She remembered pictures of American bombers targeting Vietnamese peasants, a little girl screaming in pain, hit by napalm. Just images from a bygone age, a few years before she was born. Had it touched her emotions? Not much. But what had the voices said? 'You're made of this stuff, it's the very fibre of your existence.' The distance in time between the little Vietnamese girl's experience and her own childhood was a tiny fragment of world history. They were connected – that was the point of the vision. They were part of the same tragedy and, if there was salvation to be found in the bloody history of the twentieth century, they shared that too. In Wei Chi they had come together, that little Vietnamese girl and Frances. They had met. The little girl was Wei Chi's daughter; even if not in actual fact, she might as well have been. Frances had not thought of herself as a victim, not until the last few months. Yes, as a woman in Leeds, she had to watch out, but there were ways of being streetwise and keeping away from trouble. Any sign of violence and she was off. But the phone stalker had changed all that and now the visions confirmed it. Frances, the women in the refuge, Debs, the Vietnamese girl, Wei Chi, they were all potential victims. But would they accept it and leave it at that? *No. Never. That's what witchcraft's about. It's a way of fighting back.* Not with napalm, not with blows and threats, not with menace and plotting but by becoming the people they were meant to be. *Women with control over their lives. Not victims.*

'You've not gone back into that depression, have you?' asked Nathan, breaking into her silence.

'No,' replied Frances. 'I feel really great. I know that she's with me, you see.'

All four adventurers gathered to look over at the nearby town of Vodable, perched on a volcanic hill rising above the rolling fields.

An evening in Besse. It seemed quiet for the time of year; most of the visitors were day trippers. The pretty medieval centre of the town – open only to pedestrians, except for the odd delivery van – quickly became familiar. The clock tower above an old city gate. A few gift shops for those touring the mountains. A little statue of the Madonna in a niche on a street corner holding a Jesus without a face. There were several restaurants, rough and ready but always friendly and comparatively cheap. While in France, they had developed a liking for the *galettes*, savoury pancakes with a variety of fillings. In the near-empty *crêperie*, a young slim waitress with dark curly hair and large earrings, almost pretty but with the appearance of already having a fair share of the ups and downs of life, brought the food quickly. After the day together, there was not a lot left to say. So Frances took the opportunity to read to them a few lines from Wei Chi's *Before Completion*. She chose a section which seemed relevant to the legend of the dragon of Ronzières.

'The Many-Headed Dragon

The Greek and Hebrew myths of old can inform us a great deal about our society today. Take the hydra, for example, a beast with many heads. This figure can tell us something about the way in which the powers in society work. Although we need governments and some measure of social order, human power can easily become monstrous. It can become like a many-headed hydra. If you concentrate all your fears on a possible attack by one power, this will make you put all your attention on it and so forget the threat of the other powers. If you are worried about communism, you will run into the jaws of capitalism; if you fear atheism, you will let religious leaders do whatever they want with you. The hydra works like that. One head says, "Stick with me or you will be destroyed by another one of the heads". You must choose this religion or that one; between this nation or that nation; this cause or that cause. But we need do nothing of the sort. They are all aspects of the same monster, dividing us from one another, ruling by making us fearful of the enemies in the shadows. We can choose to be free of the hydra by not allowing ourselves to be coerced into a choice between false opposites. We must remain sceptical when someone tries to win our loyalty by making us fearful of what will happen if we don't put all our trust in them alone.

The New Testament has its hydra creature too. This is the dragon of the book of Revelation, which had seven heads. It tried to devour the Messiah as he was being born, but it was defeated by St Michael. This tells us that the human powers that divide us one from another are the enemies of what God is trying to do for us. When Jesus said, "My kingdom is not from this world", he was confirming for us that God has no love for human power, because it so often stands against everything that God wants for us. It is very hard for humans to exercise power over one's fellows, whether in the government, or church, or workplace, without striving for their own interests against the well-being of others. To serve the needs of their own power, the powerful demand loyalty from others. The dragon's many heads scare us into agreeing to be ruled by one of them. The dragon or hydra is a tricky monster. But if we want to find the kingdom of God within ourselves, we have to refuse to bow down before it. God's power is not like human power. We will not be loyal only to certain groups of our fellow human beings but to all of them as a whole. Even when we discern something to be evil in our society, we will not regard ourselves as righteous, cutting ourselves off from the evil but, as a community, we will seek to engage with the people involved and attempt to free them from it. "Judge not." We are all in this together, although the hydra will tell us otherwise. In Revelation, it was the Earth that rescued the mother of the Saviour from destruction by flood; by being citizens of the whole Earth, we can resist the dragon with many heads, who wants us to serve one of the heads while fearing the others...'

'Wow,' said Frances. 'Do you think that *Before Completion* could be a new bible for people like us?'

Nathan looked up, having been swilling his lager round in the glass while Frances was reading.

'The trouble with bibles and any books that are given ultimate authority,' he commented, quietly but firmly, 'Is that people then regard their own interpretations of them as authoritative. That's how fundamentalism develops.'

'Oh.' Frances felt deflated for a few seconds. Her reading hadn't quite engendered the interest and discussion for which she had hoped. Everyone expressed their respect for Wei Chi and admiration of her wisdom, but the tiredness after a summer day on holiday; the downbeat atmosphere of the *crêperie*; people's private thoughts – all conspired to bring back the silence. But Frances didn't dwell on the disappointment. Her thoughts were racing with the idea of the Goddess facing the dragon or the hydra. A few months ago, she wouldn't really have engaged with all this head stuff but the visions, particularly the great blue Earth, had changed all that. She had seen the beast that was humanity. The Goddess was doing battle against the dark forces of the world, the negative tendencies of the human race. It wasn't an easy conflict, a straight Hollywood fight between goodies and baddies, but instead it involved tricky decisions and avoidance of simple answers. And it involved dilemmas, of course. It was ultimately the very tough challenge of being in solidarity with the whole Earth and not just a part of it. So Frances resolved to ask the Goddess about this when she saw her next. But the real excitement welling up inside her was not inspired by intellectual propositions about human power but by a deep emotional energy that wrapped itself around all the symbolic entities – Goddess, dragon, black, Mary Magdalene – and refused to allow itself to be pinned down in logical answers. It was that energy that was so attractive, so exciting and so stimulating.

# 38

## Clothed in Gold

On Monday, the thirty kilometre car journey to Orcival passed through some spectacular mountain views, including the great fortified château at Murol perched on a rock above the town. From behind the wheel, Nathan looked at the strange volcanic formations of the hills in the near distance and the undulating lines of the mountain ranges further off.

'This *is* fairytale country, isn't it!' he exclaimed. 'The kind you read about as a kid. Castles on hills, volcanoes, mountains as far as you can see. All we need is a princess in a tower.'

Frances suddenly sat up and switched on. *Dragons again?*

'Yes, it is, wi' beasts and dragons. We've met some o' them, haven't we? But instead o' princesses, Goddesses. They seem to go out and beat dragons up instead o' being shut in towers, waiting for some guy to rescue 'em.'

'Right on,' agreed Debs. 'Princesses who drill a hole in wall and kick dragon's teeth in.'

'It takes more than a good kicking,' pondered Nathan, quietly but with conviction. 'Remember Wei Chi's book? The hydra is very subtle. It'll tell you to kick one of its heads in, while getting you to rely on another one.'

'Maybe Goddess has several feet,' Debs responded, gaily.

*She's in jolly mood today, looking to find jokes in everything. It in't normally her job!* This thought was interrupted as Frances' attention suddenly came to bear on one mountain that was greater than the rest. It stood like a giant mound of earth, a huge Christmas pudding, the top just hidden by a low cloud.

'What's that?' she asked. 'Must be one o' biggest volcanoes of all!'

'It is,' replied Jose, who was map reading. 'It's the Puy de Dôme, the highest peak of the northern Auvergne. We should try and go up there at some point.'

'Yeah, we must. Puy de Dôme. Where the dragons live. I think I'm up to fighting 'em now.'

Orcival was a large village in a pleasant valley, not like the high gorges of the Alagnon or Allier but rolling countryside reminiscent of an English dale. A great Romanesque basilica with its octagonal tower, similar to the one they had seen in Brioude, stood at its centre. Orcival was quite touristy, with several hotels and restaurants; it was one of the traditional pilgrimage centres of the Auvergne. The basilica was austere and dark inside, without the artefacts around the walls at Brioude or in the nave at Le Puy. This concentrated the pilgrim's attention on the Madonna and Child in Majesty sitting under spotlights in the roped-off choir behind the altar, on a square pillar several feet high. The statue was not large, no more than a couple of feet high, yet it dominated the surrounding space. Flowers were placed all around her. Here was an active and passionate devotion. She was one of the prettiest and best-crafted of the Virgin statues that they had seen, in gold except for the white faces and hands of the two figures.

'Would you believe, it's a black virgin,' said Jose, in an awed whisper.

'How?' asked Frances. 'She's golden as far as I can see.'

'Probably at one time she would have been painted black,' replied Jose. 'But whatever the reason, they call her a *vierge noire*. Black Virgin. I'm not sure that anyone really knows why. But, like the Madonnas of Le Puy and Besse who actually are black, the title *vierge noire* suggests that she has great spiritual power.'

'Look at her hands,' said Frances. 'So large and protecting her Child on each side. She's quite awesome.'

Frances remembered that the Goddess of her visions, in one of her many guises, was sometimes clothed in gold like the Virgin of Orcival. She found herself standing leaning against a pillar in rapt concentration, staring at the figure. She didn't need to think or pray anything in her mind. Just be there. The statue signified a spiritual presence, which fixed itself in Frances' intuition more powerfully than ever. It was the same presence that she saw in visions and felt was with her even in the most mundane of situations. She was lost to everyone around her. As she had at Saugues, she went into the vision spontaneously, without any ritual to prompt her…

She was back in the room behind the old door. So much light, it was difficult to look. Predictably, the Goddess was all in gold this time. However, the face was again indistinct, difficult to pin down. It was not one face but many. Frances remembered that she had questions to ask. She sat on the Goddess' lap once more. Bliss, peaceful bliss. The conversation was again like telepathy – was it really words? Or what? She could only recall it as speech, although it wasn't exactly that.

'Talk to me about the dragon.'

'What can I tell you – you know everything about it.'

'But tell me anyway.'

'It's part of you, didn't you learn that at the Madeleine chapel? It's within you, it's the human desire for power over others: the great dragon.'

'So the dragon is in *me*. How can I fight it then?'

'You have to know it's in you before you can fight it.'

'OK, but there's more to me than the dragon. You're in me too, aren't you?'

Frances somehow sensed that the Goddess smiled on that impossibly shifting and unknowable face.

'Yes, Frances – now, no more questions. Just stay with me for a while. It'll be OK.'

The vision continued as a moment of pure joy as Frances exulted in the fact that her attendance was required by the one who *was* the great Presence herself. *Maybe I've got the dragon inside, but she wants to spend some time wi' me...*

Frances came to. This time, neither her comrades nor any of the visitors to the basilica had noticed the trance. The pillar had kept her from falling and she was swaying back and forth against it. She rested there a while longer and contemplated what she had seen, felt and heard. She was happy, ecstatic actually, but there was something which unsettled her. Despite all these powerful apparitions and their insights, Frances felt she hadn't changed much. She had experienced the great vision at Massiac but life went on, food was eaten, beverages were drunk, people were irritating, the weather was 'bad', Nathan wasn't attentive enough, beds were uncomfortable, people at home in Leeds were forgotten, prices were double-checked to make sure she wasn't getting overcharged. She had stepped into the chamber of the wonderful Goddess, but she was still the grumpy, grotty, greedy, ungrateful wretch that she had always been. Then it came back to her: 'It's part of you.' The dragon. Human power, the sum total of all the little grumps, grots, greeds and lack of grace. Us. *Even the Goddess can't charm us. She can tame lions and unicorns but not us. Dragons are much tougher than lions.* Frances sighed. But the mood swung back. *Despite all that, she wants to spend time wi' me! I'm blessed. It'll be OK, Frances!*

Debs had found a guide book and told them about two sacred sites up the hillsides on each side of Orcival.

'There's "Tomb of the Virgin" on one side, which is the site of an ancient chapel and, on t'other, a little chapel with a spring, *Notre Dame de la Source*. On Ascension Day each year, processions come down from each side by candlelight, each singing in turn back and forth across valley. It must be really impressive.'

'OK,' said Jose. 'Let's visit those places and choose the place where we can have our ritual.'

They decided to go first to what was known as the 'Tomb of the Virgin'. The path up the hillside was a 'Way of the Cross' with fourteen 'stations' at intervals, each of which depicted a scene in Christ's walk from Pilate's Palace to Calvary. At the top, the view of the great basilica and the surrounding buildings was enhanced by the brightening of the day, the sun breaking through thinning clouds. The shrine itself was a little nineteenth-century covered monument in stone with a Madonna statue, all behind green railings. It looked rather like the kind of structure one would see above a wealthy person's gravestone or a family vault.

'Could the Virgin have been buried here?' asked Debs, inspecting the edifice.

'I once read a book that claimed her body was hidden somewhere in Anglesey,' chipped in Nathan, his tone suggesting that the theory hadn't impressed him very much. 'It was written by one of these guys who discovers something earth-shatteringly remarkable every six months or so. I would like to do that; they must make a fortune from gullible readers. Nathan Smith proves once and for all that the great city of Atlantis lies under Lake Windermere. Nathan Smith shows absolutely that Jesus' twin brother is buried under the Tate Gallery. Nathan Smith has found that British librarians are descended from the Egyptian pharaohs; his arguments are irrefutable. Nathan Smith...'

Jose cut in.

'The great Nathan Smith might like to be aware that, according to Catholic teaching, the body of the Virgin is *in heaven*,' he declared. 'It was taken up by angels. I don't know why this place is called the "Tomb of the Virgin", but if they believe her to be buried here, then it's not Catholicism as we know it.'

'Well, it's not her body that's important,' said Frances. 'It's her *presence*.'

Then she went back into dreamy mode, reflecting on her vision which, until now, none of the others knew she had already experienced. She stood enjoying the view of the hill opposite, beech trees in massed ranks forming little collections or lines here and there, punctuating the light green of the grassy bank, with pines at the summit.

On the other side of the valley, the little chapel of *Notre Dame de la Source* was locked, although it was possible to peer through the grille at the holy well; the fact that it was surrounded by strange crystalline rock formations created an aura of otherworldliness and mystery. The area outside, hidden in the woods, would be a perfect place for the ritual. Frances admitted to the others that the vision had already occurred, in the basilica. As at Saugues, this led to a somewhat restrained ritual without its centrepiece. They called again for the spirit world to enter into the G8 summit and influence the delegates towards a more radical approach to the environment. They built their altar of flowers and twigs and later, at the end, scattered them back into the surroundings as if nothing had ever been built there. There was silence. However, despite the muted atmosphere of the rite, Frances felt excited: it was the eleventh and there was only one to go. It was the climax of the journey to the Auvergne, one week before the summit began. Soon they would know if their magic had been successful. Soon too, Frances felt, she would enter into a new and exciting stage in the visions as she approached nearer and nearer a powerful intimacy with the Goddess. Then, with the return home, the anticipated relationship with Nathan could begin, when they had a chance to be alone. The cards had decreed it. The Ace of Cups. He looked really good today, like a beautiful golden-headed boy who was about to become a man in taking the step towards a proper relationship. She felt an almost painful tenderness for him as she watched him go through the actions of the ritual. He always put everything into it, even when others were not in the mood. He always took the lead; by far the tallest member of their group, he was always the one to offer to carry something, place something, build something. He was the one to try and inject humour and optimism where there was gloom. She smiled. What a wonderful partner he would make! He had been resistant but, like the delegates at the summit, he would submit to the Goddess' designs. In each ritual, Frances secretly included a little prayer for their relationship to be fruitful. She felt that she shouldn't; it seemed a bit self-seeking, but the card reading had encouraged her in thinking that it was appropriate after all.

The mood stayed low-key, the adventurers seemed a little weary and so, after lunch and a look round, they returned to Besse. An afternoon reading novels perhaps? They found a café where it didn't seem to matter how long you stayed. Jose had grabbed the Wei Chi book; he read sections out.

'Human life moves forward but some things remain the same. Plus ça change! In the ancient Jewish Scriptures, we see how great Empires like the Assyrians and Babylonians punished the nations who were their vassals. If the subservient regime failed to play the right tune, or make the right speech, the troops would come in and the foundations of that regime would be cut from under it. Probably they found their own rationale for it but it was the force of power all the same. Ancient Israel suffered many times like this: the north fell to the Assyrians, the south to the Babylonians and later the nation was put to the sword by the Romans. Is it any different today? No. Then it was the Romans, now it's the Americans and their allies. Then it was the Jews, now it's the Iraquis. The little men on their power trips who foolishly snub their noses to the truly mighty empires, thereby condemning their people to destructive invasion. Then Jehoiakim, the Jewish king, now Saddam Hussein. Did Jehoiakim threaten Babylon with the "mother of all battles"? Just as the destructive nature of human power systems continues unabated in our world of the 21$^{st}$ century, so does the potential of the human heart to love its neighbour and seek a better life for them. But it needs awakening. The Hebrew prophets argued for justice and righteousness then, and they do so again today. They call us.

Their spirit is with us still. They were herders of flocks and strange eccentric priests of a bygone society but somehow they saw into our world of tanks, pollution, cheap labour and the force of international economic systems. They speak to us, to urge us not to be misled by the great powers of the modern world and not to regard them as if they were morally superior to those of ancient times...'

'She takes the words right out of my mouth,' said Jose, approvingly. 'She makes sense of the problems of today's world.'

Debs grunted. Her relationship with her latest novel brooked no interruption, even if she would have agreed with every word that Jose was saying. Nathan said nothing. His head was buried in a travel guide to the area. There were only a few days to go. What unmissable sight or location had they overlooked? Frances heard but did not listen. The problems of the world sat light on her shoulders just for the moment. She just couldn't shake the upbeat feeling that all was extremely well. Everything was ready like a great banquet; today, the preparations had finally been completed. The table was ready, silver cutlery and cut glass goblets awaited the guests; the kitchen was on standby to bring in the first courses. The red wine was uncorked, the white in the fridge. The hostess looks through the window; in the distance, she sees the headlights of the first car making its way up the drive of the mansion. The silence in the house is testimony to its expectation and its readiness. The next vision would be the twelfth.

# 39

# Pagan Mass

The high sense of expectation in Frances lasted throughout the Tuesday as the adventurers took a drive through the area around Besse. The nearby valley of the Couze de Valbeleix and Gorges de Courgoul was spectacular; its closed-in narrowness, depth and verdancy made it seem like a French Shangri-La, a paradisiacal location in which to live. It was the kind of place where, if finances allowed, the city dweller might be tempted to buy a small property and retire from the trammels of urban existence. A million miles from traffic queues with people desperate to just get past the next traffic light; from litter blowing past rows of shops embedded in plains of concrete, which always included a newsagent's, a betting shop and a place that sold fast food of some kind; from small piles of rotting garbage that everyone seemed to have abandoned to the responsibility of someone else; from badly lit alley ways; from shadowy patches of greenery that punctuated the urban scene but which no one dared cross after dark; from unnecessary hooting of car horns; from the carpet of fag ends; from advertising on large billboards. None of these seemed to feature in the environs of the Couze de Valbeleix; what rural hells might possibly have replaced them weren't apparent to the tourist driving through. In the depths of the gorge, the village of Valbeleix; high up opposite, its sister settlement of St Anastaise. They seemed to call to each other across the intervening space like mountain shepherds checking each other's welfare or herds of cows spontaneously communicating with tinkling bells.

For Frances, however, paradise was not to be found in the beauty of Valbeleix. It resided in her future, in Leeds. Time was rushing on towards the inevitable journey home. Like all vacations, this one had started slowly, the first few days seeming like an eternity, but the last two thirds – in this case, the period after Wei Chi's death – were passing like a flash. She nursed no regrets about the impending end of a sensational holiday and a return to G.R.C. as she would have done were she sunbathing, reading romantic novels, drinking cheap wine and partying by night on Ibiza or Mykonos. The mystical Auvergne was not about transient pleasures, lost in an inkling and forgotten after a morning slaving over files, but about what was to come, what the Goddess was preparing for her.

Waking up on Wednesday brought with it a special thrill of anticipation. The twelfth vision was here, the completion of the great magical task! The day of the transference of the Black Virgin from her winter home in the church at Besse up to her summer residence in the mountains at Vassivière. A symbol for Frances' life as she went forward to embrace her destiny.

Early rising was necessary in order to catch the beginning of the procession at 8 a.m. in the medieval church in Besse. Some prayers were taking place so the adventurers waited outside. Then people started coming out and in their midst was the Black Virgin in her circular glass case mounted on a bier, carried by four strong-looking men of the countryside. The top of the case was adorned by a golden crown and several large white feathers. The statue went through the narrow medieval streets and up towards the old gate, which had its own Madonna statue below the clock tower.

'Where's that voice coming from?' asked Debs, grumpily.

She was not the happiest bunny if involved in public events at eight o'clock in the morning.

'It's the priest,' replied Jose. 'He's leading the prayers and hymns over a radio link through speakers carried in the rucksacks of some of the participants.'

'He hasn't got the most wonderful voice,' grunted Nathan.

'Maybe someone's suffering after several glasses of Auvergne wine?' suggested Jose.

'Actually,' replied Nathan, with a grimace, 'His voice would annoy a teetotaller saint.'

'You'll never know, because that doesn't describe you,' riposted Jose.

'Well, OK, I'm an *alcoholic* saint,' Nathan went on.

'St Nathan the Legless,' interjected Frances, grabbing the comic opportunity.

She giggled, enjoying the good humour but secretly feeling too emotionally intense about the occasion to want to overdo the joking.

'How far does St Nathan the Legless have to walk without his legs this morning?' asked the newly canonised saint. To puzzled looks, he added, loudly: 'How far's the procession?'

'Erm, about eight kilometres,' replied St Jose the Slightly-Nervous-That-He-Hadn't-Mentioned-This-Earlier. 'Five miles in English money.'

Frances and Debs looked alarmed.

'What!' cried Debs. 'That's a crazy distance to walk first thing in morning!'

But if Debs had real concerns about the demands of the procession, Frances privately did not. It was all part of the plan. Pilgrimages were supposed to be arduous, weren't they? Then you'd be rewarded. You did it out of devotion to the Madonna and she paid you back.

The procession left Besse and began to climb along the road out to the south. There were in the region of a hundred people present; apart from a group of teenagers from a school in Clermont-Ferrand, most were aged fifty plus. The adventurers' presence was clearly very welcome judging by the smiles and nods of approval. Debs, however, was not that gracious, flinching as the rucksack bearers spread out among the crowd so that everyone could hear the priest.

'I cannot *believe* how loud that awful voice is,' she exclaimed. 'How can the Church expect young people to want to join in, apart from a few school kids who've been dragged along by their teacher? Isn't this supposed to be a community event, a cultural happening? Where are groups o' women singing Auvergne songs in traditional costumes? How long can this kind o' male priest-dominated activity survive in modern world?'

'You've got a point,' agreed Nathan, who got a dirty look from Jose for encouraging the critical talk among strangers, many of whom might have understood some English, although there was no sign of it. 'The lack of young people, the fact that there's nothing traditional relating specifically to the local area – it's a real problem. If this has been going on for hundreds of years, I'm sure it wasn't always like this. They should tap into people's desire to be in contact with their cultural roots, as well as encouraging more leadership by the ordinary people. If they don't, it'll die out.'

And so, and so... Frances heard, appreciated the points made, but it really didn't matter to her. No matter what the context, the single fact remained that this was the climax of her visionary journey through the Auvergne. The black doll-like Madonna in a glass case was only an image of the wonderful Goddess with whom she had a relationship. *Really I'm black, Frances.* Even the fact that she had forgotten to bring water for a five-mile walk on a hot day did not compromise her good mood.

They walked on as the route wound up through pleasant hilly country. Gendarmes controlled the traffic so that the procession could take up half of the road, which was the main route south to the Cantal mountains. Every so often the procession would stop as part of a traditional prayer cycle. Debs now seemed to be in a better mood as she had started a conversation with the school children, who looked about fifteen or sixteen and welcomed the chance to talk to an Englishwoman. Then there was expectation in the crowd. The gold crown and white feathers that could be seen above the crowd changed direction. The bearers of the glass case had turned off the main road onto a wide farm track. It was clear that this was the turning leading up the hill to the shrine of Notre Dame de Vassivière. After a few yards, the procession also left the track and starting climbing up a muddy path through scattered trees. Everyone stopped at a cross, a tall slender piece of iron protruding from a hexagonal concrete block. Prayers were said, led by the ubiquitous projected voice of the priest.

'Another thing strikes me about what you were saying earlier,' said Nathan to Debs. 'The main problem here is modern technology itself. Without the wireless short wave radio system, the priest would not be able to dominate so much. In a bygone age, the mountain wind would have prevented his voice carrying and there would have been more communal leadership and participation.'

'Good point,' agreed Debs. 'Church is not so oldy-worldy as we often think; maybe it would be best if it were.' She turned to Jose. 'Are we nearly there, Dad?'

'Well,' replied Jose. 'In distance terms, yes, I think so. But we're doing the stations of the cross. It's a traditional way of approaching a shrine, particularly one on a hill; remember the Virgin's Tomb at Orcival? We're on the first station and there are fourteen altogether.'

'Oh, goody,' said Debs, sarcastically, her dark frizzy hair getting loose from its ribbons and flying in the upland breeze, restoring the familiar hairstyle that had been replaced by a neater version over the last few days. Frances remained in the daydream state that she had been in for most of the procession. *No problem wi' having thirteen stations to go; it's worth waiting for.*

Finally, the chapel at Vassivière came into view. Behind it towered the mountains leading up to the great Puy de Sancy, hidden by the surrounding peaks. In the distance stood the modern ski town of Super-Besse, somewhat spoiling the illusion of remoteness. Outside the grey-bricked chapel, the fourteenth station of the cross took place. The procession circled around to the west end under the bell tower and past a small well house, in which was placed a shrine with a tiny black Madonna.

'That's the holy spring,' said Jose. 'Did you know that this place was sacred to the Celts before Christianity came? Its traditions are ancient. Probably the black Virgin here inherited the cult of a pre-Christian goddess.'

'A familiar theme,' commented Nathan.

Meanwhile, the statue in the glass case made its way towards the chapel door and had to be lowered by its bearers to get it through the entrance. It was clear that the chapel was packed; many people, particularly the elderly, had come directly in vehicles, thus not having been part of the procession.

'What'll we do in there?' asked Debs, clearly reluctant to push her way in.

'It'll be a Mass after which the Black Virgin will be placed in her summer position,' replied Jose.

'A Mass like we did in Poissy?'

'Similar, but not exactly the same – that was a Requiem Mass, for the dead.'

'I don't really want to go to a Mass,' Debs went on. 'I'm only one who understands what they're saying, and I don't know what it's all about.'

'OK,' said Jose. 'But it would be the climax of the procession.'

Frances was adamant.

'In that case, we must go in.'

Debs frowned. She wasn't comfortable. Nathan came up with a solution.

'We'll do our own Mass,' he said. 'The twelfth ritual. Somewhere out on the hillside. I've got some bread and a bottle of wine in my rucksack that I brought for lunch.'

'Brilliant!' exclaimed Jose. 'We can come back afterwards and see the Black Virgin in her chapel.'

*Well done, Nathan,* thought Frances, *you've just earned the Jose 'brilliant' award for July.* Loath as she was to desert the Madonna, she could see that Mass in the packed church would not be the kind of ending that would be appropriate for their pilgrimage journey with its small-scale rituals in lonely places.

'OK,' she said. 'But we'll come back later, won't we?'

Makeshift Mass. At least, the familiar Pagan ritual with bread and wine added. A sacred circle. The calling of the quarters and the spirits of the mountains. An altar constructed from leaves and branches from hillside bushes...

They reflected on it afterwards, sitting in the sunshine and finishing the bread and wine as lunch along with the locally produced St Nectaire cheese and some peaches.

'We've done our own Mass! What would the Pope have thought, or the good Catholics in the chapel just a few hundred yards away?'

'Blasphemy!'

'It were a Pagan Mass really, if there can be such a thing. Not a Black Mass, that's more of a Satanist thing, where you say everything backwards – sounds hard to do!'

'Maybe a Black Mass would have been appropriate for a Black Virgin.'

'There's no doubt we had the best view.'

'Yeah, it did seem a bit crazy to cram into a small building on a warm day with mountains all around.'

'I really like it when we offer bread and wine; after all, they're Nature's gift to us.'

'Debs is turning into a Catholic. I always knew that's what she was secretly.'

'Yeah, maybe I'm a Catholic witch.'

'Interesting idea. Broomsticks, cassocks and incense. Frances, you seem a bit down. Is it something to do with the apparition you had?'

'I'm really confused. I saw Goddess in that room again. She were beautiful but, as usual, I couldn't make her face out. I said,

"This is the twelfth vision." She said, "It's not complete yet, Frances. You haven't finished." I said, "Do you mean that we have to do more rituals?" She just said, "You need Notre Dame de Zion." Then it were over. It seemed like a strange end to the visions. So it can't be, can it? There must be more to come.'

The visionary was then seen to have a tear running down her cheek. Debs put an arm round her. All the excitement, then anticlimax. This was going to be the big day. She was like a little girl who turned up to the party only to find out that it had been postponed.

They returned to the chapel to see the Black Madonna on a high pedestal behind the altar of the church; several people were still milling about, some praying before the bright bank of candles. Frances sat down to pray too. She needed some guidance. She decided that it would take some time and stayed for several minutes.

'She looks more pious than most o' people here,' Debs whispered to the men.

Nathan nodded but Jose hadn't heard. He had gone into 'mystery solving' mode. As someone with a fair deal of knowledge about the world of symbols and religious images, he felt that the Goddess was merely giving them a stimulating challenge rather than letting them down.

As they went back down the hillside to Besse in a minibus organised for the occasion, he turned into a cross between Miss Marple and Sherlock Holmes.

'Let's think about this. We did twelve rituals. Why? Well, because of Frances' dream. She saw twelve crescent moons. But did you see twelve, Frances? Or did you *think* you did?... Right, you thought you did, then we decided that because there were twelve months in a year, that was right. OK, let's think about that...'

Jose was enjoying this. He even started wagging his right index finger like a master detective in deep thought. Frances sighed.

'I don't know what to think.'

It was beyond her. She looked out at the mountain tops to see if any inspiration would come from there. After a period of a few minutes in contemplation, Jose continued.

'Well, of course, there are *not* twelve cycles of the moon in a year. There are twelve and a third. To be precise, 12.37. Although twelve was a sacred number for many ancient cultures, including the Jews, they knew that the lunar cycle was a bigger number than twelve. I recently read about an example in the New Testament. Twelve was an important number for the Jews: twelve tribes, twelve months, etc., and they used the number 144 to represent a great number, as it is 12 times 12. However, after the resurrection of Jesus, there's a story about the catching of – not 144 – but 153 fish in a net all at the same time. This must have been a symbol: the net was absolutely full because of the miracle of the resurrection. The 153 fish represent the souls that would be saved by it; in other words, a great number, not literally 153. But why are 153 fish representing the great number, not 144? Well, 153 is 12.37 times 12.37: the lunar cycle. So, in this story, they used the precise number for the lunar cycle, 12.37, rather than the approximate one, 12.'

Debs and Frances looked at one another and shrugged. Nathan was impatient.

'OK, interesting, but cut to the chase! What does it mean?'

'It means...' replied Jose, pausing, as if about to reveal the murderer, 'It means that we have to do one more ritual so that we include the full twelve and a third. Frances thought she saw twelve; in a dream, it would be difficult to get a sense of twelve and a third. But she said it herself, it was the number of moons in a year that was the crucial thing.'

Nathan was trying to turn Jose's mystical ranting into something simpler.

'Fine. What you mean is we do a thirteenth ritual. We've got three more days here. So that's no problem.'

'But there *is* a problem,' Jose continued. 'We have to do the ritual at the shrine of Notre Dame de Zion. That's what the vision implies. All of our rituals have been at shrines of the Madonna, starting with Notre Dame de Le Puy...'

'Notre Dame *du* Puy,' interrupted Debs. Sherlock wasn't very good at French.

'Yes, *du* Puy,' agreed Jose. 'Then Saugues, Estours, etc. etc., up until today at Notre Dame de Vassivière.'

'Good,' said Nathan. 'So we just have to do the thirteenth ritual at the shrine of Notre Dame de Zion.'

'That's all very well,' replied Jose. 'But I checked the internet via my phone when I could get a signal. There's no such shrine, certainly not in the Auvergne. We've been sent to a sanctuary that doesn't exist.'

# 40

# Notre Dame de Zion

'What exactly did she say about Zion?'
Jose was interrogating a tired and rather deflated Frances as they sat over another *galette* with salad in Besse that evening.

'You need Notre Dame de Zion.'

'Zion as in Jerusalem, or Zion as in *The Matrix*? Or maybe as in the Prieuré de Sion from *The Holy Blood and the Holy Grail*?'

'No, don't let's go down that bestseller mysteries road,' said Debs, raising her eyebrows. 'I didn't know we were chasing Grail. Spare us that hocus pocus.'

'Yes, the Zion in Jerusalem, I suppose,' replied Frances, a bit put out but at the same time thinking that the Ace of Cups might represent the Grail, maybe. 'But no, not like all those sensationalist books.'

'It is a mystery, though,' reflected Jose. 'Tell me, do you think that Notre Dame de Zion is in the Auvergne?'

'I think so.'

'It's just that there *is* a shrine called Notre Dame de Sion in Lorraine, another region of France. Mind you, that Sion is not named after Zion as in Jerusalem. It has a different derivation. Anyway, going to Lorraine would take us several hours by road, and then we'd have to come back south to take the car in and catch the train. There's also a Sion over near the Atlantic coast, again a long drive.'

Debs looked very sceptical. Driving all over France to save the environment? However, Frances said the right thing.

'No, I'm sure we're supposed to stay here.'

'Not anything to do with Israelis who want to claim the biblical lands from the Palestinians?' wondered Nathan, a minute or two behind the conversation. 'Not *Zionism*?'

'No, definitely not that,' answered Frances. 'I don't know what. Just Notre Dame de Zion, that's all.'

'What does Notre Dame de Zion look like?' asked Jose, still playing the super-sleuth. 'Is she black?'

'Don't know,' replied Frances. 'I think she's really interesting though. I just feel it. It could be another name for Goddess.'

'Right, we need to find out by Friday, our last day, don't we?' said Jose. 'I can't seem to find anything meaningful via the phone. Tomorrow, I'll scoot down to the library in Clermont-Ferrand. It's not far. I can read some French if I go slowly.'

The next day, all the adventurers went to Clermont-Ferrand, the largest city in the Auvergne with its busy centre, residential suburbs, factories and an airport. After the customary urban struggle to find a car parking space near the centre, Jose disappeared off to find the library, armed with a French dictionary. Frances, Debs and Nathan wandered around shops; had lattés and pastries in a café, sitting *al fresco* as was normal in the pedestrian precincts of the French city; looked at an exhibition of photos of the area in the Tourist Information Office; went to the Cathedral and to the Romanesque basilica of Notre Dame du Port in both of which they found several more Madonnas. Frances noted how Debs and Nathan were now careful to be attentive to her feelings at every turn; this worried her somewhat. Was she giving off signals that she was especially vulnerable at the moment? True, she was feeling quite emotional but she was desperately trying to hide it. She attempted to appear on top of things by engaging Debs in a conversation about their future partnership. Maybe Nathan would like to hear about it. It started well.

'Debs, what do you see yourself doing as part of our little venture when we get home – you know, the one we talked about by the Alagnon?'

'Yeah, I'm keen! Let's set up summat very soon. We can advertise ourselves as Tarot readers and creators o' rituals for people. We can do baby namings, handfastings, maybe even burials. I've got a friend who can do a website for us.'

'Sounds great!' exclaimed Nathan. 'I can spread the word at the University.'

'How many hours a week could you spend on it, do you think?' Frances asked Debs.

And then it lost a little of its momentum suddenly.

'Well, not as much as you, maybe one day a month over weekend,' replied Debs. 'We can have a diary and book people in.'

'Oh,' exclaimed Frances. 'That isn't as much as I were maybe expecting.'

'Well, it's just that... you see,' stuttered Debs; she was clearly about to make an announcement. Then she let it out, all in a rush. 'I've decided to do a part-time degree. Women's Studies. Put a bit o' theory behind my job. I could get some funding from Council.'

'Wow,' said Frances, trying to sound pleased and simultaneously suppress the disappointment that her new partner was going to take on a very large distraction from their work. 'That's sudden.'

'I've been thinking about it for some time,' Debs continued. 'You've both got degrees, haven't you?'

'After a fashion,' replied Nathan, reflecting on his undistinguished academic career.

'Well, I'm sure it meant *summat* to you,' Debs said with a smile. 'Jose hasn't got one but he's so full o' facts that he might as well have. He's worth ten University graduates.'

'That's true,' agreed Nathan. 'I know the other nine personally and, like me, they're not very bright.'

'Ha ha,' laughed Debs, clearly now in a relaxed mood. 'But you see, I think it's *my* turn. When I were eighteen, I were in such a mess that University degrees belonged to Never-Never Land. Now I need to prove that it can come true for me. It's like the last piece o' jigsaw.'

'I understand,' said Frances, picking herself up a little. 'Anyway, I'm sure you can do both.'

'Certainly can,' agreed Debs, patting her encouragingly on the arm.

The rendezvous with Jose had been set for 3 p.m. in the square by the Cathedral. Unusually for a holiday meeting, they and he were there bang on time, each sensing that ritual matters were at a crucial stage. A bar with a great host of outside tables under parasols provided seats and coffee.

'Have you worked it out, maestro?' asked Nathan, grinning as he remembered the comment about Jose and the ten graduates.

'I think so,' replied his companion, predictably.

'Where is Notre Dame de Zion, then?' asked Frances. 'Maybe here in a little church off a side street?'

'Yes, here,' Jose stated, looking at her intently, enjoying his air of mystery. 'But not in a little church.'

'Wow, in Clermont itself! But where, exactly?' Frances couldn't stop herself looking round the square, wondering in which direction the shrine would be.

Jose didn't answer immediately. He was going to milk this one for a few moments more.

'Zion...,' he said eventually, interrupted by the newly arrived coffee, '...is the most famous of the hills on which Jerusalem is built. It was so important to the Jews of pre-Christian times that sometimes they referred to the whole city as "Zion". Because of this, it gained a kind of mystical reputation, the most holy mountain in the world. It's where the crusaders built a great abbey and so its reputation comes down from the ancient world through the medieval period too.'

'And as I said this morning,' added Nathan. 'It gave its name to the modern Israeli programme of re-conquering the Holy Land, i.e. Zionism.'

'Yes, true,' replied Jose. 'The crusades aren't over yet, it seems. So it's a mystical centre in both Judaism and Christianity. Both faiths have, in their time, planned to recapture the land from the Muslims, for whom Jerusalem is holy too. Zion is much desired and has been fought over. Hence there is the belief that "Zion" represents something very sacred, which might hold the key to the future of western spirituality.'

'However,' interrupted Frances, wanting to get the Goddess back on the agenda. 'We're looking for a Madonna, aren't we, *Notre Dame* de Zion.'

'Absolutely,' agreed Jose. 'But let me continue. You might want to know that Zion was important to the Jews because it was a fortified hill. Jerusalem is in the mountains, a strategic site difficult to conquer. Before the really powerful empires came along, the Jews did have some success in defending it. So "Zion" is also associated with "fortress".'

'Right,' said Debs, keen to get into the conversation and confirm that she had the ability to discuss things like any graduate. 'So Notre Dame de Zion might represent the Goddess defending something that's very important and sacred. Like the environment, for example.'

'You might have something there.' Jose sipped his coffee. 'But let me go one step further. According to the literature, the word "Zion" does have an original meaning. As far as scholars can make out, it comes from a root meaning "dry or parched place".'

'That doesn't sound very positive,' commented Nathan. 'Was it in the desert?'

Jose was still very much relishing his role as the one who solved riddles.

'Well, not strictly, although Jerusalem is a hot dusty place not far from desert areas. The dryness of Zion may have had a more positive meaning, in that the Jews of ancient Israel equated the sea with chaos and so a dry place would have been a refuge from the waters, which symbolised the mess of life, the dangers of the world out there. For the Jews, foreign conquest of their land and cultural contamination were terrible to contemplate; Zion was intended to be a refuge, according to the Hebrew Scriptures.'

At this point, Jose breathed in deeply; clearly, he had reached the climax of his little lecture.

'Come on!' urged Nathan, tired of the dramatic effects.

Jose obliged.

'OK. So, for "Zion", we have "fortress" and "dry place". Let me turn that around and play with those words as if we had a crossword puzzle. What is a fortified town in good old Anglo-Saxon? Well, it's the origin of many place names: "burg". So two and two making five, we have "dry burg" which becomes "dry borough" in later English – have you heard that before?'

Frances looked astounded. She hadn't seen this coming.

'Well, it's my surname, of course,' she stammered.

'Yes, it is,' said Jose; the *coup de grâce* was about to be delivered. 'Your surname is English for "Zion". It all comes back to you, the visionary herself. I can only conclude that you, Frances, are the person indicated by the expression "Notre Dame de Zion". Frances Dryburgh is synonymous with Frances Zion. You asked me if Notre Dame de Zion was here in Clermont-Ferrand and I say, yes, right here drinking a cup of coffee.'

Debs almost choked. Nathan just kept saying, 'Crikey'. Jose looked smug. Frances stared back at him.

'Don't tease me,' she implored him. 'You know I can't be Notre Dame de Zion, whatever my name is. I'm not the Madonna. I'm not the Goddess.'

But Jose didn't budge.

'All I can offer you by way of explanation is that, in modern Goddess worship as far as I see it, the point is that there is no longer the great distance between deity and humanity as in traditional religions. You *are* the Goddess, so are other women, so is Debs, so even are men like Nathan and me. Maybe that's the lesson of the play on words: Notre Dame de Zion. Notre Dame de Dryburgh. You and the Goddess are one.'

Debs had recovered, although there remained a coffee stain on her white vest.

'Jose's right,' she agreed. 'We shouldn't worship a Goddess above us and too great for us to imagine. Goddess is in nature and in human beings. She shows us what we can be. In that sense, yes, Frances, you *are* Notre Dame de Zion.'

'I go along with that,' agreed Nathan. 'But it doesn't help us locate the shrine where we are supposed to hold our thirteenth ritual.'

'I've been thinking about that,' replied Jose. 'It seems to me that it doesn't matter. As long as Frances herself is present, we *will* be at the shrine of Notre Dame de Zion. So perhaps we should let Frances choose the location and hold the ritual there tomorrow, on our last day in the Auvergne.'

Frances could hardly get a word out in response to all this. She was still trying to take it in. *My awful name, 'Dryburgh', that kids used to mock? Miss Dryfanny? The name that made me feel like I were boring and lacking personality? It means 'Zion'? It means summat great, summat spiritual, summat mystical? I can't believe it. It's fantastic. What else can happen in this dragon country?*

She finally composed herself and tried to regain control of the situation.

'OK, so I've got to choose the place,' she said. 'Have you finished your coffee?'

They had.

'Come with me,' she ordered, grandly. 'This way.'

*If I'm Notre Dame de Zion, I might as well behave like it. I'm Queen Alice; the pawn has got to the end of the board and been crowned. Or maybe it were a queen all along.* She led them towards the front of the great blackened gothic cathedral on one side of the square, to the west end with its tall twin spires. They stood on the steep steps leading up to the west door. Frances pointed away from the cathedral. Opposite the door was a long pedestrian street, lined with small shops. Signs indicating a 'Patisserie' or a 'Salon de Thé' could be seen protruding out, hanging invitingly above the shoppers. There were book shops, gift shops, food shops. Above hung lines of bunting, alternate blue and yellow triangular pennants. Yet Frances was looking way beyond into the distance. Framed between the buildings on the two sides of the street, several miles from the city, was the great pudding shape of a volcanic mountain. It dominated the peaks around it and, from Clermont-Ferrand, it was a distinctive and unmistakable landmark. The Puy de Dôme.

'Up there,' she announced. 'On the volcano. It's the nearest thing we have to Mount Zion. That's where we'll have our thirteenth ritual.'

## 41

## The Temple of Mercury

A night with interrupted sleep followed for Frances. Her mind would not stop racing, ideas flowing back and forth. She was thrilled by Jose's revelation in Clermont-Ferrand. It was as if her whole life now made sense. It had an inner purpose that linked her to the very core of the greatest spiritual mysteries. She was not just plain Miss Dryburgh. She was Notre Dame de Zion! She had a destiny, which would soon become clearer both to her and everyone else. The night air seemed enchanted, full of near-visible dancing imps whose task it was to keep her awake. When she found herself still in that wide-eyed manic state at 4 a.m., she tried to feel the presence of the Goddess around her in the same way as she did during the visions. *Why can't I speak to you like that now? OK, you're probably silently speaking and telling me that I can, actually...* Suddenly, 8.30. She woke with a start. That calculation familiar to all poor sleepers followed: *How long were I under? I don't feel great. But then, I'm Notre Dame de Zion, think on that. I can put up with a bit o' tiredness! And today we're going to Puy de Dôme!*

The Puy de Dôme, from afar, was a mountain that suggested a great mystery, the lonely peak set a good deal higher than its volcanic neighbours – the capital of Dragon Country, the Mount Zion of the supernaturally charged Auvergne. It wooed and invited the adventurers onto its slopes; seeing it from a distance, they longed to climb to its summit and breathe in the rarefied spiritual air. There was a discussion at breakfast about mountains as sacred places. Jose suggested Sinai, where Moses met God, as an example; Nathan contributed the site of the rendezvous with aliens in *Close Encounters of the Third Kind*. 'Encounter' seemed the right word as, in such a location, surely one could not help but come face to face with deity. Although Debs disliked any notion that God was 'up there', she too agreed that prominent peaks had a kind of symbolic quality, promising to be sites of strange and wonderful experiences. The lonely pilgrim faced the terrors of the wild, the dangers of the climb and the ravages of the cold, wind and rain, as she or he ascended to the awe-inspiring heights, that is, if the gods and spirits deigned to allow her or him within the holy boundaries. If they did not, she or he might be overcome by the weather or fall to a tragic doom. But it was worth the risk. Great spiritual rewards were available to the one who left the madding crowd and roamed, staff in hand, towards the hostile terrain of the mountain top.

However, closer at hand, all these notions turned out to be overly romantic and quite inaccurate in the case of the Puy de Dôme. It turned out to be a sacred mountain that the madding crowd quite enjoyed visiting too. Tourists, hikers, dog walkers, hang-glider pilots, parascenders all made their way to the summit. Visitors had to park their cars at the foot and go up by minibus – in French, the *navette* – unless they fancied the daunting walk up the footpaths, the Puy de Dôme rising sharply and majestically from the surrounding wooded country. There was a discussion about making the journey on foot – in favour, one (Nathan); against, three (Frances, Debs, Jose). Motion defeated; the *navette* it was, then. Frances sat in the rather cramped space of a window seat next to Debs, the sun particularly hot through the glass and the diesel fumes caused by the motor running while stationary making her feel slightly queasy. *Not environmentally friendly. Diesel smell's not very sacred.* She reflected on the disparity between the wonderful ideal and the mundane reality of pilgrimage and had to battle to maintain the excitement that she had been feeling about her moment of destiny. It was so easy to get irritated with entrance fees; crowded minibuses; fumes; people talking rather loudly nearby; a child that didn't want to stay in his seat; Debs yawning widely without covering her mouth. Why was this great journey so compromised with all the more dreary aspects of communal human existence? Then an insight popped up among her whirling thoughts that made her smile with pleasure. *My name 'Dryburgh' is dull and ordinary too, in't it? Yet it hides an amazing secret: it really means 'Zion'. Perhaps this tortuous minibus trip up mountain is also just a surface appearance. The whole event is wonderful and spiritual beneath. So sit back and enjoy it!*

The *navette* wound its way up the road coiled around the mountain cone. The first views were towards the south, where the peaks towards the Puy de Sancy made jagged the horizon. The Puy de Dôme was one of the chain of volcanoes running north to south, the backbone of the Auvergne. The vista rotated to the west, undulating hilly tracts of countryside going goodness-knows-where into the distance. Then the north, where nearby volcanoes stood, distinctive crater tops filled with grass-topped earth and rock. Finally, the road swung round to the east affording a panoramic view of Clermont-Ferrand, the city stretching out across the plain through which the Allier flowed, its dark hilltop cathedral clearly identifiable. The summit of the Puy de Dôme was adorned, not with a volcanic crater, but with a more conventional mountain peak on which stood a transmitting station with a tall mast, standing high like a great white syringe pointing into the air as if injecting radio waves into the atmosphere or awaiting take-off like a rocket. The *navette* came to a stop in a turning area on a plateau several tens of yards below the peak, next to an expansive building which turned out to be a restaurant and visitor centre. As they got out of the vehicle, Frances felt the mountain winds flow around her, taking away the worst of the heat of the sun. Being on the Puy de Dôme was like standing on a miniature version of Everest, as it dwarfed the surrounding terrain, the roof of its neighbourhood. The mountain top was busy with people enjoying the view and the thrill of looking down on the world. Around the plateau, hang-gliders hovered in the air; it was a perfect launching pad for the sport with nothing around to impede free movement.

'What's that?' Frances asked Jose, pointing at the outline of a ruined building a little way below the transmitter.

'It's the ancient Temple of Mercury,' he replied, well informed as ever. 'From the Roman period. They're doing some archaeological work on it, I believe.'

'Wow!' exclaimed Nathan. 'So this was a sacred site going right back.'

'Yes,' replied Jose. 'The Puy de Dôme is a perfect place for it, don't you think?'

As they walked up towards the stones of the ruin, Jose was clearly deep in thought. When they reached it, he shared his reflections with them, the delivery passionate and engaging like a TV presenter on location. *What'd he do without us,* wondered Frances. *He needs a group o' listeners!*

'It's amazing when you think about it,' he proclaimed. 'We think that Mercury was a god of ancient times, no longer relevant. Those ruins there are to do with something gone forever, a site of worship long forgotten. Yet look at the transmitter. Is that not the modern rebuilding of the Temple of Mercury, the god of communication, the messenger of the gods? He receives devotion and adulation today far more than anything offered him in Roman times. Communication systems are the very hub of our society: television, telephones, the internet. We hold them in such great esteem; we cannot do without knowing what is happening on the other side of the world, sharing news, ideas, entertainment. Hail Mercury! Of course, he's also the prince of tricksters and thieves. Our modern communication industry is a testimony to his skill in deception. We don't know whether things on screen are actually as they seem; we get persuaded to buy products because we are fooled into thinking we need them; we have to beware of scams and viruses in our e-mails, of websites that plant listening devices into our computers.'

Debs turned to Jose with a grin and broke into song.

'You're so right, you're so very, very right, you're the rightest person in the world!'

Frances was struck dumb for a moment. Hearing her own little piece of silliness – that she assumed to have been disregarded by her more serious friend – warmed her heart. She started to laugh out loud, Debs soon joining in. Nathan tried to look disapproving but couldn't suppress a smile. He then rescued the disconcerted Jose.

'You're right. The old gods describe forces that are still very powerful in our world of the twenty-first century. Mars loves warfare; he gets his own way pretty well, doesn't he? Aphrodite, love and sexuality – need I say more?'

As they stood together looking over the stonework that formed the outline of the ancient temple, Frances voiced a concern that was nagging her.

'There's too many people up here for a ritual. It'll more difficult than anywhere we've been, even centre o' Le Puy.'

'Yes,' agreed Nathan. 'Maybe we could walk to another one of the volcanoes; look down there, you can see the crater and everything. What a brilliant place for a ritual!'

'It doesn't look easy to get there,' countered Jose. 'Too difficult for me and my bad legs, and I don't think Debs and Frances love long difficult walks, do they?'

'Maybe it'll get quieter here when evening comes,' suggested Frances.

'True, but if we leave it too late, we might have to walk back down,' said Nathan.

'I could live with that,' replied Jose. 'But if we went to another volcano, it would be climbing down *and* walking a distance.'

It was decided unanimously. They would wait for evening and the reduction of the numbers of people at the top of the mountain. They would take their chance with the availability of the *navettes* and go down on foot if necessary. Anyway, the Puy de Dôme was not a bad place to spend the last day: a magnificent view and pleasant in the sunshine without being too overwhelmingly hot. A day for lying on some patch of grass and reading novels; somebody could take a turn with *Before Completion*. Reading material and food sufficient for the day, plus some plastic raincoats for lying on, had been placed with forethought in Nathan's rucksack. Frances was prepared to wait. The thirteenth ritual with its much anticipated vision could be the climax and ending of the holiday, on its final evening. But she could not fight off anxieties that honed in on her like incoming bombers on a radar screen and which had to be picked off one by one. *What if I'm wrong about Nathan? He's given no clue that he's about to make a move. Well, he wouldn't, not with Debs and Jose around and rituals still happening. He probably thinks he mustn't disturb me while I complete this great task. What'll I do after visions have finished? Will there be more? Will I go on having 'em throughout my life?*

'Penny for your thoughts,' called Nathan, lying on his stomach a few feet away, having noticed that Frances was not reading a single word of her book.

'It'll cost you more than that. They're a special and rare collection, my thoughts.'

'Perhaps I could just take some on loan and see what I think of them,' he went on.

'No, we don't allow 'em out o' library; *you* should know that, seeing as you work in one.'

'OK then, I'll just photocopy one or two for personal use.'

'Fine, here you are then. One, Nathan's a git; two, he's round bend, hanging about wi' women who have visions.'

'Shut up, you two!' pleaded Debs, taking her iPod earpiece out. 'You're giving me earache, I can even hear you through headphones.'

Frances laughed. She scrambled to her feet.

'I can't relax. I'm going to walk round that visitor centre.'

She knew that it wouldn't really interest her – history, archaeology, all that kind of thing. *There'll be nowt about spirit of the place.* Nothing of winged Mercury hovering invisibly above the mountain, laughing capriciously like a James Bond villain as he contemplated his victory over all the other gods. Nothing of the dragons who stalked the land of volcanoes, taking heed of nothing and nobody until, one day, they were tamed by a passing Virgin. Nothing of Mount Zion and its ancient and enduring mysteries, with no one, not even the secret societies in certain famous novels, realising that Frances herself was the person to whom they all pointed. What kind of visitor centre would include that sort of information? She grinned to herself about finding three exhibits as she went in: Mercury, a Black Madonna confronting a dragon, and herself. *That would be an interesting display, wouldn't it? I could go up to an attendant and say: Hello, I'm Notre Dame de Zion, whose image you have on your wall there. Bien sûr, madame!*

After a whistle-stop tour round the centre, which included buying an ice cream in the restaurant, Frances re-emerged to go for a walk around the mountain summit. It was clearly circumnavigable, with people disappearing off and others emerging all the time on the paths that wound around it. And then, as she meandered about, watching the hang-gliders, avoiding the dog walkers and enjoying the high cooling breezes that swirled round the peak, she saw something for which there had to be a perfectly rational explanation. She stiffened when she saw it, and she was anxious for a few seconds before she realised that there had to be a perfectly rational explanation. Clearly he was just comforting his friend as she fretted about some problem or another. Perhaps she had stumbled and needed support. After all, he was a sympathetic man who didn't mind physical contact with his friends when they needed it, wasn't he? She knew that. Yes, indeed there had to be a perfectly rational explanation, so it wasn't worth getting overwrought about it. The promise was hers alone and it would be untrusting of the Goddess to think anything else. So she didn't need to be too taken aback by the sight of Nathan and Debs – who had wandered away from Jose round to the far side of the mountain to survey the view to the north with its intriguing volcanic craters – standing together hand in hand.

## 42

## Twin Sisters

Guided by some instinct, Debs turned round soon after Frances saw her. She smiled, let go of Nathan's hand and beckoned Frances to join them.

'You OK?' asked Frances as she approached.

'Yeah,' replied Debs, matter-of-factly. 'Just enjoying amazing view. Look at them volcanoes. It's like a fictional country. Beats Almscliffe Crag, anyway.'

*Fine, she's not sharing her problem, that's OK. Nathan's dealing with it.*

'We must come back here,' said Nathan, suddenly.

'Where, to Puy de Dôme?' asked Debs.

'Well, maybe, but I was meaning the Auvergne as a whole. There must be so many wonderful little places we haven't discovered yet: river valleys, old chapels, hilltop views. I'd like to hike across it instead of driving. I think I've sort of fallen in love with the region. I never fully appreciated countryside, food, culture and a foreign people until this holiday. The sights, tastes and smells. The guide book said that the people of the rural Auvergne were taciturn, but I've found them so hospitable and friendly.'

Frances and Debs winked at each other. Frances felt a warm flush surging through her. *Nathan finally falling in love wi' summat! That's a good sign. He's opening his heart at last. What a character he is. I really love him. Ace o' Cups is overflowing.*

The evening came on and the Puy de Dôme gradually became quieter. The sight of the setting sun from such a high vantage point was a wonder, red sky in the west, dark blue in the east. The few light clouds streaked across the heavens in sharp, angular shapes, like giant quill pens. The artwork they created with their random arrangements was unlikely to be matched by anything produced by a human designer. There was little sound on the summit except for the constant but gentle rustling of the breeze. And so the adventurers began to prepare for the thirteenth ritual, staying on the north side away from any continuing activity at the coach stop and heritage centre. They approached it with a solemnity that they had not managed to conjure up at Vassivière, despite the fact that they had thought that occasion to be the last. It was as if each had known in their hearts that one more was to come, one final rite to complete the journey they had made through the Auvergne. The panorama from Puy de Dôme was more open and far-ranging than that from Vassivière and, although the shrines were not actually in sight, it gave an impression that they could view back in time across the three weeks, back to Le Puy; Saugues; Estours; Chazes; Entremont; Vauclair; the chapel of the Madeleine high above Massiac; Laurie; St Gervazy; Ronzières; Orcival; Vassivière. Frances felt that there was something about the shrines collected together that felt like a full experience in which no one location could be omitted, each part contributing to the whole. The fullness of twelve: a clock, a zodiac, a calendar, the tribes of Israel, a Last Supper table surrounded by disciples. And yet, the thirteenth provided the crown, the centre of the circle of twelve. It was Christ in the midst of the apostles, breaking the bread.

They stood apart in a wide ring, then Debs left it to draw a wider circle around them: the sacred circle. She had found a long twig with which to inscribe lightly into the grass-covered clay of the mountain top. Then they called the spirits of the quarters. Frances felt that the whole earth was responding as she peered across the great distances still visible to her. Her imagination began to work overtime as she carried through her determination to live every moment of the adventure's climax. The spirits of the east dragged a dark curtain with them as the bringers of night, as blue turned to black across the plains of the Allier. The lights of Clermont shone more brightly, paralleled above by the emergence of a myriad stars joined by the planet Jupiter rising above the horizon, a minor king triumphant with the temporary waning of the dynasty of the emperor Sun. The spirits of the north leapt out of the now shadowy volcanoes, earth daemons linking the windy heights with the red hot depths of the earth's core. Molten lava had been absent there for many centuries, but it was present in spirit as it poured into the sacred circle, the Goddess' gift of warmth and inspiration. From the west came spirits of light from the departed Sun, sending its messengers to remind the world that it still ruled from just around the horizon's corner. In the south, the peak blocked out the view, but there stood the great transmitter. The spirits of the south were the agents of Mercury, blending in with the invisible but all-pervasive waves of radio communication, genii extending their reach across great swathes of space, land and sea. By the time the quarters had been called, Frances' consciousness had melted into a trance kingdom of faerie folk, milling all around the mountain top in an array of colours and energy patterns. She revelled in their dancing around her like the little people of so many traditional folk tales. They were celebrating because *she* was coming. The Goddess. It was the sacred moment, her advent into the circle...

From the horizons of east, north, west and south she approached, flying regally through the air: four goddesses. From the east, she appeared as majestic Isis with the horned helmet; from the north, Mary Magdalene of the dark hair and red cloak;

from the west, the golden-hooded lady of Almscliffe holding a lion by its mane; from the south, a mighty winged angel, a female Mercury hanging in the air above the aerial. They all merged into one shimmering being on the mountain peak. Frances was taken up by invisible hands so that she seemed to be alone with only the Goddess present, who became once again the shining lady of the room behind the old door, the Madonna on the throne, constantly shifting in appearance, so difficult to focus eyes upon.

'Frances, tonight, I'm going to show you my face.'

'Yes, I want to see you more clearly. You're so beautiful.'

'You'll soon see how beautiful.'

Gradually, the many transformations began to slow down and the colours of the cloak settled into a radiant gold, the hair a soft light brown under a garland of many flowers. The Goddess turned her head away and then back, in gentle, graceful movements, the fine strands of hair swirling. Finally, her face could be seen clearly and distinctly, strong eyes looking straight into Frances' own. The encounter was fully realised and it was overwhelming. Frances gasped.

'I don't believe it, I really don't believe it, how can it be true?'

She was staring as if into a mirror. The visage reflected back to her was her own. The red-brown suntan, the freckles on the bridge of the nose, the cheeky smile. She realised that the voice too was her own right down to the intonations of the Leeds accent. Heart-shatteringly familiar, yet there was a poise and dignity that Frances did not recognise in herself. The Goddess Self revealed her identity.

'I'm Notre Dame de Zion.'

'Yes I see. Notre Dame de Zion. You're me.'

'I'm you and I'm not you.'

Somehow Frances understood without there being any speech communication between them. She sighed.

'It's incredible. Frances Dryburgh and Notre Dame de Zion.'

'Yes, and we love each other intensely like twin sisters and sometimes hate each other too.'

'I'll never hate you. I love you, absolutely love you.'

The Frances Goddess smiled, so tenderly that it was almost more difficult to stand than the great Earth vision of Massiac. Then she spoke one last sentence.

'It's done, Frances. The thirteen rituals. They're complete.'

Frances suddenly became aware of the faerie beings around her, gathering around like small bundles of light. They lifted the golden Frances Goddess into the sky. She swiftly grew in size to become a giant gowned lady hovering above the Puy de Dôme; she filled the sky, the stars shining through her cloak. Her golden dress turned dark blue; then, for an instant, she transformed herself into the great sphere of the Earth. Finally, she was gone...

'Don't go,' whispered Frances. 'Don't let that be the last time.'

And then she found that she was saying it to Nathan, supporting her as she found herself back down on the grassy northern slope of the volcano.

'Did she say anything about the G8 summit?' asked Jose, with urgency, while Frances was still coming round.

'Just that rituals were complete. You don't suppose I'll never see her again, do you? It were so brilliant. And she were... were *me*!'

'What do you mean, she were you?' demanded Debs.

'She looked like me, I mean. Notre Dame de Zion. That's me... and her!'

'I always knew you were a Goddess,' Nathan teased her.

'Well, not quite. She said she were me and not me.'

'Explain?' inquired Debs; they were all very keen to find out every last detail of the vision tonight.

'Well, it's like this, I think. If I were exactly like her then I'd have nothing to aspire to. Goddess would just be me with all my worries and weaknesses. I need her to be strong. If she were beyond my reach, completely different like maybe God is in most religions, then it wouldn't be worth me making the effort to change my life. I'd just wait for Goddess to do it. That's no good either. So she's close to being me, but she's still greater than who I am now; she's what I can become.'

'Well, I seem to remember, at Avebury, people saying that you looked like the Goddess when you were in the trance,' said Nathan.

'And when they did, I said you were like Bernadette of Lourdes, whose trances were so powerful that she attracted thousands to watch her and convinced the most sceptical of onlookers,' added Jose. He looked at Debs, who didn't like linking Goddess spirituality to Catholics and nuns but, fortunately, she was in too good a mood for an argument, so he continued. 'Bernadette is like you in another sense. She saw a figure of the same height and age as herself, of short stature and fourteen years old just as she was. It *was* herself, in an exalted sense. At first, the figure did not call herself Mary; she just spent time with Bernadette. On the strength of that, Bernadette turned from being an illiterate backward teenager to becoming one of the great saints of the nineteenth century. She corresponded with popes. Millions visit her shrine even today. Of course, the Catholic Church commandeered the experience; they made all the statues look older and more maternal and then sent Bernadette to the convent. Nevertheless, her story is still remarkable. She saw her potential self and the experience helped her express her powerful spirituality.'

'Where is Lourdes?' asked Frances, wondering whether it was close by.

'In France, in the Pyrenees, not the Auvergne,' replied Jose. 'Several hours' drive from here. But I bet that there have been many lesser known Bernadettes in the Auvergne over the centuries!'

The spirits were bid farewell and the sacred circle was closed. The spirits of the east had now gained the ascendancy, the sky almost completely dark and full of stars.

There was no moon to guide as it was only just past new. With Nathan leading the way, holding a torch, the adventurers found their way to the footpath winding back down the volcano. There was silence. The great journey was over and now the homecoming was about to start. The Auvergne would leave an indelible mark in each soul; like Wei Chi at her funeral, the whole holiday loomed larger than any single part of it now that it had come to an end. Driving the next day to Lyon, then taking the train back under the Channel would be like separating the opposite poles of two magnets; it would be a wrench and the heart would oppose it. While the lights of Clermont-Ferrand dominated the eastern view, it was the city of Leeds that was now re-emergent in the reflections of the four ritual-makers who trudged quietly down the mountainside, down from the sacred temple of the great Mercury, whose kingdom never slept and whose dominance in the twenty-first century world was assured. Frances was lost in her thoughts about the thirteenth apparition. It was the one that had thrust its way into her gut more than any other, more deeply even than the great Earth vision of Massiac when Wei Chi fell to a liberating death. This was because the Puy de Dôme vision was the one in which she had been asked that most poignant of questions: who am I? The little girl, anxious and sensitive, looking for the approval of her father and craving greater strength in her mother? The young adult, caught up in a whirl of sexual attraction, music, fashion, dull jobs, keeping at bay the dark forces that lurked in the domain of the pleasure-seeker – but only just? The as yet unrealised woman of the future, hopefully a married mother and, at the same time, a priestess of the Goddess, someone who would grow in wisdom and share it with others? The elderly lady, peering nervously through the curtain, wondering why the world had changed so much but looking back contentedly over a busy life? Which of these most clearly identified Frances Dryburgh? She had seen her soul sister, Notre Dame de Zion, her twin full of light, and she wanted to be like her. How could she hate her? That part of the vision made no sense. *I'll be like you more and more as I grow older, that's my ambition,* thought Frances as finally they reached the car park at the base of the volcano. She took one last longing look over her shoulder at the great black mass above her. *I'm sure I'll be back. Wi' Nathan. Hiking across Auvergne and visiting Puy de Dôme again. Maybe one day we'll take some little ones up to enjoy view and they'll shout with excitement at hang-gliders. And I'll tell 'em: that's where your mum met Notre Dame de Zion. Where she came face to face with herself.*

## 43

## News

Good news and bad news. That's how Frances remembered the journey home. Leaving Besse-en-Chandesse at 8 a.m.; returning the car, unscratched, in Lyon; taking the train, changing at Lille and then St Pancras for King's Cross; arriving in Leeds Station around 9 p.m. on Saturday night; hiring a taxi for the short final leg home without thinking of doing anything other than going straight to bed. Good news and bad news. First, the good news. Surely the most important? The news that will affect so many people.

The good news came at Lille station in mid-afternoon. There was a TV in the departure lounge for the Eurostar train, with news on in English. They read the headline several times on the text rolling across the bottom of the screen, before the call came to board the train to St Pancras. 'G8 summit will tackle global environmental challenge...' The latest scientific research findings, it seemed, would galvanise the world's greatest polluting nations into pulling together for the sake of the human race and its future. Next week would surely see radical action. *For our grandchildren, so that they can visit the Auvergne and still see its beauty,* thought Frances. The verdant luxury of its river valleys; the abundance of its wooded gorges. The Dales, too. Puy de Dôme and Almscliffe. Frances' descendants would do rituals on them and enjoy the clean air.

'We did our bit, didn't we?' said Frances proudly, as they stared in rapt wonder at the newsreader. 'Thirteen rituals in three weeks.'

She nestled back in the waiting room chair, tired but content with her paper container full of coffee from the machine. She pushed off her shoes as if she had arrived home after a hard day, stretched out her bare legs and wiggled her toes. The departure lounge was cool despite the humid warmth of the early afternoon outside, but light with the rays of the sun invading through the windows at one end and spreading across the welcoming space of the interior.

'Yes, throughout the Auvergne, from one end to the other,' agreed Nathan.

'Well, there were areas of the Cantal region that we didn't…' Jose started to say before Nathan did some mock slapping to shut him up.

'Pedant! But we'll be back,' announced Nathan, having reasserted the right to speak. 'We'll come back next year to celebrate the anniversary.'

'You've done really well,' said Debs to Frances, adding seriousness to the general high spirits. 'For a few days, I thought visions might be doing you harm. I said so to Wei Chi but she thought it were OK. You came through that really well.'

'It were to do wi' Wei Chi dying,' replied Frances. 'I've had nowt to worry about since then.'

Not exactly the truth – she had experienced little moments of anxiety and strange feelings in her body, but she had suppressed them in her belief that it was all right now. Certainly the out and out panic of the first week had gone.

'I can't believe that when we were going in opposite direction, arriving in France, we'd never heard o' Wei Chi,' said Debs. 'Little did we know.'

Whenever new and life-changing things come unexpectedly, it's strange to remember the time of ignorance just before their arrival, Frances reflected. When crossing Paris to board the Lyon train, she had not met Wei Chi. Frances boarding the London St Pancras train at Lille was on a high. But Frances had not yet heard the bad news.

They told her as the train from King's Cross pulled out of Wakefield, just fifteen minutes from Leeds. They wanted to leave it in case it spoiled the holiday, they said. But they couldn't leave it any longer, they said. Hopefully, the fact that the rituals went so well and the summit was likely to be a success would make it easier, they said. It happened in Paris when they were there for Wei Chi's funeral, they said. Happened when they went off together but completely unexpected, they said, not at all planned. Frances was very important to them both, they said... He had known how much he respected Debs because of her life's struggle, he said. Couldn't believe how someone could come through such a childhood to be the amazing person she was, he said. But somehow in the Auvergne it finally turned into love, he said. Came from the blue and surprised him, but when he knew, he really knew, he said... Didn't think I could ever really love a man, she said. Everything that happened in my youth made me think that relationships weren't for me, she said. It's taken this long for me to really trust Nathan, she said. But when I did, I really did, she said... Could she forgive them, they asked? They were desperate to stay close friends, they said... Of course, she said. Good luck to you both, you deserve it, she said. I'm just a bit surprised, she said. Might take a little while to get used to it, she said... Yes, it's great news, Jose said. Two really good people getting together, he said... *I'm numb,* she thought. *Lucky for me that I am, because I mustn't cry until I'm on my own,* she thought. *I can't take it in,* she thought... Here we are at last, she said. I'll just get a taxi and see you all soon, it's been great, she said... Are you sure you want to be on your own tonight, they asked? Oh yes, no problem, she said. *God, yes, as soon as possible,* she thought. My own bed at last, she said. *To cry myself to sleep and hope I die before I wake up,* she thought. We'll all get together and have a photo evening, there are so many memories, they said. Yes, great, I think I've got some good ones, she said. *But none of you two doing the dirty on me in Paris,* she thought.

In the taxi, the tears came and they flowed unrelentingly. As it passed Hyde Park Corner, the memory of that evening in February: the first night out with Nathan and his unexpected companion. The relief when it turned out to be Debs, Debs of the wild hair, Debs of the fierce stare, plain Debs who couldn't possibly be a rival. Not a contender to be the lover of a drop-dead gorgeous man. Women like that couldn't hope to be any more than friends with drop-dead gorgeous men, could they? The irony! She had discounted Debs that evening. Like Nathan, she had then grown to respect Debs for who she was, finally grown to love her. But not like he was loving her now. *Surely he's got it wrong, hasn't he? He's gone a bit mad and he'll regret it in a few days time. Probably just felt sorry for her. He's too cold to fall in love, one o' them commitment dodgers.* Then she recalled how intense and sure he was when he said that 'he really knew'. More tears fell. She remembered how Debs had smartened herself up since Paris, seemed to be a different woman. More tears. Finally, she recollected that card reading by the river Alagnon with the Ace of Cups. 'One or both of us is going to get into summat interesting, no doubt about it!' Debs' words. She didn't let Frances draw another card for explanation. The Ace of Cups was for Debs alone, maybe she knew it then. Treachery by the Alagnon. *My friend, my future business partner, my betrayer!* It was not a cup, pentacle or stave that was on the cards right now but a sword. A sword in the back and through the heart! If she did a reading now, she knew she would see only swords.

The environmental issue got sidelined in her mind, washed away by the floods caused by the disaster in her heart. The wonderful vision on the Puy de Dôme, just twenty-fours hours ago, blown away in the night wind. Goddess, where was she?

Why did affairs of the heart always become dominant over things that should matter more? *I can't let this destroy me. There's too much other stuff happening. Maybe a little prayer before I go to bed. No, I need to sleep. Maybe I'll dream of a different ending to our holiday... Frances! Yes, Nathan? Frances, while Debs and Jose are dozing on the train, there's something I've got to tell you. I wanted to leave it in case it spoiled the holiday. But I couldn't leave it any longer. The fact that the rituals went so well and the summit is likely to be a success makes this a wonderful moment to tell you. It happened in Massiac when you looked so beautiful during your trance on the crag top by the Madeleine chapel. It happened when I caught you in my arms to stop you falling, and it was completely unexpected, not at all planned. I realised how important you were to me. I already knew how much I respected you because I knew you were special from the time I saw you. Couldn't believe how an ordinary young woman from the Leeds suburbs could be the amazing person you were. But somehow in France it finally turned into love. It came from the blue and surprised me but when I knew, I really knew. I knew, I really knew...*

*But I didn't know, Nathan. Maybe it were obvious wi' Debs glamming herself up and wi' you holding her hand on Puy de Dôme, but still I didn't know! Stupid, aren't I? Maybe if Debs had been beautiful, I'd have expected it, or if you'd only just met her. But she's near to being ugly and you've known her for years. Why did you wait till now, Nathan? Why not just before I met you in February? Then I wouldn't have fallen in love with you. And I did fall in love with you, Nathan! And I came to love Debs too. After only a few months. But how can I love you both now?*

Treachery by the Alagnon. She couldn't get that idea out of her mind. Debs, her partner in the great new plan, the soul mate with whom she had said goodbye to Wei Chi with a little ritual on the riverside. 'Women should gather to mourn when a woman passes.' Now she was mourning all right, mourning for the bright and innocent Frances full of love and hope, who had just passed away. She felt the Ace of Swords plunging right through her, she started to sob and she rushed to bed with a bottle of vodka in hand to make sure she fell asleep soon and stayed asleep. Treachery by the Alagnon... Stabbed by her sister... Wrong ending...

# 44

## Sun in Scorpio

Frances woke at 5 a.m. with a headache. The weather must have been in deepest empathy with her bitter tears of the night before, as she could hear the rain pounding on the window. It was clear that going straight back to sleep was not going to be an option. She tried focussing on anything other than Nathan and Debs. *Right. Let's get organised, take my mind off it. What shall I do today? Call Mum and Dad and ask 'em to bring Cass home. Then maybe some Sunday shopping to stock up wi' food. After that, I'll phone Irene. It'll be great to see her; I need someone to talk to and get it off my chest in private. I can't let it take over my life. I'm twenty-nine, not a teenager; it's not right to make a big scene. I don't want to lose Nathan, Debs and Jose, so I've got to put up with it.*

Somehow remembering the fact that she was twenty-nine didn't help the stoical attitude that she was trying to inculcate. Twenty-nine! Single. How much had Nathan seemed to have been an answer to an urgent prayer that she had uttered on reaching that age last November? *Dear God, don't let me reach thirty without being in a steady relationship with a really good bloke.* Every young woman's nightmare. Thirty and single. *On shelf, body clock ticking ominously like a terrorist bomb. Fodder for lonely old men looking for someone a bit desperate. No longer in the hunt for Mr Right, just seeking Mr Anybody. Oh God, I feel like I'm sinking into a black hole. I can't believe this has happened to me. I remember how I sniggered about thirty-something women on their own when I were eighteen. It's not going to happen to me, I thought. I'm not beautiful but I've got a way about me, someone'll see I'm worth pursuing. But I've had my chances, haven't I? There were Gary, and I pushed him away mainly because Nathan were in background and because I thought I'd changed too much to be with a bloke like Gary, he belonged to my past. But maybe I were foolish. I don't suppose I could phone him? No, it's too late. He weren't the one. A whole wide world with billions of men in it and the 'one' in't in it, not here, not anywhere, not to be found, not Nathan, not anybody. How can I live in a world without him, without the 'one'? It's like a desert.*

*Twenty-nine. I might as well die. Come on, be positive. What about my new career? That's what I should concentrate on for a bit. A relationship will come when I'm good and ready. OK, let's do summat about it today. I can go to big bookshop in town, they're open Sunday, and look for some good stuff. On spiritual healing, visions, witchcraft, all that. I need to be properly informed. Then I can plan to go professional. Leave work, put ads in free paper, set up website. I can't push Debs away, because I need her. She's more streetwise than me, knows how to do things. She'll be my business partner even more so now, because she owes me one. It's weird not waking up in same room as her, that's what I've been doing for three weeks. My soul sister. It's not her fault. She didn't plan it. She must've felt terrible, especially after everything I said to her about how I love Nathan. We've shared so much. Like at the Alagnon.* The thought of that moment caused the river to gush in, through the doors of her heart, to flood every positive thought. *Maybe Debs fell in love wi' Nathan because she knew how much I wanted him! Some women are like that. Deep within 'em, they can't help it, it's a competitive thing. Another woman wants him, so they've got to have him. Even if it destroys best friend. She'll probably drop him when it's too late for me.*

*Stop it!* The waters receded. *I'm twenty-nine. I'm a fully grown adult. I can do better than hurting myself wi' jealousy and anger. She's had a hard life. She deserves a break. She's going to stay my friend. I can do this.* In order to reinforce the determination she was trying to build up, she swung her legs out of bed and strode purposefully to the kitchen to make a cup of tea. *Oh, no bloody milk! Always happens after a holiday.*

She was so keen to get on with the positive aspects of her life that she put off her parents and the cat until the afternoon and marched straight down to the bookshop to be there at ten, which she thought was opening time. Except that it opened at eleven. *Oh well, I'll buy a paper, see if there's owt about G8 summit next week and stay in the café for an hour.* The newspaper seemed to confirm the good news of Lille. *Come on, Frances. You've just saved world and you're fretting over bloke! It were me. I did that. Me and Notre Dame de Zion. I'm a powerful magician with a great future.* Debs had said to her: 'Magic's not about conjuring tricks, it's about changing the world through changing your attitude to it.' *OK, then, let's get to bookshop and see what's there...* Twenty minutes later, she strode out with three items: *Witchcraft for Healing*; *Starting Your Own Business*; *Visionaries*. She postponed the food shopping and went home with the books, a large bar of chocolate and a litre of semi-skimmed milk.

Milky tea and a lovely soothing therapeutic block of choc now in hand, *Visionaries* was the book that grabbed her attention. She was a visionary, wasn't she? The book was out of date already; they should add a chapter on her. 'Visionaries are remarkable people; it's no exaggeration to suggest that they have changed the world.' *Yes, we have!* 'All cultures have celebrated those special people who see into a spiritual realm that others can only dream about.' *Yes, we do!* Then a picture held her attention. A faded 1860s photo of a young woman in peasant costume. St Bernadette of Lourdes. The visionary Jose kept talking about and likening her to. The phone rang; she ignored it. *Probably Debs, she's bound to call today to see how I am. Leave her for a bit. St Bernadette of Lourdes. So young. She were quite a looker, weren't she?* Dark hair; intense, beguiling eyes; straight features. 'Bernadette entered the convent at Nevers soon after the visions ended and was a nun until she died there aged thirty-five.' A nun. *Maybe she wanted to find a bloke too, but visionaries are called to higher things, aren't they?* Read on. 'Bernadette said that the beautiful lady of her vision told her: "I don't promise to make you happy in this life but in the next." And so it turned out. She was kept in obscurity in the convent and died young from a painful tuberculosis, but she became one of the best known and most loved saints of the modern era.' A sob came from somewhere inside her; she put down the tea and chocolate. *So that's the deal. I get visions but I don't get owt else. So, Notre Dame de Bloody Zion, you think a few visions make up for a lifetime o' loneliness, do you?*

The phone began to bleep; a text was coming through. 'Pls phone – Debs.' But Frances was on a single track. A thought had entered her head; she ran over to a drawer. She pulled out a large brown envelope. Inside was a horoscope, sent to her from somewhere in London for £29.99 plus postage. The ciphers and squiggles inside the circle, carved as it was into twelve pieces of pie, meant little to her, but accompanying the horoscope was an interpretation. 'Prepared for you personally by Orion, astrologer to the stars… Frances Dryburgh, born in Leeds, 5$^{th}$ November 1978, at about 9 a.m.' She scanned the lines furtively. She hadn't taken it all in when receiving it a few years ago. Then, every small reference to the possibility of future romances had been eagerly gobbled up, the rest ignored and the horoscope discarded until now. Now, every reference to a *lack* of relationships stood out starkly from within the lines. 'Sun in Scorpio near to the 12$^{th}$ cusp. This signifies your strong interest in spiritual, other-worldly affairs… Venus in Scorpio, close conjunction with Uranus. Your romantic relationships will be intense and passionate but often unstable, impermanent and subject to separations… Moon in

Capricorn trine Saturn in Virgo. The prominence of Saturn in the affairs of the Moon, which concern emotions and day to day relationships, may make you seem reserved, perhaps more than you intend. You will be someone for whom relationships take time to develop. You often prefer your own space...' Frances threw the envelope back in the drawer without reading further. *So, it's written in stars too. Why didn't the astrologer just write: 'You're not going to do very well with men, are you? If you get a good relationship before you're thirty, it'll be a miracle. After that, all the good men will be gone. I'd settle for the cat and a lifetime of spirituality if I were you.' Thanks, Notre Dame de Zion, you've really sorted it all out for me, haven't you?*

Now she was mad. She ran over to the icon of the Madonna of Iviron, took it off the wall and hurled it across the room. It crashed into the bureau and landed face down on the floor, where she left it. Part of her wished the picture had not been a plain wooden icon but instead framed; she might have felt better to hear the smash of breaking glass. It was all she could do not to damage the other Madonnas, but a reluctance to devastate her own living space held her back. She took them down roughly and placed them, like Iviron, face down.

'Now see what your visionary thinks o' you!' she hissed at the overturned portraits. 'You don't want me to have a man, to feel warmth of another human being in my bed! You just want me for yourself! You don't want me to have sex, that's it, in't it? Just because you're a fucking virgin, you want everybody else to be! Well, I'm going to show you. I'm going to have sex today. Visionary or no visionary. Who'll have sex wi' me? Who do I want to have sex with? Oh yes, I know. This'll really annoy the Goddess.'

She called Irene.

'Hi Irene! I'm back! I really need to see you today, are you free?... Oh yes, I understand, a bit fraught right at the moment... Will you get off tonight maybe?... Excellent, seven... I'll be there, love! Can I stay over? It's not easy to get home without a car... I can go straight to work in morning... Great, you're really good to me. Bye!'

OK, girl on girl. She'd never tried it, now's a good time as any. So, Goddess, I forsake you for another woman! Suddenly, Frances recalled the last vision. *Yes, and we love each other intensely like twin sisters and sometimes hate each other too.* The words cut through Frances like the sharpest kitchen knife. *Yes, I do hate you right now. I need to let off some steam. I can't bear the way my life's going. You can't keep me all to yourself. I'm going to do summat mad!... Another call. Yes, Debs again. She's got to show me she cares. OK, let's get it over with. Twenty-nine. I can handle it. No need to show bitterness. What were it that Nathan said? It don't matter what you feel inside, only what you show to others.*

'Hello Debs! Sorry, I missed you. I were just in bathroom... Yeah, I'm all right. OK, I can't pretend it weren't a shock, but that's love, in't it? You can't predict it... I know you didn't mean me to get hurt... I'm sad for me but really glad for you... Of course I'll stay friends wi' you two... Look Debs, let's not meet today, I've got to see Mum and Dad, but I'll be there next Friday in pub as usual... We'll soon get back to normal... OK, bye!'

*Magnanimous,' weren't I? Debs sounded surprised. Almost like she was a bit put out that I weren't more upset. She's had several sleepless guilty nights, but I'm saying, cool as you like, there's no problem. But there is, dear Debs. A big, big, ginormous problem.*

Frances stayed hyper for the rest of the day. Everything she did was carried out with a trembling hand and a manic expression. Jose texted to ask if he could come round, but she put him off. Sal and Jo phoned, but she didn't call back. It was crazy. She had abandoned her old friends for new ones who hurt her. Sal, Jo, Cyn, all in the recycle bin. They weren't spiritual. They just enjoyed life without looking beyond it. Crazy. *When did any o' them hurt me like this? Never. Any woman who did the dirty, like that Becki, got shunned forever. And here's me saying, of course I'll stay friends. Of course I'll hang around to get shafted by whoever wants to hurt me. Crazy, crazy, crazy.* She was about to break something, anything, with that demon energy tingling in her hands, when the door bell rang. There stood Mum and Dad holding Cass.

'Hello, dear, we've brought love of your life back to you.'
*Oh yes, nearly thirty – single – spinster – loves cats. Logical.*
'Hi, good to see you!'
*I'd give up on grandchildren if I were you.*
'Did it all go really well in France, dear?'
*Yeah, brilliantly, I saved the world and my travelling companions destroyed me.*
'Fantastic, Mum. It were a really beautiful place.'
*Lovely views, like bloke you really love holding hands with your best friend.*
'We didn't get a postcard, dear.'
*No, Mum, couldn't see any postcards o' Chinese women throwing themselves off crags or me having a nervous breakdown.*
'Sorry, I don't think they have that many postcards over there.'
*Liar – you saw loads.*
'Don't worry, love, expect you had lots o' fun and didn't have much time to write.'
*Well, packing in thirteen visions o' Goddess does rather cut down on postcard time.*
'Yeah, totally. Gorgeous food, great places to visit.'
*And dragons to slay, only I were the one who got slayed.*

Mum and Dad left, having not got a great deal of information out of her but without seeming to notice. *Just me and Cass, that's how I like it.* 'You often prefer your own space.' *Got it in one, Orion! Me and my black cat. The witch o' Hyde Park.* She looked at the pictures lying face down. *It's you who's the witch, Notre Dame de Zion!* A peculiar thought struck her like a flash of revelation, her angry manic moods being very productive in creative thinking. She recalled her earliest memory: the witch in the dream who had come down from the wall to attack her. While the witch was on the wall, she had held a baby in her arms. Well, of course the witch and the Goddess were one and the same person. Maybe Frances had put the pictures of the Madonna up on the wall because of the residing fear of the nightmare. The pictures kept her high on the wall with her baby, frozen in the portrait, preventing her from beginning the threatening descent. So the fear was relieved. That's where the witch had stayed for years. But now the witch had come down and was tormenting Frances like she had in the dream, taunting her with her spinsterhood. So today Frances had removed the pictures; they were no longer doing their job. She couldn't keep the witch on the wall so she had to fight her instead. Begin the fight by sleeping with Irene. *Let battle wi' wicked witch commence! Who'll be strongest witch, me or her? Which witch? Witch, witch, witch, witch. My final battle. Wi' Wicked Witch o' the West. I've conquered beast and dragon, now I've got to do battle against my evil twin. Whose magic will be most powerful?*

And so it's off to Irene's. *I can be who I want to be, have sex wi' who I want to, stars can't dictate. Goddess witch can't dictate either. Sorry, Cass, we've only just been reconciled and I'm off again. Never mind, as long as I feed you, do you really care? Maybe I should bring you with me, to help me do black magic. Back to Hyde Park Corner, to get bus. Like I did last February, to meet Nathan and his future girlfriend. Now it's July. I'm a lot wiser. And madder...*

## 45

## No Goddess

Frances knocked at the familiar door of the refuge house. She managed a forced grin at the sight of little Lucy's one visible eye staring at her from behind the door. *Does she still allow Lucy to open door in a refuge house? It's mad. What if I'm a big skulking wife basher?*

'Can I come in, then?'

'Yeeessss' accompanied the disappearance of Lucy with the sound of running feet and the door swung open gently, enough for Frances to see Irene come inquiringly into the corridor. Now it was Frances' turn to feel breathlessly nervous, just as Irene had a few weeks before. She tried to look at her friend with new eyes. Irene was going to make this easy. Her dark skin had caught the sun in the recent warm spell and her black hair was tied back in two bunches, making her look much younger than her forty years. She looked gorgeous, whatever the observer's sexuality. Her smile was ready and warm as ever; it fondly held whomever it met and took them into its care. Then her body, in perfect step with the approachability of the face, reached eagerly forward to give a hug, an embrace like Baby Bear's porridge, not too tight, not too loose, just right. Frances wouldn't have to work too hard at this one. It would be fine. She relaxed into those welcoming arms and didn't let go until Irene eventually pushed her back.

'Are you OK?' asked Irene, suddenly concerned.

*Is it so obvious that I'm screwed up, then?*

'Yeah... yeah, it's just been a difficult holiday, that's all. Mostly good but with a funny ending. But I'm here now, that's all that matters. Are you free all evening?'

'Yes, my friend has come round to take Lucy back to hers – she always enjoys going there to play with other children. There's a new crowd in the house now, not the ones you knew when you were here. Always a problem! But I think they're settled enough now; I can give you some time. It's great to see you! Where shall we go?'

'Nowhere,' replied Frances. 'Can we stay here? I've brought some wine.'

'Yeah, of course,' said Irene, knowingly. 'You want to talk, don't you?'

'I do, yes,' conceded Frances, at the same time giving Irene a really warm smile so that her host wouldn't think she had only come there for a shoulder to cry on. 'But I also want to see *you*.'

'OK, go to my room,' said Irene. 'I'll be up as soon as Lucy's gone, shouldn't be long.'

The 'shouldn't be long' seemed like an age, although it was just under twenty-five minutes. At first, Frances could do nothing but stare into the fireplace on one wall that focussed everything in the space into a navel, as if the room had grown organically from that point. It stood resiliently, a vestige from a day gone by when the only form of heating was wood, coal and a good flame. Something about it stirred Frances into reflecting: *I haven't had sex for so long, it's not right. Must be about nine months now, given that I didn't do it wi' Gary. I weren't meant to be celibate.* She uncorked the bottle and glugged a few mouthfuls from it. *I didn't think I were a lesbian but I can change, can't I? I can learn. Irene's so wonderful.*

She started to look around the room, which was familiar but she hadn't had such a long time to study it. It covered a medium-sized fourteen foot square which always looked bigger because of the high ceiling and Irene's penchant for large, framed pictures of open fields of poppies; the woods; the sea. She was a spirit of the outdoors, was Irene, not that her lifestyle allowed much open air activity, although she had a decrepit old bike for short journeys. *She would really love the Auvergne,* thought Frances. *When Nathan goes walking wi' Debs, I'll take Irene and Lucy there.* Images flashed into her mind: Irene looking at the view of Massiac from the Madeleine chapel on the crag; standing on the great staircase at the entrance of Le Puy cathedral; electing to forego the *navette* and walk to the top of the Puy de Dôme with Lucy on her shoulders (Irene always seemed so physically strong); gasping with delight at the great wooded gorge at Estours; sitting by the Alagnon and dangling her feet in the gurgling stream – perhaps they could do a Tarot reading together. In all of these imaginary cameos, Irene was looking lovely, brimming with good health and laughing with pleasure.

The pictures on the wall spoke of Irene as a virgin goddess of nature, a huntswoman Diana free from the demands of men, rescuing other less fortunate women from their degradations. The nature motif was everywhere. Irene's curtains displayed an old-fashioned floral motif with the brighter colours rather faded, each pattern surrounded in frames of green and brown. The carpet was brick red. The untidiness of the bedroom told against Irene as a goddess of the hearth, like Hestia. It wasn't Lucy, whose little bedroom was next door, who could be held responsible for the jumble of clothes and bed linen. Irene's motto seemed to be that, if something was used regularly, it was better out of a drawer than in. Irene's few dresses, which Frances could see through the open wardrobe door, were predominantly blue, brown, white or lemon yellow. No red; no black. This was not a lady who dressed to impress; her beauty was natural. A photograph of her stood above the fireplace, stunning as a slimmer twenty-something year old in just one of those blue dresses, receiving some kind of award from a grey-haired man in a suit. The donor was looking straight at her, admiringly; she, however, gazed directly at the camera with those large enchanting dark eyes engaging the viewer. She was photogenic to the extreme. The camera caught the line of the splendid bone structure; the face integrated strength and gentleness as far as any person could combine them. *This is my goddess. No need for visions, for rituals. A goddess in the flesh. This is her shrine. I don't need to worship here, I can just lie back and sink into luxury and warmth.* And she stretched her arms out, fell back on the king-size bed that was just perfect for two and closed her eyes. But her heart was still pounding; all the softness and comfort of the room could not take away the nervous anxiety that continued to rage in Frances' head. With her eyes shut, she did not notice Irene slip through the door. Nor did she realise that she was mumbling to herself.

The wine was poured. Irene wanted to find out what was going on. Frances made light of it, mentioning disappointment that was quickly fading and instead began the process of seduction. *It should be easy, shouldn't it? She were really into me. Signals? Yes. Lots of smiling, fond looks, intimate conversation. So, here we go. She's lovely, she really is. Don't know why I didn't do this before. I'll just touch her cheek gently, then lean over and kiss her...*

'What're you doing?' asked Irene, pulling away a short distance after their lips met.

There was no hint of rebuke, just a straight question, very Irene-like.

'I love you,' replied Frances, with tenderness. 'I realised it in France. I should've responded when I were staying here.'

'You realised it in France?'

Irene's jet black eyes were searching right inside of her, sending lasers through her own. Her ability to pin down the untruth so quickly was scary. Frances squirmed.

'Yeah, well, it slowly became obvious to me when I knew how much I missed you.'

Irene was direct but continued the cross examination with sensitivity as if the prosecution lawyer decided that this was the best tactic to break down the witness for the defence.

'Did it become obvious just after Nathan rejected you?'

'Yeah, it were all part o' same process really.'

'Don't lie to me, Frances, we've become too close for that. You know I love you but I'm not going along wi' you when you're deceiving yourself. You're in a mess today, aren't you? This is not the time for us. Probably it'll never come, more's pity. I couldn't take advantage of you when you're so low. Come on, tell me what's happening.'

Frances' chin trembled and the tears were not long in coming.

'Now *you*!' she exclaimed. 'Now *you're* rejecting me. Everybody does, sooner or later.' Irene, stroking her hair fondly, let her gabble on for a while. 'Nathan said he thought I were special, but actually he thought I were unattractive and he wanted to encourage me. He likes the underdog, Debs said so. Do you know what my old boyfriend Jason said? He said there were three kinds o' people. "Yes please" people; "maybe but then maybe not" people; "definitely no way" people. "Yes please" people are gorgeous, so they always have lovers; if a relationship finishes, they can decide how long it is before they take up another. "Definitely no way" people are seriously ugly and have to find someone else in same category or stay lonely. "Maybe but then maybe not" people look OK at nightclubs and when they're out, so they attract lovers, but there's summat about 'em, looks or personality or both, that just makes 'em not so attractive on a day to day basis. They have to settle for other fairly boring people but it takes ages for 'em to realise it. I knew Jason didn't love me, so I said stupidest thing ever. I said, Maybe I'm a "maybe but then maybe not" person. He rolled around laughing for absolutely ages and told all his mates. I were really humiliated. But I am, aren't I? I'm a "maybe but then maybe not" person.'

Irene smiled; laughter was trying to break through the corners of her mouth at the absurdity of this, but she suppressed it for Frances' sake by taking hold of her forlorn guest and shaking her.

'Stop! Don't do this to yourself! Jason sounds like biggest creep you had misfortune to meet! Immature self-possessed young idiot! He's got no idea o' real life or real people. They can't be pigeonholed so easily. Don't let him or any other man tell you what you're worth! I *did* fall in love with you. You're not a "maybe" as far as I'm concerned! But I'm not going to be part o' your plan to avoid pain, that's all. Come on, I'll help you go through it. You can spend night wi' me but not as lovers. You wanted a mum, remember? I'm it.'

'You're right, you're always right,' sighed Frances, breathing deeply to try and regain control of herself. 'Like Wei Chi. You're so right, you're so very, very right, you're the rightest person in the world.' Irene looked blank, so Frances moved on quickly. '*You're* my Goddess, not woman in visions.'

'I'm no Goddess, but I'll deal with that later,' said Irene, firmly. 'Now tell me whole story, from beginning to end.'

...From Le Puy to Massiac, beasts, shadows, the demise of Wei Chi, then to the Puy de Dôme, through the land of dragons, all thirteen visions and finally the King's Cross train crawling into Leeds station – it all came out, Frances lying snugly with her head in Irene's left armpit.

'Ooh!' exclaimed Irene. 'You've been through a lot. But it's all going to work out for you now; what a good idea to start up in business on your own away from that G.R.C. place. I'll send loads o' people to you. It really will be OK, you know, Frances.'

'That's what Goddess says,' laughed Frances, much calmer after the cathartic experience of telling it all. 'Proves what I said, you're Goddess in flesh and blood.'

'We're going to have to deal wi' that,' replied Irene. 'This Goddess business. I'm Goddess only as far as all women are; I thought that were *your* theory. It's democratic, not just a matter o' setting some people up to be idols. If you do, you'll get disappointed, as they'll let you down sooner or later.'

'But you're so kind and you do anything for anybody. What about Lucy? You took her in.'

'I do what I do because I need to do it. I need Lucy as much as she needs me, maybe more. I need to be loved; I need to be needed. So I help people. I need to see them happy. I'm meeting my own needs. That don't make me a goddess!'

'It does to me!'

'OK, so to you, women are goddesses if they're meeting everybody's needs! Not sounding very liberated!'

Irene sighed good-naturedly and went to the loo. But her argument had struck home – Frances was having her doubts now. *Irene's right (yet again!), I should stick to idea that Goddess is in everybody. It's just that Irene fits my own understanding o' what Goddess is like, a kind and wonderful mother. But, of course, Goddess is like me too, in't she? Even if I'm not as fantastic and caring as Irene.*

With Irene out of the room again, Frances began to feel a strong emotion stirring within her. Somehow, through this discussion with Irene, she was making peace with her twin sister. *Goddess is like me too, in't she? Yes, and we love each other intensely like twin sisters and sometimes hate each other too.* Frances floated back on the wind of her imagination to the Puy de Dôme. An overwhelming love for the Goddess hit her without warning; it was so intense, she was doubled up with the pain of it. It flooded through her more acutely than the visions themselves; it was as if her soul were laid bare, as though heaven and hell were transcended in that feeling – they were neither high nor low enough to encompass it. In her mind's eye, she saw the great blue Earth, then Notre Dame de Zion in her gold and Mary Magdalene in her red. They made an extraordinary rainbow trinity of beings, who seemed in one unified movement to reach out and touch her; there was no other way to describe it. And their power on contact was so immense that Frances cried out. She fell into a state of ecstasy; an orgasmic feeling rippled through her entire body, an electric tingling in all the nerve endings causing the hairs on her arms and legs to stand on end. Everything seemed to be clear, at least for a brief moment. The meaning behind the heavens; the sun, moon and stars; her existence; her place in the destiny of the human race. *Am I dead?* She could not stop sighing and moaning. *What are you doing to me, Goddess? I can't escape from you, can I? There are times when I hate you but most of all I love you.*

'God, what're you up to?' asked Irene, coming back into the room. 'I really thought you were masturbating when I heard you from outside, you know. Sometimes people under stress do that scarcely realising they're doing it.'

Frances just managed to gasp out a 'no' and shake her head. She opened her eyes and looked at Irene; love surged through her, not sexual love primarily but a powerful feeling of empathy and fondness. It was ecstatic love for another human being rather than for Irene herself in particular; she was a representative of the human race. From Irene's point of view, Frances simply looked spaced out, so she resumed her position on the bed and put one arm around her.

'She's touched me,' murmured Frances, slowly, as if in a waking dream.

'You're worrying me,' replied Irene. 'Come on now, calm down.'

'I am calm, really calm, calmer than I've ever been.'

'I think you've been through a lot recently. It's bound to catch up with you.'

'I love you, Irene. I'm not trying to get off with you now; I just want you to know that I love you.'

'I love you too, babe. This is quite hard for me, lying here so close. But I'm not going to get into a situation that *you* then regret.'

'I understand. Anyway, I thought I were into sex but I'm not now. It's Goddess. I'm suddenly seeing things through her eyes and, whichever way life goes, I think I might be able to bear it.'

'Maybe she's made it hard for you so that you see it that way.'

Frances laughed feebly.

'You're really wise, aren't you? Just like Wei Chi...'

'Just like Wei Chi. Whoever she were, she made quite an impression on you,' whispered Irene to the now sleeping Frances.

'God, you're suffering from nervous exhaustion, aren't you? You really are a strange girl, do you know that?'

## 46

## Ace of Swords

*I'm spending Monday night on my own, me and Cass. You haven't seen much o' me, have you, darling? That's right, sit on my warm lap. Another day done. I thought work would be worse after three weeks away, but it's OK what wi' Carson in charge. I screwed up and he just laughed. It'll take you a couple of days to get your head back from holiday, won't it, Frances? Maybe you should check lost luggage! Haha! Good one! Katie's assistant manager now – that feels strange. She's not as scary as Taylor were, not by a long way. She didn't push me a' all, almost seemed... well, nervous of me! I just wonder whether Ballard mentioned to her that I were a witch! A witch, yes. I've got powers, me. So don't mess wi' me if I don't concentrate on my work or I could cause you mischief! Anyway, I did next to nowt and it were still OK. I'll work harder tomorrow. But I mustn't get settled, it's only a temporary thing now. I'm going to leave and get set up in business. Rituals, readings, maybe a bit o' counselling? People just need someone to be caring and listen to 'em. Nowt fancy; no special magic. Help 'em find their inner power, changing the world through changing your attitude to it.*

*Through power o' Goddess. She'll help me. On Friday, I'll talk it over wi' Debs, about how we're going to start.*

*Thinking o' Debs makes me feel uneasy. This morning, when I woke up at Irene's, I still had that wonderful feeling o' love in me. I were touched by the Goddess last night, touched right in my soul and it stayed with me. As I lay there in Irene's bed for a few minutes, I loved Nathan and Debs. I wanted 'em to be happy. I were glad they'd found each other and didn't care about myself any more! But now it's worn off a bit. I keep feeling frustrated; it's quite a physical thing, I suppose. I were really into Nathan and just put up wi' my celibate period because I were saving myself for him. That's why, when I knew I'd lost him, I wanted sex, any sex! Poor Irene. I shouldn't have done that, but she knew what it were really about, didn't she? Wise old owl. I've managed to live without sex for months because I kept thinking o' what it would be like if he... well, it kept me warm at night! But I should stop that now. He's somebody else's. Shit! How can I sit there on Friday if they've got their arms round each other? Shit, shit, shit. If they start cuddling, I'll turn to Jose and talk about Poulenc. Bloody Plonker! If it weren't for him, Debs and Nathan would never have gone off together that night. I hate you, Monsieur Plonker!*

*I can't stop looking at text I got this morning. 'Hope u r OK u r really important 2 me cant wait 2 c u Friday – N.' Is it insensitive? Does it keep me hanging on in hope when he should be cutting me off? Is it a pathetic attempt at an apology? Shall I do the normal 'men can't help saying and doing wrong thing' routine? Or should I just be glad he's texted? He's thinking of me, but what could he say to make me feel better? He's put it as well as it could be put. I'm his friend. That's how he wants it. That's how he always wanted it. I can't complain that he misled me. I just misled myself, that's what I did. Right from that day in February when he agreed to meet me. He thought I were special. And I guess I am. Thanks to him, I found out. I should be grateful, shouldn't I? But it's so bloody, bloody painful.*

*I feel at a loss. What am I going to do? All my old friends are drifting further away and my new ones are hurting me. I can't hold on to that sublime feeling o' love every minute of the day; sometimes it comes back, then it goes again. Last night and this morning, I thought I had it all sorted for a few brief moments. My head were sorted, completely. But you can't keep it going, can you? Getting up, showering, washing hair, putting make up on, travelling to work, looking at your computer screen all day, typing boring letters, remembering to update files when new 'directives' come round; well, how can anyone continue to love humanity fiercely through all that? And if I don't love humanity, I'll find it hard to accept Debs and Nathan. To put them first, above my own desires. I want him, bitch! Maybe I could do a little magic on you, Deborah! You started me on it, but I'll turn it on you! Apprentice bewitches sorcerer. I could get some o' your hairs and do some spells. Keep 'em apart, your hairs and lover boy's, in little sealed metal boxes. That should do it. But no, I know it's not right, I wouldn't want to. It's not just that law saying that evil you do in witchcraft comes back to you three times over, it's not that. It's just that I really wouldn't want to do it.*

*No bad spells then, but I need summat to get me through. Calling on Goddess, perhaps, wi' my candles lit. I've put Virgins back up even though Iviron's got a little battered. Well, I read that some o' the most famous black Virgins were damaged, that one in Poland for instance. Czesto... summat. But people still revere them despite that. So it's a holy dent, is that! Hang on though, maybe I could do some Tarot. OK, now I'll light candles and do reading after a short meditation.*

*The past: Ace of Swords. Wow. That's third ace: Debs and I had aces o' Staves and Cups by the Alagnon. Cups were hers though, weren't they? Swords went right through me! What does it read? 'Pure understanding and wisdom... clarity and good judgement.' Oh, that were everything I learnt in visions leading up to yesterday, weren't it? Love for humanity and acceptance of Debs and Nathan being together. All o' that stemmed from my love for Notre Dame de Zion, my higher self. That seems to me to be understanding and wisdom. Now I'd better find out about present.* Temptation. 'The seductive mermaid Nyai Loro Kidul. Her powers reflect the temptation of illusion; of beauties which may be enslaving; of obsessions which control... Tempted by forces one cannot control... Sensual desires. Gluttony or envy.' *Yep, guilty as charged. Yesterday's feelings were good, today's have started going back to being bad. I must try and resist the temptation to feel jealous o' Debs. Yeah, it's an obsession. Cards are right. But I need to know more about present.* Three of Pentacles. 'Constructive and pragmatic building – career, relationships, home. Ability to transform talents into material goods or business success.' *That's better. It's not all about sex and envy, then. I'm coming up to thirty, I need to think o' future. I've got talents and they're not being realised at G.R.C.*

*OK, I see what that's about. On to future.* Four of Pentacles. *Oh, are these shuffled properly? Well, I've got to stick by it, it's drawn.* 'Wealth and prosperity. Stabilizing material forces in life. A family inheritance – this could be a talent, money, land.' *Logical. If I use my talents now, they'll bear fruit in future. But I'd like more information about how that'll work out. Another card:* Love. Venus. *Yes! This is my reading now, in't it? Not Debs'. Mine alone. No sharing it.* 'A renewed awareness of the nature of passionate love and what is needed to encourage it. Artistic creativity. Sexuality. Integration of the masculine and feminine. A new, important relationship.' *Mega-wow. Maybe by doing what I'm good at, I'll find a decent relationship at last. Or it could be relationship wi' Goddess. One last card. I just need to know a little more.* Six of Cups. 'Six cups... are filled with flowers as an offering to Venus.' *Yes. It fits!* 'Harmonious home. Children and childhood memories. Longing for the sweetness and innocence of the past.' *Not sure about that. Will I be having children quite soon? I haven't met* him *yet, the 'one'. And how can I start a family and become a priestess all at same time?*

*Let's think about future cards again. Pentacles, good, that'll encourage me to work and make summat of my business.*

*Love/Venus? I've made so many mistakes. Hadn't I better be careful about falling in love? I don't want to do it all again, do I? I don't think I could pick up on any romantic thing, not quite yet. I'll just stick to my new venture and let love come naturally, if it wants to. No more waiting for future, I'm going to hold on to present. Well, I say I will. But I probably won't! Finally, six o' cups. Longing for sweetness and innocence o' past? Were there ever such a time? Don't understand that really. Childhood memories. Not sure what that's about, most o' my childhood were filled wi' fear and inhibition. I prefer being nearly thirty! It's not so bad, is it? Probably, one day I'll wish I were back here at this age, just starting the interesting bit o' my life. So I'd better make most of it. I'm going to cut down on drinking as well. Wei Chi said it: 'Stop drinking, it won't help!' I've been a bit of a binge drinker up to now, haven't I? It's not good. Come on, Cass, get off my lap, you witch's familiar, you! No claws, please! Keep them to yourself and I'll not use mine when I next see Debs. That's a deal!*

## 47

# Higher Self

Friday. *One week after Puy de Dôme. Life goes on.* Back at the *Airedale* after a four week absence. 'Haven't seen you lot in here for a week or two,' commented the barman. 'Been to France,' replied Frances, stopping to see whether a question would follow. *Oh yeah, what were you up to there? Saving world wi' magic, actually.* But the prompt didn't come. He just pulled the two pints and poured one red wine, one orange juice. *Debs keeps looking nervously at me. Why is she doing that? Maybe she's scared I'll bewitch her, after all. Stop it, Debs! I love humanity, you're safe. Jose looks shifty too. The only one with his usual cool bearing is Nathan, typically not sparing my feelings and managing to look great as usual. Oh God, hell is so much more terrible when heaven's only a few inches away. Thanks for being so handsome, darling! You'll look so much better wearing your pint o' beer with a few prawn cocktail crisps rubbed into your blond locks for good measure! Stop that! OK, I'm sorry, Higher Self, lover of humanity. I'll hold that thought right there. You can rely on me. Be kind to everyone, wish 'em well.*

After the 'what a crap week it was at work after such a great holiday' routine, Jose made an announcement.

'The G8 summit seems to have been a decisive step towards reducing carbon emissions. All the major nations appear to be on board.'

'Yes, that was my reading of it too,' agreed Nathan. 'We did it! Particularly you, Frances.'

*Yeah, you're right, I shouldn't sit here thinking about lost love.*

'No, particularly *all* of us. It's fantastic, in't it?'

Then, apparently with nothing much more to say on that topic, Jose made a second announcement.

'I've met this guy.'

'God, Jose, brilliant, mate. How long's it been since you were last in a relationship?'

'Years, Nathan, bloody years.'

'Where'd you meet him?'

That was Frances, Higher Self now fully in control and asking polite questions, holding down the 'what a time for this to happen, everybody but bloody me' personality in a strong headlock.

'On Wednesday night, I finally plucked up the courage to go to that gay bar down by the river. I've been too scared to go after a friend got knifed there by gay-bashers. But after Paris, well, I felt it was time to risk having a life despite Leeds being home to lots of good citizens who don't like Asians or gays.'

'His name? Come on, tell us about him!'

'Terry, or Tel-boy he says his friends call him. Anyway, you'll meet him later; I asked him to meet us here. I hope you don't mind.'

'Not a' all. We don't, do we, Frances?'

*Debs, why ask me? You're being oversensitive. You've just given the inner juvenile delinquent another bit o' provocation. She might come out and murder everyone.*

'Absolutely not, it'll be great to meet him,' replied the Higher Self.

The Higher Self was then rewarded by being put centre stage.

'I wanted to say this to you, Frances,' said Jose. 'I'm sure the others will agree. Since we met you, everything seems to have gone really well for us all. You're a catalyst for good, Frances, one of those people who makes things happen for others.'

*Yeah, others but not myself. Cut that out! OK.*

'That's nice of you to say so,' replied Frances, Higher Self still winning out. 'But surely catalyst were Wei Chi. It were after her death that I felt better and all you guys suddenly found yourselves.'

*Found yourselves in bed with one another, that is. Last warning! OK. Shtum.*

Debs smiled. She had a chance to show her disappointed friend that she was on her side.

'While Wei Chi may have been important, it's you who's the catalyst, Frances. We wouldn't have gone to France if it weren't for you, wouldn't have met Wei Chi. She were drawn to *you*, remember. Fact is that you've got a gift and you can use it when you start your new career.'

Frances began to ask Debs about the 'partnership' while the men listened politely. A website's what's needed; some photos and a little biographical info. Rituals done for every occasion: welcoming babies, outdoor natural weddings (handfastings, as Pagans call them) or just rituals to greet a new season. Advice, using a little positive thinking and maybe some witchcraft. Tarot readings. Maybe they could learn some astrology. And *I Ching* too, in memory of Wei Chi. Debs could sound out some of her friends to see what was already out there in the 'witch advisor' field and make contacts with any willing clients to get the thing started. It was all very exciting, jobs allocated, and Frances felt that even the inner delinquent was beginning to forgive Debs. She was really enthusiastic. The memory of the rippling Alagnon needn't be betrayal, after all. Its spirit was the initiative of a new venture, real friendship and partnership. *That's good,* thought Frances. *Too beautiful a place to be ever after associated with anger and pain.* And then, just as the plans were as good as done, in walked Tel-boy. Smooth timing. And, as it turned out, smooth guy.

The first impressions were that Tel-boy was tiny. A very small white man, even shorter than Jose, scarcely more than five feet but nicely proportioned with it, very sleek and neat. Black hair gelled, short and spiky in a carefully styled arrangement, clean shaven. Square jaw, fine cheek bones, snub nose, large round dark eyes, fair clear skin. *If he were a few inches taller and wider, he'd be really handsome,* Frances reflected. *Probably older than he looks, thirty-something.* Short-sleeved black shirt, unostentatious gold necklace and gold watch to match. Very clean black jeans with a gold belt and smart black shoes. All in black and gold, a real cowboy, but understated in a planned sort of way. Jose was glowing. This guy was a real catch. How had he done it?

'Terry's an environmental scientist at the University,' Jose declared, in a proud voice that would only be possible with really good friends. 'He's doing a PhD on the effects of urban pollution.'

'Do you know, I think I've seen you before,' said Nathan. 'I work in the library.'

The look that was returned suggested that Tel-boy had *certainly* seen Nathan before. *Don't worry, Jose. You can't lose out like I have; Nathan is definitely not into men.*

'Yeah, I've noticed you working there. I'm in there a lot,' affirmed Tel-boy, with what sounded like a mild north-east accent.

'Environmental scientist! Shall we tell Terry what we've been up to?' asked Debs, excitedly. 'Did you tell him, Jose?'

'Not really,' replied Jose. 'But go ahead.'

Frances sensed that this was a moment of truth for Jose. He didn't know yet what his new boyfriend thought of magic and Pagan ritual. He was nervous, but he knew that it was a hoop that had to be jumped through. Debs recounted the story. Tel-boy listened intently and nodded from time to time. At first sight, he seemed to approve.

'Well, that's great,' he said. 'Your hearts are certainly in the right place; I've never been one for spiritual things myself but, if you're going to have rituals, why not for good reasons like that?' General relief, although Frances wondered whether the 'hearts being in the right place' implied that the heads weren't. Then Tel-boy added a postscript, demonstrating a wonderful ability to pour cold water in a polite matter-of-fact kind of way. 'However, I should add that the G8 summit was not really a decisive moment in the environmental debate. They discussed it, yes, and it seems like the major industrial powers might finally begin to work together to reduce carbon output and limit global warming. A step in the right direction but, according to experts, not anything like enough. So far, there's nothing definite in terms of political action. We might find out more at the Copenhagen summit next year. Mind you, I guess that the media played up the environmental bit, so I can understand where you're coming from.'

*We've been here before, haven't we?* The Ballard and Taylor decision. You thought that your magic caused something to happen and then it turned out you were just short on information. Frances looked at Debs, trying to make their minds meet. Debs answered for them both, desperately trying not to sound put out.

'I'm sure you're right. We don't know all the details. But you never know, whole thing could still've gone wrong at last minute. So maybe we were just making sure. Anyway, point is that we did our rituals, then we got good news. In a sense, that's all we need to know.'

'Good point,' replied Tel-boy, trying to underscore the genuine nature of this polite comment by pointing his alcopop bottle at Debs before sipping it.

Jose looked as if he wanted the 'spirituality and the environment' part of the conversation to stop there, but Nathan hadn't spotted that.

'So tell me, Terry, why aren't you into spirituality? It seems like a natural thing for an environmentalist to have a sense of the sacredness of the Earth.'

'I see what you're saying,' said Tel-boy. 'But I happen to believe that we can appreciate the wonder of the universe with a scientific view rather than believing in something else "out there".'

Nathan liked a good friendly argument about religion; he wasn't stopping at that.

'For us, you know, the "out there" and the universe we see are two parts of the same coin. Unlike the traditional religions, we don't separate them and make the invisible superior to the visible. The Goddess is in us and in nature. She also has a spiritual, invisible dimension, which only a few... (leaning over and putting his hand on Frances' shoulder, making her feel tense)... can actually perceive. But this doesn't mean a denial of the empirical, tangible, physical world and all its beauty.'

Tel-boy was into the robust discussion thing too.

'Yeah, I respect your view. But, for me, there isn't any dimension other than those that are scientifically observable. Maybe one day, we will know that there are more dimensions than we understand now, but that's just a gap in science, not an "otherworld" with gods, goddesses and spirits. Of course, I can't rule out the possibility that science will one day discover the things you regard as spirits to be entities beyond our present knowledge but that's the key phrase: beyond our present knowledge. I can't believe in things that I can only imagine.' Nathan was about to say something, but Tel-boy, finishing off the alcopop in one quick gulp, was keen to continue. 'I have some reservations about this New Age thing. It sounds all very democratic and personal but, in many respects, it's just a new form of the old religious sentiments that have been around for centuries. There are new authorities and gurus, you have to buy this book and that book, visit this website and that one, and people still make a lot of money out of other people's needs... (*oops,* thought Frances)... I'll give you an example. Take Russia. It was ruled by a tsar, then communism, then capitalist democracy, but the country has always chosen to have an authoritarian government, no matter what kind it was. Religion is like that – it changes and adapts to new circumstances, but it is still essentially the same beast. Certain people decide what the supernatural world is like, others believe them but, doing so, give them power.'

'Not in this case,' replied Nathan, not at all fazed, rather enjoying himself. 'You've missed the point. Goddess traditions, Neo-Paganism – the things we're into – don't give power to anyone. We decide what the supernatural world is for ourselves.'

'Well, if it's truly like that,' conceded Tel-boy, graciously but with a hint of scepticism. 'Then good luck to you all. I'm not one for telling people what to believe, either.'

Jose just sat through all this with a frozen expression. He was in an uncomfortable place. Conservative Christians and Muslims did not like being mated with unbelievers, but was it any easier for a Neo-Pagan with a Catholic background like Jose? Could he cope with a scientific atheist? If not, it would prove Tel-boy right, wouldn't it? Alternative spirituality would be just like the traditional religions, dictated by boundaries. Anyway, Tel-boy was too good-looking to let a little religious argument or two get in the way. Jose resolved to move the conversation on, just as soon as he had gone to the loo and got the next round in. That would give him a minute or two to work out what topic was the most suitable to bring everyone together. When he returned, he had the answer.

'Hey, everyone. Did you see the line-up for this year's Leeds Festival? Makes me want to get the tent back out and pitch it in a muddy field. We must go!'

'Jose!' exclaimed Tel-boy. 'You read my mind. Now *that* would be a spiritual experience.'

Frances just sat there, smiling. Firstly, she had lived up to her resolution about cutting down on the alcohol by joining Debs on the orange juice after only one glass of wine. Secondly, she had discovered an inner certainty over the last few minutes. Her 'spirituality' would have crumbled in face of the arguments by Tel-boy, PhD boy, smooth-talking boy, just a few weeks ago. But Wei Chi, umpteen visions, being touched by the Goddess and being given the gift of loving all of humanity, even if for only a few odd moments in a busy life? Well, all that made her a believer. She was sure of her experience and it was an experience that Tel-boy simply hadn't had. That's why he thought the way he did, Goddess bless him. There was no need to feel defensive about it. The inner conviction felt good; it really took the bitter edge off the whole business with Debs and Nathan.

'You know what,' she said to Tel-boy. 'I'm really pleased you and Jose have got together. We need to think about what we believe in. You're going to be good for us all.'

The cowboy in black and gold smiled back. He looked slightly smug, as if he had made a convert. *Quite the opposite, Tel-boy,* thought Frances good-naturedly as she took a sip of the fruit juice.

# 48

# Washing

Frances' lie-in on Saturday morning was interrupted by a call on the landline.

'Yeah, what? Who's that?'

'It's me – *Irene*.'

'OK, hi, Irene, I'm not really with it yet. What time's it?'

'Just after ten, Frances.'

'Oh, that's late for you, in't it? Sorry.'

'No problem, I weren't getting at you. I just need to know whether you're free tomorrow afternoon.'

'Yeah, I suppose so. It's always great to see you. Are you planning summat?'

'It's Kelly. Remember her?'

'Yeah, I do. I must admit I found her difficult to get on with.'

'I know, but you did get through to her, Frances. Remember that ritual you did? She's always going on about it whenever I see her.'

'That's true, she did seem moved by that. Summat about her Nan being Catholic and lighting candles.'

'Yeah, that's it. Well, she wants you to… well, she says, *baptise* her two boys.'

'Baptise? How can I do that? I'm not a vicar.'

'Maybe, but I told her you were thinking o' going self-employed, like. So she says great, *you're* the one who's got to do it and she wants to pay you for it. She says if you're free, she can invite a couple o' people round tomorrow afternoon for a little ceremony.'

Frances felt apprehensive and would have loved to have found a way to postpone, but she knew that this was an opportunity that she couldn't miss. It would mark the beginning of her new career.

'Can I invite Debs too?'

Some help would be needed. Who better than her business partner?

'Sure, no problem. Kelly knows Debs, anyway. She's always been a great support to all the women in refuge.'

'Will *you* be there?'

'Of course I'll be there, Frances. Keep me away!'

'OK, where does she live? She's not in refuge now, is she?'

'Seacroft. In flats. I'll give you her address and mobile number. If we meet there, she says we can go to a patch of open land a few miles outside city. Her brother Derek'll drive us.'

'Fantastic, I'll call her. Thanks, Irene, this is great. Just what I've been waiting to do.'

*Scary. So soon. Got to start sometime. Call Debs... OK, sorted. She's coming. We can meet for lunch today and plan it. But she says we shouldn't invite Nathan and Jose, not with Kelly's past. More vulnerable than she seems. If strange men turned up, she couldn't cope. OK, now I'll have some brekkie and then phone Kelly herself. A ritual, eh? First one since Puy de Dôme, except for a few moments o' meditation. Shouldn't have left it so long. I should do these things regularly. Will I get a vision? I really miss seeing Goddess. It scares me that now thirteen visions in France are done, I'll not see her again. Couldn't bear that...*

'Hello, Kelly? Frances here. Nice to speak to you again. OK, I'll hang on... yes, I see, you need to be near window to get good reception. Anyway, I'll gladly do rituals for your boys. Do you really want baptism? In Paganism, we call it baby-naming, it's a different thing.'

'Frances, I don't mind what we do, but we must do some kind o' baptism for 'em. You know, washing away sins. They're… (hesitation, sounding tearful)… well, they're screwed up. Both of 'em. Jake's cruel little bugger and Danny's scared of everything, still wets bed.'

'I understand, Kelly, but it's not their fault, is it? You've all been through it. I'm not sure about this "sins" business.'

The word had a strange resonance in Frances' ears: the revelation of the corpse in the nightmare and its association with her threatening phone caller.

'I just want them to be innocent, Frances. Like little kids should be. Not screwed up any more.'

'OK, Kelly, I get what you're saying. But you know that rituals don't produce miracles, don't you? Even baptisms in churches don't stop people going astray.'

'I know they'll not change overnight but I want them protected, do you see what I mean? You were so… well, great, that night in refuge. I think you've got power. You put up with everything I threw at you when we were there.'

Frances remembered how shaken she had been; if it was Kelly's perception that, on the inside, she had remained calm and serene in the face of provocation, it was a wrong one. Only with Irene's guidance and support had she been able to deal with it. But no point in saying all that.

'No, you were fine, love, just a bit harassed at times, that's all.'

'I were a bitch, Frances, and you know it. I were testing you.'

'Irene always believed in you, Kelly. I just trusted her, that's all. Anyway, I'd really like to help; it's what I'm planning to do, rituals and all that. It'll be a great chance to practice. I hope it'll be OK.'

'It will, Frances, I know it will. See you tomorrow.'

Frances got ready to go and meet Debs. She wanted to talk about this 'washing away sins' idea. It bothered her. *How can kids like that be expected to be innocent? Is any kid innocent, even those from a loving home without violence?* These thoughts stirred up a recent memory in Frances. Innocence. She looked up the Tarot reading from the previous Monday. 'Harmonious home. Children and childhood memories. Longing for the sweetness and innocence of the past.' *Ah, the past, not mine but Jake and Danny's. It's about them and about my new career.*

The café in the city centre where she met Debs was the same one they visited when Frances had been desperate about her mystery caller. It was full of the bustle of Saturday shoppers, people getting recently purchased goods out of bags to admire them with friends over a cappuccino, resignedly devouring pastries which temptation had insisted were to be bought and consumed. The strip lighting was too bright and made Frances feel somewhat light-headed. A wonderful variety of mobile ringtones punctuated the noise of conversation, uniting owners in their desire to sport something distinctive and amusing. The tone that replicated a 1930s telephone ringing in a grainy black and white movie; the theme from Popeye; one that sounded like the inside of an aviary, causing heads to turn and seek out birds sitting on perches near the ceiling. *Very funny,* thought Frances, shaking her head at the young man responsible. Then in came Debs; it was the old Debs, hair flying in all directions, not the transformed lady. Clearly, Nathan was not on the programme for some hours, not until she'd had a chance to do some grooming of her appearance. The old Debs to look at, but it was the new Debs who gazed into her face with a show of fondness and attentiveness, betraying the discomfort from the week before that had not subsided yet. The best thing to do was to launch straight into the business of tomorrow and avoid Nathan-talk.

'She wants baptism. To wash away sins. We don't believe in sins, do we? It's just a way o' churchy people trying to make everyone feel guilty.'

Debs' answer was surprising.

'Yeah, it's true that Christians use the idea o' sin to ram their religion down everybody's throat. But that don't mean there's no such thing as sin. What about sin against women? Sin o' violence. Sin o' politicians lying. Sin o' wars against weaker nations.'

'OK, but Jake and Danny aren't guilty of all that, are they?'

Debs sipped her cappuccino, leaving a little line of froth on her upper lip.

'No, but they're *victims* o' sin.'

Frances leaned over and gently wiped the milk off with a serviette.

'You can't sit there saying wise things wi' crap on your face, Debs, love. Would they've listened to Sermon on Mount if Jesus had a large bogey hanging from his nose?'

She smiled mischievously. Debs poked her tongue out. It was milky too. She tried again.

'What I'm saying is that Jake and Danny are *victims* o' sin. So is Kelly. So are many women and children; men too. Sins o' violent males and unfair social systems. So what's wrong wi' ritualistically washing it away?'

'I hadn't thought of it like that. Washing away sins you've suffered rather than ones you've committed. Why don't the churches do that in their baptisms?'

'You'd better ask *them* that. Maybe some do, I don't know. But even if not, we don't need to do things like them, do we? We're free to do it our way. We're spiritual adventurers, remember? Trying things out, thinking o' new ideas. And another thing – we should include Kelly in the baptisms, not single out the kids. They'll feel weird. Kids and Kelly are all in it together. Let's ask her to be part of it.'

'You're amazing! Really clever. I can see why you want to do a degree. Only don't forget me and our partnership, will you?'

'Of course not. Anyway, most people could do degrees if only they had confidence and encouragement. You've got one, haven't you?'

Did that sound like a put-down, even if unintentional? Frances refused to be fazed by it anyway.

'I were a bit young. Everybody wanted me to go. First one in family and all that. I didn't make most of it. I weren't clever like you are now.'

'And like *you* are now, too. Except, unlike me, you don't have to do a degree to prove it, because you've already got one!'

That was better.

Frances was keen to get on with the business in hand despite the rather large lady trying to get into a seat at a nearby table and, without being aware of it, her shopping bags brushing Frances' head.

'OK, let's work out what we're going to do.'

'Normal things, Frances. What we're used to is best thing. Creating circle; making an altar o' flowers; calling quarters; spirits. We can include baptism as centrepiece. Get kids involved. They can help with making altar and we can get some drums for 'em to bang. We have to make it fun; it can't be heavy and I don't think we can go on about "sins". That word'll have to stay in our heads and Kelly's.'

'OK. But drums? From where?'

'There's a shop in Merrion Centre. It's worth investing if we're going to do this a lot.'

'What words are we going to use? For baptism, I mean? All that "Father, Son and Holy Spirit" stuff, that's not us, is it?'

'No. But what, I don't know, what do you think?'

'OK, I think we should call on Goddess. I'll think o' some words. We'll talk about the kids being looked after by Goddess, who's there to protect them. That's near to what Kelly wants.'

'That's great, Frances. You're a natural!'

'Is anybody natural at this? It's quite hard, making up rituals, in't it?'

'Yeah, I agree. But if anyone can do it, *you* can.'

'*And you*! We're a partnership, aren't we?'

At this, Frances took Debs' hand. Remembering the two of them talking by the Alagnon triggered in her an urge to forgive, to let her friend know that they could move on. It wouldn't be easy but it had to be done. Bitterness washed away. Like sins. Washed away down river to the Atlantic. It had to be done before the ritual. The priestesses needed to purify themselves first.

Frances took a deep breath and opened up the can of worms.

'I'm glad Ace o' Cups came true for you.'

Debs bit her lip, looked away and then forced herself to look back into Frances' grey-green eyes, the penetrating look emanating from them shining like a searchlight into her own. It wasn't often that she was the weaker party in a meeting of eyes. When she spoke, it was in a hushed whisper.

'It'll come true for you as well. It were your reading too.'

'Maybe; I'm sure that it will one day. I thought I wanted it to be Nathan but if it weren't meant to be, then I'm glad he's with you.'

Frances spoke with a conviction that belied the inner struggles of the past week.

'I wish my happiness hadn't come at your expense,' replied Debs. 'That's last thing I wanted. I had no idea that it would turn out that way, not until Paris.'

'Didn't you feel for him at any time before then?'

'Yeah, for ages. But I couldn't believe that he would like me, not in that way. I thought I would never find happiness with a man, not after everything that's happened to me. I were wrong. At Massiac, after Wei Chi died, I just noticed him getting closer. I didn't dare hope – anyway I felt like I were trespassing on *your* territory.'

'He's not anyone's territory; you can't own people. That's the one thing you can't demand from them, a committed relationship.'

She remembered Gary saying that.

'True, but you know what I mean. I knew you loved him and wanted to be with him. So I would've stayed out o' way. But... I couldn't do it. I loved him too much. I had to be selfish.'

'I wouldn't say you were selfish. Just in love, that's all.'

Having said this, Frances smiled and squeezed Debs' hand. She didn't take her eyes away from Debs', in order to assure her that she was being honest. Debs looked down; she couldn't hold Frances' gaze any longer. But neither could she hide the fact that tears were appearing in her dark brown eyes. Frances seized the opportunity and went on.

'Go for it, Debs. You deserve it. Nathan must really love you; he doesn't commit himself easily, does he? I love you both and I give you my blessing. I would say I forgive you, but there's nowt to forgive, is there? You've followed your heart; remember how important hearts are to witches?'

Debs nodded and glanced up, wetness now apparent on her cheeks. She quickly looked down again. Frances felt that ecstatic feeling of Sunday night coursing through her body. She had let go, she had let circumstances take her where they would and she had blessed others who stood in the way of her own dreams. Notre Dame de Zion had used her to bring Debs and Nathan together, that's the way she saw it now. She spoke to the Goddess in the quiet space of her imagination, miles from the clanking cutlery and crockery of the café. *OK, twin sister, happy now? You've got your own way again, haven't you? You owe me one, well maybe several more than one. If I say jump, you'll jump, won't you? So you'd just better help me and Debs get this ritual thing together and help me start a new life. OK, twin sister? I don't hear you saying too much! Am I just talking to myself?* The Goddess sister replied sheepishly in the imaginary conversation. *Yes, OK, Frances. I've got your drift. I'll make it up to you. I won't make you be celibate. I won't make you be a nun. I'll find you a gorgeous hunk, I really will. Make sure of it,* insisted the inner Frances. *I won't tell you again.*

'What're you smiling about?' asked Debs, bringing Frances back to planet cafeteria. 'Where have you gone in that mind o' yours? You're bananas, aren't you?'

'Bananas, what a good idea,' replied Frances, still grinning broadly. 'Do they serve fritters here, do you think? Even goddesses like comfort food, you know.'

## 49

# Gift of Seeing

The prospect of a Saturday evening in was not normally a welcome one; it made Frances feel as if she were now well over thirty instead of a few months short. But it made sense: time to relax and think about tomorrow. She wanted to write some words for the baptism ritual and work out how it would all come together. However, Saturday night wasn't going to be quiet, after all. Dad phoned.

'It's your mum. A little turn. Not sure what. They're keeping her in hospital overnight. Could you pop down and see her, Frances? She's in L.G.I. I'm there now.'

'What's the problem, Dad?'

'Not sure, love. Come down and maybe you can ask doctor.'

*Oh no. Good timing, Mum. Is it just one of your little anxiety attacks? Or summat else, a serious illness this time? Well, I've got to go and find out. Oh God, I can't help thinking about my mum's death. What if this were it? How would I feel? Would I be choked, really upset? Yes, of course I would. But would I miss her? Every conversation I have with her is to support her and cheer her up; I don't share my own little secrets any more because my life don't seem to mean much to her. Did I tell her about that business wi' phone calls? No, would've worried her too much. About my spiritual adventuring? No, she wouldn't have understood it. About Nathan? No, she would've just assumed I were close to getting married. That's the trouble with a mum so much older.*

As Frances scuttled round Hyde Park Corner and up past the University towards the hospital, she played through the hypothetical scenario of her mum's death. The announcement: 'I'm sorry to tell you that your mother passed away last night. There was nothing we could do, I'm afraid'… 'Oh, Dad, I'm so sorry.' The funeral. Aunts and uncles; brother Colin returning with the latest girlfriend for support; the women from Mum's old workplace. She remembered Wei Chi's requiem. Her spiritual mother whom she had known for just a few days. The insight that a whole life stood before you at a funeral, that's why the occasion was so powerful. Her mum's story presented itself: *born in War, house in danger o' bombing, moved away as a baby from suburbs o' Leeds, then came back in '45; girlhood in time o' rationing; smog; the fifties. It's all nostalgia now, but I bet those times were hard for factory girls. Met Dad at eighteen. He were doing National Service. Nice smart uniform. That turned a girl's head in them days, didn't it? He were from mining family south o' Wakefield, but he decided to leave mines because o' Mum's worries about him getting lung disease. Got a porter's job in Leeds; he were head of security in a large hotel by time he retired. They were married in early sixties. Same month as Cuba crisis. Everybody thought that World War Three were coming, nuclear bombs and all. No wonder she were neurotic. She told me about it: 'We all thought balloon were going up, I'm not kidding you – didn't seem worth getting married!' What made her so scared? Other women got through it OK. More money around; people started having cars; holiday camps; Beatles; Summer o' Love; rock music. But she lived as though she were a generation older than she is. And what made her so scared? Whatever it were, it interfered with her fertility, so me and Colin, we didn't appear for years. Some drug or other did the job.*

*Thank God she didn't take Thalidomide. Then being a mum scared her even more: take your coat in case it gets chilly, don't talk to strangers, there's bad people about, hurry home. She didn't teach us, she instilled fear into us. No TV with any scary content to be seen round our house, no X films! Even Coronation Street got turned off if it got a bit racy. Friends used to laugh at us. Did you see Psycho's on tonight, Frances? Will you be watching it with your mum? No, I really don't think so!*

*Oops, lost in thought. I'm already here. L.G.I. Leeds General Infirmary. Last time I were here, it were when Jason broke his ankle. Not so cool then, were you, Jason, love? 'Come with me, Frances, I need you there, I hate it when they take the plaster off, my ankle really hurts, I don't like hospitals, it's the smell.' Yes, you loved me when you needed me, didn't you? During your bad times. There were one time I wished you were in wheelchair, so you'd need me every day. Crazy ideas come when you're in love...*

*OK, now I've seen her. She's sedated, couldn't get much sense. They've not found owt wrong, but they're keeping her overnight just in case and because she's so distressed. It's just one of her panic attacks, I'm sure of it. Feels giddy and sick and gets confused. Maybe this one's a bit worse than normal. There's no end to 'em though, is there? How many times will this happen? When will National Health give up on her? They can't have unlimited resources for this kind o' thing. Anyway, I'll just sit wi' Dad for a few minutes before I go. He's upset. I'll get him a cuppa in hospital coffee bar. It's still open...*

'Now, Frances, I've got you to me sen for a change, tell me, what's going on wi' you?'

'Well, Dad, nowt to speak of.'

'Come on, Frances. I know there's summat, you've been odd lately.'

'Just fell in love, Dad. It's over now. I'm just getting over it.'

'It's more than that, Frances. Falling in love – you're always doing that!'

*OK, you want to know. Let's see what you make o' this. You'll probably change subject and start talking about rugby league.*

'Well, I've been going through some changes in my life. You see, I've had these... these *visions*.'

'Visions! Visions o' what?'

*He looks surprisingly interested. Not visions o' Leeds Rhinos winning Superleague, if that's what you think.*

'Well, visions of a beautiful, kind lady. I think she's... the *Goddess*, Dad. She's calling on me to help people more, maybe get a job, well... helping people more.'

'Well now, Frances, that's what happened to your mum. Strange that. She were about your age – no, maybe younger, I think.'

*What? What? What?*

'Tell me about it, Dad! You've never mentioned it before.'

*I don't believe this.*

'We'd not long been married. She were worrying that she couldn't have children. She told me that she'd had these visions... of a lady, a kind o' mother figure. This lady were going to help her.'

'Oh, my God, what did she do?'

'I suggested we went to local vicar and tell him about it. We used to go to church on and off in them days, Frances. I were sure he could help, tell her what it all meant.'

'And did he?'

'He told her to ignore visions. Said they were dangerous, could make her ill. Probably came from her anxiety, he said. Best to pray to Jesus and forget about 'em. They might be from devil, he said.'

'No, that's so unfair! Goddess would've made her less anxious!'

*Typical, bloody vicars! What do they know?*

'Well, she were so scared after that, she's refused to talk about it since. Frances, you mustn't raise subject. I shouldn't have told you. She'll be furious. Promise me, please.'

*Great, finally one subject that me and Mum have got in common and you want me to keep quiet.*

'OK, Dad, leave it to me, I'll not say more.'

*He's probably right. Would just upset her. If she still thinks it's from devil, she'll worry about me; if she's thinks it were a good thing after all, she'll fret that she were put off all those years ago.*

'Well, better get back. Golf highlights on telly tonight. I'll come in and take her home tomorrow. Will you come round?'

*That's better. Back to normality.*

'Sorry, Dad, I'm really busy. Can you manage while Monday evening? I'll phone.'

*Now I'm home, I'm deep in thought, but I should be thinking about tomorrow! Still, I've got a whole morning to do it. I just can't get over that business wi' Mum. I thought only thing we had in common were fear. Not a great thing to inherit from your mum, fear of everything that moves. Fear o' success, fear o' failure. Fear o' being hurt, fear o' hurting others. I try to keep it hidden, unlike her. I just wonder if blokes see that fear in me, that's why I'm not married? Not that attractive, is it? I'm too scared to have your kids, darling! But Goddess is helping me get past it, that business wi' Jonathan, I think she arranged that. Led him to me but made him harmless. Then I managed to get through my own anxiety attacks while Wei Chi were dying. Now I'm stronger, just like Jose after Paris. I think Goddess arranged that too. Pushed yobs in our direction but didn't allow 'em to hurt us. So, I'm fighting to overcome my mum's fear, handed down like an inheritance. But now I find out she's given me summat else. My ability to see visions. Gift of seeing into other world. Except she were frightened off using that gift. That weren't her fault. It would've happened to me if I were thirty-eight years older. It's all changed since sixties. Now people can believe what they want. The New Age, they call it. You can be a Pagan or Witch or whatever you want. Of course, some people were already doing it long ago but not ordinary working folk in*

*Leeds suburbs. Still went to churches then, 'on and off' as Dad puts it.*

*But she's still my mum. OK, I suppose I look down on her, sometimes despise her if I'm honest, but still she's my mum. She represents everything I don't like about my own life; things I try and keep suppressed. Worrying about trivial things, she likes this and dislikes that, doesn't like loud music, doesn't understand modern world, can't operate mobile phones. So I look for a mum elsewhere. Irene. Goddess. I want to start again, be re-born from a new mother so's I can be strong, choose a career, not just get stuck in rut. Maybe it's good I didn't get married yet. It'd be more difficult with a couple o' kids. How would Jason have reacted to me finding myself? He would've mocked me, that's what. Then if I took it too far, he would've got mad.*

*But she's still my mum. How can I love Goddess, who's my spiritual mother, a fantastic mother maybe more like an older sister, and not love my natural mum? That would be quite wrong, wouldn't it? So maybe I've got to say thanks, Mum, for giving me what you have. Without you struggling wi' fertility drugs, without you agreeing wi' Dad when he begged you not to give up on kids, without you still managing to go to work and run our home even though you were near mental breakdown most o' time, without all that I wouldn't exist. I wouldn't be here to have visions, to find my spiritual mother. I'm really sorry. I've not had many kind thoughts about you these last few years. I've worried about you, yes, and I've been loyal but inside, there's been no appreciation o' who you are. You never knew what I were thinking, o' course. Nathan says thoughts don't matter. Maybe that's partly true. I've been loyal on surface and you didn't know what I were thinking. So from your point o' view, maybe it don't matter. From Dad's point o' view, it don't matter either, he were glad to share moments when we sighed and moaned about you, gave him a chance to let it out, but he were also glad that I stayed loyal like him. Unlike Colin. How many times does he come home these days? Can't really blame him, he's started a new life somewhere else. But, anyway, what I think does matter to me. I've got to light a candle, say sorry for being so down on you in my mind, try and accept you for who you are. Maybe I can do a little magic for you, Mum. Get well soon. Get well forever and enjoy rest o' your life. Goddess'll come and visit you again, I'm sure she will. This time you'll let her help you…*

After spending a few minutes in front of the candle and wishing her mum well, Frances started to feel anxious about the next day, then laughed as she realised that she had been spending the whole evening thus far deriding fear. *OK, a little bit o' nerves is fine, keeps you concentrating, but don't overdo it. Of course you can do it, of course you can.* She pulled the curtains with purpose, as if to express her resolve in every physical action. As she wandered thoughtfully into the bedroom, she wondered to herself, was she just doing her own thing tomorrow and helping out a friend, or was she taking her place in centuries of religious tradition, no less significant than all those who had gone before her? Frances Dryburgh, from the inner suburbs of Leeds, with an undistinguished degree, a dad who spent all his time watching sport and a mum who had attacks of anxiety? Frances Dryburgh the priestess. Did she really have the right to baptise those children? Did she need to do a training course? Sit before a selection board? Or was it just that the Goddess had called and, for once, Frances Dryburgh was listening?

# 50

# Contact with the World of Spirit

S unday lunch and the preparations were done; now the Citroen snaked its way through the Leeds streets. Jose drove with Nathan next to him in the front, there to provide moral support on the journey. Jose was cursing the poor old car: 'it's pinking again', not that Frances knew what that meant. *It's amazing that it's still going,* she thought. She felt nervous and she could see that Debs was too. To add to the normal apprehension of meeting several new people, this time she was the centre of attention at an event, the priestess with a special role. No longer the person on the periphery, watching on. No longer allowed the surreptitious yawn, whispered criticisms of the proceedings or looks in the wrong direction at some incident or object that diverted the eye. She was responsible; the yawning and carping would be at her expense this time. *What about that cousin's wedding in Ossett last year? All wrong, weren't it? Photos took too long; didn't get drinks quickly enough; seating plan were crap; you couldn't hear speeches too well. But now it's my turn under spotlight – me and Debs are running things.*

'Here we are,' announced Jose, clearly relieved that the Citroen had survived another battle against the road with four passengers on board.

'Phew,' breathed Debs tensely, looking at Frances.

'You should be used to coming to places like this in your job,' said Frances, hoping for some sign that Debs was in charge, but she didn't get it.

'Yeah, but not to do baptisms!'

Nathan's wit to the – erm – rescue?

'Don't worry, girls, they don't burn witches these days – except in Seacroft, of course. Oh, hang on a minute, this *is* Seacroft.'

'Shut up!'

The great square beige tower blocks of Seacroft, trimmed in white, were several stories high. They looked down on the new arrivals imperiously, disdainfully. Silly people trying to invade the impregnable cultural fortress of an urban estate. Don't bring your fancy 'spirituality' here! We'll spit you out. Graffiti greeted them as they climbed the stairway, deciding to forego the terrors of the lift. Nathan alone used it to take up the box of accessories. Then he and Jose left before they rang the doorbell.

'Just give us a call when you want picking up.'

The anticipated hostility turned out to be a figment of the anxious imagination. The welcome in the cramped third floor flat was worthy of members of the royal family or Hollywood stars. Kelly was first to the door, a warmly smiling Kelly looking so different from the woman Frances met those weeks ago. She had glammed herself up with a green off the shoulder low-cut dress, some dangly earrings, glistening make-up and an old locket around her neck, supported by a thin silver chain. Behind her came the lovely Irene, resplendent in a new T shirt in bright electric blue. Into each visitor's hands was thrust a can of lager and a glass; Debs had to do some persuading before she was given a fruit juice instead. They went into a rather Spartan fourteen-foot-square room with many chairs and a dining table but little else in the way of furniture. The eyes that met them were not suspicious and distrustful but open and expectant. The room was full: three women of different ages – mid-twenties, middle-aged, elderly – and two men, both in their thirties. A brown and white springer spaniel lay in front of them, looking up through beseeching eyes, hoping that the newcomers brought food or a chance of some exercise. The small two-person faded red Dralon-covered settee was quickly vacated for Debs and Frances, despite their protests, while the elderly lady stayed in the armchair and the others perched on dining chairs or leant against the table. The boys Jake and Danny played some kind of DVD zoo game in one corner of the room with Lucy and two other children, one very small boy about two and the girl nearer Lucy's and Jake's age, occasional disagreements being heard above the adult chatter. Several people were smoking, which made the flat claustrophobic, although the French windows were fully open onto a small balcony. Outside, the cloudy but dry weather promised a good setting for a ritual. The day was bright enough to splash light around the flat with its recently painted magnolia walls.

'Right, let's do some introductions,' said Kelly, in a loud but uncertain voice. Her apparently aggressive persona hid a shy vulnerability. She spoke quickly and jerkily. 'Everybody, this is Frances and Debs, who's going to do baptisms for boys.'

'Hello, everybody!' They waved to each person in turn round the room.

'OK, now, this is my friend Kirsty… (she pointed to the young woman, pretty in a sundress with her brown hair swept back)… and her two kids are over there, Sadie and Will. This is Sue, my mam, and Auntie Beryl, my Nan's sister. And my big brother Derek and his friend John, who I've known since I were a kid.'

Frances' attention was focussed on Derek and John for a moment. *Derek's OK-looking, strong and square like Kelly, shaved head, wi' a cute smile, but John's not likely to be a babe magnet, is he, wi' bad teeth and unwashed hair that badly needs to decide whether to be long or short.* Her thoughts were interrupted by Aunty Beryl asking her where she lived. Then there were some pleasantries exchanged around the gathering, which preceded an awkward silence.

'OK, where're we going?' asked Debs, taking the initiative. 'Weather's fine for an outside do.'

'Quiet little field out beyond Thorner,' replied Derek, flashing that smile again.

'Fantastic,' said Frances. 'Can we have a quick word wi' you on your own, Kelly, just to make final arrangements, like?'

'Yeah,' replied Kelly. 'Just come through to bedroom.'

The bedroom was even emptier than the lounge; Kelly had not lived there long and she had few possessions. In fact, the clothes scattered about all over the floor were welcome to the eye, otherwise the room would have been very bare and devoid of colour. There were no curtains; no bedside table; no carpet; a single MFI wardrobe had seen better days. The wallpaper, a plain pattern in lemon yellow, was torn here and there and needed removing; the lino was ripped in places too, revealing bare floorboards.

'We've not got round to decorating in here,' Kelly declared, realising that her guests had noticed the mess. 'Derek's part done lounge but Council take time, you know.'

'That's *not* a problem,' replied Debs, firmly. We know you've not been here long and it won't be done overnight. Don't worry about it. Let's sit on bed.'

'Kelly, love, I guess you've been baptised,' said Frances. 'What wi' being a Catholic and all that.'

'Yeah, I have. When I were baby. My Nan insisted. This were her locket, you know. It's got Immaculate Heart o' Mary in, look. I should've had my boys done when they were babies.'

Frances launched into a little prepared speech.

'We think we should include you in baptisms, Kelly. Else boys might feel awkward. You can all do it together. Maybe it's you, as much as them, that needs a new start. And we'll try to make it fun. It's a celebration.'

Kelly thought for a few seconds; with that firm, stubborn-looking chin thrust into the air, it seemed as though she would refuse. Catholics didn't get baptised twice, did they? But Kelly's stern demeanour was once again misleading.

'That's great. It's for all of us, in't it? Me and them together.'

A few tears welled up in her eyes. Frances and Debs sat on either side of her, tenderly holding one arm each. They told her a little more of what they had planned for the ritual. She just nodded without speaking. Then, all at once, she pulled herself together and resumed the strong woman appearance.

'Let's go,' she said. 'We'll get off before kids start playing up.'

Derek and John both had cars; John's was a four-by-four so, between the two, there was just about room for everyone, the kids and dog squeezed in the back. 'It's only a couple o' miles,' Derek told them, 'Just up A64, turn left, and we're there.' The cars went on their way and were soon out of the city. The countryside was pleasant and verdant: woods and fields. *Don't remember ever being out here*, thought Frances. *Only a few minutes from Leeds. Must come again another time.*

Twenty minutes after leaving, the packed vehicles pulled off the road into a lay-by and the men led everyone into a field, surrounded by trees on three sides. The dog and children leapt out like escaping prison camp internees and raced into the open space.

'That's good, no one here, no lads playing football or owt,' said Derek, looking pleased with himself; he'd done his homework.

'It's the perfect place,' exclaimed Frances. 'Look there!'

In the far corner stood a great oak which spread its sturdy branches several yards away from the trunk, so that part of the field was kept in shade.

'It must be hundreds o' years old!' cried Debs. 'A brilliant place for a ritual.'

The oak must have been waiting for an opportunity like this. The gathering sauntered over, the boys arriving first, finding acorns and little twigs to throw at each other. The dog executed several perambulations of the area at speed. John carried the box. Under the tree, they got out the contents, Lucy and Sadie showing particular interest. First, Nathan's bodhran along with recent drum purchases: a pair of bongos, two djembes, castanets and a tambourine. Then a blue ceramic goblet, a large plastic bottle full of water, some flowers – germini and chrysanthemums from the supermarket, in red, yellow and green sprays – and several small brooms made of twigs tied together with string. Debs asked everyone to form a circle; the boys were bribed to join in by the promise that they could play the drums later. Frances placed the flowers just behind her. Then Debs explained in a clear, steady voice, what was going to happen.

One, she would create the sacred circle, sweeping round behind the company in a clockwise direction – the children would be asked to help;

Two, they would call the spirits of the quarters (they had given Irene and Sue some words written on pieces of paper for north and west);

Three, they would ask the children to bring the flowers into the circle and make an altar;

Four, they would ask Kelly, Jake and Danny to stand by the altar, while they poured water in the goblet;

Five, the baptisms would be carried out by Frances, with some words read out by Debs;

Six, Jake and Danny would then be asked to splash everyone with just a little of the water (they had planned this so that people would feel included);

Seven, to celebrate, everyone would be asked to bang drums and move round in the circle;

Eight, Frances would thank the Goddess for everything that was good and ask her to protect them from everything that was harmful;

Nine, the spirits of the quarters would be called on to depart;

Ten, the circle would be closed by Debs and the children moving round anticlockwise.

Ten actions – easy to remember, neat and symmetrical. Short, sweet, right. Take time on each step, no need to rush.

The kids loved the creating of the circle; Frances was glad that they had thought to make several brooms to avoid arguing. The quarters were called. The air was still and warm, perfect for speaking out to a group. *Now Irene's reading her bit, she does it well like she should've been an actress or summat. OK, now kids are enjoying themselves bringing flowers into centre o' circle for our homemade altar. I just hope Jake don't do summat weird. Yes, little Will, you can bring twigs and acorns and put them in middle. You're very young but you've got the hang of it, an altar made from nature. Here while we're here and gone when we're gone.*

Then, at last, the baptising. Danny looked nervous; Jake giggled; Kelly had the stalwart look of someone who didn't want to cry. The water was poured into the goblet. Frances put her hand into the goblet and took out a handful of water, which she poured over Kelly's head. Debs spoke the words they had written together earlier that day.

'Kelly, we dedicate you to the Goddess and ask her to guide you and protect you from all harm.'

This was repeated for Jake and Danny. Then it was their turn to do some baptising. As the boys splashed the water round, taking small handfuls from the goblet that Frances held down for them, there was an eerie quiet amongst the people in the circle. No one reacted to having the drops thrown at them, no one made a fuss; each adult bent down so that whatever little water the boys still held, it fell on heads and faces. Even the children were calm. Nature itself provided the perfect atmospheric background: no breeze, just the occasional chirping of a bird in the nearby branches. Frances began to feel strange. She knew that sensation, a tingling as though a small current were being passed up her back. She had felt it at several places: Almscliffe, Le Puy, Massiac and the Puy de Dôme among them. *She* was coming.

Frances looked around. No sign of an apparition, no celestial being, no cloaked woman, no dancing, no lions, no faeries, no blue Earth, no moon, no ancient doors, no light. Frances felt disappointed. Surely she hadn't already experienced the final vision? OK, on with the ritual. She retook control.

'Now we're going to celebrate by making a noise! As many people as possible, take a drum and bang it. Shake a tambourine, rattle a castanet. As we do, we can walk round in a circle. Each person can thank Goddess for her gifts in whatever way they want, or they can just enjoy drumming!'

She glanced anxiously at Derek and John, then at Kirsty and Sue. Would taking part be embarrassing for them? Had they been content to stand and watch, for Kelly's sake, privately thinking how stupid the whole thing was? If so, would they accept participating in it themselves? But there was no sign of discomfort; all the adults joined in with some gusto. John had grabbed the bodhran and looked like he'd played one before; Auntie Beryl had the tambourine and shook it lustily, as if she had just left the Salvation Army. Will ran around with the castanets in hand, making a joyous racket. Kirsty and Irene were helping Lucy, Jake and Sadie with the bongos and one djembe. Kelly had the other and was slapping it with Danny in attendance, clinging to her. Derek held nothing but was clapping, looking contentedly at the floor as he circled round. Frances glanced at Debs and breathed a sigh of relief. No problem. It was all going well. The hard part was done. The banging and clacking filled the summer afternoon air. Strangely, for such a ragbag group, there was a certain rhythmic pattern to all the tapping. It seemed to connect with thousands upon thousands of rituals across centuries and continents. Just ordinary groups of human beings doing their best to make contact with the world of spirit...

With that profound thought, the tingling feeling came back to Frances more strongly. Yet still no apparition. She looked around again. *Now, just who is this?* A woman was walking across the field towards them. Just an ordinary person. From fifty yards or more, Frances could make out a young woman with brown hair tied back in a ponytail, a white T-shirt, blue jeans and white trainers. Probably a passer-by who'd got curious. But then Frances remembered that she herself was wearing a white T-shirt, blue jeans and white trainers. Her brown hair was also tied back in a ponytail. The woman came nearer; she sported a distinctive silver bracelet on her right arm. Frances glanced down; she wore an identical silver bracelet, one that she pulled out on special occasions. She looked up again, expectantly. The woman was smiling. Frances smiled back. Things became clear. She was being approached by her mirror image.

## 51

## Blessed Be

'Oh, God, it's you!' exclaimed Frances to her twin. 'I'm so glad to see you again! I wondered if I ever would.'

'One more time only,' replied Notre Dame de Zion. 'This is last time you'll ever see me, Frances.'

The Goddess walked purposefully straight up to Frances through where the circle of people should have been but, in the trance state, no one else was to be seen. A very ordinary English field in the summer, not notable in any way except for the magnificent large oak under which they were standing; yet the newcomer's presence brought light to every part of it, every blade of grass, every leaf in the hedgerow. Frances was aflame with passion for her, but the thought of never seeing her again was like the pouring of icy water onto the fire. Summer turning to winter. Frances was on the verge of weeping.

'No, don't say that. I need you to be with me. I didn't know you existed just a few month ago. I can't live without you now.'

Notre Dame de Zion moved closer and reached out with her right hand to touch Frances gently on the left cheek. This sent waves of ecstasy through her, wonderful sensations of energy, spreading feelings of calm and well-being. The Goddess came right up close so that their identical breasts, pushing out the T-shirt fabric in exactly the same way, brushed together. She spoke softly, in the way that Frances imagined herself to speak to a friend needing consolation.

'I said that this is last time you'll ever see me. I didn't say I wouldn't be with you.'

'OK, I get it; you'll be with me in spirit.'

'More than that. I'll be in your very being.'

'Then why won't I see you?'

'You can only see me because I'm separate from you, can't you? That's only reason you see anything, because it's some distance from you.'

'Yes, I get that, I think.'

'So if I'm in you, right inside you forever, you won't be able to see me, will you?'

'No.'

'But I'll be closer than anyone can be, nearer to your heartbeat even than the breath you take.'

'Of course. I want that.'

'Then let me in, Frances.'

The Goddess now moved up very close. Frances could feel the Goddess' arms around her, the rhythms of her body flowing through its every small movement. Their eyes gazed at each other, the faces touched and then – she was gone…

'Don't worry, everybody,' Debs called out in a confident, clear voice. 'This is quite normal. She has visions during rituals, you know.'

She had moved towards Frances when she saw the eyes rolling upward in order to hold her from the front, providing a support against her friend falling. In alarm, the drummers had stopped their banging and there was quiet underneath the great oak. Frances looked at Debs with the expression of a person just waking up.

'She's in me,' was all she could say.

'Who's in you? Goddess?'

'Yeah, Goddess. Notre Dame de Zion. In me forever.'

'OK, Frances. That's great. But she's in all of us, all time. From birth to death.'

'Yeah, I know. But I've seen it, that's all. That's only difference between me and everyone else. I've seen it.'

'You're very lucky then.'

'Yeah, but I'll tell you all about it. Then you'll know too.'

'*Is* everything OK?' asked Irene, walking up to the two of them, as they stood like statues in the centre of the circle, clasping each other like two marionettes whose puppeteers had dropped the strings.

'Yes,' replied Frances, pulling herself together and giving her a reassuring smile. 'We'll finish ritual now.'

Frances had prepared the thanksgiving that morning. She was even inspired enough to say it from memory so she didn't have to pull out the piece of paper carefully placed in her jeans pocket. But now that she felt the Goddess inside her, part of her, the way she spoke the words differed from previous rituals. Rather than shouting off into the open air, to a deity somewhere out there among the trees, she addressed them clearly but intimately into the core of her being. She understood that among the trees and in the core of her being were in essence the same place; all-pervasive Nature, of which she was constituted, of whom she was a child, connected and merged them.

'Goddess, we thank you for your gifts to us: the beauty of the countryside, the warmth of summer and for us being together in this ritual today. We ask you to protect the children here and to shield them from those things which cause them harm. We dedicate them to you, now and forever.'

And then she added words ad-lib, words that she had not written on the paper.

'Because you are in them, they are part of you. You are in us all. Blessed be.'

Spontaneously, and for reasons unknown to her, she finished the little piece of liturgy with a dramatic gesture, thrusting her right hand straight up in the air towards the oak branches – and beyond them, the heavens – and pointing the left at the earth beneath her feet, the arms straight and the index fingers of each hand outstretched. Somewhere in her imagination, she felt a surge of lightening connect the heavens and the earth through her. The words 'Blessed be' took on energy and power; she had spoken them and so they came into being, illuminating the circle of participants. Her actions had gained their rapt attention, even the children. She felt that all the faces were shining with light as the ritual was finished with the departing of the spirits and the closing of the circle.

The party relaxed and enjoyed the sunshine that had begun to break through the greyness of the clouds. Drums were left lying around. Snacks were produced; the children dashed off with the dog in tow towards the promise of secret places among the trees. Frances noticed that even Danny seemed uninhibited enough to leave his mother behind and join the frolicking. The adults chatted and generally agreed that they thought the ritual had gone well; Irene and Kelly were fulsome in their praise for the ceremony and how good it had made them feel.

'You were *radiant*, Frances, just like that time at refuge.'

'Thanks, Kelly, but you looked radiant too. You really love your boys, don't you?'

'Yeah, o' course I do. I just want them to be happy, that's all. Live their lives without fear.'

Debs raised her face towards Frances and they exchanged a glance. The look said that fear was part of the package; you could no more remove it than eradicate love, hunger, desire, pain, energy, ecstasy, embarrassment, hope. But they knew what she meant. Keep it in its place; don't let it become king and lord over the other human experiences and emotions, just make it one of the courtiers.

'Well, maybe life will get a little easier from now on,' Frances found herself saying to Kelly. 'Remember, just call on Goddess when it gets tough. And call on us too.'

'Are you *witches*?' asked Kelly. 'If you are, I'd like to be one too. How do I do that?'

'Just by being one,' answered Debs, gently. 'By understanding that Goddess gives you power, power to change your life and others too. By making up little rituals for yourself. By joining us when we do. We can celebrate Lughnasadh together, if you like, at beginning of August.'

'Yeah, I'd like to,' agreed Kelly.

'I thought you had to go through initiations in witchcraft,' said Irene.

'Yeah,' replied Debs, reflectively. 'I were initiated once. But I didn't ask Frances to do that. I could see that she had magic in her naturally. Then I thought maybe initiation as a fixed thing in't necessary; it happens whenever Goddess decides. Initiation is what religions have; it makes 'em into clubs, societies wi' membership, which means that people have power over who's in and who's out. So I say: initiate yourself when you're ready!'

'I think my initiation were kind of at Avebury,' added Frances. 'When we drew down Moon. I were welcomed into circle, Debs' circle. That's all I needed.'

As the picnic progressed, Frances felt that Debs wanted to be close to her, closer than she had ever been. It was there in the body language, in the little codes of communication, in the responsiveness and attention with which Debs picked up on her cues and comments. Maybe it was down to a little jealousy of Irene, for whom Frances' devotion was all too obvious; maybe it was a little residual guilt over Nathan, waiting with Jose for her call to come and pick them up; but then maybe it was just sisterly love, plain and simple. There was something intangible about Debs that reminded Frances of Notre Dame de Zion, the Goddess who had turned into her twin. In Debs, Frances recognised a lost part of herself that she had been invited to recapture by finding it in another. In the same way as taking the Goddess within herself, the embracing of another woman emotionally made her feel complete; the jigsaw came together and the missing pieces were supplied. Then she realised, with some force, how much she loved Debs. And, clearly, it was a two-way thing. As she was thinking this, Debs grabbed a brief opportunity to speak to her quietly and alone, while the other women were distracted by Lucy running over and saying that Will had fallen over and was crying.

'It's true what they said. You were *transformed* today. Shining. Especially at the end when you said those words. I really saw Goddess in you, I thought I'd say that. You're a high priestess, that's what you are.'

Frances felt the contrasting emotions of proud excitement and unease at being put on a pedestal. She remembered Irene's reaction to adulation. She needed to climb down for the sake of their relationship.

'I saw Goddess in you too, Debs. You brought me into all this, remember. You're *my* high priestess. When you were holding me up today, I saw Notre Dame de Zion in front o' me but, in fact, it were you standing there.'

Debs' pleasure at the mutual appreciation could not be concealed; she beamed warmly. As she had with Kelly, Frances glimpsed the vulnerable woman beneath the tough exterior and ready arguments; inside, Debs was all too quick to disregard herself. She needed the inner demon to be contradicted by others, and often.

'OK, then, we'll be high priestesses for each other.'

'Agreed!'

The exchange was ended as Irene and Kelly rejoined them, having soothed Will in a few seconds; he resumed all the unsteady running around that had caused him to fall in the first place.

As they began to pack up, Frances noticed Beryl hovering around her.

'Were it all right?' she asked the short, stocky, chain-smoking lady, whose carelessly cropped white hair contrasted strongly with her bright green cardigan.

'It were marvellous, dear. Me and my sister, you know, we were brought up Catholics. We loved candles and Virgin Mary, you know, all that stuff.'

'Yes, Kelly told me about her Nan.'

'That's right. Well, we stopped going to Mass, I'm afraid. It seemed to lose summat as we got older. Just got a bit boring. But I really liked what you do – we all need rituals, don't we?'

'I think so, yes.'

Derek and John, cigarettes in mouths, were gathering the drums up nearby and putting them back in the cardboard box. Frances looked across.

'What did you men think? Were it all a bit girlie for you?' she asked with a twinkle in her eye.

Derek laughed, a genuine good-hearted guffaw which put her at her ease instantly. John smiled too, his blackening teeth showing through, although he seemed to have no self-consciousness about it.

'It were fine,' said Derek. 'Religion's not really my thing normally, you know, but anything that'll perk Kelly up a bit, well, I'm right behind it. And John likes to bang a drum, don't you, John?'

'Aye, well, I were in band,' replied John. 'We were going to be famous but well, you know how it is. A few arguments and we weren't new Oasis after all.'

'No, they stayed in desert instead,' quipped Derek.

*Nathan's here after all,* thought Frances.

'He's right, we're so pleased that Kelly's looking a bit better these days; she's been through hell these past few years,' added Sue, standing nearby, taking the conversation back to the more earnest levels. 'That were great, Frances. Maybe we could get you to do more.'

Frances was now grinning broadly; she was enjoying all this, the centre of attention of a pleasant little group of people, the mistress of ceremonies. Short of dominating girlie pub conversations when she was a little drunk, she had never seen herself as a leader or organiser of anything much. Just an ordinary sit-at-the-back kind of person. Other people did things, managed things. She glanced around. The only person she hadn't really spoken to was Kirsty, who was so busy with the children, but an opportunistic look found the young woman's eye and they exchanged a warm smile. She was onside too – *why did I ever worry about all this?* Then Irene came over and hugged her. From that point, she could barely stop herself grinning all the way back to Seacroft. *It's worth being alive for days like these!*

Later, reunited, the adventurers went to the *Airedale*, Irene along with them. The mood was exultant. Frances and Debs were full of reflections, thoughts and also relief.

'So, here we are, the four musketeers again,' announced Frances, beaming at everyone.

'What about me?' interjected Irene, then she laughed to show that she didn't mind really. 'Maybe I'm Queen o' France.'

'You can't be Queen o' France, you've not been to France,' smiled Frances. 'You can be Queen o' Leeds.'

'Yeah, OK, I'm happy wi' that. A great title – Queen o' Leeds.'

Frances couldn't be stopped tonight.

'The Queen o' Leeds, she made some... er... *seeds*.'

'Grew some seeds?' suggested Debs.

'Yes, the Queen o' Leeds, she grew some seeds, all on a summer's day. The Knave o' Leeds – that's you, Nathan – he stole the seeds and took them right away.'

'I'll release them for a reasonable ransom,' said Nathan, always game for some stupidity.

'Yes, you will, my man, or high priestess'll strike you down wi' lightening,' shouted Frances above the din of the pub, suddenly realising that she had introduced her private memory of the ritual into the banter.

Debs joined in.

'The *two* high priestesses will strike you down wi' lightening.'

'The *three* high priestesses!' added Irene.

'Too many high priestesses spoil the beer,' smiled Nathan.

'Yes,' agreed Jose. 'But maybe guys can be high priestesses too, so it's five.'

'Here's to that,' said Frances, clinking glasses together rather hazardously. 'The five high priestesses. Beats four musketeers any day.'

'Even beats a royal flush,' added Jose with self-conscious wit, before nipping off to the loo...

Back home alone as midnight approached, Frances glowed with the warmth of success and sat contentedly stroking Cass. *What a day for celebration!* This triggered a memory of the dream of several months ago. CELEBRATE OFTEN, the words written on a banner. *They've come true. I am going to celebrate often in rituals, just like I did today. And when I do, Goddess will be celebrating inside o' me.* She recalled that, in the same dream, the Goddess' dancing had been replaced by her own, a prophecy telling her that she would be united with the Goddess. She was just an ordinary person going through life changes but she was lucky enough to be guided by powerful spiritual experiences, dreams and visions. *Well, not everybody has visions,* she thought, *but they do all have dreams.* Maybe they guide us more than we realise.

Wei Chi's book was lying beside her on the sofa. She flicked through a few pages. Synchronicity came into play. The word 'visionaries' suddenly stood out from among the thousands of words, although she had never noticed it before in *Before Completion*. Her heart leaped. She had to scan back through the pages to find it. She read the paragraph with eagerness.

'There have been many visionaries in the modern period. Strangely, in this scientific age, visions are more popular than ever. People flock to Lourdes, Guadalupe, Medjugorje. However, against the popular conception, visionaries aren't holier than anyone else. They are merely given the gift of perceiving the spiritual realities which are true for us all. They see Jesus and Mary as if they were present with them alone but of course Jesus and Mary are with us all. Now, visionaries are just as likely as any other people to be misled by personal and political agendas. So we have to discern carefully what they are saying to us. If they tell us what spiritual reality looks like and they are truly inspired, they may give us insights to help us on the spiritual journey. But if they are being deluded by their own self-importance, then we will be fools to heed them. They might be the eyes of the spiritual body, but eyes can play tricks. As Jesus says in the gospel of Matthew, "The eye is the lamp of the body. So, if your eye is healthy, your whole body will be full of light; but if your eye is unhealthy, your whole body will be full of darkness. If then the light in you is darkness, how great is the darkness!" So beware of visionaries; do not suspend your critical faculties when you listen to their prophecies.'

Frances pursed her lips and frowned. She had expected Wei Chi to wax lyrical about visionaries and instead she had warned her readers about them. *Hmm!* She then thought about Kelly, Sue, Beryl, Kirsty, Derek and John. They had enjoyed the baptism ceremony, but none of them had ever read, or was ever likely to read, Wei Chi's words of wisdom. They might possibly believe whatever was told to them by someone who had visions, looked radiant, read Tarot cards, carried out baptisms, played the part of the high priestess. Like Frances. She had a huge responsibility. With exultation and celebration came the need to be aware, to learn things. To strive to be a spiritually healthy and clear-sighted priestess of the Goddess and not a misleading one. Debs was right to do some study. Maybe Frances needed to as well. Her Chinese teacher had popped in just at the right time. Like all good teachers, she didn't get carried away with her pupil's success but saw it as an opportunity to impart a new lesson, to move things forward by one more step. 'All right,' said Frances in mock irritation to the face in the photo on the back cover. 'All right! You're so right, you're so very very right, you're the rightest person in the world!' Then she smiled and placed the book on the mantelpiece, covers spread so that it stayed standing there with the photo looking out authoritatively into the room.

*People don't forget a good teacher,* she thought. *So I won't forget you.*

## 52

# No Place like Home

*Monday morning at work. God, God. So boring. I keep daydreaming about weekend and baptisms. Phone's bleeping! It's a text from Jo to me, Cyn and Sal. 'Lets meet, Tues eve – r u on? Its bn ages.' The old guard. Not musketeers nor high priestesses, just the girls. No talk o' visions or baptisms, just shopping and men. Except I've got no man, have I? Not that I mind right now, yesterday were so great, but meeting wi' girls'll put me back in that needy kind o' mood. But you can't just throw away your friends. They're part of you, aren't they, part o' your history? It's just one evening. I can tell 'em about France – they'll like to hear about wine, good food and hunky French men. Not that I noticed any, I were thinking about Nathan all time! I'll make summat up. OK, text back. No one's looking. Wine bar wi' Mexican food. Greek Street. Tuesday, seven o'clock. For old time's sake...*

*Tuesday. It's arrived so quick. They're all glammed up, anybody would think they're the ones looking for a guy and not me. Their blokes have been parked for the evening. Girls' night out.*

'So what you been doing all this time, Frances? I hardly get to speak to you these days.'

*Jo looks great tonight, what's she done with her hair? She's gone a shiny blonde colour. Shorter than usual, tapered forward on each side of her face. The bob's on a comeback! Suits her. She looks so much more on top o' things these days. Leaving G.R.C. were making of her!*

'I've been away, Jo. Three weeks in France. Brilliant holiday. I were wi' Debs, Nathan and Jose. We met loads o' people.'

'OK, now which man are you with? Nathan or Jose?'

'Neither as it happens. Jose's gay and Nathan's wi' Debs.'

'I thought *you* fancied him.'

'I did. That's how it goes. But we're all friends. No problem.'

*I can see Cyn trying to get in. She's holding back from putting in another mouthful o' fajitas. She's obviously keen to get into conversation.*

'Did you hear owt more about Jonathan?'

'No, I'm still waiting on court case.'

'God, it takes time, don't it?'

'Yeah, don't know what's happening, to tell truth.'

*We've all gone quiet for a second; the chilli is starting to burn mouths. Now Sal's looking at me quizzically.*

'Come on, Frances, what's going on wi' you? It's been months since you had a steady guy. What happened to that Gary?'

*Thanks very much, we're on blokes trail again, are we? It's a dead end for me and you know it. Steady, I can love these girls, I really can. I can love everyone. Goddess is in me, remember?*

'He weren't right. I'm just going through a celibate period. Got to sort myself out. Then I'll be back in there!'

'What're you sorting out, love? Job's OK now, in't it?'

'Well, my mum's not been well. Knocked me back a bit.'

*Mum's neurosis can be useful at times.*

'That's great, Frances, but get back in there. After all, you're nearly thirty, aren't you? Body clock and all that. Need to find Mr Right soon!'

*Cyn, you always were one to turn screw. Notre Dame de Zion, help me, stop me strangling her!*

'I'll find him, don't worry.'

'You've been saying that for ages! Ten year ago it weren't so serious!'

*OK, forget last instruction, Notre Dame de Zion, kill bitch with massive thunderbolt.*

'Come on, Frances, tell us more about this France thing? What were that all about?'

*Phew! Change o' subject. Thanks, Jo.*

'We went to France because we wanted to be there just before G8 summit took place.'

'Come off it – they didn't let you take part in summit, did they?'

*Leeds woman chokes on fajitas. Witchcraft suspected.*

'No, we thought that we could maybe influence meeting so that it found solutions to the environmental crisis.'

'Influence it how?'

'By… erm…' – *Foot's already in, so just get ready for splash* – '…magic.'

'Magic? The witch thing's for lovesick teenagers, surely?'

*Yeah, let's ditch witchcraft. Leeds woman stabbed to death wi' cutlery.*

'Come on, girls, give me a break! I really care about environmental issues now. It's worth trying everything. It's all for our future. What's point in finding guys and having kids if human race is going to die out in fifty years?'

'What happened at summit meeting anyway?'

*Sal's not very well informed.*

'Well, major industrial nations are going to take measures to cut carbon emissions and stop mass dumping o' waste.'

'That really pisses me off, you know, that idea o' charging us for excess waste. What're you supposed to do? Don't we pay enough tax?'

*They're really testing me tonight…*

*OK, I feel better. It were just nerves that made us annoy each other at beginning of evening. We hadn't got together for a bit. Now we're remembering old times, good times. Being a priestess doesn't mean turning your back on past and all the hanky-panky we got up to. I'm not entering a convent, am I? God, that reminds me o' when I were so angry about Debs and Nathan. Wouldn't it have been brilliant if I could've turned up here wi' Nathan? That would've sorted them out, wouldn't it?*

'What're you thinking about, Frances? You've gone all strange again.'

'I were thinking that I'm happy Debs is wi' Nathan. I care about 'em both, I'm glad they're happy.'

'Care about 'em? They screwed you, didn't they? I'd have scratched her eyes out.'

'Yeah, well, for a short while, I did want to do that and worse. But I moved on, you know, got over it.'

'OK, but you don't need to hang around 'em so's they rub it in, do you?'

*Life's so simple for you, Cyn. You either love someone, that is, if they do what you want them to, or hate 'em.*

'I stick with 'em because they're my friends. Just like I stick wi' you lot, too.'

*Now, real friends are people you can tell about your life and what's going on for you. Take a deep breath. Don't be apologetic. Look 'em straight in eye. Put knife and fork down, forget Mexican food for a moment.*

'I can accept what's happened because I've become a spiritual person. I suppose probably I were always that way inclined but I never knew what to do with it. Truth is, I've had experiences, visions. They've convinced me that in all of us, every single one of us, is a great Goddess. For each of us, she's probably different, just like a mother seems different to each of her kids, but she's in all of us anyway. I've seen her. I've seen her in Leeds; in Yorkshire Dales; in France; on volcanoes; by rivers; on crags. I saw a Chinese woman die, a brilliant woman, who taught me more in knowing her for one week than schools and colleges could ever do. So yes, it hurt me when Nathan chose Debs, but in great scheme o' things it's summat I can live with. Go wi' flow as they say. I'll find a man, at least I think I will and, if I don't, I imagine that I'll still be happy, somehow, some way. I couldn't have said that just six month ago but now I can. All I know is my bloke's got to be special, he's got to accept what I believe in and he's got to be a spiritual person too. Maybe I'm expecting too much. But, after Gary, I don't know how it could be any different. Good bloke, Gary. But not the man I need. If that special guy don't exist, no one else will do.'

*OK, silence. Is anyone going to speak? Tumbleweed blowing down street. Cyn quiet? No, can't be. She's got to say summat Here it comes.*

'I'm sorry, Frances, but are you saying that we're just settling for our blokes because we're not prepared to wait for a special one?'

'No, not a' all. Each of us must do it her own way. Look, Cyn, I'm just speaking about myself, that's all. I'm not making any judgement about your guy. I've not met him, have I?'

*I see it now in her face. She* is *settling for a bloke that don't excite her any more, even after only a few weeks. Then she were in love. Now she's bored already.*

'OK, maybe my relationship's not perfect.' *You can rely on Cyn to be honest. Blunt with you but honest about her own feelings too. Good on you, girl.* 'But what am I to do? I understand you, Frances, I really do. You don't want to make do. Nor do I. But you need a bloke, don't you? Life in't right without a man in tow. Mine's a good-looker, you know. Not too bright upstairs, though. Likes a fight in town if he can get one. Don't matter whether you're with him or not. Still fights. Pisses me off. It really does.'

*Cyn looks a bit tearful. Come on, Goddess, what shall we say?*

'You're worth more than that, Cyn, you know you are. You've not been lucky just recently, have you? But you're gorgeous, you'll get there. Try to look for someone more gentle and caring, not necessarily so good-looking.'

*I'm saying that? The woman who put everything on hold for Nathan? Well, at least he is gentle and caring, despite his crap sense o' humour. Now Jo's coming in.*

'My man's OK. But it's not all grippingly exciting either. He's sometimes too peaceful – I could do wi' fighter!'

*No, you couldn't, Jo. You'd be in pieces within minutes. Cyn's a tougher cookie than you. Sal's only one of us who's married, although we're all near on thirty. Mind you, Jo's been living with hers for a few month now. But none of us has kids. What're we like? Career girls, want cash for fun nights out, not nappies and sleepless nights. Not yet. Somebody'll have to crack and pop a bun in their oven soon. When clock ticks past thirty, Sal and Jo will, I'm sure of it. Not Cyn though. Maybe never for Cyn. She hasn't found a likely father for her children yet.*

'Tell us more about Goddess, Frances.'

*Wow, Jo! I'm a missionary now.*

'She's in all of us; she's the whole Earth and she's our mother who cares for us, but she's also our sister. She wants women to be strong and stand up for themselves and for peace and the environment. We can try to achieve these things by magic if there's no other way. Magic in't rabbits out of a hat; we can change things and people just by our attitude to the world. That's expressed in ritual. I'm going to leave my job and do rituals for people. Mainly women, I expect!'

'So Goddess is like a caring mother? In't that a bit old-fashioned?'

'Maybe, Jo, but women don't have to stop being caring. It's just that men have to be caring too! It's not all up to us! We don't have to be womanly in old-fashioned sense, over-emotional and weak and leaving men to run things and wreck world.'

'We're not womanly really, are we, Frances? None of us are mothers. We just work and go out, like blokes really.'

*OK, Sal, you read my mind.*

'We *will* be mothers, Sal. One day. And then Goddess will help us look after our kids. And in all violence and mess o' society, we might need her help.'

*Maybe I should tell them about Kelly. Maybe not, I met her in refuge and there's a confidentiality rule.*

'So you're worried about Planet Earth, are you, Frances? All this global warming business?'

'Yes, I am, Jo. The Earth *is* a Goddess. She's our mother. We can't abuse her. She feeds us, clothes us, gives us shelter, nurtures us from birth to death. Without her, we have nowt. She's our home.'

*Cyn's smiling at me, a bit mischievous, like. I can see she's going to change subject by cracking a joke. It's got too serious for her.*

'There's no place like home!'

Laughter. *Cyn's good at that Judy Garland impression, damn her!*

## 53

# Before Completion

The next evening, Frances and Debs sat in the flat, busily scribbling things on pieces of paper. They were starting on the planning of the new venture: designing a website with a catchy heading; a few photos; some descriptions of themselves; a commendation from Kelly and Irene saying how good the ritual had been. People would definitely respond. And they'd pay money too. Professional ritual-makers. OK, in Debs' case, semi-professional. Magic-makers. Witches.

Wei Chi stared at them from the back cover of *Before Completion: Spirituality in the 21$^{st}$ Century*, still standing on the mantelpiece. The word 'spirituality' jogged Frances into remembering something she had read a few days before.

'Debs, do you believe in guardian angels?'

Debs sighed. Frances was not the best person for a concentrated effort.

'Not really. It's just a New Agey thing, in't it? All nice and cosy for middle class New Agers; they've got everything in life but they want angels caring for 'em as well! No there's just a Goddess in us and in Nature, not always sorting things just as we'd like, but sometimes she does when we ask her.'

Frances nodded and uttered a faint sound of agreement, yet she hadn't finished.

'True, but Goddess might have angels, kind o' messengers looking out for us on her behalf, mightn't she?'

'They don't seem necessary to my way o' thinking.'

'It's just that I keep getting this funny sensation every time I think of angels.'

'You're a bit touched, aren't you?'

Frances laughed and gave Debs a friendly push.

'Yeah, you're very, very right, I think I am.'

She looked up through her grimy window and out at the soft grey of the cloudy summer evening.

'I just wonder, that's all.'

\*\*\*\*

Of course there are guardian angels, Frances! I'm yours. I've looked after you from your first breath and I'll be there for your last. I've been especially busy during these last few months, bringing you nearer and nearer to the Great Goddess, so that you finally let her in. Who am I? Does it matter? I can recall that I was a man in human life, not that it makes any difference when you become an angel. The only facts that I remember with any certainty are that I'd just turned fifty-three, I was driving down a road, then an accident occurred. I skidded, the lorry skidded, I don't know which. My time had come. One moment, you're there in the world and the next, you're an angel. Like the scene changing in a movie. Somebody else's life, not your own, moves to the centre of your concern. Maybe I could try to bring to mind my job, my family, where and when I lived, the things I did, but it's not necessary. It's *your* life story that became important to me. I was trapped in a wrecked car on a road; one instant later, I was looking down on you becoming a new person entering the world. Frances Dryburgh. Ever since then, I've been calling you. It's taken you a long while to answer, hasn't it, Frances?'